Flying Off Course

Aviation is one of the most widely talked about industries in the global economy and yet airlines continue to present an enigma. Between 2010 and 2018 the global airline industry experienced its longest period of sustained profitability; however, huge global profits hid a darker side. Many airlines made inadequate profits or serious losses while others collapsed entirely. This fifth edition of *Flying Off Course* explains why.

Written by leading industry expert, Rigas Doganis, this book is an indispensable guide to the inner workings of this exciting industry. Providing a complete, practical introduction to the fundamentals of airline economics and marketing, it explores the structure of the market, the nature of airline costs, issues around pricing and demand, and the latest developments in e-commerce. Vibrant examples are drawn from passenger, charter and freight airlines to provide a dynamic view of the entire industry. This completely updated edition also explores the sweeping changes that have affected airlines in recent years. It includes much new material on airline alliances, long-haul low-cost airlines, new pricing policies and ancillary revenues in order to present a compelling account of the current state of the airline industry.

Offering a practical approach and peppered with real examples, this book will be valuable to anyone new to the airline industry as well as those wishing to gain a wider insight into its operations and economics. For undergraduate or postgraduate students in transport studies, tourism and business the book provides a unique insider's view into the workings of this exciting industry.

Rigas Doganis is a former airline chief executive and was a non-executive director of both easyJet and South African Airways. He has worked as an aviation consultant and adviser to numerous airlines, governments, banks, the European Commission, the United Nations and the World Bank. He was also Professor and Head of the Air Transport Department at Cranfield University, UK.

Flying Off Course

Airline Economics and Marketing

Fifth Edition

Rigas Doganis

LONDON AND NEW YORK

Fifth edition published 2019
by Routledge
2 Park Square, Milton Park, Abingdon, Oxon, OX14 4RN

and by Routledge
52 Vanderbilt Avenue, New York, NY 10017

Routledge is an imprint of the Taylor & Francis Group, an informa business

First edition published by HarperCollins Academic 1985
Fourth edition published by Routledge 2010

British Library Cataloguing-in-Publication Data
A catalogue record for this book is available from the British Library

Library of Congress Cataloging-in-Publication Data
Names: Doganis, Rigas, author.
Title: Flying off course : airline economics and marketing / Rigas Doganis.
Description: 5th Edition. | New York : Routledge, 2019. |
Revised edition of the author's Flying off course, 2010. |
Includes bibliographical references and index.
Identifiers: LCCN 2018039625 (print) | LCCN 2018042218 (ebook) |
ISBN 9781315402987 (Ebook) | ISBN 9781138224230 (hardback : alk. paper) |
ISBN 9781138224247 (pbk. : alk. paper) | ISBN 9781315402987 (ebk)
Subjects: LCSH: Aeronautics, Commercial. | Aeronautics,
Commercial--Marketing. | Airlines. | Airlines--Marketing.
Classification: LCC HE9780 (ebook) |
LCC HE9780 .D64 2019 (print) | DDC 387.7/1--dc22
LC record available at https://lccn.loc.gov/2018039625

ISBN: 978-1-138-22423-0 (hbk)
ISBN: 978-1-138-22424-7 (pbk)
ISBN: 978-1-315-40298-7 (ebk)

Typeset in Bembo
by Integra Software Services Pvt. Ltd.

Contents

12   The impact of ancillaries   271

BY DR JOHN F. O'CONNELL

13   The economics of air freight   287

14   Strategies for success   317

Figures

Tables

Acknowledgements

The international airline industry is complex, dynamic and subject to rapid change and innovation. To understand the industry's economic and operational features one must be close to its pulse. In this I have been fortunate. I have been able to work both within the airline industry itself and as an academic and consultant in air transport.

In February 1995, while a professor of airline management, I was lucky enough to be suddenly invited to Athens to be chairman and chief executive of Olympic Airways, the Greek national airline. Olympic had been losing money heavily. My task was to implement a restructuring plan and turn the company around. Fourteen months later my Greek colleagues and I were able to announce that Olympic had produced its first profit for 18 years. Managing a state-owned airline was a roller-coaster ride, which can best be described as 'long period of crisis management interspersed by short periods of catastrophe management'.

After Olympic I spent four years in the early 2000s as a non-executive director of South African Airways, another state-owned airline, which manifested several of the same problems as Olympic. From December 2005 to the end of 2014 I spent an exciting period as a non-executive director of easyJet. This was a period of rapid growth which saw easyJet become the second largest low-cost airline in Europe and a big player. My experiences of these three airlines has enlivened and enriched my understanding of the airline business. I have learned a great deal from colleagues and executives at Olympic, SAA and easyJet.

Over the last 30 years I have also been closely involved in the industry's problems and aspirations as a professor, researcher and consultant in air transport. I have taught many in-house air transport seminars or led executive workshops for airlines such as Aer Lingus, Finnair, Emirates, LOT, Malaysia Airlines, Royal Jordanian, SAS, Thai International, Vietnam Airlines and most notably Malaysia Airlines and Singapore Airlines. For both of these I ran management short courses for 20 years. These seminars and workshops provided an open forum for frank discussions of airline trends and problems, where established truths were constantly challenged. In the process I learned much about the airline industry. I am indebted to the countless participants from these and many other airlines who helped me gain a deeper insight into their industry.

For the same reasons, I would also like to thank my numerous post-graduate students at the Universities of Westminster and Cranfield, many of whom now hold key positions in aviation.

In the long years of my involvement with air transport there have been so many who have influenced my thoughts that it is difficult to mention them all. I would like to single out some of my former colleagues at the Department of Air Transport at

Cranfield University, who have been enormously helpful not only while I was at Cranfield but in the many years since: Dr Fariba Alamdari (now at Boeing), Prof. Peter Morrell, Ralph Anker, Prof. Keith Mason, Dr Romano Pagliari, Dr Frankie O'Connell (now at Surrey University), Ian Stockman and Andrew Lobbenberg (now aviation analyst at HSBC). Beyond Cranfield I should mention John Balfour, Paul Clark, Brian Pearce, Chief Economist at IATA, Dr Nigel Dennis at the University of Westminster, Dr Michael Hanke, Dr Conor Whelan, Andy Hofton, James Halstead, Tim Coombs, Chris Tarry and Peter Harbison. The numerous discussions I have had with them all on a variety of air transport topics in recent years have contributed significantly to the current edition.

I am also indebted to Boeing, Airbus and the International Air Transport Association who have provided some key diagrams, also to Edward Greenslet who gave me access to 'Airline Monitor' and its amazing data. Finally, I must thank Dr Conor Whelan and Dr John F. O'Connell, both of whom have gone out of their way to help with several diagrams. I am especially grateful to the latter, who also wrote a new chapter on ancillaries, a valuable addition to this book.

Abbreviations

ACMI	Aircraft, crew, maintenance and insurance (type of aircraft operating lease)
AEA	Association of European Airlines
ANA	All Nippon Airways
ASEAN	Association of South East Asian Nations
ATB	automated ticket and boarding pass
ATK	available tonne-kilometre
BA	British Airways
CAA	Civil Aviation Authority
CAB	(US) Civil Aeronautics Board
CASK	cost per available seat-kilometre or CASM cost per seat mile
CRM	customer relationship management
DOC	director operating cost
EASA	European Aviation Safety Agency
EDI	electronic data interchange
EEA	European Economic Area
EU	European Union
FAA	(US) Federal Aviation Administration
FFP	frequent flyer programme
GDP	gross domestic product
GDS	global distribution system
GNP	gross national product
IAG	International Airlines Group (BA, Iberia, Aer Lingus and Vueling)
IATA	International Air Transport Association
ICAO	International Civil Aviation Organization
IFE	in-flight entertainment
IOC	indirect operating costs
IT	inclusive tour (holiday package)
ITC	inclusive tour charter
JAA	Joint Airworthiness Authority
JAL	Japan Airlines
JAR	Joint Airworthiness Requirements
JIT	just in time
MTOW	maximum take-off weight
OPEC	Organization of Petroleum-exporting Countries
OTA	online travel agency
PAL	Philippine Airlines

RASK	revenue per available seat-kilometre or RASM – per seat-mile
RPK	revenue per passenger-kilometre
SAS	Scandinavian Airlines System
SIA	Singapore International Airlines
SITC	Standard International Trade Classification
td	time-definite cargo
ULD	unit load device
UPS	United Parcel Service
VFR	visiting friends or relatives

N.B.: ATK and RPK are referred to in the Glossary and some abbreviations are already shown there.

Introduction

The airline industry presents an enigma. Over the last 50 years it has experienced fluctuating but steadily falling unit costs combined with continuous and, at times, rapid growth in demand for its products. This should have been a recipe for financial success. Yet the airline industry as a whole has been only marginally profitable in most years. It was not until the period 2015 to 2018 that the industry's financial returns, at last, more than covered the cost of capital. But even during this period of golden profits there were many airlines that were loss-making, some technically bankrupt and many more generating marginal or inadequate profits.

The performance of the airline has also been markedly cyclical. In the three decades up to 2000, five or six years of profit were followed by three to five years of losses. It was the loss-making years which ensured that long-run profitability was only marginal. This was despite the fact that technological improvements in aviation led to falling unit costs, which in turn allowed airlines to cut fares. Declining fares, growing personal incomes in most leading economies and rapidly expanding world trade generated a growing demand for both business and leisure travel. A seemingly insatiable demand. But this has failed to ensure long-term profitability.

The marked cyclicality of the industry was evident again in the early 2000s as losses returned, but the downturn this time became longer and deeper than during any previous period of losses. The United States' airlines posted huge losses. The airline industry as a whole took seven years to recover fully from the world economic slow-down in 2000, the attack on the Twin Towers in New York in September 2001, the Iraq war in March 2003 and the SARS epidemic that followed. These were external shocks. They resulted in the airline industry as a whole making substantial losses in the six years 2000 to 2005, breaking even in 2006 and posting the first industry-wide profit of US$12 billion in 2007. Then came the world economic crisis of 2008 and losses returned. (Figure 1.1 in Chapter 1.)

The 2000s were a difficult decade for airlines but the industry's failure to generate adequate profits sooner was due not only to the external shocks but also in part to internally inflicted wounds. Liberalisation and the increased opportunities for competition led to over-capacity in many markets and induced airline managements to cut fares and tariffs even when costs were rising. But it was the airlines themselves who had created the over-capacity in the first place, either by over-rapid expansion or by failing to cut back capacity in markets where they were no longer competitive. By the end of the decade the airline industry appeared once more to be flying off course.

Losses in 2008 and 2009 were short-lived, however. The traditional cyclical pattern described earlier appeared to be broken. In 2010 the airline industry entered a decade of profit. The industry as a whole generated reasonable profits for the following five years though they were not sufficient to cover the cost of capital. Then, following the collapse in the price of aviation fuel in mid-2014, the industry recorded super-high profits until 2018 and for the first time began generating returns greater than the cost of capital. Almost a decade of continuous global airline profits was unprecedented.

But high overall profits hid the reality that there were many airlines around the world that regularly made losses or very inadequate profits. In Europe alone in mid-2017 three reasonably sized airlines collapsed or went into bankruptcy – Air Berlin, Monarch and Alitalia. Elsewhere, others such as Air India, South African Airways and Malaysia Airlines needed government financial support to keep flying.

There is no simple explanation to the apparent contradiction between the industry's high overall profitability in recent years and the poor financial performance of so many airlines. For the individual airline, financial success depends on matching supply and demand in a way that is both efficient and profitable. This is the underlying theme and focus of the book. While airline managements have considerable control over costs, they can influence demand but cannot control it. Hence the matching process is not an easy one. To help in understanding the process this book provides a practical insight into key aspects of airline operations, planning and marketing within the conceptual framework of economics.

The book works through the issues logically. First it explores key trends and characteristics of the airline industry including its regulatory structure. Then it examines various aspects of the supply side of the industry. This is followed by several chapters concerned with the demand side of the industry and with the process of matching demand and supply. A brief final chapter covers air freight economics.

The airline industry exhibits some unique features and characteristics which colour and affect its operations. These and key trends are outlined in Chapter 1. Any understanding of the economics of the industry must also start with the regulatory framework that circumscribes and constrains airlines' freedom of action. On many international air routes a traditional and highly regulated market environment still persists, though such routes are declining in number. Elsewhere, in some major markets the economic regulation of air transport has been progressively relaxed as a result of pressure from the United States, the European Union and several other states. Thus, regulated and so-called 'open skies' markets co-exist side by side (Chapter 2).

In the next part of the book the focus is on understanding both airline costs and the factors that affect them (Chapters 3 and 4). Such understanding is essential in order to successfully match the supply of air services with demand.

Until the late 1990s, airline economics was primarily concerned with the more traditional or so-called network airlines operating hub-based radial networks; but then a new airline business model emerged, that of the low-cost or budget no-frills airlines. Growing fast and profitably, these LCCs have proved a real threat to the network airlines. The particular economics of this model needs to be assessed (Chapter 5). There is a much older low-cost model, that of the charter or non-scheduled airline. It is of some importance in Europe and to a lesser extent in North America. Its characteristics and advantages require special attention (Chapter 6).

A key feature of the airline industry during the last 25 years has been the growth of a multiplicity of inter-airline alliances of various kinds from simple bilateral commercial agreements or multi-national alliances to joint ventures or even equity cross-share holdings. They have become a crucial element of the supply side of the industry (Chapter 7).

The book then examines the demand for air services and the processes, such as marketing or pricing, which enable airline executives to match demand and supply in a way that generates adequate profits. Understanding demand is the first step in the marketing process (Chapter 8). A thorough appreciation of demand must also be used to develop traffic and other forecasts, since every activity within an airline ultimately stems from a forecast (Chapter 9).

Supply and demand are brought together in a number of ways, but most crucially through effective product planning (Chapter 10). Price is a key element of the airline product or service and deserves particular attention. Alternative airline pricing policies and strategies need careful consideration, especially as low-cost airlines have introduced new pricing concepts (Chapter 11). In recent years, airlines have introduced additional sources of revenues, the so-called ancillaries, to complement fare revenues. Ancillary incomes are generated from a wide range of services and products and are of growing significance for the financial performance of many airlines (Chapter 12).

While the book focuses on passenger services, the importance and role of air freight should not be forgotten. For several airlines it is crucially important both in output and revenue terms. Freight requires special attention since many of its economic and operational characteristics are different (Chapter 13).

Based on the foregoing analyses it is possible to draw some conclusions as to the strategies airlines with different models should follow in pursuit of longer-term success (Chapter 14).

This book is concerned primarily with international air transport, which accounts worldwide for about two-thirds of the industry's output. Only for the airlines of a few large countries such as the United States, the Soviet Union, Brazil and China are domestic operations of greater significance than international, though most of their major domestic airlines also operate internationally. In most countries the larger airlines are primarily concerned with international air services while several of them operate only internationally. Nevertheless, the economic analysis which follows is in many respects equally relevant to domestic air transport.

There is no magic wand to ensure success within the international airline industry. This book attempts to flesh out the economic and operational issues which must be understood in order to match supply and demand. Only when this has been done can airlines ensure some measure of success in this most dynamic of industries. So come, fly with me.

1 Characteristics and trends in the airline operations

> We have to adapt to low margins and high investments. In a life and death business that is a crazy combination.
>
> (Carsten Spohr, CEO Lufthansa, May 2016)

1.1 The nature of the airline product

The airline industry has three key characteristics. First, the demand for air services, whether for passengers or freight, is a derived demand. Second, the product is very homogenous and, third, it cannot be stored. These are fairly obvious features but are crucial to understanding the economies of airline operations. They also ensure that the airline industry is dynamic and exciting.

As far as passenger services are concerned, the air journey is seen not as an end in itself, but as part of a business trip, a two-week or two-day leisure trip, or a weekend visit to see relatives. The air journey is a part of a variety of other products or services. A number of important considerations flow from this. The demand for passenger air services is a derived demand. It is dependent on the demand for these other activities. This means that to forecast the demand for air services one needs ideally to forecast the demand for all these other types of expenditure. It also means that there has been strong pressure on the airlines to expand vertically into other areas of the travel industry, such as hotels, travel agencies, car hire or tour organisers, in order to gain greater control over the total travel product. There is also a direct effect on airline marketing techniques in the sense that these are frequently oriented towards selling and promoting the total product, whether it be a business or holiday trip or a weekend excursion, rather than selling a particular airline. In newspaper and television advertisements airlines often try to interest the reader or viewer in a particular destination or a particular type of trip, and only as an afterthought, almost, do they suggest the airline that might be used.

On the other hand, airlines have to face the realisation that one airline seat is very much like another and that from the passenger's viewpoint there is little difference between one jet aircraft and another. Equally, for the shipper or freight forwarder the major decision will be whether to ship by air or surface and having taken the decision to use air he may have difficulty in perceiving any significant difference in quality of service between one airline and the next serving a particular route with similar frequencies.

Thus, while air journeys may be only one part of a variety of heterogeneous products or services with different market structures, the air service part of these products is itself fairly homogeneous. One airline seat is very much like another and one freight hold is no different from the next. Even when airlines wish to differentiate their products, competitive forces and the fact that they are flying similar or identical aircraft have meant that they often end up offering very similar products. This is especially so in Economy class cabins and on shorter sectors.

The consequences of the homogeneous nature of the airline product are two-fold. First, in competitive markets, it pushes airlines into making costly efforts to try to differentiate their services and products from those of their competitors. They do this by being first to introduce new aircraft types, by increasing their frequency of service, by spending more on ground services, by focusing on their premium cabins, by building a more user-friendly website, by advertising and by effective use of social media. Moreover, much of the advertising is aimed at trying to convince passengers or freight agents that the product they offer is appreciably better than that of their competitors because of the friendliness of the hostesses or the culinary expertise of their chefs, the comfort of their seats, or because of other claims, all of which may be dubious and difficult to assess. In the end, because of the difficulties of substantiating many claims related to service quality, airlines very frequently resort to competing on price, which is tangible and price differences are demonstrable. This is the strategy most clearly adopted by the low-cost airlines.

Second, the homogeneous nature of the airline product makes the emergence of entirely new airlines or the incursion of new airlines on existing routes relatively easy.

This dichotomy between the heterogeneity of the various products, of which the air service is only a part, and the homogeneity of the air services themselves is a constant constraint in airline planning, a constraint which often results in apparently contradictory decisions and actions by airline managements.

A third defining characteristic of the airline industry, one which it shares with other transport modes but also with hotels, is that its product cannot be stored. It disappears the moment it is produced. Once a flight takes off, any empty seats or unused cargo capacity is lost forever. It wastes immediately. This is costly for airlines. As a consequence, airline executives make great efforts to reduce such wastage by pushing up the occupancy or load factor of each flight. They use whatever means they can, but most critical is pricing. Different pricing strategies have been used to push up occupancy of both passenger and all cargo flights. One clear consequence of having unsold seats is that those passengers who are on a flight must meet not only their own costs but also cover the costs of the unsold seats. This further complicates pricing and tariff structures.

In short, the airline industry is characterised by trying to meet a demand for its products, which is a derived demand dependent on demand for other products and services. Its products are largely homogenous and difficult to differentiate. Worst of all, they cannot be stored.

1.2 Airline business models

The priciples of airline economics discussed in the chapters that follow are relevant to all sectors of the industry. But one needs to be aware that not all airlines are the same. For historical reasons and especially because of the impact, in the past, of both domestic and international regulations, quite different airline business models have emerged.

The traditional regulatory regime, as described in Chapter 2, ensured that airlines could only fly from and to their own country. With a few exceptions they could not operate air services and carry passengers between points in two countries outside their own. This inevitably meant that airlines developed both domestic and international routes that radiated from their home base. In most cases, the home base was the airport of their own capital city. These bases became 'hubs' where passengers could transfer from one flight to another to fly between two points, which the airline could not serve with direct non-stop flights. The vast majority of traditional scheduled passenger airlines around the world operate radial networks.

In the United States, for somewhat different reasons, the larger airlines also developed hub-based radial networks though they often operated from two or more major hubs and several smaller hubs. The larger number of hubs resulted from the numerous mergers of airlines with complementary radial networks. Scott Kirby, president of United Airlines, early in 2018 summed up the essence of hub networks as follows: '*A hub-and-spoke airline is really a manufacturing company and it is about manufacturing connections*' (quoted in Airline Leader, Jan–Feb 2018).

Airlines whose business model is critically dependent on operating radial networks based on one or more hubs, where passengers can be transferred between flights, are referred to in the following chapters as '*legacy*' or '*network*' airlines.

The network airline model enjoys numerous economic advantages but also suffers some cost disadvantages (Chapter 5, Section 5.7). This model contrasts with that of the 'low-cost or budget' airline model which has emerged over the last 30 years or so. Low-cost airlines (LCCs) have been launched and grown rapidly in response to the progressive liberalisation of both domestic and later international air services. Freed from the constraints of out-dated regulations, they developed networks based on offering direct non-stop services between many points both within and outside their own country or state. They have services radiating from their major base but these are integrated into a matrix of services that criss-cross the country or the region in which they operate.

The low-cost carrier Southwest, the fourth largest US airline, has somewhat distorted the simple point-to-point low-cost model, because it has developed such high frequencies on many of the routes between its various airports that they provide convenient and fast connections for passengers wishing to fly to points not served from their own airport. Effectively Southwest operates 20–25 mini hubs and attracts a significant share of transfer passengers.

Basically, the LCC model's network structure and shape is quite different from that of the traditional scheduled network airlines. This a fundamental difference that affects many aspects of the operations and economics of both models. This will continue to be so even if in some respects the two models appear to be coming closer (for instance, by not offering free on-board catering or charging for seat allocation).

In addition to these two significant business models there are a number of other airline models that have their own distinctive characteristics and are discussed in later chapters.

The third model on the passenger side of the industry is that of the '*leisure or charter*' airline. These are airlines, many of them owned or linked to holiday companies, whose primary business is to sell holiday packages that include flights, hotel rooms and/or car hire or other holiday elements such as sea cruises or tours to historical sites. The holidays are put together and sold by the parent holiday company or any other holiday company that buys seats from the leisure airline. The latter may also sell some of its seats without a holiday package directly to passengers. Leisure or charter airlines are important in Europe and less so in North America but play an insignificant role elsewhere in the world.

Finally, there are two distinct airline business models concerned with the carriage of freight. The most significant in terms of volume of freight transported and size of fleets are the so-called '*integrators*'. These companies are essentially door to door carriers. They not only fly freight between key points but they also provide surface transport to collect freight from its actual origin and deliver it to its ultimate destination. For the air freighting part, the integrators will use freighter aircraft but also book space on passenger services operated by network carriers. The second air freight model is that of the specialist '*all-cargo*' airline whose business is to transport cargo on dedicated freighters.

While most network airlines carry both passengers and freight, some are much more heavily involved in air freight, which may represent up to 40–50 per cent of their total traffic in terms of tonne-kms performed by weight (Section 1.9). Unlike most passenger-focused airlines, these airlines heavily involved in the carriage of freight also operate a small but significant number of freighter aircraft. Do they perhaps represent a different business model?

1.3 A high-growth industry

For the last 60 years the airline industry has been characterised by continued high though declining growth rates in demand for its services. Annual growth in global passenger traffic was much faster in the 1950s and 1960s when aviation was a new industry, but over time growth rates declined as the industry became more mature. But growth rates were still impressive. In the 1970s the annual growth was close to 10 per cent. This meant that passenger traffic, and the airlines with it, doubled in size every seven years or so. In the following decade growth declined to around 6 per cent annually and during the 1990s growth was down slightly at around 5.2 per cent on average each year.

The first decade of the new millennium was a difficult time for the airline industry. It was hit by a world economic downturn early on in 2001–2 and a further global financial crisis signalled by the collapse of Lehman Brothers, the large US bank, in September 2008. This pushed many key economies into recession. Passenger traffic declined sharply on both occasions but then recovered. Despite these setbacks, in the decade 2000 to 2009 passenger traffic worldwide grew annually at an average rate of just below 4 per cent. Of course, there were marked regional variations with traffic growing well above 6 per cent per annum in many Asian markets, but much slower for instance in North America or parts of Africa.

In the years that followed annual growth rates picked up, averaging around 6.5 per cent from 2010 to 2017. By 2017 air transport, and particularly passenger traffic, seemed to have recovered from the impact of the world financial crisis that began in 2008. Not so the air freight market, which, after a huge jump in 2010, then grew only slowly though there was a 9 per cent spurt in 2017.

The steady long-term, though fluctuating, growth in the demand for air travel has been generated by many drivers, several of which reinforced each other. Four developments seem to have been particularly significant.

First, in the second half of the twentieth century rapid technological developments in airframe and engine technology resulted in larger, faster and more economically efficient aircraft. As their hourly productivity (measured in terms of passenger-kms per hour of flying) increased so the unit cost per passenger-km declined. This in turn meant both lower fares and faster and more attractive journey times. (For more on technological change see Section 1.7.)

Second, in Western Europe and North America rising household incomes in the 1960s and 1970s enabled a growing proportion of their population to take advantage of the lower fares and new destinations accessed by flying. But in the 1990s and after 2000 it was in South and East Asia that household incomes were growing fastest. As a consequence air travel from and within countries such as China or India was then growing the fastest. Meanwhile, European and North American air travel was reaching a more mature stage and growth rates slowed.

The third development which stimulated demand for air travel was the progressive liberalisation of the many international and domestic regulations that had previously constrained the expansion and growth of both cross-border and, in many cases, domestic air services (see Chapter 2). In the 1980s and 1990s many of these regulations and rules were loosened. This process, which is still not complete everywhere, had a double impact in stimulating air travel. First, it resulted in flights to more destinations with more direct point-to-point services thereby opening access to new and attractive markets. Second, it increased competition between airlines. This, together with the relaxation of fare or price controls in many markets, created strong downward pressure on air fares. New destinations and lower fares further stimulated the demand for air travel.

Finally, a more recent change which undoubtedly had a major stimulus on air travel growth has been the emergence of a new airline business model, that of the so-called low-cost or budget airlines. In the United States, Southwest launched its low-cost model beyond its Texas heartland into wider domestic operations following deregulation of US domestic air services in 1978. In Europe, low-cost airlines grew rapidly after the creation of the single European aviation market in the mid-1990s. In South-east and East Asia, international low-cost airlines emerged during the new millennium as regulations on market access and pricing were gradually relaxed. The growth of the low-cost airline sector was directly linked to the progressive deregulation of air services.

The low-cost airlines launched fares that were often 40–60 per cent lower than those of the traditional, so-called legacy or network airlines, and they simplified the fare structures and rules. They also opened up new routes, in many cases flying to airports that had previously had few or no scheduled air services. Substantially lower fares and the offer of many new destinations have generated rapid traffic growth in many markets. This has been so not only on new routes but also on routes already served by existing legacy carriers. In previously dense markets such as London–Barcelona total passenger traffic doubled in five years after low-cost carriers entered this route in 1997 (see Chapter 5 for economics of the low-cost model).

Low-cost carriers had a twin impact on air fares. Not only were their own fares low, but in offering competitive low fares they forced the legacy carriers to lower their own fares and make them more flexible. This further stimulated demand.

1.4 Declining fares and yields

Technological innovation, increased competition following progressive deregulation and the emergence of low-cost airlines have together been the key drivers pushing down the real price of air transport in the last 50 years. The revenue generated by airlines per tonne-km carried is a good indicator of how fares and cargo rates have fallen over time. Average revenue per tonne-km, in current values, for the world's airlines fell from US $2.40 in the early 1970s to around $1.30 15 years later in 1985: a drop of almost half. By 2000 it had dropped further to less than $0.80 per tonne-km.

Current yields subsequently fluctuated around this level until 2010 when they started rising but then fell sharply after 2014 in line with falling fuel prices and declining costs. By 2017 they were around $ 0.76 per tonne-km and expected to rise moderately in 2018.

In real or constant value terms, that is adjusting for inflation, average yields more or less halved between 2000 and 2018 falling particularly sharply after 2012 (Figure 1.1). Yields declined initially because of growing competition and the impact of low-cost carriers and, after 2014, in response to falling oil prices. Falling real yields have posed a constant and critical challenge for airline executives.

1.5 The paradox – marginal profitability

The airline industry appears to be strongly influenced by external factors. This inevitably means that growth rates fluctuate from year to year. Nevertheless, the underlying trend has been one of consistently good growth in demand, but at a declining rate. Industries or businesses faced with steady long-term growth of demand for their products or services should be basking in substantial profits. Not so the airlines. This is the paradox.

The financial performance of the world's airlines taken as a whole has been very marginal, even in the early years when the industry was highly regulated and largely protected from internal competition.

One measure of profitability commonly used among airlines is the profit margin (or operating ratio), which is the annual operating profit or loss or the net profit or loss, after tax, expressed as a percentage of the total annual revenue. This is calculated annually for the world's airlines by the International Civil Aviation Organization (ICAO). The profit margin for the years from 2000 to 2018 is shown diagramatically in Figure 1.2. This figure also shows the global airline industry's net profit after payment of interest and other non-operating items.

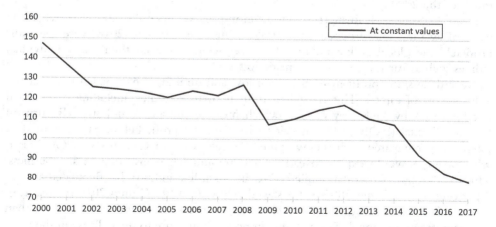

Figure 1.1 Average yield IATA airlines in US cents per tonne-km, 2000–18

Source: Brian Pearce. *Airline Industry Economic Performance: Mid-2018 Update*. Geneva: IATA

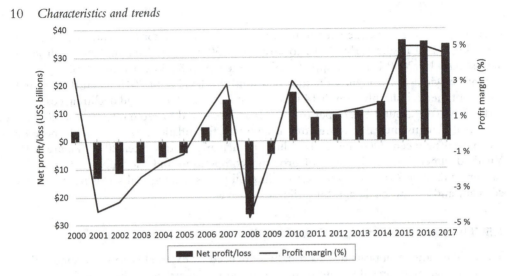

Figure 1.2 Net profit/loss and profit margin of world's airlines, 2000–17
Source: Compiled using ICAO and IATA data

In the 30 years prior to 2000, the airline industry's financial performance was clearly evident. Four to five years of poor or bad performance were generally followed by an upturn and five or six years of improving results and profits. But the profits after interest and tax rarely exceeded 2 per cent of revenues.

This neat cyclical pattern was broken in the new millennium because it started with five years during which losses were deeper and longer-lasting than ever before. (Figure 1.2). Then two years, 2006 and 2007, when financial results began to improve before another major collapse in 2008–2009 following the US and European banking and financial crises, which caused a drop in both leisure and business travel in many key markets. This was the worst decade the airline industry has experienced, though some airlines such as Cathay Pacific, Singapore or British Airways were profitable for much of the 2000s.

From 2010 onwards financial results again improved, especially after 2014 when the price of aviation fuel dropped dramatically. The years 2015 to 2018 were the most profitable the global airline industry had ever seen. Yet even then many individual airlines such as Air India or Alitalia made losses.

Nevertheless, the profit margins remain low and until 2015 have failed to cover the airlines' cost of capital. This is evident from numerous studies, including one carried out for IATA by McKinsey & Co., which measure the airline industry's Return on Invested Capital (ROIC). This is calculated from the profit before payment of debt interest and compared with the Weighted Average Cost of Capital (WACC). This is what investors would expect to earn as a minimum when investing in any business. This IATA report shows that while ROIC in the airline industry has fluctuated around 4 per cent since the mid-1990s it has stayed below the WACC until 2015 (Figure 1.3). It was only in financial years 2015 to 2017 that at last the airline industry was more than covering its cost of capital. This was due in no small measure to the collapse in the price of fuel in the second half of 2014.

Figure 1.3 Global airline returns below the cost of capital until 2015
Source: Brian Pearce. *Airline Industry Economic Performance: Mid-2018 Update.* Geneva: IATA

Conversely, over the same period since the mid-1990s many sectors providing goods or services to airlines were more than covering their cost of capital. This was particularly true of travel agencies, freight forwarders and computer reservation system providers, and to a lesser extent of ground-handlers, in-flight catering and aircraft maintenance organisations.

Numerous factors may help explain the airline industry's marginal profitability and its failure to cover its cost of capital in the years prior to 2015. Key among them was the long-term decline in average fares or yield, as highlighted in the previous section. While unit costs have also declined over the last 40 years, the industry as a whole has proved unable to ensure that its revenues more than adequately exceeded its costs. Several airlines have managed to generate adequate profits, but the airline industry as a whole has not done so, at least not until 2015–18.

1.6 Three drivers of airline profitability

There is no simple explanation of the apparent contradiction between the airline industry's relatively rapid long-term growth and its cyclical and marginal profitability, but for the individual airline overcoming this contradiction means matching supply and demand for its services in a way that is both efficient and profitable. This is the essence of airline management and planning. It is about matching the supply of air services, which management can largely control, with the demand for such services, over which management has much less influence.

To be successful in this an airline can be a low-cost operator or a high-cost operator. What determines profitability is the airline's ability to generate unit revenues higher than its unit costs. An airline, within any regulatory constraints, can itself determine the level and nature of services it offers and choose the various markets it wishes to serve. In turn, the way it organises these services and manages the inputs required to supply them impacts directly on its costs. Though the cost of some inputs, such as fuel or airport charges, are externally determined, an airline can have a significant impact on its unit costs both by the way it uses those inputs whose costs are externally determined and the control it exercises over other more controllable inputs. But cost efficiency and low unit costs do not guarantee profit if an airline is unable to generate even the low unit revenues necessary to cover such costs.

Airlines' unit costs vary enormously. Some have average unit costs two or three times as high as those of some of their competitors. Does this mean that they are inefficient high-cost operators? Not necessarily. As will become apparent in the course of this book, high unit costs for some airlines may be a function of the nature of their operations and/or the high externally determined costs for some inputs, rather than be the result of poor management. For example, other things being equal, short-haul operations will have higher unit costs than long-haul services. Equally, smaller aircraft are likely to generate higher costs per passenger-km than much larger aircraft.

The challenge for any airline is whether, given the level of its unit costs, it can plan and market its services, for passengers or cargo, in such a way as to generate unit revenues higher than its unit costs. In other words, low unit costs alone do not necessarily ensure profitability though, clearly, they make it easier to achieve.

During the last decade, two Asian airlines, Air India and Pakistan International Airlines, operated with unit costs (CASK) which were relatively low when compared with many traditional legacy airlines. This was in part because they benefited from low unit costs of labour. Yet in most years, their product and marketing strategies failed to ensure that their unit revenues (RASK) were sufficiently high to cover their low unit costs. As a result, they made substantial losses and required successive injections of cash from their governments to keep flying.

Even very low-cost airlines may fail in meeting this challenge. In Europe in the early years of the twentieth century one of the lower-cost operators was SkyEurope, a low-cost or budget airline launched in 2002. Yet by 2009 it had collapsed, despite operating at relatively good load factors. Its fares were just too low! Conversely, since 2008, many airlines with relatively high unit costs, such as Delta or American or British Airways, have managed to be profitable in most years.

Airlines can be low cost and very unprofitable or high cost and financially sound. Unit costs or unit revenues are not critical in themselves. For airline executives the key to financial success is to ensure that unit revenues exceed unit costs and by as much as possible.

CASK is the unit cost of a single seat-km. It is arrived at by dividing the total costs of an airline or a route by the total seat-kms flown. RASK is the revenue generated per seat-km. It is a function of the average revenue or fare per passenger (i.e. how much is earned from each passenger on a flight travelled) and the seat factor (i.e. the proportion of seats filled by passengers). In other words, the average revenue per passenger multiplied by the number of passengers produces the total revenue. The total revenues divided by the total seat-kms generated (i.e. the seats multiplied by the distance) produces the RASK (the revenue per available seat-km). This calculation can be done for a flight, a route or an airline's total network.

It is the total revenue that determines the RASK. But the total revenue itself is a function of the average revenue per passenger and the percentage of seats sold. If the seat factor is low, then the fare or revenue per passenger needs to be much higher to compensate for the smaller number of passengers. Conversely, if a flight is very full a lower average revenue per passenger may still generate a higher total revenue and therefore a higher RASK

It is important to bear in mind that the revenue per passenger is not just the average fare paid or the so-called yield but may also include the revenue generated from ancillary revenues such as fees for baggage, ticket changes and so on.

In brief, airline executives and planners must juggle with three variables in trying to generate profits, the CASK (cost per seat-km), the revenue per passenger-km and the occupancy factor, which, together, produce the RASK (revenue per seat-km). These are the three drivers of success.

The difficulties faced by airline executives in trying to match supply and demand by balancing these three variables are compounded by the fact that the airline industry is very dynamic and subject to structural instability. The industry's fortunes oscillate wildly in response to both external factors such as rapid changes in the price of fuel and internally induced problems such as over-supply of capacity.

While the discussion has focused on passenger costs and revenues, the same is also true of air freight. To generate profits, cargo executives must balance cargo revenues per tonne carried, cargo load factor and costs per available tonne-km.

1.7 Rapid technological change

Continuous technological innovation has been a key feature of air transport. In the early years, innovation centred on the development of the jet engine for civil use, first in a turbo propeller form and later as a pure jet. Successive developments in the jet engine have consistently improved its efficiency and propulsive power. The emergence of larger and more powerful engines in association with improvements in airframe design and in control systems has resulted over the last 50 years or so in successive and significant improvements in aircraft speed and size. Higher speeds and larger aircraft have in turn produced significant jumps in aircraft hourly productivity. (This is calculated by multiplying the maximum payload an aircraft can carry by its average hourly block speed, i.e. the distance it can fly in an hour.) In turn, higher hourly productivity meant lower costs per seat.

An appreciation of technological developments and their impact on costs and operations is crucial in understanding airline economics.

An early breakthrough was the conversion of the military turbo-jet engine for use in civil aircraft. The arrival of the turbo-jet engine had a two-fold impact. In the 1960s the turbo-jets led to a dramatic increase in speeds, while the size of the aircraft did not increase appreciably. In the later 1960s and early 1970s there was no appreciable increase in speeds, because existing speeds were approaching the sound barrier, but there was a significant increase in the size of aircraft, particularly with the introduction of wide-body fuselages. The earlier increases in speeds combined with these significant jumps in aircraft size together produced major improvements in aircraft productivity so that while the Boeing 720B in 1960 was producing 11,600 tonne-km per flying hour, only 10 years later the hourly productivity of the Boeing 747, the first so-called 'Jumbo', was three times as great. The Airbus A-300 introduced in 1974 was the first short-haul wide-body aircraft. Its productivity was about twice as high as that of the narrow-body, short-haul aircraft then in service.

The next major technological breakthrough was the production of civil aircraft flying faster than the speed of sound. But in economic terms this was a failure. The Anglo-French Concorde, which entered service in 1976, flew more than twice as fast as its predecessors yet was able to do this only through a very significant reduction in size. Because of this penalty, supersonic aircraft had a lower hourly productivity than their competitors on long-haul routes. They also burnt excessive amounts of fuel. These two features meant high costs per seat or seat-km and very high fares. This made their commercial viability very problematic, even on over-water routes where there were no noise constraints. This aircraft was only operated by British Airways and Air France, very much as a public relations exercise and only after some of the capital debts arising from its purchase were written off by the co-respective governments. Eventually, in the early 2000s both airlines grounded their Concordes to cut their losses. The last Concorde scheduled flight landed at London Heathrow on 24 October 2003.

From the mid-1970s onwards the rate of technological innovation at first slackened. Attention switched to the development of more efficient wide-bodied medium-haul aircraft such as the Boeing 767 and the Airbus A-310. Developments here were based essentially on existing engine and airframe technology, though there were major developments in avionics, in the early use of lighter composite materials, in airframe construction and in other areas. At the same time, the trend towards larger aircraft flying at the same speed continued. An example is the Airbus A-320 introduced in 1988, which, with up to 180 seats, was significantly larger than the 100- to 130-seater aircraft it was intended to replace. Again, important gains in hourly productivity resulted in lower costs per seat-km.

During the 1990s the focus was on the introduction of extended-range versions of the newer twin-engined jets, such as the Boeing 767-200 EQ, and offering 200 to 250 seats. These allowed more direct non-stop flights on thinner long-haul routes that could not support the large traditional long-haul aircraft such as the Boeing 747 with 400 seats or more. This trend towards medium-sized aircraft for long-haul services led to the introduction of the Airbus A340 in 1993 and the Boeing 777 in 1995.

Technologically, more significant was the development of small, efficient and light jet engines that could be used to power smaller passenger aircraft. Such aircraft had hitherto been dependent on turbo-propeller engines, but they were noisy and aircraft speeds were very low. The 50-seater Canadair Regional Jet (CRJ), which first entered service in November 1992, and the Embraer ERJ 145, also with 50 seats, which launched services in 1997, revolutionised regional air services. They offered faster and more comfortable jet travel on thinner short-haul routes previously the preserve of turbo-prop aircraft. They were followed in the early 2000s by larger versions such as the CRJ 900 with 86 seats and the 98-seater Embraer 190.

While technological improvements in all areas of both engines and airframes have continued in the years since 2000, more recently the focus has been on two developments, both of which would have a significant economic impact. The first was the more extensive use of lighter composite materials in airframes. By reducing the weight of the aircraft, such composites, if used extensively, could reduce fuel consumption and consequently operating costs. This was critically important in periods when fuel prices were especially high as in the years 2006 to 2008 and again in the years up to another peak in 2014. Reducing fuel burn per aircraft-kilometre flown was also critically important in view of growing concern about the impact of aircraft emissions on the environment. Leading in the adoption of this new composite technology has been the mid-sized, long-haul Boeing 787 Dreamliner, in which as much as 50 per cent of the primary structure, including the fuselage and wings, is made of composite materials. All Nippon Airways was first to launch the Dreamliner into service in 2011. Boeing claimed that the extensive use of lighter composites plus improved engines would result in a reduction of up to 20 per cent in fuel consumption per passenger carried, compared to existing aircraft types.

Four years later, in January 2015, the Airbus A350 entered service with Qatar Airways being the launch customer. Similar in size to the Boeing 787 it, too, had a large proportion of its fuselage and wings made from carbon-fibre composites.

The second major development in recent years has been in new engine technology for single-aisle aircraft. Using different approaches, the Pratt and Whitney geared turbofan engine and the CFM International LEAP engine were initially developed for use in short-haul aircraft such as the Airbus A320 and Boeing 737 families. These engines were combined with the use of composites in the Airbus A320neo (entered service 2016) or the Boeing 737 MAX (in service 2017) and resulted in reducing fuel consumption per kilometre flown by up to 15 per cent. Embraer in the Embraer E2 and the Bombardier CSeries also introduced the newer engine technology in their smaller aircraft.

Another notable innovation was a quantum jump in aircraft size, spearheaded by the Airbus A380, which first entered service with Singapore Airlines in October 2007. With a maximum take-off weight of around 40 per cent greater than that of a Boeing 747-400, it can carry up to 550–600 passengers in a three-class cabin or up to 800 in an all-economy configuration. This major increase in size marked another jump in hourly productivity and a further reduction in cost per seat-km. However, sales of this aircraft have been disappointing. Except for use on a few trunk routes, where airports at one or both ends are congested, it has proved too large. Also, the newer-technology Boeing 787 and Airbus A350 aircraft offer seat-km costs that are almost comparable while offering the flexibility of being operated on thinner, longer routes or denser routes needing higher frequencies. Emirates remains, by far, the largest operator of the A380 fleet.

1.8 Impact of technological innovation on costs

These developments described so briefly above, which were matched by equally rapid innovations in other areas of aviation technology in the air and on the ground, were due primarily to the increasing efficiency of the jet engine. For a given level of propulsive thrust successive engines were able to carry a larger payload and to carry it faster as well. This, combined with other economies arising from the greater size of aircraft and the increasing use of lighter composite materials, resulted in ever-decreasing costs per capacity tonne-kilometre (see Chapter 4, Section 4.6 for the impact of size and speed on unit costs). Herein lies the significance of the technological improvements in aviation and of the increase in aircraft productivity they made possible.

Helped by both the switch to larger aircraft and the fall in the real price of fuel, airline costs declined steadily in constant value terms during the 1980s and the 1990s. This trend was helped by the airlines' own strenuous efforts, especially in the early years of the latter decade, to drive down their non-fuel costs. They were under pressure to reduce costs because of the increased fare competition between airlines as more and more international markets were liberalised. In constant value terms, global unit costs per ASK fell by about one-third between 1990 and 2000, as shown by the upper line in Figure 1.4.

The economic downturn in the early years of the new millennium resulted in the collapse of yields in many markets and rising losses increased pressure on airlines to further reduce costs, especially non-fuel costs, that were more controllable. The focus was on reducing staff numbers, in order to reduce wage costs, and on reducing distribution costs by switching to direct airline online sales, by cutting or eliminating agents' commission, where possible, and by introducing electronic ticketing.

In the United States, several major airlines filed for Chapter 11 bankruptcy protection. This enabled them to cut staff levels dramatically, by up to one-third, while also cutting average salaries by around 30 per cent. The US majors also renegotiated leasing and other contracts. Non-fuel costs dropped.

The trebling of the fuel price between 2002 and 2006 (solid bottom line in Figure 1.4) reinforced the need to cut all other costs. For the airline industry as a whole, reductions in non-fuel costs more or less balanced the increasing cost of fuel. As a result, airline costs were more or less stable in real or constant value terms in the period 2000 to 2006. But when fuel prices doubled between 2007 and mid-2008 airline total unit operating costs shot up.

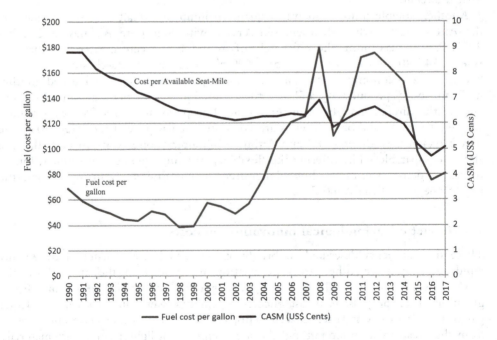

Figure 1.4 Trends in real unit costs and fuel costs, 1990–2017

Note: CASM is at constant 1982–84 US dollars. Fuel costs per gallon are at constant 1987 US dollars

Source: Compiled from Airline Monitor October 2017 (based on ICAO data)

Since then airline unit costs have tended to mirror movements in the price of oil. As the latter moved down after 2008 so did airline costs, but then climbed slowly. When this collapsed in late 2014 airline costs went down too. The price of aviation fuel oscillated around a very low level from 2015 to 2017. This, combined again with drastic efforts to cut non-fuel costs following the economic crisis of 2007–8, helped the airline industry to lower costs and produce record profits in 2015, 2016 and 2017.

Technological innovation has clearly facilitated a long-run trend towards lower unit costs in real terms per seat-km or tonne-km carried. This trend has been reinforced when the price of aviation fuel has declined and when airlines have made strenuous efforts to reduce non-fuel costs. Inevitably, such efforts were particularly marked when fuel costs were rising.

1.9 A passenger and freight business

It is generally assumed that airlines are primarily concerned with carrying passengers and that freight and mail traffic are relatively unimportant both in terms of output and of revenue. This is far from being the truth. In 2017 around 26 per cent of the world's scheduled airline output was concerned with the carriage of freight and mail, though mail itself is tiny (Table 1.1). Passenger traffic accounted for the rest. On international routes, where distances are greater and air transport becomes more competitive, freight comes into its own, generating almost one-third (32 per cent) of the world's tonne-kms. However, in recent years this share has tended to decrease. Conversely, freight's share is very much lower on domestic air services. This is because surface transport, road and rail, is generally more competitive in domestic freight markets.

These global figures hide considerable variations between airlines. A few large international airlines, such as Federal Express and UPS or Cargolux, are exclusively concerned with the carriage of freight. They are the exceptions. Most airlines are combination carriers, that is they transport both freight and passengers on their international services. But their degree of involvement in the carriage of freight varies enormously (Table 1.2) and does not change much from year to year.

At the bottom of this table are Asian carriers such as Korean Air, Cathay Pacific, Qatar Airways or Singapore Airlines for whom air freight represents close to half or even well over half of their total global production in terms of revenue tonne-kilometres, that is traffic carried. These big air freight carriers invariably bolster their cargo capacity by operating fleets of all-cargo freighters.

Table 1.1 Passenger and freight traffic mix on scheduled services of world's airlines, 2017

	Traffic share			
	International traffic (%)	*Domestic traffic (%)*	*Total traffic (%)*	*Total revenue All services (%)*
Passenger	68	89	74	85
Freight and mail	32	11	26	15
Total	100.0	100.0	100.0	100.0

Note: For conversion of pax.kms into pax.tonne-kms see Glossary
Source: Compiled using ICAO/IATA data

They are clearly quite different airlines from those at the top end of Table 1.2, for whom freight and mail together account for less than 20 per cent of their total traffic. Interestingly, the US major carriers, American, United and Delta, are in this latter group generating around 10 per cent or less of their business from freight. This is largely because they have lost much of the US international and, for that matter, most of the domestic, freight market to the integrators; that is the all-cargo door-to-door carriers such as Federal Express and UPS (see Chapter 13), or to foreign airlines such as Korean Air or Lufthansa.

Low-cost budget airlines are the least involved in the carriage of freight. Most carry no freight or only limited amounts. Their prime focus is passengers and their operating and economic model requires fast turnarounds at airports, which is often incompatible with off-loading and loading cargo.

It is significant that while freight accounts for about one-quarter of total airline production it generates only about 15 per cent of total operating revenue (Table 1.1). This means that the average revenue per tonne-kilometre of freight and, incidentally, of mail, must be very much lower than the average revenue or yield generated by passenger tonne-kilometres. Despite this it is evident from Chapter 13 that freight revenues make an important contribution to many airlines' overall profitability (to convert passenger-kms into passenger tonne-kms see Glossary).

Table 1.2 Passenger and freight traffic mix on sample of combination airlines, 2017

	Distribution revenue tonne-kms carried			
	Passenger	*Mail*	*Freight*	*Total*
	%	%	%	%
Delta Air Lines	91	1	8	100
Aeroflot	89	1	10	100
American Airlines	88	1	11	100
United Airlines	86	2	12	100
Aeromexico	85	*	15	100
Air Canada	80	1	19	100
Qantas	80	2	18	100
Air France	77	1	22	100
British Airways	76	1	23	100
Turkish Airlines	73	1	26	100
Global Airlines' Average	**74**	**1**	**25**	**100**
China Eastern	73	*	27	100
Emirates	68	1	31	100
Ethiopian Airlines	67	*	33	100
Lufthansa	67	1	32	100
Air China	65	1	34	100
Singapore Airlines	58	1	42	100
Qatar Airways	54	*	46	100
Cathay Pacific	49	2	49	100
Korean Air	46	1	53	100

Note: * = less than 0.5%
Source: Compiled by author from IATA Statistics

Over the airline industry as a whole, the carriage of freight is a significant factor, both in terms of the amount of productive resources absorbed by it and in terms of its contribution to overall revenues. For an individual airline the split of its activities between passengers and freight clearly affects both its marketing policy and the structure of its revenues. As Tables 1.1 and 1.2 show, the importance of mail as a revenue is very limited and declining. Inevitably, much of the discussion that follows, except in Chapter 13, concentrates on the passenger aspects of both supply and demand. However, this should not mask the significance of air freight for the international airline industry as a whole.

When assessing or comparing passenger airlines' performances one must take account of the degree to which and the way in which they are involved in air freight. This impacts many aspects of their operations, and their labour productivity, as well as their cost and revenue performance.

2 International regulation – bilateralism or 'open skies'

Our goal is very simple: to gradually and securely open the skies between the remaining restrictive European markets and my country, Qatar.

(Akbar Al Baker, CEO Qatar Airways, October 2016)

2.1 Two regulatory regimes

Airline managers are not free agents. They must cope with another characteristic of the airline industry, namely the extensive and complex domestic and international regulations that constrain it. It has been argued earlier that airline planning and management is the process of matching the supply or provision of air services, which airline managers can largely control, with the demand for such services, which they can influence but not control. It is not as simple as that. Traditionally, the airline industry has been one of the most highly regulated of industries. As a result, the actions of airline managers are circumscribed by a host of national, bilateral or international rules and regulations. These are both economic and non-economic in character and may well place severe limitations on airlines' freedom of action. An examination of the scope and impact of such regulations is crucial for an understanding of the economics of international air transport.

In the period 1919 to 1949 a framework of international regulation evolved in response to the technological, economic and political developments in air transport. It was uniform and, broadly speaking, worldwide in its application. For the next three decades until the late 1970s this international regulatory framework remained largely unchanged. It was based on hundreds of bilateral air services agreements between pairs of states and supported by inter-airline pooling agreements and the tariffs and pricing agreements negotiated through the International Air Transport Association (IATA). This so-called 'bilateralism' created a highly regulated operating environment unlike that of any other international industry – an environment, moreover, that stifled innovation and change. But a review of the United States' international aviation policy in 1979 inaugurated a trend towards gradual liberalisation of the economic regulations affecting international air services. This liberalisation became more rapid after the mid-1980s when it was adopted by key European countries and eventually by the European Union. It reached a peak with the March 2007 'open skies' agreement between the European Union and the US.

As a result, by the end of the 2010s there were, broadly speaking, two different regulatory regimes in the world. On the one hand, many major and secondary routes to and from the United States, those between the member states of the European Union and some routes between a few European states or the United States and some Asian countries, such as Singapore, were operated under what might be termed 'open skies' regimes. On the other, international air services in many parts of the world were and still are operated with the traditional regulatory structure based on more restrictive bilateral air services agreements. In practice it is not a simple twofold division. There are gradations in each of the regulatory regimes. Some traditional bilateral agreements are very restrictive while others are much more open and allow more effective competition. Equally, in some liberalised markets, such as that between the European Union and the United States, economic deregulation has removed most of the constraints on inter-airline competition, while some vestiges of traditional regulation survive, for example, restrictions on foreign ownership of airlines.

It is also the case that most states have a mixture of bilateral air agreements with some being more or less liberal while others may be restrictive. Member states of the European Union provide a good example. One finds that most European states, whose airlines now operate in an open, deregulated market on services within Europe, have some very restrictive bilateral air services agreements with non-European states, which are protective of their own airlines.

2.2 Non-economic technical and safety regulations

The advanced level of aviation technology, the need to ensure passenger safety despite the rapidity of technological innovation and the international nature of much of the airline industry have all created pressure for the introduction of more complex and more wide-ranging external controls and regulations than are found in most industries. These are broadly of two kinds. First, there are those discussed in this chapter, which are economic in nature and are concerned with regulating the business and commercial aspects of air transport. Second, there is a whole host of technical standards and regulations whose prime objective is to achieve very high levels of safety in airline operations. Such regulations cover every aspect of airline activity (see Appendix B for more details).

These various technical standards and safety procedures undoubtedly constrain airline managers and, at the same time, impose cost penalties on airline operations. But such external controls are inevitable if high safety standards are to be maintained, and significantly all airlines are equally affected by them. No major international airline can enjoy a competitive advantage by operating to airworthiness standards below the generally acceptable level. The implementation of ICAO standards and the safety oversight procedures together ensure that, unlike the shipping sector, there are very few 'flags of convenience' in air transport, that is, states that allow airlines to circumvent national or international safety or manning regulations as a way of reducing costs. Those few airlines that bend the rules tend sooner or later to find themselves banned from flying to the major markets.

While the large number of technical rules and regulations have safety as their primary objective, they have economic repercussions. Two examples: very high temperatures at an airport may limit the number of passengers or freight an aircraft may load thereby reducing the potential revenue for that flight. Safety regulations also determine how many cabin crew must be carried in a passenger aircraft, irrespective of the number of passengers boarded, which impacts on operating costs. The possible impact of technical and safety regulations must be borne in mind when considering airline economics

2.3 The growth of economic regulation

When the Paris Convention, signed in 1919, accepted that states have sovereign rights in the air space above their territory, direct government intervention in air transport became inevitable. A country's air space became one of its valuable natural resources. As a result, the free-trade laissez-faire approach towards air transport of the early years of aviation was gradually replaced by an incomplete pattern of bilateral agreements between countries having airlines and the countries to or through which those airlines wished to fly. But the restrictive character of 'bilateralism' was soon apparent. Even before the Second World War was over, 52 member states met in Chicago in 1944 to consider some form of multinational agreement in three critical aspects of international transport:

(i) the exchange of air traffic rights, or 'freedom of the air' (see Appendix A); i.e. market access
(ii) the control of fares and freight tariffs
(iii) the control of flight frequencies and traffic.

From an economist's viewpoint these three aspects together effectively determine the nature of any industry, for they regulate the entry of firms into each market (through traffic rights), the degree of pricing freedom and the nature of controls on the capacity or level of production put onto the market. If there is a maximum exchange or traffic rights, which means open market access, combined with little or no control of tariffs or frequencies and capacity offered then a market could be considered to be very competitive; provided, of course, there were no other barriers to market entry. If, on the other hand, traffic rights, tariffs and frequencies are all tightly regulated then such markets will be uncompetitive or even monopolistic.

At Chicago there was a clash between those few states led by the United States who wanted no control of tariffs or capacity and the maximum exchange of traffic rights, including Fifth Freedom rights, and the United Kingdom and most European countries who were more protectionist. They supported tight controls on tariffs and capacity and the limitation of the so-called Fifth Freedom traffic rights (see Appendix A for definition of traffic rights). These two conflicting views could not be reconciled. No multilateral agreement was reached on the three key issues of traffic rights, tariff control and capacity.

The most significant result of the Chicago Conference was the signing of the Convention on International Civil Aviation, known subsequently as the Chicago Convention. This provided the framework for the orderly and safe development of international air transport. It did this through its various articles and the 'annexes' that deal with every aspect of the operation of aircraft and air services both in the air and on the ground. The Convention also set up the International Civil Aviation Organization (ICAO), an inter-governmental United Nations agency that provided the forum for further discussion of key aviation issues and the basis for the worldwide co-ordination of technical and operational standards and practices. ICAO also provided crucial technical assistance to many countries, especially newly independent states in Africa and Asia, helping them to establish airport and air navigation facilities and to organise other aspects of civil aviation infrastructure.

In time, governments and airlines together found a way of circumventing the failures of Chicago. The exchange of traffic rights became a matter for bilateral air services agreement between states; the control of capacities and frequencies became a matter for inter-airline agreements, and sometimes was also covered by bilateral state agreements; and tariffs came to be regulated by the International Air Transport Association (IATA).

2.4 Bilateral air service agreements

From the mid-1940s onwards, each country negotiated a series of bilateral air services agreements (known as 'bilaterals') with other states aimed at regulating the operation of air transport services between them. The prime purpose of such bilaterals has been the control of market access (points to be served and traffic rights) and of market entry, by determining which airlines could be designated by each of the two countries to use the traffic rights granted. Some bilaterals also control the flight frequencies or the capacity that can be offered by each airline on the routes between the two countries. Such bilateral agreements, and there are over 1,500 of them still today, became and, in much of the world, remain the fundamental core of the regulatory regime. This is so even when the bilaterals have been renegotiated and have become very liberal or 'open skies' agreements.

Air service agreements have three distinct parts. First, there is the bilateral itself. This consists of a number of articles covering a variety of administrative provisions to facilitate the operation of air services. These include articles dealing with exemption from customs duties on imports of aircraft parts, with airport charges, with the setting up of sales offices or the transfer abroad of an airline's sales revenues and so on. Of greater significance are the articles dealing with the economic provisions of the agreement. The key articles are those dealing with the regulation of tariffs and those on capacity. Most of the traditional bilaterals specified that passenger fares and cargo tariffs should be agreed by the designated airlines, due regard being paid to all relevant factors, including cost of operation, and a reasonable profit. But in the early years airlines were encouraged to use the tariff-fixing machinery of IATA to reach agreement on fares.

Even states such as Singapore or Malaysia, whose national airlines did not become members of IATA until 1990, agreed in their bilaterals to approve where possible tariffs agreed through IATA. Approval for the IATA tariffs procedures was therefore enshrined in most bilateral agreements. It was this that gave the IATA tariffs machinery such force until liberalisation set in after 1978. However, both governments were required to approve such fares and tariffs. In other words, ultimate control of tariffs rested with governments, though in practice the vast majority of governments automatically approved the IATA agreed fares. On capacity, some traditional bilaterals require very strict control and sharing of capacity by the airlines of the two countries while others have minimal control.

Another economic issue covered in the bilateral is the number of airlines which will be designated to operate between the two signatory states. Originally, in most bilaterals only 'single designation' was envisaged, that is one airline from each state on each route. However, a few bilaterals, especially those with the United States, allowed for 'double' or 'multiple designation'. More recently, more airlines have been allowed by other states too. Irrespective of the number of airlines to be designated by each state all had to be 'substantially owned and effectively controlled' by nationals of the 'designating state'. This so-called 'nationality rule' found in virtually all the traditional bilaterals has proved the biggest obstacle to the normalisation of the international airline industry.

The second part of the bilateral is the annex containing the 'schedule or routes'. It is here that the traffic rights granted to each of the two states are made explicit. The schedule specifies the routes to be operated by the 'designated' airline(s) of each state. Airlines are never mentioned by name. It is up to each state to designate its airline or airlines subsequently. The points (towns) to be served by each designated airline are listed or, less usually, a general right might be granted such as from 'points in the United Kingdom' without specifying the points. If a town or country is not specifically listed in the route schedule a designated airline cannot operate services to it unless the bilateral is amended.

The schedule will also indicate whether the designated airlines have been granted rights to pick up traffic in other countries or from airports lying between or beyond the two signatory states. These are the Fifth Freedom rights, but they cannot be used unless the third countries involved also agree. Thus, if the US–Singapore bilateral granted the Singapore designated airline Fifth Freedom rights between London and New York as an extension of its services between Singapore and London, which it did, then the London-New York rights could not be exercised until the UK government agreed to this in its own air services agreement with Singapore.

The final part of the bilateral may consist of one or more 'memoranda of understanding' or 'exchange of notes'. These are agreements, often confidential, that amplify or subsequently modify particular aspects of the basic air services agreement. Bilateral air services agreements are government-to-government trade agreements. Once negotiated and signed their validity is indefinite until they are renegotiated.

Many of the traditional type of bilateral agreements reflect protectionist attitudes. They insist on prior agreement on the capacity to be provided on the route and may also specify that the agreed capacity should be shared equally by the designated carriers of the two states, normally only one from each state. At the same time few if any Fifth Freedom rights are granted.

Some slightly more liberal, but still traditional, bilaterals are frequently referred to as being Bermuda-type agreements, after the air services agreement signed in 1946 between the United Kingdom and the United States in Bermuda. They differ from the protectionist or 'predetermination' type of agreements described previously in two respects. First, Fifth Freedom rights are more widely available. Second, there is no control of frequency or capacity on the routes between the two countries concerned. Bermuda-type bilateral agreements became quite widespread.

The traditional air services agreements were and are essentially restrictive. They prevent airlines from operating to points or on routes they may wish to enter, even if it makes economic sense for them to do so, either because those points are not included in the bilateral agreement or they have not been designated, that is chosen, by their own government to serve these points. If their government is unable or unwilling to renegotiate the relevant bilaterals to obtain the additional rights then airlines have only one option left. They could try to purchase such rights by paying royalties or 'revenue compensation' to the airlines whose 'rights' will be affected. Such royalty payments were most common when airlines have wanted to pick up Fifth Freedom rights on medium- or long-haul multi-sector services, but are much less common today.

2.5 Inter-airline pooling agreements

Prior to liberalisation, the vast majority of international sectors had only two major carriers, the designated airlines of the two countries involved. This is still the case today on many routes, especially short-haul international routes and on long-haul routes to/from Asia, Africa and Latin America. As in many duopolistic situations, there is a strong incentive for formal or informal agreements between the duopolists to share out the market. In the years up to the early 1990s such agreements generally took the form of revenue-sharing pools or, less frequently, revenue- and cost-sharing pools.

Pooling agreements were forbidden on routes to or from the United States by that country's anti-trust legislation. But they became very widespread in Europe, where until the early 1990s 75 to 80 per cent of intra-European passenger-kms were operated on pooled services. They were also common in South-east Asia and to a lesser extent in other parts of the world. Agreements could cover a single route or sector or, more normally, all the routes on which the two signatory airlines operated between their two countries. In general, airline pools covered Third and Fourth Freedom traffics. While most pool agreements involved two airlines, three or four airline pools were not uncommon, especially in South-east Asia.

In revenue- and cost-sharing pools *both* airlines operate on one or more routes between their countries and all their costs and revenues are shared on the basis of an agreed formula. The flight numbers often carry the code of both airlines.

The most widespread pooling agreements were those involving revenue-sharing. In these, all revenue on a route or sector is shared by the participating airlines in proportion to the capacity, that is the agreed number of seats, they each offer on the route or routes involved. Complex agreements establish how to calculate the revenue earned by each airline on the route and how much of that goes into the revenue pool to be shared.

The effect of all pooling agreements, once entered into, was to reduce the freedom of action of the airlines involved and to reduce or even blunt any competitive tendencies. Since revenues are shared there is little incentive for pool partners to compete. Another feature of pooling agreements which was anti-competitive is that they required the pool partners to agree jointly on the capacity and frequencies offered. This enabled them to push up load factors and tariffs by limiting seat capacity offered or frequencies.

It is precisely because they were deemed to be restrictive and anti-competitive collusion agreements between suppliers of air services that pooling agreements had never been permitted on routes to and from the United States. This was also the reason why in its December 1987 decisions on air transport liberalisation, the so-called 'First Package', the European Council of Ministers deemed that pooling agreements would be illegal unless granted specific exemptions by the European Commission. During the early 1990s European Union airlines gradually unwound their pooling agreements. Today, a limited number of traditional-style pooling agreements can be found only among some Asian, Middle Eastern and African airlines.

A key issue is whether, in recent years, the earlier inter-airline pooling agreements have been replaced by other forms of airline co-operation that may also manifest anti-competitive features. Code share, block space or other inter-airline commercial arrangements seem to have similar objectives to pooling agreements – namely to co-ordinate schedules, reduce capacity or frequency competition and thereby push up load factors and, hopefully, fares and yields. More recently, the metal-neutral joint venture agreements entered into by some airlines on long-haul routes, such as the North Atlantic, appear to be very similar to the revenue cost-sharing pools previously banned by the US government and the European Commission. Yet most have been granted immunity from prosecution under US anti-trust legislation by the United States Department of Transportation and have also been accepted by regulators elsewhere.

2.6 Limited regulation of non-scheduled air services

Unlike scheduled rights, non-scheduled traffic rights were traditionally not regulated by bilateral air services agreements. Whereas under Article 6 of the Chicago Convention scheduled air services specifically required 'special permission or other authorisation' from the destination countries, Article 5 left authorisation for non-scheduled services at the discretion of individual states (ICAO, 1980).

In practice, prior to liberalisation, most countries insisted on giving prior authorisation to incoming non-scheduled flights, but attitudes towards authorisation varied significantly. Some countries, such as India, have historically been restrictionist in their approach and refused to authorise charter flights unless they were operated by their own national carrier or unless it could be shown that no scheduled traffic would be diverted. In contrast, many other countries, particularly tourist destinations such as Morocco or Tunisia, followed a more liberal policy and have readily authorised non-scheduled services.

Countries with non-scheduled or charter airlines, including the United States, brought non-scheduled operations within some form of domestic regulatory control. Such regulations varied by country but aimed at clearly delineating the area and scope of non-scheduled operations so as to protect scheduled airlines, while giving non-scheduled operators considerable freedom of action within their defined area.

As charter flights grew in the 1960s and 1970s, IATA and many governments, under pressure to protect their own scheduled airlines, imposed arbitrary and often restrictive regulations on charter services. But as the tide of public opinion in many European countries and in North America swung strongly in favour of cheap charter flights governments were forced to gradually dismantle the various domestic controls on charters.

The gradual liberalisation of non-scheduled services and the dismantling of often arbitrary regulations led to a rapid growth in charter traffic. By 1977, nearly one-third of passengers flying across the Atlantic were on inclusive tour or affinity group charters. This was the peak year. Then in 1978 the long-haul charter market collapsed. This was a direct result of deregulation of scheduled fares and the entry on many North Atlantic routes of new scheduled airlines, such as Laker Airways. Competitive pressure pushed both new and existing scheduled carriers to offer fares that were charter competitive. With little price advantage to offer, charter airlines found their traffic shrinking rapidly. Today charters account for well below 5 per cent of North Atlantic passenger traffic. However, in other areas, especially in European holiday markets, charter operations have continued to play a role but a diminishing one. They too were undermined by the European deregulation and the emergence of low-cost airlines after 1996 (see Chapter 6 for more on charter economics).

2.7 The role of IATA

The International Air Transport Association (IATA) was founded in Havana in 1945 as a successor to a pre-war association that had been largely European. Its primary purpose was to represent the interests of airlines and to act as a counterweight to ICAO, which was an inter-governmental agency primarily concerned with government interests in aviation. Through its various committees and sub-committees, which bring together airline experts for a few days each year, IATA has been able to co-ordinate and standardise virtually every aspect of international airline operation. Thus, the Financial

Committee has harmonised methods of rendering, verifying and settling accounts between airlines while the Traffic Committee has standardised aircraft containers and other unit load devices as well as many other aspects of passenger or cargo handling. IATA produces invaluable statistics, surveys and research reports covering many areas of airline activity. IATA also represents the airlines in negotiations with airport authorities, governments or ICAO on matters as diverse as airport charges or anti-hijacking measures. IATA works both as a forum for inter-airline discussion and resolution of key issues and as a pressure group representing the interests of international airlines.

One of IATA's most important functions is to operate the Clearing House for inter-airline debts arising from interline traffic, that is the carriage by one airline of passengers (or freight) holding tickets issued by other airlines or associated companies. The sums involved are enormous. In the year 2017 the nearly 300 IATA and non-IATA airlines using the Clearing House, together with 80 or so airlines of a United States-based clearing house and over 100 other aviation associated participants, submitted inter-company claims amounting to US$56 billion. The Clearing House settles inter-airline accounts by offsetting members' counter-claims against each other. Normally over 70 per cent of all claims can be offset without the need for any cash transaction. The Clearing House speeds up and simplifies the process of clearing inter-airline debts and substantially reduces the cost. IATA also operates a 'Billing and Settlement Plan' (BSP) that simplified the selling, reporting and remitting procedures at IATA-accredited travel agents. There is a similar clearing system for settling accounts between cargo agents and airlines (Cargo Accounts Settlement Systems – CASS).

IATA has made and continues to make a vital contribution in establishing common standards and recommended practices for the selling and distribution of air services. This is crucial, given the vast number of very different airlines involved in international operations and the large number of different countries each of those airlines may be flying to. It is IATA that has made it possible for a passenger to buy a round-the-world ticket from American Airlines in New York involving travel on several different airlines and for the passenger to have his ticket accepted for the sector from, say, Borneo to Bali by an airline he may never have heard of.

Historically, IATA's most important function has been to set airline fares and cargo rates. Up to 1979 the process for establishing fares was rather rigid. It involved the so-called Traffic Conferences; one covering North and South America, the second covering Europe, the Middle East and Africa, and the third the Pacific region and Australasia. Airlines operating in or through these areas belonged to the relevant conference. The conferences, meeting in secret and usually about four to six months in advance, established the tariff structure that would be operative for a specified period, usually one of one year. The conferences also agreed on fares between the conference regions. About 200,000 separate passenger fares and over 100,000 cargo rates were negotiated together with complex conditions of in-flight service associates with each fare, such as seat pitch, number of meals to be served, whether they were hot or cold, charges for headphones and so on. Since such detailed service conditions had to be strictly applied by IATA member airlines there was little scope for competition in service standards or fares.

From the airlines' point of view the Traffic Conference system had clear advantages: it produced a coherent and worldwide structure of interrelated passenger fares and cargo rates, together with tariff-related rules and regulations. The Traffic Conferences were also instrumental in developing standard documents and contracts of air carriage – tickets, waybills, baggage checks, etc.

IATA tariffs were accepted worldwide because, as previously mentioned, many bilateral air services agreements governments had explicitly agreed that they would approve fares negotiated through the IATA process.

Since IATA airlines were not allowed to deviate from the IATA tariffs, no price competition was possible. There can be little doubt that IATA was effectively a suppliers' cartel whose object was to maximise its members' profits by mutually fixing prices at which they sold their services.

But if IATA was a cartel it was failing to achieve the prime objective of any cartel, namely high profits for its members. In the 1970s and 1980s the industry was characterised by poor financial results. Nevertheless, pressure began to build up on governments in Europe and North America to allow greater pricing freedom. At the same time IATA tariffs procedures began to prove too rigid and inflexible to deal with two new developments. The first of these was the growth in the 1960s and 1970s of non-scheduled or charter air services offering much cheaper fares and making serious inroads into scheduled markets in Europe and on the North Atlantic. The second development was the expansion in the 1970s of new dynamic airlines such as Thai International, SIA and Korean. As non-IATA carriers they captured market share either by offering much higher levels of in-flight service than was permitted under IATA's 'conditions of service' or through greater flexibility in their tariffs.

Faced with these external competitive pressures, IATA was forced to change. But attempts by IATA in the 1980s and 1990s to introduce greater flexibility in setting fares and greater freedom for airlines to opt out failed to halt the erosion of its influence.

By the start of the new millennium IATA's role in the setting of passenger and cargo tariffs was seriously diminished. The market environment had changed drastically on many major international routes. In long-haul markets competition had increased as a result both of the development of more effective hubs and the growth of global alliances. In many short-haul markets the rapid expansion of low-cost carriers had totally undermined attempts to control fare levels. By the early 2000s fares in many markets were determined by competitive pressures rather than IATA tariff setting. At the same time the regulatory authorities were increasingly concerned about the anti-competitive character of IATA tariff processes.

The European Union adopted a Regulation in September 2006 that ended the block exemption from competition law, which had been previously granted to IATA fare conferences. The US Department of Transportation followed suit with a March 2007 decision withdrawing the exemption from US anti-trust laws previously granted to IATA tariff conferences in the transatlantic and US–Australia markets. According to its final order the Department believed that '*Pricing discussions among competitors ... at the IATA Tariff conferences are inherently anti-competitive and likely to increase the fares paid*' (DOT, 2007).

IATA was forced to change. The IATA Traffic Conferences continued to agree tariffs though this was done electronically, not at annual meetings. United States carriers dropped out and in time IATA tariffs were only used as a guide or by a small number of airlines that did not have bilateral agreements on fares with other airlines. In 2018 IATA decided to discontinue tariff co-ordination altogether as from November of that year. There have been no IATA tariffs since.

The creation of 'open skies' within the European Common Aviation Area and on the North Atlantic (see later sections) has negated the need for IATA or any other tariff-fixing in two major markets. Elsewhere progressive liberalisation and increased competition especially in Sixth Freedom markets, such as those between Asia and Europe via Middle East points, have made it virtually impossible to control tariffs. That is so in the majority of the world's aviation markets.

2.8 The impact of bilateralism

The regulation of international air services through a system of restrictive bilateral agreements still exists in many parts of the world; for example, in much of South America and on routes to and from China. But the system has changed in two important respects. First, IATA no longer determines the level and structure of air fares and cargo tariffs worldwide. Second, inter-airline revenue-sharing pools are less widespread, even where bilateralism prevails, though in a few major markets they have been superseded by joint ventures.

The bilateral regulation of international air services posed, and still poses, severe constraints on the freedom of action of individual airlines. First, their markets are restricted. They can only fly to points in foreign countries specified in the bilateral agreement made with their own home state. Even then they can only do this if they are designated by their home government to operate on specific routes. Then they may or may not have Fifth Freedom rights to or beyond the points they serve. Second, the level of output of each airline is not entirely at its own discretion. The bilateral agreement under which it is operating may limit the number of frequencies it can offer each week or the number of seats; if there is no limit it may only be allowed to increase frequencies or seats if the airline(s) of the foreign country agrees. Finally, at least until progressive liberalisation in the 1980s, most fares have traditionally been set through the IATA tariffs.

Two examples may illustrate the constraints faced because of restrictive bilaterals. Under the UK–China air services agreement the number of flights between the two countries was limited to 80 for airlines of each country. Because of this restriction and flights by other Chinese airlines, Hainan Airlines could not fly to London, though it had four flights weekly between Beijing and Manchester. In October 2016 a revised bilateral came into force increasing weekly flights to 100 by each country. Only then could Hainan Airlines launch sustainable services to London from Changsha, which it did in 2017.

Up to 2015 the France–Qatar bilateral also limited weekly frequencies between Doha and France to 18 by airlines of each state. Qatar Airways flew 15 times a week to Paris and three times to Nice. The airline, through the Qatari government, asked for more flights because with only three weekly flights the Nice service was not viable. The French refused to increase the 18 weekly limit and in 2015 Qatar Airways pulled out of Nice. Then in 2016, Airbus sold 35 aircraft to Qatar Airways and, not surprisingly, at about the same time, France agreed to increase the weekly limit to 23 flights. As a result Qatar Airways was able to relaunch five-times-weekly services Doha–Nice from June 2017.

2.9 Towards open markets 1978–91

The bilateral system was and remains restrictive, but had been justified on the grounds that air transport was a public utility or at least a quasi-public utility. The social and external benefits of air transport were such that the industry needed to be regulated to ensure its continued operation in the public interest in order that such benefits were not jeopardised. This in turn meant protecting the established scheduled airlines from the rapid development of charters and non-scheduled operators in the 1960s and 1970s and also from price competition from non-IATA scheduled carriers.

Whatever the economic arguments, political and consumer pressures for liberalisation of the tight regulatory regimes was building up during the 1970s. Consumers in the United States and Europe could not understand why various rules were needed to prevent them from having free access to much cheaper flights or cheaper and unrestricted fares on scheduled services. Then in 1978 the newly elected President Carter, who had made support for consumers a key part of his election platform, signed the Airline Deregulation Act into law on 24 October.

The Act provided for the complete elimination of the Civil Aeronautics Board by 1985, bringing an end to virtually all controls over US domestic route licensing and fares. Other aspects of the Board's responsibilities would be taken over by other branches of the Federal government. The significance of US domestic deregulation, which was so rapid and total, was that the pressures for change inevitably spilled over to international air transport.

Progress on liberalising international regulations was at first slow but then gathered pace. Under President Carter, US international aviation policy was reversed. The United States set out to introduce greater competition through renegotiating a series of key bilaterals in the period from 1978 to 1991. The changes became apparent in the first revised bilateral signed between the United States and the Netherlands in March 1978. This broke with the traditional bilateral agreements in several ways. It allowed for multiple designation, i.e. more than one airline from each state. It increased the number of points in each country to be served with no restrictions on frequencies or seats. There were no restrictions on Sixth Freedom rights, and it granted unlimited charter rights. More US bilaterals followed, especially in East Asia, with Singapore, Thailand, Korea, the Philippines and others.

In Europe, consumer pressure for liberalisation was also building up in the 1980s. The United Kingdom led the way, renegotiating most of its key European bilaterals in the period 1984–93. The key features of these new bilaterals were free entry of new carriers, access by designated carriers to any point in either country, no capacity controls and no control on fares unless both governments disapproved. The latter became known as the 'double disapproval' concept and effectively meant little control of tariffs.

Outside Europe and North America, a number of other countries also began to move cautiously towards reducing controls on their air transport industries. In Japan, JAL's effective monopoly of international air services was broken when from 1986 onwards domestic carriers All Nippon Airways or Japan Air Systems were designated as the second Japanese carriers on a number of key international routes. In several Southeast Asian countries new airlines were allowed to emerge to operate both domestic and international air services often in direct competition with the established national carrier. In South Korea for instance, Asiana Airlines was formed in February 1988 and launched domestic services at the end of that year and regional services to Tokyo, Bangkok and Hong Kong in 1990. The emergence of Eva Air in Taiwan and Dragonair in Hong Kong were other examples. In Australia in 1987 a new government aviation policy heralded a complete deregulation of domestic air services from October 1990. This meant that the government would withdraw from regulating domestic fares or capacity.

In the East Asian-Pacific region such attempts at liberalisation were often localised, haphazard and uncoordinated as between neighbouring countries. Their impact was fairly limited. On most routes single designation continued to prevail (except on routes to Japan), Third and Fourth Freedom capacities and frequencies were still regulated and many services were covered by revenue-pooling agreements. On tariffs there was more flexibility. In many countries governments, aviation authorities and airlines turned a blind eye to illegal discounting of government-approved IATA fares. In this way de facto liberalisation of tariffs was introduced on many international routes.

The effect of all these renegotiated bilaterals was to open up many markets and routes previously restricted in a variety of ways. The new regulatory features to emerge during this period of opening markets included the following:

- access opened up to more specified points (airports) in each state
- extensive Fifth Freedom rights granted
- no limits on non-scheduled flights
- multiple number of airlines could be designated by each country
- no limits on frequencies or seats offered, i.e. no capacity controls
- double disapproval of fares, i.e. only if both governments disapproved could a fare be blocked.

2.10 'Open skies' – launched 1992

The large US airlines such as Delta, American or United felt that the new 'open market' bilaterals still limited their scope and freedom of action. They pushed for further liberalisation. They felt that in a fully liberalised open skies environment they would do better than their foreign competitors because of the traffic feed that they would obtain from their huge domestic US networks and from their sheer size. The US State Department and the Department of Transportation also felt that open skies would benefit both American consumers and their airlines. At the same time, developments within the European Community, later to become the European Union, were also pushing inexorably towards open skies.

In the case of the United States bilaterals, the first key breakthrough came in 1992 in negotiations with the Netherlands, whose government and airline, KLM, were also keen to adopt open skies. In September 1992 the US and Dutch governments signed what was effectively the first 'open skies' agreement thereby inaugurating a new phase in international deregulation. Compared to the previous US–Netherlands bilateral the new agreement introduced the following changes:

- open route access – airlines can fly between any two points in the two countries
- airlines had unlimited Fifth Freedom rights
- no control of tariffs – unless too high or too low
- airlines free to code share or make other commercial agreements.

These new features represented a further and significant easing of the regulatory environment. Open and free market access together with no pricing controls when added to the absence of capacity restrictions and multiple designation, already granted in the earlier 'open market' bilateral, meant that one moved to a regime that appeared to be deregulated. But not quite. As discussed later, the open skies agreements still leave some regulatory issues unresolved.

Shortly after the 1992 'open skies' agreement with the United States, KLM applied for and obtained anti-trust immunity from the US authorities to enable it to exploit more fully the potential benefits from its partnership with Northwest. Immunity provided KLM-Northwest with considerable freedom jointly to plan their code shares, schedules and pricing policy on routes from the US to Amsterdam and beyond. This later became a joint venture in which the two airlines shared costs and revenues.

By 2017 over 120 new 'open skies' agreements similar to the one with the Netherlands had been signed by the United States. They all included the same basic provisions, but in some cases with some limited modification to reflect local realities. Thus, the US–Japan 'open skies' bilateral gives US airlines the right to fly to any point in Japan but there are restrictions on additional flights to the two Tokyo airports. Equally, the revised US–Mexico agreement signed at the end of 2014 lifted restrictions on flights between the two countries with the exception of flights to Mexico City.

Open skies policies have also been adopted and actively pursued by a few other states. New Zealand, which signed an open skies bilateral with the United States, had secured similar deals with Singapore, Malaysia, Brunei, the UAE and Chile by the end of 1999. This was in addition to the Single Aviation Market pact concluded earlier between New Zealand and Australia. The latter country pursued its own open skies agreements and signed the first one with the UAE. This represented a major policy shift. Australia was prepared to offer not only all the key features of US-style open skies agreements but was also willing to consider granting Seventh Freedom rights to UAE airlines for stand-alone air services between Australia and a third country on a case-by-case basis. Domestic cabotage, however, was not negotiable. In a new aviation policy, Australia also relaxed its ownership rules to allow foreign interests or airlines to own up to 100 per cent of Australian domestic airlines.

The 'open skies' agreements, generally very similar to the US–Netherlands agreement described earlier, were a significant improvement on the 'open market' agreements they replaced in several respects, most notably in relation to market access and tariff regulation. They opened route access to any point in either country whereas the earlier bilaterals had tended to limit the number of points that could be served by foreign carriers in the United States. Additionally, mutual Fifth Freedom rights were granted without restraint compared to the more limited Fifth Freedom in earlier bilaterals. On tariffs, double disapproval or the country of origin rule were replaced by a clear decision that governments should not meddle in tariffs except *in extremis* to prevent discriminatory practices, to protect consumers from unreasonably high or restrictive prices or to protect airlines from artificially low fares due to government subsidies or support. The significant changes under 'open skies' bilaterals compared to the traditional bilateral agreements are summarised in Table 2.1.

A further innovation was the inclusion of an article dealing specifically with inter-airline commercial agreements such as code-sharing (this is when airlines add their partner's code to their own flight number) and block space or leasing agreements. This was critically important. Close-knit commercial agreements, which went further than simple code-sharing on routes between the two countries, risked falling foul of US anti-trust legislation unless an open skies agreement had been signed. Later, after 2007, the US Department of Transportation went a step further. It offered anti-trust immunity (ATI) to allow US airlines to enter into approved joint ventures with airlines from states having an open skies bilateral with the US. Airlines within an approved joint venture could legally set joint prices, allocate routes and capacity, share revenues and costs and effectively act as one airline. They could do this without fear of prosecution under US anti-trust laws. ATI is not granted easily and may be refused,

Table 2.1 Key features of traditional and 'open skies' bilateral agreements

	Traditional bilateral	*'Open skies' bilaterals*
Market access	Only to points specified (few)	Open access – airlines can fly between any two points
	Limited Fifth Freedoms granted in some bilaterals	Unlimited Fifth Freedom rights
	Charter rights not included	Unlimited charter rights
Designation	Single – one airline from each state	Multiple
	Airlines must be 'substantially owned and effectively controlled' by nationals of designating state	
Capacity	Capacity agreed or shared 50:50	No frequency or capacity controls. Co-operative arrangements such as code-sharing, blocked space or leasing allowed
	No capacity/frequency controls in liberal bilaterals, but subject to review	
Tariffs	Double approval by both governments required	No tariff controls

N.B.: Neither traditional nor 'open skies' bilaterals permitted domestic cabotage or granted Seventh Freedoms (see appendix for definitions)

which prevents the joint venture from going ahead. This happened in November 2016 when a JV between Qantas and American Airlines on the Trans-Pacific was turned down on the grounds that the proposed partnership would account for nearly 60 per cent of the US–Australia market, and would be too dominant.

2.11 The European Common Aviation Area

In parallel to the United States, Europe was also moving towards open skies, but the approach was structurally quite different. The US strategy was essentially bilateral. The implementation of open skies was being promoted by one country through a series of bilateral air services agreements. In contrast to this the development of a single open aviation market in Europe was to be achieved through a comprehensive multilateral agreement between the member states of the European Union. This multilateral approach to opening up the skies enabled the Europeans to go further in pursuit of deregulation than was possible under the US bilateral approach.

Within the European Union the push towards multilateral liberalisation of air transports among the Member States was driven by two complementary lines of approach. The Directorate General for Transport espoused airline liberalisation early on while the Directorate General for Competition was trying to ensure that competition between producers and service providers within the Union was not distorted by uncompetitive practices imposed by governments or introduced by the industries themselves. The twin objectives of air transport liberalisation and fair and open competition were only achieved in stages. In the late 1980s, the first two packages of liberalisation measures did not go very far. The major breakthrough was achieved only through the so-called 'Third Package' of aviation measures, which came into force on 1 January 1993.

The Third Package consists of three inter-linked regulations, which have effectively created an 'open skies' regime for air services within the European Union. First, there is *open market access*. Airlines from member states can operate with full traffic rights between any two points within the EU and without capacity restrictions even on intra-EU routes entirely outside their own country (CEC, 1992b). Thus, easyJet, a UK airline, can base aircraft in Milan and, with Italian pilots and cabin crew, operate both domestic and international flights from Milan, entirely outside the UK. Governments may only impose restrictions on environmental, infrastructure capacity, regional development or public service grounds, but any restrictions would have to be justified. Second, there are *no price controls*. Airlines have complete freedom to determine their fares and cargo tariffs but there are some limited safeguards to prevent predatory or excessive pricing (CEO, 1992c). Finally, the third Regulation *harmonises the criteria* for granting of operating licences and air operators' certificates by EU member states (CEC, 1992c). Apart from technical and financial criteria that have to be met, the airline must be majority owned (i.e. over 50 per cent) and controlled by any of the member states or the nationals of any member state. But they do not need to be nationals or companies of the state in which the airline is registered. In addition, henceforward, all regulations applied equally to scheduled and charter services with no distinction being drawn between them.

The Third Package went further than the US-style 'open skies' bilaterals in two important respects. First, it was a multilateral agreement to open up the skies covering not just pairs of states but a whole region. Second, whereas the open skies bilaterals did not change the nationality rule at all, the Third Package for the first time explicitly allowed cross-border majority ownership. It gave to EU nationals or companies, majority owned by EU nationals, from any member state, the right to set up and operate an airline in any other EU member state or to buy such an airline.

In the 1990s this enabled British Airways to own and manage Deutsche BA in Germany, though it was later sold and became Air Berlin. However, this so-called right of establishment was restrictive in one important sense. While Deutsche BA could operate freely within the area of the European Union it could not, as a British-owned airline, operate international services from Munich to, say, Moscow because the Germany–Russia air services agreement contained the traditional article regarding substantial ownership and effective control by nationals of the designating state. A German airline flying from Germany to Russia had to be German owned!

While the European Common Aviation Area was created by the European Union a number of countries joined it by accepting the union's various aviation Directives and Regulations. Switzerland, in 2002, Norway, in 2006 and Iceland were important additions. These were followed by several Balkan states who were not members of the European Union. In the last 10 years a number of non-EU Mediterranean states such as Morocco, Jordan and Israel have joined, but on a looser basis. These latter countries gain progressively more access and rights to European markets as they accept and enforce more of the EU's aviation Regulations.

In parallel with the liberalisation of air transport regulations, the European Commission felt that greater freedom for airlines had to be accompanied by the effective application and implementation to air transport of the European Union's so-called 'competition rules'. These were designed to prevent monopolistic practices or behaviour that was anti-competitive or distorted competition to the detriment of consumers. The competition rules cover three broad areas, namely cartels or restrictive agreements, monopolies and mergers, and state aid or subsidies to producers. The basic principles on competition were originally laid down in Articles 81 to 90 of the Treaty of Rome and the separate Council Regulation on Mergers of 1989 (Regulation No.4056/89).

The subsidisation of airlines by central or local government clearly distorts competition. Articles 88 and 89 of the Treaty of Rome specifically prohibit 'state aid' of any kind, yet during the 1980s and early 1990s most of Europe's numerous state-owned airlines were being heavily subsidised by their governments. To overcome this contradiction, the European Commission, in a series of decisions in the 1990s, approved major injections of government aid to a number of airlines but with strict conditions whose purpose was to ensure their transformation into profitable enterprises. Moreover, the state aid was approved on the basis of a 'one time, last time' principle. In other words, no further requests for approval of additional state aid would be considered. With the exception of the authorised state aid schemes, no direct or indirect subsidisation of any kind by governments of their airlines is now permitted within the European Union.

But it appears that in emergencies state aid may be authorised to deal with unexpected crises! For example, early in 2005 the Commission also approved emergency state aid to Cyprus Airways in the form of a government-backed loan. But late in 2014, the Commission ruled that additional state aid given to Cyprus Airways in 2012–13 was illegal and had to be repaid to the government. This effectively bankrupted the airline and in January 2015 it closed down.

A key element of the competition rules is the EU's Regulation on Mergers first agreed in 1989 and subsequently modified in 1997 (Regulation 1310/97). Any mergers or acquisitions which exceed the stated permitted limit in terms of turnover must be first notified to the Commission. It will only give its approval if the transaction does not lead to the strengthening or creation of a dominant position. To ensure that this does not happen the Commission may impose demanding conditions, including the surrender of airport slots that may be used by competing airlines. The Commission did this in the case of Lufthansa's purchase of Swiss Airlines in 2006 and its purchase of 45 per cent of SN Brussels Airlines in 2008. The Commission may also block a merger on the grounds that it would harm consumers by creating a dominant position. It did this early in 2013 when it stopped the proposed takeover of Aer Lingus by Ryanair.

In addition to its decisions arising directly out of the application of the competition rules, the European Commission, acting through the Council of Ministers and the European Parliament, has passed various Directives, Regulations or Codes of Conduct both to ensure greater competition in areas where competition was previously limited and to ensure that competition is not distorted through unfair practices. Both the Code of conduct for slot allocation at airports (Council Regulation 95/93, amended 2009/0042 COD) and the Directive on ground-handling services (Council Directive 96/97) were aimed at ensuring greater competition. Later, the Airport Charges Directive in March 2009 aimed to ensure a level playing field for airlines at different airports (Directive 2009/12/EC). On the other hand, the Code of Conduct for computer reservation system was aimed at avoiding unfair practices (Council Regulations 3089/93). Such Directives and Regulations were in addition to the numerous measures introduced to protect consumers directly (e.g. Regulation No.261/2004 on passenger compensation rights) or to ensure safety of aircraft and so on.

If the aim of transport deregulation and open skies is to encourage much greater competition, then competition rules appear to be necessary to ensure that the increased competition is effective and is not undermined by anti-competitive practices or the abuse of dominant market positions. Hence, the parallel but contradictory development in the European Union of an intra-European open skies regime and a raft of new competition rules.

The 'Third Package' and the various EU Directives, Regulations and Codes of Practice have created a truly 'open skies' regime for air transport within the European Common Aviation Area. By 2018 this covered an area with a population close to 600 million, not only the 27 EU member states but several other European countries such as Norway and Iceland, which had adopted these various measures into their own regulations without joining the European Union.

The decision of the United Kingdom, following a referendum, to leave the European Union threatened to blow a hole in the large European open skies market. The UK government formally launched the process of 'Brexit' in March 2017, which should have entailed the UK leaving the EU on 29 March 2019 though a transition period to end December 2020 was agreed. As a result of leaving the EU, all the aviation-related agreements which the UK was party to, as a result of being a member of the EU, would no longer hold. These included (i) open access to all intra-EU markets including Seventh Freedom rights granted to EU airlines, open ownership rules and other liberal measures included in the Third Package of liberalisation measures; (ii) the 250-plus EU Regulations and Directives that take effect in UK laws (some are aviation-specific while others, such as the competition rules, are not but affect aviation – they were likely to change over time but not in the UK); (iii) the EU bilateral air services agreements with numerous countries outside the EU, such as Morocco, as a result of which UK airlines enjoy access to these markets – the most significant is the EU–US open skies agreement, and it and others will no longer cover services by UK airlines; (iv) the various EU institutions, such as the European Aviation Safety Agency and others, in which the UK was a full member as an EU state (Doganis, 2017). The UK's position in all these areas will need clarification and renegotiation.

As far as aviation is concerened, the UK would like to keep things as they were before. In theory this could be done through a new bilateral agreement with the EU covering most of the issues listed above. In practice the European Commission has stated that it does not want a separate aviation agreement. Aviation must be part of a comprehensive agreement covering all issues – trade, migration, fisheries, budget contributions etc. There must be some doubt whether this can be done as a single package. By April 2018 the negotiations had not progressed far. An agreement by the end of March 2019 seemed unlikely but was possible before the end of the transition period. For the time being uncertainty would prevail.

2.12 The nationality rule re-defined

In November 2002 the European Court of Justice (ECJ), in a key judgement relating to individual bilaterals with the United States, declared that traditional clauses in bilateral air services agreements infringed Article 43 of the European Community Treaty. This article requires each EU state to allow nationals or companies of any other state to establish and operate businesses within that state. Yet for air transport services the traditional ownership and nationality clause is clearly very restrictive. For instance, under the then existing open skies bilateral between Germany and the United States the German government could only designate airline(s) that were 'substantially owned and effectively controlled' by German nationals. Only German airlines could use the traffic rights granted by the bilateral. To conform with Article 43 any EU airline should have the opportunity to be designated to fly on routes between Germany and the US.

While the November 2002 ECJ judgements referred specifically to bilateral agreements with the US, it was clear that all other bilateral agreements between EU member states and third countries faced the same legal problem. Thus, the ECJ decision meant that not only would bilaterals with the US have to be modified but so would hundreds of bilaterals between each of the then 25 EU states and third countries around the world. A daunting task.

In June 2003, the European Council of Transport Ministers adopted two decisions to tackle the complex task of renegotiating so many bilaterals. The first measure was to give the Commission a mandate to negotiate with the United States to fully liberalise air transport between the EU and the US. This had been a European objective for some time.

The second measure was another mandate to the Commission to negotiate so-called 'horizontal agreements' with third countries in order to correct the legal problems in their then existing bilaterals with EU states that had been highlighted by the European Court's judgements. In order to avoid a very large number of separate renegotiations by individual Member States with numerous third countries, this horizontal mandate empowered the European Commission to open negotiations with individual third countries in order to replace certain provisions in all their existing bilaterals with any EU states by a single Community agreement bringing all these separate air services agreements into line with EU laws. This would mean, for instance, replacing existing nationality clauses by an article in which third countries would accept designation by individual EU states of any carrier owned by EU nationals. By 2018 the European Commission had signed 'horizontal agreements' with more than 40 states around the world.

Even before the Commission began to implement its various negotiating mandates the longer-term implications of the ECJ judgements became starkly clear. In September 2003 Air France and KLM announced a proposed merger of the two airlines, which was realised in April 2004 following approval by the Commission's Competition Directorate and acceptance by the two airlines of the Commission's conditions. This marked the start of the long-awaited consolidation of the European flag carriers. The ECJ judgement, by relaxing the strict definition of nationality, opened the door for cross-border acquisitions and mergers among European airlines. After Air France-KLM, Lufthansa was next, purchasing the ailing Swissair in 2006, Austrian Airlines in 2009, 45 per cent of Brussels Airlines in 2009 and the remainder in January 2017. In 2011 British Airways and Iberia came together under a joint holding company which in 2015 bought the Irish airline Aer Lingus. It had earlier bought the Spanish low-cost carrier Vueling.

2.13 'Open skies' on the North Atlantic

After nearly four years of negotiation the EU–US Air Transport Agreement was signed in April 2007 and came into force on 30 March 2008. This agreement replaced all the existing bilateral air services agreements between individual EU states and the US. Its key provision was to open up all traffic rights between the US and EU member states to any US or European Community airlines. The latter can fly from any point within the EU and not just their own country, to any point in the US. The US airlines can do likewise. All airlines have Fifth Freedom traffic rights on behind, intermediate and beyond points on their services to or from the US or Europe. There is no control of frequencies or capacity or of tariffs. The US accepts designation on any route of any 'Community airline' whose substantial ownership and effective control are vested in nationals of any member state of the EU and whose principal place of business is within the EU (Official Journal of the European Communities, 25 February 2007).

In essence, the US agreed to this wider definition of nationality. But it did not agree to granting Community carriers domestic cabotage rights in the US nor to relaxing the strict ownership and control rules for US airlines that would have allowed European companies to gain control of US airlines or to establish their own subsidiaries in the US. Foreign ownership of US airlines continues to be limited to 25 per cent. However, franchising and branding agreements between US and European airlines would be permitted.

It is because of these shortcomings that a provision was included for negotiations to re-start 60 days after the agreement would come into force in March 2008 with the aim of examining further liberalisation of traffic rights, foreign investment opportunities (i.e. ownership), environmental issues and wet-leasing of aircraft in order to conclude a second stage agreement. A Second Stage Agreement was signed in March 2010 but failed to resolve the issue of foreign ownership restrictions. Its focus was on strengthening EU–US co-operation in areas such as safety, security and environment.

Despite any shortcomings the 2007 EU–US agreement represents a major breakthrough in two respects: first in relaxing the very strict definition of 'nationality' used in traditional European bilaterals; second, in creating a vast 'open skies' market between most of Europe and the US. The effects would be a wider range of point-to-point services across the Atlantic with new carriers on new routes, lower fares and increased opportunities for mergers and consolidation between European airlines.

The impact has been dramatic. An additional 88 new direct city pairs were launched between 2010 and the end of 2016, many of these due to the entry of new airlines. The number of direct city pairs increased by 40 per cent as a result.

There was a breakthrough elsewhere in the North Atlantic in May 2009 when the European Union and Canada announced the signing of an 'open skies' agreement similar to that between the EU and the US but going even further in some respects. Notably, it would allow European investors to acquire up to 49 per cent of Canadian carriers. In the longer term full ownership rights were envisaged.

Thus, since 2010 'open skies' have prevailed in the North Atlantic aviation markets between Europe and the US and Canada. This is one of the world's largest international markets; it is 'open' in all respects but two. First, there are still restrictions on foreign ownership on both sides of the Atlantic. Second, domestic cabotage by non-national airlines is not permitted. That is, a European airline cannot carry passengers between two US cities, but nor can a US carrier between London and Athens; although, of course, within the European Common Aviation Area Lufthansa can operate between any two cities even if outside Germany.

2.14 Liberalisation spreads

Since the early 2000s air transport liberalisation has been accelerating both bilaterally and multilaterally in other countries too. First, many governments that had previously followed a protectionist domestic aviation policy began to appreciate the benefits of a more open competitive aviation environment for both their airline sector and their tourism industry. India is a good example. It liberalised domestic air services and as a result several new low-cost airlines, such as Indigo, SpiceJet and Air India Express, were launched in 2005–6. In time, they were allowed to operate internationally too, as India renegotiated several bilaterals opening up new points to be served from India and also increasing frequencies. China, like India, also began opening up its bilaterals in the mid-2000s. For example, in June 2007 the earlier 2004 air services agreement with the United States was amended to allow more frequencies and three new US carriers. As mentioned earlier, Australia went furthest in deregulating aviation both domestically and on international routes.

Second, one has seen several plurilateral regional agreements aimed at furthering liberalisation. In May 2001 five Pacific states – the United States, Brunei, Chile, New Zealand and Singapore, later joined by Peru (for a time only), Samoa, Tonga and Mongolia – entered into a multilateral 'open skies' agreement. This was notable in that it allowed these states to designate, on services to the other signatory states, airlines that are not owned by their own nationals. But such airlines must be incorporated in and have their principal place of business in the territory of the designating state. The United States, which brokered this agreement, known as the 'Multilateral Agreement on the Liberalisation of International Air Transport' (MALIAT), hoped that other states would accede to it. None have!

Other multilateral agreements have attempted to move in the same direction. For instance, in May 2009 the Association of South East Asian Nations (ASEAN) approved a multilateral agreement for the phased establishment of a regional 'open skies' area between the ten member states. The aim was the gradual liberalisation of passenger and cargo rights. The agreement was finally ratified by all 10 ASEAN member states in May 2016. It removed any restrictions on Third, Fourth or Fifth Freedom traffic rights for airlines based in ASEAN states. Seventh Freedom and cabotage rights were not included at this stage; nor were ownership rules relaxed. More opening up, including establishing the concept of an 'Asean Community Carrier', would be negotiated in the period up to 2020.

Earlier, meeting in November 1999 in the Ivory Coast, African states had adopted a new policy framework, the so-called Yamoussoukro Decision, for the liberalisation of the continent's air transport industry. The agreement was to liberalise market access by the year 2002 in order to create a single African aviation market. It was far-reaching. Though ratified by many states, in practice Yamoussoukro failed to be effectively implemented, though it was bypassed by some smaller regional initiatives within Africa. Then in January 2018, under the auspices of the African Union, the Single African Transport Market was established by 23 African states. The aim was to implement the provisions of Yampussoukro and create an African open skies area similar to that in Europe. It was hoped that the remaining 32 African states would sign up in due course.

2.15 Brexit and aviation

In 2017 and early 2018 negotiations were in progress to finalise the UK's exit from the European Union. The potential repercussions for UK and intra-European aviation were far-reaching. At stake were the participation of British airlines in the European open skies aviation area; the future role, if any, of more than 250 EU Directives and Regulations affecting the operation of airlines in the UK; and the impact on UK airlines of the numerous air services agreements signed between the EU and third countries to which the UK would no longer be a party once outside the EU. The most significant of these are the open skies agreements with the US and Canada.

Clearly all these issues could be negotiated by entering into a separate and new air services agreement between the UK and the EU. However, the European Commission stated that a separate aviation agreement could not be considered until the overall agreement specifying the terms of the UK's separation from the EU had been agreed to and signed. Since by mid-2018 little progress appeared to have been made on reaching such an overall agreement, great uncertainty prevailed among airlines.

A key area of uncertainty related to the nationality rule. If the UK left the EU with no aviation agreement then only airlines being owned by nationals of EU member states could fly between EU airports. UK airlines such as easyJet would no longer be able to operate numerous services from Berlin or Munich to other points in Europe. To overcome this problem, easyJet obtained an Austrian AOC and ensured that a majority of its shares were held by EU nationals. But could it then operate domestic services in Britain if it was no longer a British airline? Virgin Atlantic, where UK shareholders are in a minority, would no longer be able to use British traffic rights to fly between London and the US.

To overcome nationality issues facing easyJet, IAG, Virgin Atlantic and other airlines the UK government took a bold move. In May 2018 it tacitly 'agreed' that easyJet would continue to be treated as a UK operator, after Brexit, even if the majority of its shares were to be owned by EU nationals. The latter ownership was needed so it could operate freely within and between EU states. Effectively, in adopting this approach, which would apply to other UK-based airlines, the UK government was abandoning the strict nationality rule based on ownership. It made it clear that airlines such as easyJet, whose principal place of business was in the UK, would be considered as UK airlines for traffic rights purposes.

The UK thus became the first major aviation power to 'de facto' base nationality on primary place of business rather than nationality of owners. This was a major break-through on the nationality issue and would inevitably influence other countries to follow the same path.

2.16 The significance of the regulatory environment

It is perhaps surprising that a book on airline economics starts with a chapter that appears to be legal in character and to be dealing with the international regulation of air transport. The reasons for this are clear. Airlines, especially those operating internationally, are constrained in where they can fly to and how they operate by a complex web of domestic, bilateral and international rules and regulations both technical and economic in character.

To make matters worse, the regulatory regime, as we have seen, varies from country to country and market to market. Within the European Common Aviation Area, airlines have the freedom to operate as they deem commercially attractive while the major constraint appears to be airport or ATC capacity shortage. Across the North Atlantic, the same European airlines can fly between any points in Europe and the US with whatever flight frequency they wish and offering fares of their choice. But they cannot buy a US airline or set up a fully-owned subsidiary in the United States or operate domestic services there. On routes to many Asian, South American or African countries a European airline may be limited as to the points it can fly to or the number of flights it can offer. It may not be able to fly at all, because another European airline has already been designated for that route. It may even have to share capacity (i.e. the number of flights or seats offered) with the foreign carrier on the route. Almost everywhere there may be restrictions on who can own an airline, that is on the nationality of ownership. On the other hand, controls on pricing are rare.

The ASEAN member airlines are moving towards an open skies area, but ownership restrictions continue. To overcome them Air Asia, a Malaysian airline, has had to set up subsidiaries in other ASEAN countries in which it has less than 50 per cent of the shares but management control. This is in order to bypass the nationality restrictions. Its ASEAN subsidiaries include Air Asia Philippines, Thai Air Asia and Indonesia Air Asia.

Despite the liberalisation that has taken place, the European example illustrates the difficulties faced by managers of international airlines. In other parts of the world the constraints faced by airline executives may be even worse. On each route, what managers can or cannot do is circumscribed by the regulatory regime prevailing on that route. Some routes will be governed by very restrictive traditional bilaterals, as are many Chinese bilaterals; elsewhere a more liberal 'open skies' regime may prevail, as is the case on several routes to the United States. An appreciation of the regulatory environment is fundamental for an understanding both of airline economics and of the reasons why airline operating decisions sometimes appear to be irrational or even contradictory.

3 Understanding the structure of airline costs

If we want to succeed, we need to know that cost-cutting is never, ever ending. Airlines just breed nonsense costs.

(Peter Bellew, CEO Malaysia Airlines, March 2017)

3.1 The need for costing

The airline industry is dynamic, fast-changing and subject to sudden and unexpected variations in the cost of many of its inputs. This is why a clear understanding of the costs of supplying airline services is essential to many decisions taken by airline managers. But there are many ways of looking at costs. How an airline's costs are broken down and categorised will depend on the purpose for which they are to be used. In airline planning, cost information is generally needed to meet four key requirements. First, airlines need an overall breakdown of their total expenditure into different cost categories as a general management and accounting tool and in order to produce profit and loss accounts, balance sheets and annual reports. Second, airlines require a general breakdown of costs to show and monitor cost trends over time, to measure the cost efficiency of particular functional areas such as flight operations or maintenance. Third, airlines require very detailed cost information by flight and route in order to make operating decisions such as whether to add more frequencies on a sector or reduce them, or whether to operate that route at all. Such cost identification, by route or even by flight is crucial in the development of pricing policies and pricing decisions, for both passengers and cargo. Finally, an assessment of aircraft-related costs is essential in any evaluation of investments, whether in new aircraft or in new routes or services.

No single cost categorisation is capable of satisfying all of these management requirements simultaneously. A cost breakdown developed for general management and accounting purposes may be useless as a guide to pricing strategy and may be of little help in making operating decisions or deciding on aircraft purchases. As a result, most airlines break down their costs in two or more different ways depending on the purpose for which the cost analysis is required.

While the approach to cost categorisation used by each airline is strongly influenced by accounting practices in its home country, it has also been influenced by the cost classification adopted since the 1970s by the International Civil Aviation Organization (ICAO). This classification was in any case based fairly closely on prevailing costing practices in the United States and among several European airlines. Thus, worldwide throughout the airline industry, there tends to be a fairly standard and traditional approach to the categorisation of costs for general management use.

The cost classifications developed in the following sections are widely used and are helpful in making operating, pricing or investment decisions. While they may be used in preparing airline accounts they do not necessarily conform with international or national accounting standards, which may be more detailed and disaggregate.

3.2 The traditional approach to airline costs

It is normal practice to divide airline accounts into operating and non-operating categories. The aim is to identify and separate out as non-operating items all those costs and revenues not directly associated with the operation of an airline's own air services. Following ICAO and US practice, most airlines have adopted this approach, which identifies as *non-operating* the following five items:

1   The gains or losses arising from the retirement of property or equipment, both aeronautical and non-aeronautical. Such gains or losses arise when there is a difference between the depreciated book value of a particular item and the value that is realised when that item is retired or sold off.

2   Interest paid on loans, as well as any interest received from banks or other deposits. It is considered that bank interest paid or received has little to do with the business of flying. For some costing purposes, however, such as aircraft evaluation, some airlines would include interest paid on aircraft-related loans as an operating cost.

3   All profits or losses arising from an airline's affiliated companies, some of which may themselves be directly involved in air transport. In some cases, this item may be of some importance in the overall financial performance of an airline. Thus, in 2017, Singapore Airlines was part of a larger SIA group including SIA Engineering, SIA Cargo and the airlines SilkAir, Scoot and Tigerair (later merged). The group also had investments in over 60 aviation-related companies including a 20 per cent shareholding in Virgin Australia and 49 per cent in the Thai airline Nok Scoot. While the SIA group produces consolidated accounts, in examining the performance of Singapore Airlines itself the dividends, profits or losses of these various linked companies are best treated as non-operating items, otherwise the true performance of the core airline will be distorted.

4   An assortment of other items that do not fall into the previous three categories, such as losses or gains arising from foreign exchange transactions or from sales of shares or securities. In recent years airlines have from time to time made large losses or profits as a result of sudden marked fluctuations in exchange rates. These are clearly a non-operating item.

5   The final item includes any direct or indirect government subsidies or taxes on profit or other corporate taxes. In the case of some airlines, subsidies have at times been very substantial. Thus, in the 10-year period after 2008, Air India received massive injections of state funds, estimated at over US$1.5 billion, to enable it to reduce its debts and restructure its operations. State financial support in various forms has also been paid periodically to many other government-owned airlines in Europe, Africa and Asia. Such subsidies should appear as non-operating items. Similarly, profit taxes or other corporate taxes should also be categorised as non-operating.

For some airlines non-operating items may have a major impact on their financial results. Singapore Airlines (SIA) provides a dramatic example. In the financial year 2015–16 the SIA Group produced an overall net profit before tax of S.$736 million. Of this, slightly less than two thirds (63 per cent) was generated from airline operations, which here include cargo operations and SIA engineering. The remainder (37 per cent) came from non-operating items made up primarily of profits from subsidiaries, dividends from investments and interest earned from bank deposits. Though in subsequent years SIA's non-operating income dropped sharply, the SIA example amply illustrates why it is essential to separate out non-operating items so as to get a true assessment of how well the core business, which is flying aircraft, is doing.

Non-operating items are not necessarily profits or surpluses. They may well be losses or costs. Most airlines normally pay out a great deal more in interest charges on their loans than they receive from their own cash deposits at the bank. This is particularly so of state-owned airlines whose development has been financed by a succession of loans rather than through injection of equity capital. But even many privatised airlines face large interest payments on their debts, which may not be off-set by interest they may earn on their cash in hand.

The nature of each airline's non-operating costs and revenues is probably unique, in that many non-operating items are influenced by circumstances very particular to each airline. As a result, inter-airline comparisons of net profits or total costs including non-operating costs are of limited value.

In fact, in years when their profits decline, many airlines 'massage' their non-operating costs or revenues to improve their bottom line results. For instance, it is common for hard-pressed airlines to sell some of their aircraft and then lease them back. This generates a substantial cash inflow, which appears as a positive non-operating item and may offset any operating losses. Because of such anomalies and complexities it is better when assessing an airline's costs or revenues to leave non-operating items aside and to focus on its operating costs or revenues. These are the best descriptors of its performance as an airline.

On the operating side, airline accounts are divided into *operating revenue* and *operating costs*. The latter can be further subdivided into direct operating and indirect operating costs, but direct and indirect have a different meaning in the airline industry from that in normal accounting usage.

In theory, the distinction between these two cost categories is fairly clear. *Direct operating costs* should include all those costs associated with and dependent on the type of aircraft being operated and would change if the aircraft type were changed. Broadly speaking, such costs should include all flying expenses (such as flight crew salaries, fuel and oil), all maintenance and overhaul costs and all aircraft depreciation costs. *Indirect operating costs* are all those costs that will remain unaffected by a change of aircraft type because they are not directly dependent on aircraft operations. They include areas of expenditure that are passenger related rather than aircraft related (such as passenger service costs, costs of ticketing and sales, and station and ground costs) as well as general administrative costs. In practice, however, the distinction between direct and indirect operating costs is not always clear-cut. Certain cost items, such as maintenance administration or costs of cabin staff, are categorised as direct costs by some airlines and as indirect costs by others. The main categories of airline operating costs are shown in Table 3.1. The cost categories shown are those currently accepted and used, with some modification, by most international airlines around the world. US carriers use slightly different categorisation of costs, but the overall approach is similar.

Table 3.1 Traditional categorisation of airline operating costs

Direct Operating Costs (DOC)	
1	*Flight operations*
	– Flight crew salaries and expenses
	– Fuel and oil
	– Airport and en-route charges[*]
	– Aircraft insurance
	– Rental/lease of flight equipment/crews[**]
2	*Maintenance and overhaul*
	– Engineering staff costs
	– Spare parts consumed
	– Maintenance administration (could be IOC)
3	*Depreciation and amortization*
	– Flight equipment
	– Ground equipment and property (could be IOC)
	– Extra depreciation (in excess of historic cost depreciation)
	– Amortisation of development costs and crew training
Indirect Operating Costs (IOC)	
4	*Station and ground expenses*
	– Ground staff
	– Buildings, equipment, transport
	– Handling fees paid to others
5	*Passenger services*
	– Cabin crew salaries and expenses (could be DOC)
	– Other passenger service costs
	– Passenger insurance
6	*Ticketing, sales and promotion*
7	*General and administration*
8	*Other operating costs*

Notes
[*] ICAO classifies airport and en-route charges as an indirect operating cost under
'Station and ground expenses'
[**] In the US and some other countries, the practice is to classify rentals under
'Depreciation'

3.3 Direct operating costs

3.3.1 Cost of flight operations

This is undoubtedly the largest single element of operating costs that is aircraft dependent. It includes, in the first place, all costs associated with *flight crew*. Such costs cover not only direct salaries and travelling and stopover expenses but also allowances, pensions, insurance and any other social welfare payments. While commercial jet aircraft have two-person cockpit crews, their salaries will normally depend on the type of aircraft being flown. For safety reasons, pilots and co-pilots are licensed to fly only one aircraft type during any period of time. As a general rule, the larger the aircraft the higher the salaries paid. So pilot costs are aircraft specific. However, cockpit commonality in some aircraft types such as the Airbus 319 and Airbus 320 are allowing airlines to use pilots who are common-rated to fly two related aircraft types. Flight crew costs can be directly calculated on a route-by-route basis or, more usually, they are expressed as an hourly cost per aircraft type. In the latter case the total flight crew costs for a particular route or service can be calculated by multiplying the hourly flight crew costs of the aircraft being operated on that route by the block time for the route (see Glossary for definition of block time).

The second and largest cost element of flight operations is *fuel*. Again, it is very aircraft specific. Fuel consumption varies by aircraft type depending on the weight and aerodynamics of the aircraft but clearly also on the number and the size or thrust of the engines and the type and age of those engines. During operations, actual fuel consumption varies considerably from route to route in relation to the sector lengths, the aircraft weight (including passengers and cargo carried), the wind conditions, the cruise altitude, and so on. Thus, an hourly fuel cost tends to be even more of an approximation than hourly flight crew costs, and it is normal to consider fuel consumption on a route-by-route basis. Fuel expenses should include any fuel throughput charges levied by some airport authorities on the volume of fuel uplifted, the fuel handling charges paid to fuel suppliers for the loading of fuel and any relevant fuel taxes or duties levied by governments, though these are not usual.

Another significant element of flight operation costs is made up of *airport and en-route charges*. Airlines have to pay airport authorities for the use of the runway and terminal facilities. Airport charges normally have two elements: a landing fee related to the weight of the aircraft, usually its maximum take-off weight, and a passenger charge levied on the number of departing passengers boarded at that airport (occasionally it may be calculated on the number of disembarked passengers). Clearly both the landing fee and, indirectly, the *total* passenger charge are related to the type of aircraft operated. At most airports a free parking period of two to six hours is covered by the basic aircraft landing fee. If an aircraft stays at an airport beyond this free time period, it will have to pay additional aircraft parking or hangarage fees. These are relatively small compared with the basic landing and passenger charges.

Airlines must also pay en-route navigation charges to cover the cost of en-route navigation services that their aircraft use while flying and during landing and take-off. The actual level of the en-route navigation charge is normally related to the maximum take-off weight (MTOW) of the aircraft and the distance flown over a country's airspace. As a result, both airport charges, where they are not passenger related, and navigation services charges will vary with the type of aircraft used and are therefore considered as a direct operating cost. On the other hand, the unit passenger-related charges do not vary directly with aircraft type. This may partly explain why ICAO suggests treating landing and en-route charges as an indirect cost, though only a few airlines follow this lead. Since landing and en-route charges vary by individual airport and country, they must be separately calculated for each flight or route.

A relatively small cost in flight operations is that of the *insurance of the flight equipment*. The insurance premium paid by an airline for each aircraft is calculated as a percentage of the full purchase price. The annual premium may be between 1.5 per cent and 3 per cent depending on the airline's safety record, the number of aircraft it has insured and the geographical areas in which its aircraft operate. If the airline wants full war risk cover, if it wants to be covered against terrorist action or if it is operating in or through an area where there is armed conflict, an additional premium of up to 2 per cent may need to be paid. The annual premium, which is fixed, can be converted into an hourly insurance cost by dividing it by the projected aircraft utilisation, that is, by the total number of block-hours that each aircraft is expected to fly during the year.

Many airlines may, in addition, have to meet *rental or lease charges* for the hiring or leasing of aircraft from other airlines or leasing companies. Lease charges are usually considered as part of flight operation costs. Small start-up airlines are often launched on the basis of leased aircraft, though over the last 20 years, leases have become widespread even among larger airlines. They are broadly of two kinds: operating leases, which are generally for one to seven years with ownership resting with the lessor, and financial leases in which after 10 or more years aircraft ownership is transferred to the airline. In the case of operating leases, rental or lease charges may be high, pushing up that airline's total flight operations costs to unusually high levels. This is because the rental charges for leased aircraft effectively cover both the depreciation and the interest charges paid by the owners of the aircraft, that is the lessors. Conversely, the airlines' depreciation charges will be low since they pay for depreciation indirectly through the rental charge. Airlines using finance leases pay both a rental fee and tend to make a depreciation charge to their accounts since they will have ultimate ownership of the aircraft involved (see Morrell, 2013, on calculating depreciation on leased aircraft).

It is because rentals include a large element of depreciation that the American practice is to categorise lease rental charges under the heading of depreciation rather than to treat them as a cost of flight operations (Table 3.1). Many non-US airlines also follow this approach. Lease costs and depreciation taken together can be categorised as aircraft ownership costs. Many airlines also include interest paid on loans raised for aircraft purchase as a cost of aircraft ownership.

Finally, there may be some costs related to flight operations that do not fall into any of the above categories. Such additional costs may include costs of *flight crew training* or of *route development*. However, if training costs are amortised over two or three years then they are grouped together with depreciation.

3.3.2 Maintenance and overhaul costs

Total maintenance costs cover a whole series of separate costs, related to different aspects of maintenance and overhaul, which ideally ought to be treated separately. In practice there are so many joint costs in the separate maintenance areas that it is difficult, if not impossible, for many airlines to break down total maintenance costs into separate cost categories. While ICAO and some airlines group all maintenance and overhaul expenditure into a single undivided cost item, the UK's Civil Aviation Authority in its own airline statistics splits maintenance into two categories, fixed and variable. The latter are those costs dependent on the amount of flying done.

Maintenance costs cover not only routine maintenance and maintenance checks carried out between flights, known as *line maintenance*, but also the more extensive periodic overhauls and major checks of airframes and engines. They encompass two major cost areas: first, the very extensive use of labour and the expenses related to all grades of staff involved directly or indirectly in maintenance work. Where possible, costs of maintenance staff at outstations should be separated out from station costs and included under maintenance. Second, there is a major cost associated with the consumption of spare parts. Most parts of each engine and airframe have a usable life measured in terms of block-hours or numbers of flight-cycles, that is, landings and take-offs. Once its certified life has expired, each part must be removed and checked or replaced; hence, the consumption of spare parts is high and costly. The costs of workshops, maintenance hangars and offices are also included. Finally, if an airline is subcontracting out to third parties any of the maintenance done on its own aircraft, then the charges it pays for any such work should be allocated to the maintenance and overhaul category.

In the United States, the Department of Transportation requires airlines to split their flight equipment maintenance costs into three categories: direct maintenance on the airframe, direct maintenance on the engines and a maintenance burden. The maintenance burden is essentially the administrative and overhead costs associated with the maintenance function that cannot be attributed directly to a particular airframe or engine but are allocated on a fairly arbitrary basis. US airlines are obliged to furnish the federal government with these three categories of maintenance costs separately for each aircraft type that they operate. These data are published and provide an excellent basis for the comparison of maintenance costs between airlines and also between different aircraft types and engines.

Outside the United States, airlines also try to apportion their maintenance costs between different aircraft types, but there is no standard way of doing this, so inter-airline cost comparisons would not be valid even if such data were publicly available. Individual airlines, having estimated the total maintenance costs for one particular aircraft type, may then convert these costs into an hourly maintenance cost by dividing them by the total number of block-hours flown by all the aircraft of that particular type operated by the airline.

3.3.3 Depreciation and amortisation

Depreciation of flight equipment is the third component of direct operating cost since it is very much aircraft dependent. Airlines tend to use straight-line depreciation over a given number of years with a residual value of 0–15 per cent. The residual value is the predicted or assumed resale value of the aircraft at the end of the depreciation period. In recent years, airlines throughout the world tended to lengthen the depreciation period of their large, wide-bodied jets and of new-generation single-aisle aircraft to between 15 and 25 years with a residual value of 5 to 10 per cent. For smaller short-haul aircraft, especially if they are turbo-props, the depreciation periods used are generally shorter.

United States airlines tend to use longer depreciation periods than their counterparts elsewhere. For instance, in 2015 Delta used 20 to 32 years for its aircraft depreciation with residual values of 5 to 10 percent. In the same year Southwest depreciated its airframes and engines over 22 to 25 years to residual values of 2 to 20 per cent.

In periods of crisis airlines tend to lengthen their depreciation period as a way of reducing their annual costs. For example, in the financial year 2014 Lufthansa changed its depreciation policy from 12 years with 15 per cent residual value to one of 20 years to a 5 per cent residual value. This brought it in line with what many other airlines were already doing. More significantly, the new policy added US$452 million to operating profits in 2014!

The purpose of depreciation is twofold. First, it aims to spread the cost of an aircraft over the useful life of that aircraft. If the full cost of a new aircraft was all debited in the year in which the aircraft was bought it would seriously inflate costs and undermine profits in that year, especially if a fleet of aircraft was bought. Instead, only a proportion of an aircraft's full cost is charged against revenues each year. The depreciation policy chosen determines how much that proportion should be. By covering its depreciation costs an airline ensures that it is also meeting the costs of owning its aircraft assets. Second, depreciation allows money out of each year's revenues, equivalent to the depreciation charge, to be put into a general reserve fund. These monies, together with any retained profits, can, in theory, be used to pay back the loans with which the aircraft were bought together with any accrued interest. If the aircraft have been bought fully or in part with the airline's own cash, then the accumulated depreciation reserve can be used to fund the new aircraft when the current aircraft are replaced.

That is the theory. Historically, the airline industry's marginal profitability combined with rising aircraft prices has meant that few airlines build up sufficient retained cash reserves to finance all their new aircraft purchases. Most then have to resort to raising loans or leasing when expanding their fleets.

The annual depreciation charge or cost of a particular aircraft in an airline's fleet depends on the depreciation period adopted and the residual value assumed. An airline that had bought several Boeing 787-800 Dreamliners in 2015 for delivery in 2017–18 might have paid, say, US$170 million for each aircraft, against a list price of $220 million because it placed a relatively large order. It may have paid another $30 million per aircraft for a spares holding, making a total cost of $200 million per aircraft.

Assuming it depreciated each aircraft with spares over 20 years to a 10 per cent residual value, then the annual depreciation charge would be $9 million:

$$\text{Annual depreciation} = \frac{\text{Price of aircraft and spares ($200m) less residual value (10\%)}}{\text{Depreciation period (20 years)}}$$
$$= \frac{\$200m - \$20m}{20} = \frac{\$180}{20} = \$9.0m$$

However, if the airline chooses a shorter depreciation period, then the annual depreciation cost will rise. Thus, if an airline followed the practice of Emirates in 2016 and depreciated its aircraft over 15 years with a 10 per cent residual value rather than the 20 years used in the example, then its annual depreciation cost for the same Boeing 787 aircraft would rise from $9 million to $12 million per aircraft. The immediate effect would be to increase annual operating costs by pushing up the annual depreciation costs for each aircraft.

So why would Emirates or any other airline choose a faster depreciation policy if the effect is to push up operating costs? An airline may wish to build up higher cash reserves by setting money aside from more rapid depreciation, so it can self-finance fleet expansion or fleet renewal more easily. Alternatively, it may wish to reduce annual profits in the short term to minimise its corporate tax liabilities.

Once the depreciation policy has been determined, the annual depreciation cost for each aircraft becomes a fixed cost, but the hourly cost is dependent on the hours of flying that an aircraft undertakes each year. The hourly depreciation cost of each aircraft in any one year can be established by dividing its fixed annual depreciation cost by the aircraft's annual utilisation, that is, the number of block-hours flown in that year. Thus, if the Boeing 787-800 aircraft in the above example flew 3,680 block-hours in a year, the average utilsation of All Nippon Airways' 787-800s in 2016, then its hourly depreciation cost would be $2,445 ($9 million divided by 3,680 hours). If the annual utilisation could be pushed up to 5,530 hours, which was the utilisation Ethiopian and Qatar Airways were achieving in 2016 with this aircraft, then the hourly depreciation cost would be cut to $1,627 ($9 million divided by 5,530). It would be 34 per cent lower. This is why pushing up the daily and annual utilisation of an airline's aircraft as much as possible is so crucial.

The more an aircraft flies each day and year the lower is the depreciation cost per block-hour. It is evident that any changes in the depreciation period, in the residual value or in the annual utilisation will all affect the hourly depreciation cost.

Developing a depreciation policy is a complex affair. This is because the prime cost of an aircraft is made up of separate components such as the airframe itself, the engines, the rotable spare parts and interior specific furnishings, including the in-flight entertainment systems. All have different operating life spans. Once an aircraft is purchased, there are periodically additonal large capital outlays needed on major airframe and engine overhauls. Airlines have to decide how to depreciate all these separate capital expenditures. As an example, in 2016 easyJet depreciated its airframes and engines over 23 years, its spares over 14 years and its prepaid major maintenance over seven to 10 years.

ICAO suggests including depreciation of ground property and equipment as a further item of direct operating costs. This practice is questionable in that such depreciation charges are not directly related to the operation of aircraft and, except where they relate to ground equipment specific and unique to a particular aircraft type, they will remain unaffected if an airline changes its fleet.

Many airlines amortise the costs of flight crew training as well as any developmental and pre-operating costs related to the development of new routes or the introduction of new aircraft. In essence this means that such costs, instead of being charged in total to the year in which they occur, are spread out over a number of years. Such amortisation costs are grouped together with depreciation but are quite small.

3.4 Indirect operating costs

3.4.1 Station and ground expenses

Station and ground costs are all those costs incurred in providing an airline's services at an airport other than the cost of landing fees and other airport charges. Such costs include the salaries and expenses of all airline staff located at the airport and engaged in the handling and servicing of aircraft, passengers or freight. These should include all costs associated with an airline's lounges for Business or First class passengers, though these could also be listed under the heading of passenger service costs. In addition, there will be the costs of ground-handling equipment, of ground transport, of buildings and offices and associated facilities such as computers, telephones, and so on. There will also be a cost arising from the maintenance and insurance of each station's buildings and equipment. Rents may have to be paid for some of the properties used, as well as charges for electricity, heating and so on. Clearly, by far the largest expenditure on station and ground staff and facilities inevitably occurs at an airline's home base.

At some airports, especially the smaller ones it serves, an airline may decide to contract out some or all of its check-in and handling needs. Handling fees charged by third parties should appear as a station expense. After the crisis periods of 2001–4 and 2008–9 there has been a strong tendency for legacy network airlines to outsource more and more of their handling, away from their major bases, to specialist ground-handling companies, as a way of reducing such costs. In this they were following the low-cost model. European low-cost carriers have done this as an integral part of their business model. An airline may contract out of all of its handling including passenger check-in, baggage and freight handling and loading, aircraft cleaning and so on, or only some of these activities. It may pay a global fee irrespective of the aircraft type actually used. However, if the fees paid for handling to be provided by a handling agent or another airline vary with the size or type of aircraft being used then such handling charges may legitimately be considered a direct operating cost.

Some limited light aircraft maintenance may be done at an airline's out-stations and the costs arising from such maintenance work should ideally be included as a direct operating cost under the 'maintenance and overhaul' category. But line maintenance expenditures are frequently difficult to disentangle from other station costs and are in many cases left as part of station and ground costs.

3.4.2 Costs of passenger services

The largest single element of costs arising from passenger services is the pay, allowances and other expenses directly related to aircraft cabin staff and other passenger service personnel. Such expenses would include hotel and other costs associated with overnight stops as well as the training costs of cabin staff, where these are not amortised. Unlike pilots, cabin crew are licensed to work on any aircraft type within an airline's fleet. They are not restricted to one or two types only; hence, cabin crew costs are assumed to be independent of the type of aircraft being used. On the other hand, as the number and grading of cabin staff may vary by aircraft type, some airlines consider cabin staff costs as an element of flight operations costs; that is, as a direct operating cost.

A second group of passenger service costs are those directly related to the passengers. They include the costs of in-flight catering, the costs of meals and other facilities provided on the ground for the comfort of passengers, and expenses incurred or compensation paid as a result of delayed or cancelled flights. The costs of airline lounges provided for premium passengers and certain members of Frequent Flyer clubs might also be included under 'passenger service' costs rather than being considered as 'station' costs.

Finally, premiums paid by the airline for passenger liability insurance and passenger accident insurance should also be included. These are a fixed annual charge based on an airline's total number of passengers or passenger-kilometres produced in the previous year. The premium rate will depend on each airline's safety record, on the regions it operates within or to and on the type of insurance cover it requires.

3.4.3 Ticketing, sales and promotion costs

Such costs include all expenditure, pay, allowances, etc. related to staff engaged in reservations ticketing, sales and promotion activities as well as all office and accommodation costs arising through these activities. The costs of retail ticket offices or shops, whether at home or abroad, would be included, as well as the costs of telephone call centres, of the computerised reservations systems and the operation of the airline's internet website. Problems of cost allocation arise. It is frequently difficult, especially at foreign stations, to decide whether particular expenses should be categorised as station and ground expenses or as ticketing, sales and promotion. For instance, where should an airline allocate the costs of ticketing staff manning a ticket desk at a foreign airport who may also get involved in assisting with the ground-handling of passengers? The same difficulty arises with the costs of an airline's 'country manager' in a foreign country, who may have overall responsibility for sales as well as the handling of passengers at the airport.

A significant cost item within this area is that of commissions or fees paid to retail or online travel agencies for ticket sales. Commissions are also paid to credit card companies for sales paid for by using cards as well as to the global distribution systems for all reservations made on their worldwide computer systems. Finally, all promotional expenditure including the costs of all advertising and of any other form of promotion, such as familiarisation visits by journalists or travel agents, also fall under this heading.

3.4.4 General and administrative costs

General and administrative costs are normally a relatively small element of an airline's total operating costs. This is because, where overhead costs can be related directly to a particular function or activity within an airline (such as maintenance or sales), then they should be allocated to that activity. Thus, strictly speaking, general and administrative costs should include only those cost elements truly general to the airline or that cannot readily be allocated to a particular activity. These are 'system'-related costs rather than aircraft- or payload-related costs. While some airlines try to allocate their central costs to different cost centres as much as possible, other airlines do not do so either as a matter of policy or because their accounting procedures are not sophisticated enough to enable them to do so.

Where airlines cannot legitimately include a particular expense under one of the cost categories discussed, they may include it as a separate item under '*Other operating expenses*'. If the sums shown under this heading for a particular airline are large, this is usually an indication of poor cost control and/or inadequate accounting procedures.

3.5 Trends in airline costs

The distribution of total operating costs between the various cost elements discussed can be seen in Table 3.2. It is apparent that in 2017 for the world's airlines as a whole close to two-thirds (63.1 per cent) of their total operating costs were direct costs. The rest were categorised as indirect costs.

Because fuel is normally the largest single input cost for airlines, variations in the price of fuel have been the most significant factor affecting both the level and the structure of airline costs. Historically, when fuel prices have been low, total operating costs for airlines as a whole have been more or less evenly split between direct and indirect; but because fuel is such a large input cost, when fuel prices rise then direct operating costs (DOC) tend to become well over half of total costs. When fuel prices rise to very high levels then DOC may represent two-thirds or more of total costs as happened in 2008 and again in 2014 and 2015. In other words, the price of aviation fuel is a key cost variable both because it may be the largest single cost but also because it changes over time and often quite rapidly.

Table 3.2 The structure of costs – IATA member airlines, 2017

		2017%
A	**Direct Operating Costs (DOC)**	
	1 Flight operations – total	47.1
	Flight crew – salaries, expenses, training	(8.8)
	Fuel and oil	(22.8)
	Airport and en-route charges	(6.7)
	Aircraft rental, insurance, etc.	(7.0)
	Other flight operations expenses	(1.8)
	2 Maintenance	9.0
	3 Depreciation – aircraft (inc. insurance)	7.0
	TOTAL DOC	**63.1**
B	**Indirect Operating Costs (IOC)**	
	4 Station/ground expenses*	7.8
	5 Passenger services (including cabin crew)	8.2
	6 Ticketing, sales, promotion	6.7
	7 Admin and other operating costs	14.2
	TOTAL IOC	**36.9**
C	**TOTAL OPERATING COSTS (TOC)**	**100.0**

Source: International Air Transport Association, Geneva

Fluctuations in the price of fuel since 1990 in constant value terms were illustrated earlier in Figure 1.4 (Chapter 1). The new century started with low oil and fuel prices. As a result, in the year 2000 fuel represented only around 14 per cent of global airline costs. But after 2003, the war in Iraq, the booming demand for oil from China and India combined with the production quotas imposed by OPEC member states led to a tripling of the crude oil price by 2006. Aviation fuel prices followed. In 2007, when the average price of a barrel of jet kerosene fuel reached US$90, fuel generated 25 per cent of airline costs. By mid-2008 aviation fuel had risen to US$126.7 per barrel before collapsing in the second half of the year and falling to US$71 in 2009. (Note prices mentioned here are at current values of the day whereas prices shown in Figure 1.4 are at constant US dollar values.)

After 2009 fuel prices rose gradually, hitting a new high of US$129.6 per barrel in 2012. At that price fuel accounted for 33 per cent of airlines' total costs. Its impact was so high partly because non-fuel costs were being successfully cut by airlines. Prices then fluctuated around that high level till mid-2014 when they collapsed sharply once more. But many airlines did not feel the full benefit of lower fuel prices because they were still locked into mid-term fuel hedges secured in 2013 or early 2014. They had bought fuel forward in the expectation that prices would rise or stay high. Those that had bought hedges found themselves paying well above market prices for much of their fuel uplift in 2015. As a result, fuel represented 28.7 per cent of total costs in 2015 and then dropped to 22 per cent the following year.

When fuel prices collapse to very low levels, as happened early in 2016, for some airlines total labour costs (covering flight and cabin crews as well as maintenance, airport and all other staff) may become the largest single cost item and surpass fuel costs.

Among US airlines, labour has tended to be their largest single cost even when fuel prices were relatively high.

Aircraft ownership costs are also one of the larger cost inputs (Table 3.2). In 2017, aircraft rentals (6.9 per cent) plus depreciation and aircraft insurance (7 per cent) taken together accounted for 13.9 per cent of total costs. This is why, as pointed out earlier, at times of crisis airlines tend to change their depreciation policy in order to reduce annual depreciation costs thereby reducing annual ownership costs. By doing this they also reduce total unit costs.

3.6 The concept of escapability

The traditional classification of costs into various types of direct and indirect costs, as described earlier, is essentially a functional one. Costs are allocated to particular functional areas within the airline, such as flight operations or maintenance, and are then grouped together in one of two categories, as either direct or indirect operating costs. This cost breakdown is of considerable value for accounting and general management purposes. This is particularly so where the organisational structure within an airline corresponds fairly closely to the same functional areas as may be used for costing purposes – in other words, where an airline has a flight operations division, an engineering (maintenance) division, a sales division, and so on. A functional classification of costs is useful for monitoring an airline's performance over time and also for inter-airline comparisons. Costs can be broken down relatively easily to produce disaggregate costs within a particular functional area. For instance, one could analyse separately labour costs in the maintenance area as opposed to the labour costs in station and ground operations.

In addition, the broad division into direct and indirect costs is especially useful when dealing with aircraft evaluation. The indirect costs of a particular network or operation can be assumed to remain constant, since they are unaffected by the type of aircraft used. An evaluation of a new aircraft type or a comparison between several aircraft for a particular network can then be based purely on an assessment of the direct operating costs. This simplifies the process of evaluation.

The great advantage of the traditional approach to cost classification is its simplicity and the fact that in allocating costs by functional area it avoids many of the problems associated with trying to allocate joint or common costs. For instance, station and ground costs common to a number of different services are grouped together and are not allocated to particular flights or services. However, the simplicity of this cost classification is also its major drawback. It is of only limited use for an economic evaluation of particular services or routes, for pricing decisions or for showing how costs may vary with changes in the pattern of operations on a particular route.

To aid decision-making in these and other related areas the concept of 'escapability' of costs needs to be introduced. The degree of escapability is determined by the time period required before a particular cost can be avoided. Clearly some costs may be immediately escapable, as a result of a particular management decision, while others may not be avoidable except in the very long run. The concept of escapability involves a temporal dimension. Different costs will require different periods before they can be avoided, but ultimately all costs are escapable.

There is also a technical dimension to the concept, in that the degree of escapability also varies with the size and nature of the airline service or activity being considered. Thus, if all services on a particular route were to be cut, the nature of the escapable costs would be different to those if only a flight on a particular day of the week was cancelled on this same route. The first course of action might involve not only a saving of flight operation costs but also the closure of a complete station or a reduction in the number of crews or even the number of aircraft in the fleet. Cancellation of only one flight a week may involve a reduction in some flight operation costs but little else. This is because many costs are joint or common costs and will go on being incurred to support the remaining flights even if one flight a week is cancelled. The interaction of the temporal and technical aspects of escapability must be constantly borne in mind by airline managers.

Airlines vary in the way they introduce the concept of escapability into their costing procedures. The most usual way is by adopting the traditional accounting distinction of fixed and variable costs. Airlines do this by taking those elements of cost generally accepted as being direct operating costs, adding to them some of the indirect costs, and further subdividing them into 'fixed' and 'variable' costs. There are several ways in which this can be done because of the temporal and technical considerations outlined previously. The larger and more sophisticated airlines may use one breakdown of costs for, say, pricing decisions and a different one for evaluating the profitability of particular services or routes. One possible approach is discussed as follows.

3.6.1 Variable and fixed direct operating costs

Variable or flying direct costs are costs directly escapable in the short run. They are *activity related*. They include all those costs that would be avoided if a flight or a series of flights was cancelled. They are immediately escapable costs, such as fuel, flight crew overtime and other flight-related cabin crew expenses, landing and en-route charges, the costs of any passenger meals, and so on. These are fairly self-evident. Less self-evident are the engineering or maintenance costs that should be classified as variable. Certain maintenance checks of different parts of the aircraft, involving both labour costs and the replacement of spare parts, are scheduled to take place after so many hours of flying or after a prescribed number of flight cycles. (A flight cycle is one take-off and landing.) Undercarriage maintenance, for example, is related to the number of flight cycles. Since a large part of direct maintenance is related to the amount of flying or the flight cycles, cancelling a service will immediately reduce both the hours flown and the flight cycles and will save some engineering expenditure, notably on the consumption of spare parts, and some labour costs.

Fixed or standing direct costs are those direct operating costs which in the short run do not vary with particular flights or even a series of flights. Essentially, they are related to *fleet size*. These are costs, such as annual depreciation or lease charges, which are not escapable in the short term but some may be escapable in the medium term. They are certainly not escapable within one scheduling period or even two scheduling periods. That is to say, having planned its schedules for a particular programme period and adjusted its aircraft numbers, its total flight and cabin crew numbers and maintenance requirements to meet that particular schedules programme, an airline cannot easily cut back its schedules and services until the next schedules programme is introduced. This is because of adverse public reaction and its own obligations towards the public. Even if it cut some services immediately, it would be unable in the short term to reduce its fixed direct costs.

New schedules might normally be introduced twice a year but will be planned more than a year ahead. If the airline decided to cut back its frequencies when the next schedules programme was introduced, it could possibly reduce its fleet by selling some aircraft and it could reduce its staff numbers and cut its maintenance and other overheads. Fixed or standing DOCs may be escapable but only after a year or two, depending on how quickly the airline could actually change its schedules and cut back on the number of aircraft operated, staff, and so on. Thus, most staff costs for pilots, cabin crew or maintenance engineers are fixed in the short term but staff travel expenses or pilots' bonuses related to flying activity would be a variable cost.

3.6.2 Indirect operating costs

While most *indirect operating costs* are fixed costs in that they do not depend in the short term on the amount of flying undertaken, others are more directly dependent on the operation of particular flights. This is particularly true of some passenger service costs such as in-flight catering and hotel expenses and some elements of cabin crew costs. Fees paid to handling agents or other airlines for ground-handling of aircraft, passengers or freight can be avoided if a flight is not operated. Some advertising and promotional costs may also be escapable in the short run. Airlines breaking down their costs according to their escapability take some or all of these expenses previously categorised as indirect costs and redefine them as fixed or variable direct operating costs. This leaves within the indirect cost category costs not dependent on the operation of particular services or routes. They are fixed in the short term but some could be escaped in the medium or longer term.

One possible threefold division of costs based on the concept of escapability is shown in Table 3.3. All direct operating costs, as categorised earlier in Table 3.2, have now been divided into fixed or variable. In addition, a number of expenses previously categorised as indirect operating costs in Table 3.1 are here re-classified as direct costs. These include all cabin crew costs, handling fees paid to others and the costs of in-flight catering and other passenger-related costs. But they too are further sub-divided into fixed and variable direct costs. Handling and passenger service costs are now deemed to be variable costs, as are those variable cabin crew costs dependent on the amount of flying undertaken. On the other hand, most cabin crew costs, including basic annual salaries, are now considered to be fixed direct costs.

It is interesting to assess the concept of cost escapability by applying it to British Airways' cost structure in the financial year to March 2015, when fuel prices were particularly high. Using operating cost data published by the UK Civil Aviation Authority (such data was discontinued subsequently) it proved possible to break down British Airways' costs in terms of their escapability. This showed that in that year over half of BA's total operating costs or 63.4 per cent were variable direct costs and immediately escapable. A further 21.3 per cent were fixed direct operating costs escapable in the medium term. Surprisingly only 15.3 percent were indirect operating costs and really only escapable in the longer term.

Because fuel is normally the largest single cost, the fuel price has a major impact on the significance of variable costs. It was the very high fuel prices in most of 2014 that

Table 3.3 Cost structure based on fixed and variable direct operating costs

Variable Direct Operating Costs	*Fixed/Standing Direct Operating Costs*
1 Fuel costs • fuel • oil consumed	**7 Aircraft standing charges** • depreciation or lease rentals • aircraft insurance
2 Variable flight crew costs* • flight crew subsistence and bonuses	**8 Annual flight crew costs** • fixed salaries and other expenses unrelated to amount of flying done • flight crew administration
3 Variable cabin crew costs • cabin crew subsistence and bonuses	**9 Annual cabin crew costs*** • fixed salaries and other expenses unrelated to amount of flying done • cabin crew administration
4 Direct engineering costs • related to number of flight cycles • aircraft utilisation	**10 Engineering overheads** • fixed engineering staff costs unrelated to number of flying hours • maintenance administration and other overheads
5 Airport and en-route charges • landing fees and other airport charges • en-route navigation charges	
6 Passenger service costs* • passenger in-flight etc. • handling fees paid to others	

Indirect Operating Costs
11 **Station and ground expenses**
12 **Passenger services** • passenger service staff • passenger insurance
13 **Ticketing, sales and promotion**
14 **General and administrative**

N.B.: *These items were previously categorised as 'Indirect' (Table 3.1)

pushed BA's variable direct costs to almost two thirds of its total costs. The same would have been the case with other airlines. In subsequent years, as the price of fuel declined, inevitably BA's variable direct costs also eased to around 50 per cent.

Variable direct operating costs are related to an airline's activity level, that is, the amount of flying it actually does. When variable costs are as high a proportion as indicated in the British Airways example, there are important implications for operations planning and for pricing. It means that revenue losses can be reduced significantly in the short term by cancelling a flight or a series of flights – if low load factors and/or low yields generate revenues that fail to cover the very significant variable costs. In other words, revenues should at least cover variable costs. If not, that flight or service is haemorrhaging money. The risks of this happening are greatest when the price of fuel is high, since this increases the relative proportion of variable costs.

Variable direct costs are those that are immediately escapable. In the medium term, that is, within a period of a year or so, many *fixed direct operating costs* previously considered fixed start to become variable. Such costs are essentially related to the size of the fleet. If the fleet size is reduced many fixed costs can be reduced too. Aircraft can be sold, cutting depreciation costs, flight and cabin crew numbers can be run down or staff redeployed, and engineering staff facilities can be reduced in size.

Indirect operating costs tend to be related primarily to the number of routes being operated, the quality of services offered and the nature of the sales and distribution systems built up to support the network. Advertising and promotion costs are also influenced by the route structure. The number of routes operated can be cut back in the medium term and over a longer period the whole network can be modified. Thus, even some indirect operating costs are escapable in the medium term and most are escapable in the longer term. In short, elements of both fixed direct costs and indirect costs are escapable in the medium term.

What is perhaps more significant and often forgotten is that as much as 90 per cent of total costs can be varied in the medium term, that is after a year or so, either by discontinuing all operations or by a partial withdrawal of certain operations. Airlines can disinvest or dramatically cut their operations more easily than most forms of public transport because they do not have fixed investments in navigational aids, runways or terminals, though there may be some exceptions, as in North America where airlines may own and operate their own terminals. But while disinvestment may be relatively easy it may also be costly if it involves redundancy payments to laid-off staff, financial penalties for early termination of aircraft leases and so on. Disinvestment is easier if the industry as a whole is doing well. Aircraft can be easily sold or leased out and staff more readily redeployed, but it is usually during industry downturns that airlines want to cut back their production. Reducing the fleet in such times becomes very difficult since no one is keen to acquire new capacity or staff.

3.7 Allocation of costs for operating decisions

In order to be able to use the concept of cost escapability in making operating decisions – such as whether to reduce or increase frequencies on a route or whether to open up an entirely new route – the various fixed and variable costs need to be allocated to individual flights or routes. Broadly speaking, the approach adopted by various airlines is similar, though there may be differences in the details.

Allocating *variable direct operating costs* is fairly straightforward since nearly all of them are specific to individual flights. Fuel costs, variable flight and cabin crew costs, airport and en-route charges and passenger service costs (as defined in Table 3.3) depend directly on the type and size of the aircraft used and the route over which it is being flown. They are clearly very specific and can be easily measured. The exceptions are the variable engineering or maintenance costs. Here some averaging out is required.

Some direct maintenance work and checks are related to the amount of flying that an aircraft undertakes, while other checks depend on the number of flight cycles. Maintenance on those parts of the aircraft most under pressure on landing or departure, such as the undercarriage or the flaps, is clearly related to the flight cycles undertaken. For each aircraft type an airline will normally work out an average cost of maintenance per *block-hour* and a separate average maintenance cost per *flight cycle*. The variable maintenance cost of an individual flight can then be calculated on the basis of the number of block-hours and flight cycles required for that flight.

An airline's *fixed direct operating costs* are normally converted into a cost per block-hour for each aircraft type within its fleet. They can then be allocated to each flight or route on the basis of the aircraft type(s) being used and the block times for the sector or route. The first element of fixed direct operating costs is aircraft standing costs, that is, depreciation and any rentals for leased aircraft plus aircraft insurance. Such costs are aircraft type specific since they depend on the purchase price or lease rate of the aircraft. They are a fixed annual cost, based on the number of aircraft of a particular type, which when divided by the annual utilisation of these aircraft produces a depreciation and insurance cost per block-hour (see Section 3.3). If aircraft are leased there is normally an annual leasing cost made up of 12 equal monthly payments. These are fixed annual costs independent of how much flying is undertaken. Therefore, the hourly lease cost, as with depreciation, depends on the amount of hours flown in each year. In addition, airlines may have to pay a separate hourly charge per block-hour into a 'maintenance reserve'. This is a fixed hourly charge. The total annual amount paid is dependent on the amount of flying undertaken. Its purpose is to build up a cash reserve for major and costly overhauls known as D checks, which normally occur every four to six years. Though ultimately needed for major maintenance checks, the hourly maintenance reserve charge is often included under rentals.

It is relatively easy to identify and allocate the fixed annual flight crew costs, since each aircraft type has its own dedicated complement of pilots and co-pilots. In many cases, if there are several aircraft of a particular type, that fleet will have its own administrative managers as well. Some flight crew overheads, however, will not be aircraft type specific and will need to be allocated on some basis between the different aircraft types, usually the number of aircraft or annual utilisation. The total annual fixed flight crew cost for a fleet of aircraft of a particular type can then be divided by the total annual utilisation (that is, block-hours) flown by all the aircraft in that fleet to arrive at a flight crew cost per block-hour for that aircraft type.

A similar approach is adopted with other fixed elements of direct operating costs. In the case of cabin crew, problems of allocating fixed annual costs between aircraft types arise because, unlike flight crew, cabin crew can work on different aircraft types at any time. Nevertheless, the annual cabin crew costs can be apportioned to different aircraft types on the basis of the number and seniority of the cabin crew they use and the sectors they fly on.

Some fixed maintenance costs will be aircraft type specific, while others will be common costs that need to be allocated between aircraft types, usually on the basis of maintenance man hours required for different aircraft. Thus, for each aircraft type, airlines can estimate an hourly flight crew and cabin crew cost and an hourly maintenance cost to cover the fixed element of such costs. Some airlines take this process a step further and calculate different hourly crew and maintenance costs for different types of routes. For instance, some carriers use a higher hourly flight crew cost for a given aircraft type when it is flying on short sectors than when it is used on longer sectors.

Since all the fixed direct costs discussed are allocated to specific aircraft types, some airlines refer to them as 'fleet' costs, associated with operating a fleet of aircraft of a particular type.

When one turns to *indirect operating costs*, difficult problems of allocation arise since by definition such costs are independent of the type of aircraft being operated. Some indirect costs may be route specific and may be escapable in the medium term if a whole route operation is closed down. If an airline operates a single route to another country, the sales and advertising costs in that country as well as the station and ground costs at the airport served can be readily identified as a cost specific to that route. Most indirect costs, however, are fixed joint and common costs that cannot be easily allocated to individual flights or routes except on some arbitrary basis. Most station costs, passenger insurance expenses and the costs of ticketing, sales and promotion as well as overhead administrative costs will normally be allocated to particular services or routes on the basis of some output measure such as the revenue tonne-kilometres or revenue generated. Each approach has its advantages and drawbacks. Using a traffic measure, such as the revenue tonne-kilometres generated on each route, may penalise long-haul routes where tonne-kilometres generated are high but revenues per kilometre are low because fares, like costs, taper with distance. Allocating indirect costs on the basis of the revenue earned on each route or flight may appear more equitable, but would bias against shorter routes where fares per kilometre are high. More than one allocative method may be used. Sales, ticketing and passenger service costs may be divided between flights on the basis of passenger-kilometres produced, while cargo-specific costs may be apportioned using freight tonne-kilometres carried.

Using an allocative methodology such as that outlined, but adapted to its own particular requirements and accounting procedures, an airline can allocate costs to individual flights or routes. Such costs would be made up of four elements:

A   All *variable direct operating costs*. These are flight specific and can be calculated per flight or aggregated to arrive at the total variable DOC, i.e. covering all flights for a particular route. (Such costs are likely to be in the range of 45–60 per cent of total operating costs if fuel prices are at the high levels of 2013–14 and will also be influenced by the sector distance.)

B   Those limited *indirect operating costs which are route-specific* such as advertising in the destination country or region or station costs. Such costs can, if necessary, be broken down further and allocated to individual flights on that route (generally 5–10 per cent of total operating costs).

C   *The fixed direct operating costs,* which are joint costs and are normally allocated to each flight or route on the basis of the block-hours flown as shown earlier (ranging between 15 and 25 per cent of total costs).

D   Those *indirect operating costs which are not route-specific* and have been allocated to each flight or route on the basis of some output or revenue measure (15–20 per cent of total costs).

By comparing these costs with the revenues generated, airline planners are in a position to make decisions as to the number of frequencies that should operate on a route or whether the route should be operated at all.

Some airlines and analysts assess flights or routes in terms of their contribution to overhead or fixed costs. This is called *contribution analysis*. In other words, a particular flight or route is expected at least to cover its variable flight- or route-specific costs (items A and B above) out of the revenues it generates. In other words, it must cover its escapable costs. If it does not do so at present and is unlikely to do so in the near future, then its continued operation must be in doubt. Revenues in excess of the route- or flight-specific costs are deemed to make a *contribution* to fixed direct costs and to non-specific indirect costs (items C and D above). Ideally, revenues should cover all of these additional costs too. Even if they do not, the key issue is the level of 'contribution' revenue generated by a particular route makes to such costs. Discontinuing flights will not save any of these fixed direct and indirect costs in the short term; thus, some contribution to meeting these costs is better than none. In the medium and longer term fixed direct operating costs can be cut by reducing fleet size, while indirect costs can be reduced by abandoning routes or downsizing the network and level of operations.

If there are many routes that cover their variable and specific indirect costs (A and B above) but make only marginal contributions to overheads, that is fixed direct and indirect costs (C and D above), then an airline is haemorrhaging. It would be wise in the medium term to cut out those routes that make only minimal contribution and have little prospect of improving and to downsize both the fleet and the operations. Unfortunately, airline managers are generally reluctant to take such corrective action, even when it becomes obvious, except at times of real crisis. But few airline executives have the nerve to cut services quickly when market conditions begin to worsen. This may be because seats are sold on flights up to nine or 12 months in advance and managers are loath to upset customers or because the routes are considered essential as feeders to an airline's hub.

While traditional legacy carriers appear slow to cut or modify routes that is not the case with low-cost or budget airlines. The latter quickly reduce frequencies or drop routes altogether when 'contribution' levels are low and show little sign of rapid improvement. The so-called 'churn' or turn-over of routes among European low-cost carriers is very noticeable. For example, in 2017 Ryanair operated only 73 per cent of the routes it had launched in the previous ten years from London-Stansted, its largest base. From Liverpool airport it operated only 41 per cent of the routes launched in the previous decade. From Shannon in Ireland this figure was down to 30 per cent (Anna Aero, February 2017).

As Peter Bellew, Chief Executive of Malaysia Airlines, pointed out in March 2017 when speaking to Flightglobal, cost cutting is a never-ending and challenging task for airline executives. To be successful in this they must have a clear understanding of the different ways of organising and structuring airline costs. This is the first step. The next step is to identify and focus on where and how costs can be reduced. This is the theme of the next chapter.

4 Determinants of airline costs

It's about the basics – you need to get your operations right; continuously work to reduce cost per seat-km; continuously work on increasing the revenue per seat-km.

(Ajay Singh, CEO, SpiceJet, India, April 2018)

4.1 Management control of costs

The theme of this book is that airline planning and management is about the process of profitably matching supply, which within certain constraints an airline can very largely control, with demand, which it can influence but cannot control. Low unit costs in themselves do not ensure efficiency or guarantee profitability if an airline fails to generate sufficiently high revenues. Nevertheless, controlling and, if possible, reducing costs is a key management objective. As more and more domestic and international markets are being progressively deregulated, competition and especially price competition has intensified. In virtually all markets average yields per passenger-km have tended over time to drift downward in real terms. This has reinforced pressures to reduce unit costs. But to what degree can airline managements influence and reduce their unit costs? Or, are such costs very largely externally determined by factors and developments beyond management control?

It is clearly evident that among major airlines unit costs vary widely. The accompanying Table 4.1 shows the unit costs per available seat-mile (CASM) for the world's 25 largest passenger carriers in 2016. Together these 25 airlines carried over two-thirds of the world's passenger-kms in 2016. The unit costs are for their total operations, that is international and domestic. The table amply illustrates both the wide range in cost levels between airlines and the existence of marked regional variations.

High-cost airlines such as Lufthansa, Air France or All Nippon Airways (ANA) have unit costs more than twice as high as the lowest-cost network or legacy airlines in their region of the world. Other notable features of this table are, first, that unit cost levels among North American airlines are closely grouped whereas in other world regions airline unit costs vary widely. Second, the global so-called 'super connector' airlines with major hubs in the Middle East have very low unit costs, especially Emirates, Turkish Airlines and Qatar Airways. Finally, Southwest, the largest US low-cost airline, appears to have unit costs only marginally lower than those of its full-service competitors. This is in marked contrast to European LCCs, especially Ryanair, whose unit costs are substantially lower than those of their legacy competitors.

Table 4.1 Unit operating costs 25 major passenger airlines, financial year 2016

	North American		European/Middle East		Asian/Pacific	
			US cents per available seat-kilometre			
1			Lufthansa	20.35		
2					All Nippon Air	18.41
3			Air France	15.20		
4					Korean Air	15.06
5					Cathay Pacific	14.98
6	Air Canada	14.40				
7			KLM	13.94		
8	Delta	12.34				
9			British Airways	12.12		
10	United	11.99				
11	American	11.89				
12					Qantas	11.83
13			Etihad	11.81		
14					China Eastern	11.36
15	Southwest	11.15				
16			easyJet	10.77		
17					Air China	10.70
18					Singapore Airline	10.56
19			Aeroflot	10.33		
20			Emirates	10.02		
21					China Southern	9.67
22			Turkish Airlines	9.45		
23			Qatar Airways	9.03		
24					Hainan Airlines	7.82
25			Rynair	5.94		

N.B.: ranked with highest-cost airlines at top
Source: Compiled using Airline Monitor (2017b) data

Many factors impact on an airline's unit costs. In order to gain an insight into the causes of such a wide diversity of unit costs between airlines one needs to assess the determinants of operating costs paying particular attention to the degree to which they can be influenced by management.

The numerous factors that affect airline operating costs can be grouped into three broad categories according to the degree to which they are under management control (Table 4.2). First, one can identify a number of external economic inputs over whose prices airlines have little control. Such input prices include the prevailing fuel prices and airport and en-route navigation charges. An airline has to accept these as more or less given and can only marginally mitigate their impact through negotiations with service providers or fuel suppliers.

Second, there are a number of major determinants of costs over which airlines have somewhat greater but still limited control. These are labour costs, the type of aircraft used and the pattern of operations for which the aircraft are used. While the latter two of these might seem to be entirely at the discretion of airline management, in practice managements' hands are tied to some extent by factors beyond their control. The geographical location of an airline's home base, the bilateral air services agreements

Table 4.2 Factors affecting airline operating costs

	Degree of management control		
Externally determined input costs	Little		
Cost of labour		Some	
Type/characteristics of aircraft used		Some	
Route structure/network characteristics		Some	
Commissions to agents/banks etc.		Some	
Airline marketing and product policy			High
Airline financial policy			High
Corporate strategy			High
Quality of management			High

signed by its government, the traffic density on its routes and in its markets and other such factors will strongly influence the type of aircraft required and the network operated. Management does not have an entirely free hand to do as it wishes. This is particularly so of national airlines in countries with only one flag carrier, especially if it is majority owned by its own government. Another smaller cost area over which airline management has some limited control is that of commissions paid to agents, global distribution systems (GDS) and banks.

The third group of cost determinants is that over which management has a high level of control or even total control. Marketing, product planning and financial policy fall into this category, as does corporate strategy. In the final analysis one must also consider the quality of management and its efficiency as a cost determinant. It is crucial because management determines the degree to which the impact of the other factors mentioned above, whether favourable or unfavourable, can be modified to the benefit of the airline concerned.

The analysis in this chapter of the effect of different variables on costs is qualitative rather than quantitative. Many studies have used various forms of multivariate analysis to establish the influence of a range of independent variables (for instance airline size, pilot wage levels or stage length) on a dependent variable such as unit cost or labour productivity. In theory, multivariate analysis should be able to establish the relative impact of the various independent variables on the unit costs of the airlines concerned.

It has been argued by some economists that such studies are essentially inductive. They can correlate events rather than establish cause and effect between them. This is an added shortcoming of such an approach.

The alternative might be to develop a deductive approach, which by using selected measures of total factor productivity allows comparisons between airlines in different countries by adjusting for differences in factor prices, network characteristics, aircraft size and so on (see for example Tae Hoon Oum and Chunyan Yu, 1995). This is an interesting and potentially valuable approach, but it is mathematically complex. While a good descriptor of an airline's overall productivity, total factor productivity is of more limited value as a management tool that can pinpoint where corrective action is needed. In order to provide a better conceptual understanding of the determinants of airline costs, a more qualitative approach would appear to be preferable to both the above techniques and has been adopted in the analysis that follows.

4.2 The influence of demand on costs

Before assessing the factors that directly impact on the costs of supplying airline services, it is important to appreciate that demand too impacts on unit costs. It is generally understood and accepted that airline costs have a direct impact on the demand for air services since they influence the prices at which those services are sold. Costs also reflect service quality and other product features. What is frequently forgotten, however, is that costs are not entirely independent of demand. They are themselves influenced by demand. There is a two-way relationship between supply (costs) and demand. Each affects the other. There are two aspects of demand, in particular, which impact on costs, namely route traffic density and sector length.

The traffic density on a route and the sector length(s) on that route will influence the size and type of aircraft chosen for that route. Aircraft type, and more especially the size of the aircraft, is a key determinant of unit costs. Route traffic density also influences the frequencies needed and will thereby affect the annual utilisation, that is the number of hours flown by each aircraft. The higher the utilisation, the lower the costs. Traffic density also affects the level of station costs per passenger or per tonne of cargo. So-called station costs do not go up in proportion to the traffic handled by an airline at each airport; therefore the greater the volume of traffic going through a station the lower will be the costs per unit of traffic. These relationships will become clearer in the following sections. There is one other aspect of demand that impacts on costs, and that is the variations in demand over time. Marked seasonal peaks create a need for extra capacity in terms of aircraft, crew, ticketing and sales staff, catering facilities and so on, which may be grossly under-utilised in off-peak periods. Carrying that extra capacity during the off-peak is costly. From a cost point of view airlines are better off if they are trying to satisfy a pattern of demand that is more or less constant throughout the year (Section 8.6).

In a truly open and competitive environment airlines would be free to choose their own markets in terms of the length of routes and traffic densities that they wish to serve. This may be the case among United States domestic airlines and to a more limited extent among European low-cost airlines or other airlines operating entirely within the European Union. But the vast majority of international airlines do not have a free hand with regard to the demand that they set out to satisfy. The routes they serve and the density of demand on those routes are largely determined by the interplay of geographical, political, economic and social factors outside the airlines' control. The starting point for any international airline is its home base. The geographical location of the home base, together with the level of business and tourist interaction between the home country and other nations, will influence the potential sector lengths and traffic densities that can be fruitfully operated. Australia and Malta represent the two extremes. A major international airline based in Australia must operate a long-haul network with some very long sectors because of Australia's geographical isolation and the long distances to key markets. Conversely the national airline of Malta, as a result of the island's location on the southern periphery of Europe and its small size, is predetermined to be a short-haul airline with only a relatively small number of rather thin routes.

Where an airline is a country's only international airline, which is frequently the case, it may also be under political pressure to operate some routes it would otherwise ignore. Conversely, where there are several international carriers, as in the United Kingdom or the United States, these may have much more choice as to the routes they can serve. For example, the UK's Virgin Atlantic has, as its corporate mission, focused purely on long-haul intercontinental services and, unlike other major European airlines, operates no short, intra-European routes.

Though constrained by some of these factors airlines have some ability to influence the patterns of demand on the routes they serve or wish to serve. First, they can as a matter of policy concentrate on the denser traffic sectors. Second, they can try to increase the total traffic on their routes through their marketing policy and their promotional activity. Third, they can try to improve their own traffic density by increasing their market share when they have competitors on the route. Many airlines place considerable marketing effort into increasing their market share on their major routes. Greater market share is seen as a key objective, not merely because it increases their revenues but also because it can help in reducing costs.

4.3 Externally determined input costs

The costs of a number of key airline inputs or factors of production are determined by external economic variables and are largely outside the control of individual airline managements. Since the external variables vary between countries and regions, the factor input costs of different airlines may also vary significantly. While airlines can try to reduce the prices of their inputs, in the case of some key inputs they can only do so to a limited extent. They have to accept the general level of these input prices as given and they have only limited scope to negotiate downwards from that given level. Another feature of these input prices is that they are subject to sudden and often marked fluctuations. Adjusting to sudden changes in the price of fuel or in the level of charges at a particular airport is a common headache among airline managers.

4.3.1 Price of aviation fuel

As shown in the previous chapter, fuel for many airlines in 2016 represented 20 per cent or more of total costs, down from a 28.7 per cent average the previous year. For most airlines, it is frequently the largest single input cost. Unfortunately, however, it is a cost over which airline managers have little control. The prevailing worldwide price of aviation fuel is directly linked to the price of oil and moves up and down in response to changes in global oil prices, which are themselves determined by the interplay of the global demand for and supply of crude oil.

At the local level, however, there may be very significant variations in the price of aviation fuel and, consequently, on its impact on airline costs. A number of factors influence the fuel price at individual airports. The prices of crude oil and of refinery costs are broadly similar worldwide, but distribution and handling costs vary considerably. While oil refineries are widely scattered around the world only a relatively small number refine jet fuel. The supply of fuel to some airports may involve lengthy and costly transportation especially if the airport is well away from a seaport. Transportation costs also rise if the total volume of fuel supplied to an airport is small. Handling costs at airports vary in relation to the facilities used and the volume of fuel uplifted. Governments may influence the price of jet fuel in two ways. They may impose duties or some other kind of tax, though most governments do neither of these things to fuel supplied for international flights. Some governments may also try to control or fix the price of fuel as a matter of government policy.

While jet fuel prices move up and down in response to changes in crude oil prices, there are quite marked regional variations in jet fuel prices as a result of the above factor (Table 4.3). In March 2018, when fuel prices were relatively low, they tended to be highest in Latin America and lowest in the Middle East and Africa. But within each region there are wide variations in fuel prices between individual airports. For example, some African airlines seem particularly disadvantaged by the very high fuel prices at many African airports south of the Sahara. Inland locations, long distances from oil refineries producing aviation fuel and relatively small volumes of fuel uplift seem to be the root cause of high fuel prices at airports such as Asmara in Eritrea or Gabarone in Botswana. In May 2017 fuel at these airports cost US$3.94 per US gallon. At Nairobi fuel was at US$1.21 per gallon and at Cairo it cost them even less, only US$1.13. At Kabul in Afghanistan the price was over US$4. In Europe jet fuel costs more at airports such as Basel and Krakow, which are inland and well away from major seaports.

The interplay of crude oil prices and oil company refining and transportation costs, as well as their pricing strategies, broadly determine the posted fuel prices at airports around the world. In addition to the basic fuel price, airlines will normally also pay a handling or so-called 'into plane' charge. This may vary markedly between airports.

The 'posted' fuel price at an airport is the price that an airline without regular scheduled services might have to pay. In practice few airlines pay the posted price. Regular users of an airport will negotiate their own contract price with the fuel suppliers. This will be at a discount on the posted price, the level of the discount depending on the total tonnage of fuel that an airline expects to uplift during the contract period. This in turn will depend on the number of daily departures an airline operates from that particular airport, and the size of the aircraft being used. Clearly an airline is likely to pay the lowest at its own home base airport as it will be by far the biggest user of fuel.

The discount will also be influenced by the number of fuel suppliers. If there is only one oil company providing fuel, the scope for pushing down the price is clearly limited. At most airports around the world there are generally only a few aviation fuel suppliers. In the United States, on the other hand, the existence of a large number of small refineries and of common carrier pipelines open to use by any company has resulted in very large numbers of companies competing for fuel supply contracts. This creates a strong downward pressure on jet fuel prices.

While the prices negotiated in individual fuel contracts are confidential there are prevailing discount levels at each airport depending on an airline's total fuel uplift. Each airline has a fairly good idea what other airlines are paying; thus, airlines each operating

Table 4.3 Average jet fuel prices by region: mid–March 2018

Region	Average jet fuel price US cents per US gallon
Latin and Central America	190.9
Europe and CIS	189.9
North America	185.5
Asia and Oceania	183.3
Middle East and Africa	181.2
World Average	186.2

Source: IATA/Platts Market Commentary

twice-daily long-haul departures from London's Heathrow airport with Boeing 787 will all end up paying very similar prices. The exact price will depend on the negotiating skill of each airline's fuel buyer. The latter might try to get a better price by negotiating with one fuel company for the supply of fuel at several airports.

Ultimately it is the prevailing market price at each airport and the accepted discount levels that will determine the fuel prices at any airport. The airline fuel buyer who is a good negotiator may shave one or two or even more tenths of a US cent off the price per gallon, but he can do little more. Fuel prices are largely externally determined by prevailing market conditions at each airport.

It is also clear that the level of fuel prices paid by airlines varies markedly between airports – even between airports in the same region – and this impacts directly on their operating costs. Air India flying out of Delhi faces the problem that fuel at its main base, where its fuel uplift is greatest, is relatively expensive, in part because of various taxes imposed on aviation fuel. Even though as the largest buyer it will be paying less than the average price, the high fuel price at its home base will inevitably push up its operating costs. On the other hand, Singapore Airlines or Malaysia Airlines undoubtedly benefit from very low fuel prices at their home airport.

Airlines can try to mitigate the impact of high fuel prices at certain airports by reducing their fuel uplift at those airports to the minimum necessary. Instead, captains may be instructed to tanker as much fuel as possible at airports where fuel prices are low. Such a policy, however, needs careful monitoring since extra fuel will be burnt during the flight to carry the additional fuel loaded. This is because fuel consumption rises as the total weight of the aircraft increases.

An added problem for airlines is that oil companies insist on escalation clauses in fuel supply contracts. These allow the fuel price to move up or down in response to changes in the price of crude oil. However, airlines can hedge against future increases in fuel prices by buying fuel forward for future delivery at fixed prices.

As fuel prices began rising in 2010 and especially in the period 2011 to 2014 when prices were very high and volatile, airlines turned increasingly to hedging to mitigate the possibility that fuel prices would rise even further. They did this by buying some of their future fuel needs at fixed prices. In the UK, easyJet has had a clearly stated policy on hedging, which was to hedge 65 to 85 per cent of fuel needs up to 12 months in advance and 45 to 65 per cent of estimated exposure from 13 to 24 months in advance.

When prices collapsed at the end of 2014 many airlines were caught out by their future hedges. During much of 2015 they ended up paying more for fuel than the then market prices. They only benefited from the lower prices when paying for that part of their fuel uplift that was not hedged. Delta Air Lines' chief executive Ed Bastian said early in 2016 that the airline had lost about $4 billion cumulatively over the previous eight years on oil hedges (Airline Business, September 2016). Early in 2016 Delta exited its 2016 hedge contracts by paying a penalty of $100 to $200 million per quarter. It forecast that it would nevertheless save about £3 billion in 2016 by buying all fuel at prevailing market rates. At the same time Southwest was estimating that its outstanding hedges would produce a potential loss of about $1.8 billion through to 2018. The winner among US airlines was American, which had not hedged at all. Having suffered when fuel prices were high it got the full benefit of dropping prices in 2015 and 2016. In Europe, the Lufthansa group suffered a €571 million loss on fuel hedging in the first nine months of 2016.

More complex methods of hedging such as the use of 'collars', whereby one tries to limit the future fuel price within an agreed range, have also emerged (see Morrell, 2013).

The differential impact of fluctuating exchange rates may also adversely affect some airlines since fuel prices in most of the world are quoted in United States dollars. If the dollar exchange rate of a particular currency drops rapidly, the cost of fuel in that country in terms of its own currency will rise equally rapidly. This will hit hardest the country's own national airline, most of whose earnings are in local currency. As with fuel, many airlines also hedge against currency movements, especially in relation to their own currency vis-a-vis the US dollar. This is because, apart from fuel, aircraft leases and loan repayments are often in US dollars too.

easyJet provides an example of the potential benefits of hedging on currency. One-third of its total expenses are in US dollars but only 1 per cent of earnings. In 2015 and early 2016 it was hedging against a drop in the value of sterling (£) by contracting to buy US dollars forward at varying exchange rates around $1.50 to one pound sterling: a wise move. After the June 2016 UK referendum on Brexit, Sterling collapsed by 10 per cent. In early 2017, 80 per cent of easyJet's US dollar needs for the whole of 2017 were hedged at $1.50 to £1; a significant benefit for easyJet, since by April 2017 the market rate was only around $1.22 to £1. For its 2018 US dollar requirements it was 53 per cent hedged at $1.43.

While unable to influence the basic price of fuel except marginally, airlines can lower their fuel costs by trying to reduce their fuel consumption. A number of options are open to them. They can try to reduce the weight of their various aircraft by using lighter equipment in the cabin, and less paint on the outside of their aircraft. They can also reduce weight by avoiding unnecessary 'tankering', that is carrying more fuel than is required to meet safety minima on a particular sector. Then they can save fuel by reducing the aircraft cruising speed. A 3 to 4 per cent reduction in the cruising speed of a jet aircraft on a sector of one hour or more may reduce fuel consumption by 6 to 7 per cent at the cost of a few minutes' extra flying. Computerised flight planning can also help. By choosing slower rates of climb or descent and higher cruise altitudes, where available and allowed by air traffic control, airlines may be able further to reduce the fuel consumed. Ultimately, the biggest savings come from switching to newer more fuel-efficient aircraft with more advanced engines.

4.3.2 User charges

For the world's airlines as a whole user charges, that is, airport charges and en-route facility charges, account for around 7 per cent of their total costs (Table 3.3 in Chapter 3). But this is an average global figure. For those international airlines operating relatively short sectors, where landings occur more frequently, the impact of user charges is much greater. Thus, in 2017, easyJet as a primarily short-haul LCC (low-cost carrier) found that airport and en-route navigation charges together represented over 20 per cent of its total costs. For British Airways, which has a more mixed network, the figure dropped to 7 per cent. For United States carriers airport and en-route charges are low, generally 2 to 4 per cent of total costs, because such facilities are funded differently in the US.

User charges, like fuel prices, are largely externally determined, but compared to fuel, user charges offer even less room for manoeuvre. While the airlines as a whole acting through IATA may try to hold down increases in landing fees or en-route charges in a particular country, an individual airline has in theory little scope for negotiating better rates for itself. All are in the same boat. This is because under Article 15 of the 1944 Chicago Convention all airlines are to be treated equally. There should be no discrimination. In practice, some airports may offer reduced charges for two or three years or longer to airlines launching new routes. But such reductions are in theory open to all operators of new services. In recent years, low-cost airlines in Europe have been able, at a few airports, to negotiate lower or special charges on the grounds that they are using cheaper or poorer facilities or because they had an economic developmental impact on poorly developed regions to whose airports they were flying. Some, such as Ryanair, have even managed to persuade smaller airports in Europe to 'contribute' to the airline's costs because of the perceived benefits they bring to the airport and its region.

The level of *airport charges* will depend partly on the costs of the airports themselves and partly on whether the airport authority or the government is trying to fully recover those costs or even make a profit. As a result, landing and passenger-related charges vary enormously between different airports. It is evident from Figure 4.1 that in 2018 British Airways, operating an intercontinental Boeing 777-300ER flight from London-Heathrow, had to pay around US$4,200 when landing and taking off at Delhi. But on returning to London the airport charges for a landing and departure, excluding government passenger taxes, would have been around US$22,300, or five times as high. Clearly airlines based in high-cost airports, such as BA at Heathrow or South African Airways in Johannesburg, face a significant cost disadvantage since a high proportion of their landings will be at their high-cost base airport. On the other hand, Qatar Airways, Aeroflot and especially Air India benefit from being based at low-cost airports.

Airport charges consist of two major elements: a landing fee based on the weight of the aircraft and a passenger charge levied on a per passenger basis (Figure 4.1). In addition to the two basic charges, there may be further charges for the use of air bridges, for aircraft parking beyond a short free period, for use of terminal air navigation services, for security, and so on. At many airports, the balance of charging in the last 20 years has moved towards generating more revenue from the passenger fee rather than the aircraft-related charges (Figure 4.1).

The position in the United States is unique. Landing fees and passenger charges, known as the Passenger Facility Charge, are generally very low, but there are a multiplicity of other fees and taxes levied on airlines or passengers (see Graham, 2008). On the other hand, at most US airports major airlines run and may even build their own terminals, which clearly increases their costs. Elsewhere in the world it is very unusual for airlines to operate their own passenger terminals, though they may have their own cargo complexes.

Unlike most other countries, the United States government has for many years levied a variety of taxes on passengers at its airports. These include an international passenger tax, plus separate charges for agricultural inspection and for immigration and customs facilities. The latter three charges are included under passenger-related charges in Figure 4.1.

In the 1990s a number of governments elsewhere also began to introduce fiscal taxes on passengers purely to raise government tax revenues. This happened first in the United Kingdom, Norway, Greece and Denmark. Several governments subsequently followed suit and more may follow. These were in addition to the normal charges levied by the airport authorities. As they are normally passed on directly to passengers such taxes are not included in Figure 4.1. In the United Kingdom the airport passenger duty levied on a

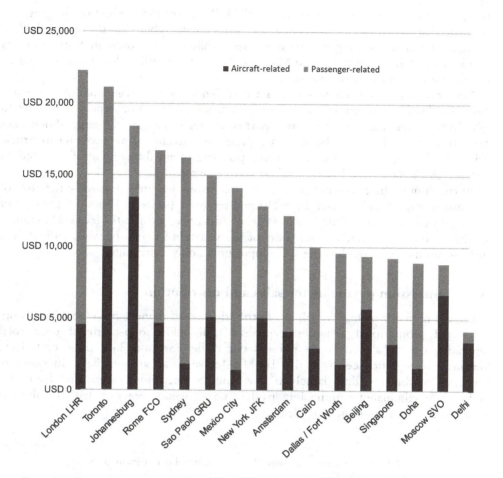

Figure 4.1 Airport charges for a Boeing 777-300ER in March 2018 (US dollars)

Note: Aircraft 352 tonnes MTOW with 332 seats and assumed seat factor of 85 per cent. International flights with three-hour parking and use of airbridge. Includes charges for use of government-run services at airport

Source: Centre for Air Transport Management, Cranfield University

flight may at some airports be higher than the airports' own landing and passenger fees. Strictly speaking such government taxes should not be considered as an airline cost, but rather a transfer of funds collected by the airlines on behalf of governments. They are increasingly identified as a separate item on tickets over and above the fare.

En-route charges are imposed by civil aviation authorities on aircraft flying through their airspace to cover the cost of air traffic control and navigational and other aids provided. The charges are generally levied on the basis of the weight of the aircraft and the distance flown within each country's airspace. But there are variations. Some countries, Egypt, India and Thailand among them, base the charge on distance alone and aircraft weight is ignored. A few, such as Japan and Kenya, have a fixed charge irrespective of aircraft size or distance travelled. Whatever the method of charging, the level of charges varies enormously, as can be seen in Table 4.4. By far the highest charges tend to be for using European air space while they are lower in North America and very much lower in Egypt and Malaysia. So where an airline does most of its flying clearly impacts on its en-route costs.

For airlines, en-route charges are a set cost. They are not negotiable. A few state-owned airlines have been able to persuade their governments or airport authorities to give them preferential treatment on airport or en-route navigation charges. Such cases are relatively few, however, because such preferential treatment runs counter to Article 15 of the Chicago Convention and to the principle of equal treatment of each other's airline, which is enshrined in bilateral air services agreement.

In conclusion, the two input costs largely externally determined, namely the costs of fuel and of airport and air navigation charges, represent between 35 and 40 per cent of most airlines' total expenditure – that is, when fuel prices are at 2017 levels. Differences in these input prices may explain some of the variation in costs between airlines. Yet airlines can influence the level of these input prices only marginally.

4.4 Commission payments for sales and distribution

For most network or legacy airlines, distribution costs, namely the cost of ticketing, sales and promotional activities, represent well below one-tenth of their total operating costs (Table 3.3). As pointed out earlier (Section 3.4), these costs have declined in significance over the last 10–15 years as airlines have increasingly switched to direct selling, largely online, and to electronic tickets, and have also reduced or eliminated commissions paid to travel agents. Nevertheless, distribution costs remain an important cost element.

Table 4.4 Comparative en-route charges in selected countries in 2018 for Airbus A320-NEO

	Charge for 400 km overflight with no landing US $
Switzerland	579
Austria	422
UK	401
Germany	397
Russia	381
France	375
Vietnam	255
Japan	229
India	221
China	206
United States	180
Saudi Arabia	156
Turkey	141
Egypt	91
Malaysia	21

Source: RDC Aviation

A major element of distribution costs is the payment of commission to third parties who assist the airlines in selling and reservations. Significant commissions are paid to three service providers – travel agents, the global distribution systems and credit card companies.

Historically, the highest commission payments have been those made to retail or online travel agents and GDSs. The rate of commission paid, expressed as a percentage of the ticket price, varies between markets and between countries. The rates for international ticket sales have tended to be between 5 and 6 per cent, but have been declining. They are usually lower for domestic tickets. Where commissions are the norm, all airlines will pay agents identical or very similar rates in any particular market in order to remain competitive.

While airlines operating in any particular market tend to end up paying agents the prevailing commission rates, pressures to cut costs have forced airlines in recent years to try to cut the overall level of agents' commissions. They have done this in two ways. First, in several key markets, airlines working in unison have cut agents' commissions to zero and now sell their tickets through agents as net of commission. They leave it to agents to add a service charge to customers for making the booking and providing the ticket. Second, airlines have succeeded in cutting intermediaries wherever they can by selling direct to customers through their own sales offices, by phone and especially online through their websites.

In the 1980s and 1990s airlines became increasingly dependent on the global distribution systems (GDS) such as Amadeus, Sabre or Gallileo (later became Travelport) that provided agents and even the airlines themselves with a worldwide computer-based reservations facility. Airlines paid the GDS a fixed charge per sector booking made, even though most of the bookings were made by travel agents using the GDS. The airlines even had to pay if they themselves booked passengers on their own flights using one of these global systems. Initially, all the GDSs charged airlines the same booking fee. In 2000 it was $3 per sector booked. But, even during the crisis years after 2000, GDS commission fees per segment continued to climb. For example, Northwest, the US carrier, claimed in 2004 that its average GDS fee was US$12.50 per segment.

The three major GDS companies, Sabre, Travelport and Amadeus, faced increasing pressure to reduce segment fees especially as the GDSs were largely ignored by the low-cost carriers, by far the fastest-growing sector of the airline industry. In response, the GDSs introduced various schemes aimed at reducing the charges or making them more flexible. For example, in 2004 Amadeus launched its 'value pricing' scheme, whereby GDS booking fees were to be set according to the value of a particular booking to the airline. This replaced a fixed fee per booking.

To reduce the impact and cost of commissions to travel agents and GDS fees, airlines have tried to focus their sales through their own websites or call centres. Nevertheless, in 2012 legacy airlines were still selling 55 per cent of their tickets through the GDSs. This compares with only 16 per cent for low-cost carriers. Legacy airlines needed to do more to reduce their dependence on third parties for ticket sales and also reduce the commissions paid.

Several took drastic action. One was Lufthansa. From mid-2015 all Lufthansa tickets sold by agents using one of the GDSs was charged €16 per ticket, irrespective of the ticket type. This would apply to sales on Lufthansa, Austrian, Swiss or Brussels airlines. The charge would be per ticket not per booking, since a booking may involve several tickets for different passengers. This charge would be passed on to the passengers or absorbed by the agents. Through this bold move the Lufthansa group was able to recoup some of the fees it was still paying the GDS for sales using their systems. It was also incentivising agents and travellers to book direct through the airline's own website or call centre so as to avoid the €16 charge. Lufthansa subsequently claimed that there was no drop in bookings after the charge came into force. Other airlines, such as British Airways, began to follow the Lufthansa strategy.

More innovation in pricing of GDS is inevitable. Most network airlines, despite developing their own reservation systems, are still dependent for much of their sales on the GDSs, especially in markets away from their own country. But as the GDSs have introduced more flexible pricing, fees paid have become a more controllable cost than they were in the past.

Finally, airlines need to pay commission to credit card companies and other handling intermediaries for any tickets bought directly from the airlines sales offices, telephone sales or internet site and paid for by credit card. Again, the commission rates have been largely non-negotiable. Commissions and associated fees on credit card sales take up to 2 to 2.5 per cent of the revenue earned on a ticket. As other distribution costs have all declined, credit card fees have become a far larger percentage of the costs incurred in handling each booking.

In Europe, in the early 2000s the low-cost airlines began charging passengers a fee per booking transaction (not per ticket) for use of credit cards when paying. This went some way to covering the cost of commissions charged by credit card companies to the airlines. In time this practice was adopted by the legacy airlines too.

Taken together, these three types of commission payments, namely those paid to online and other travel agents and to other airlines, those exacted by computer reservations systems and payments to credit card companies, may make up around 5–6 per cent of total operating costs. They tend to be highest among smaller international airlines who pay a lot of commission to agents, to the GDSs and other airlines but have limited opportunities to negotiate better deals.

4.5 The cost of labour

When fuel prices are low, wage costs and associated social security and pension payments for staff may represent the largest single cost element for many airlines. Of course, it is split between different functional areas within the airline. In 2016 when fuel prices were low, labour costs among major North American carriers, including social charges, on average accounted for around 35 to 40 per cent of total operating costs. Among European legacy airlines the average figure in 2016 varied between 15 and 25 per cent, though it was lowest for low-cost carriers. In Asia, lower wage costs mean that airlines' labour costs are significantly lower than those of European or US network carriers they are competing against. For most Asian carriers labour costs represent on average around 15 to 25 per cent of total costs. But for a few it was lower still. For example, for Singapore Airlines staff costs represented 18.4 per cent of total expenditure in the financial year 2016–17. For Indigo, the Indian LCC, staff costs in the same year were 12 per cent of total costs. Since staff costs represent such a high proportion of overall costs, variations in the average level of wages paid has a direct effect on an airline's total costs and may also lead to appreciable cost differences between airlines.

In a country with free wage bargaining it is the interplay of supply and demand for the categories of labour required by the airline(s) together with the strength of particular unions that will broadly determine the level of wages an airline has to pay for its various categories of staff. In other countries wage levels may be set by national agreements between governments or employers' associations and the trade unions. In some cases governments themselves virtually determine the levels to be paid and impose them on employers and employees alike. In all cases the prevailing wage levels are related to the standard and cost of living in the country concerned.

Comparisons of wage levels between airlines in different countries are clearly affected by currency exchange rates. What may be a very high salary for a pilot in his own country may appear low when converted into US dollars and compared with pilot salaries at airlines based in high-wage economies with strong currencies.

In addition to the basic cost of salaries and wages, airlines will normally also have to pay a variety of social charges such as social security or pension contributions or medical expenses. They are frequently enshrined in the social legislation of the country concerned and are mandatory and non-negotiable. Their impact on staff costs can be very substantial. For example, in Europe, where social security charges are very high their impact on overall employee costs can be very significant. In Germany or France such charges may add up to 40 per cent to the wages bill. In the United Kingdom or Ireland, they are much lower.

For most airlines the three most expensive groups of employees tend to be the flight crews, the cabin attendants and the maintenance engineers. For British and many European airlines, the pilots and cabin attendants alone represent on average around 10–12 per cent of total operating costs. It is inevitable that significant variations will exist in wage levels for similar categories of staff between airlines in different countries and even within the same country. Thus, in 2015 British Airways' average annual expenditure per pilot was £128,000, yet Virgin Airways only spent £104,000 for each of its pilots. Since Virgin had, unlike BA, no short-haul network and all its pilots were flying larger long-haul aircraft, one would have expected its expenditure per pilot to be higher than BA's, given that pilots flying larger aircraft generally are paid more.

When comparing airline wage levels across the major aviation regions some regional variations become apparent. Pilots and cabin crew working for airlines based in Western Europe appear to be among the highest paid in the world and are better remunerated than their American colleagues. This is in part because of the way that in the period 2002 to 2013 most of the larger US airlines, except Southwest, used bankruptcy procedures under Chapter 11 to reduce wage levels.

Airlines in South East Asia such as Malaysia Airlines, Garuda, Philippine Airlines or Thai have especially low wages. This also the case with airlines based in China. But there are exceptions. Singapore Airlines and more especially Cathay Pacific have higher per head staff costs than their immediate neighbours. In Cathay's case it is, in part, because it still employs many expatriate pilots at high salaries for whom it also has to meet living, travel or even schooling expenses. The same is also true for Gulf airlines. Low staff costs are one factor explaining why so many Asian airlines in Table 4.1 have relatively low unit costs. On the other hand, All Nippon Airways (ANA) and Japan Air Lines pay very high pilot and cabin crew salaries compared to those of other Asian carriers. These high salaries reflect the fact that Japan is a high-wage economy with a strong currency and may help explain why both ANA's unit costs are so high.

The traditional view, long held within the airline industry, was that management could do little about the unit cost of labour because salaries and social charges were largely determined by external factors such as the cost of living, the wider labour market or social policy. As a consequence, airline executives focused their attention on improving labour productivity through the introduction of large aircraft, computerisation and so on, while holding back, as much as possible, any increases in staff numbers as output increased. But in the last 30 years or so, growing domestic and international competition, accompanied by falling fares and yields, made it increasingly clear that marginal improvements in labour productivity in themselves were not enough to contain labour costs. Airlines were forced to try to reduce both the unit cost of labour and the amount of labour used.

This trend was reinforced by each subsequent cyclical downturn and the accompanying crisis. These forced airline managers to rethink their approach to labour costs: they became much more aggressive in trying to control such costs and focused on a four-pronged attack. First, they tried to freeze or even reduce wages while also renegotiating terms and conditions of employment so as to increase labour productivity. Second, they made great efforts to reduce staff numbers, which also meant increased productivity from the remaining staff. Third, many airlines reduced labour costs by out-sourcing some labour-intensive activities, such as IT development or their call centres, to low-wage countries; alternatively they fully or partly outsourced other labour-intensive functions, such as ground-handling or engineering, to specialist suppliers. Finally, some went further and reduced costs by franchising their regional or short-haul air services to smaller operators.

The United States airlines had been the first to tackle the issue of labour costs head on in the early 1980s, but it was in the period after 2001 that US airline managers had the greatest impact on their labour costs. Using the threat of imminent collapse of their airlines and, in the case of four of the majors, Chapter 11 bankruptcy rules, many airlines were able to cut staff numbers by up to one-third, while also reducing individual wage levels by 25 to 30 per cent (Doganis, 2006). This process was repeated after the 2008–9 financial crisis and explains why US airline wage levels are relatively low.

Achieving similar dramatic cutbacks in numbers and wages in Europe and elsewhere has proved more difficult because of legal, social or even political constraints. In Europe the first wave of major cuts in staff numbers came during the crisis years of the early to mid-1990s, when so many European airlines faced very large and mounting losses. This process was encouraged by major cash injections, the so-called 'state aid' granted by several governments to state-owned airlines to facilitate their restructuring (Doganis, 2006, Chapter 8). Part of the 'state aid' was normally used to offer attractive early retirement or redundancy packages to staff so as to cut staff numbers. Further waves of cutbacks in Europe came in the early 2000s and again in the mid-2010s. Very high fuel prices in 2011 to 2014 coincided with major incursions into short-haul markets by low-cost carriers. Legacy carriers fought back by reducing staff numbers, changing work conditions and freezing salaries, even when profits improved after 2010. The result was frequent industrial disputes and strikes at Air France, Lufthansa and elsewhere in the period 2014 to 2017.

A different approach has been to transfer employment to countries where wage rates are much lower. This effectively means relocating certain activities away from an airline's home base. Some European airlines have moved their call centres to lower-wage countries in Europe, such as Poland, or to Asia, even Fiji. Revenue accounting services or software development has sometimes gone to India. Another way of achieving lower wage costs is by employing flight or cabin crews who have as their base and point of employment countries with lower wage rates. Several European airlines have done this by employing Asian-based flight attendants or pilots. Norwegian employs some pilots based in Singapore. Conversely, Cathay Pacific has tried to reduce its high pilot costs by taking on pilots based in London at UK pilot wage rates rather than having them based in Hong Kong, where salary levels are very high and the airline has to meet lodging and other costs for expatriate crews.

Some airlines have tried to overcome the adverse impact of their own high salary levels by setting up or acquiring low-wage airlines, which are then used to operate services on their behalf, often with smaller aircraft. It may also be the case that the smaller carrier has lower costs in other areas as well as cheaper labour costs. Lufthansa, for instance, starting in 2013 switched all its short-haul services, not flying to/from its major hubs of Frankfurt or Munich, to its low-cost subsidiary Eurowings. In the United States, regional airlines operate scheduled services on behalf of the majors. For instance, Piedmont Airlines flies for American, while Skywest operated in 2017 nearly 150 smaller aircraft for Delta under the name Delta Connection. The effect of all of the above measures is not so much to reduce the major airlines' own unit labour costs but to mitigate their impact by utilising other airlines with lower wage rates to operate certain services.

The ultimate cost of labour depends not only on the average wage rates paid for different categories of staff but also on the productivity of that labour. This partly depends on institutional factors such as working days in the week, length of annual holidays, basic hours worked per week and so on, and partly on the ability of management to get more output per employee. This in turn is a function of the collective agreements between each airline and its staff, which determine work practices, such as number of rest days for pilots or cabin crew after long-haul flights. It is also a function of the number of staff actually employed. Many older legacy carriers have found that staff numbers have grown disproportionately over time. This was and is especially true of government-owned airlines. Earlier over-staffing meant that staff numbers could be cut significantly without affecting output or service levels.

In summary, until the mid-1980s, wage costs seemed to be largely beyond management's control. However, successive economic crises faced by the airline industry have forced airline managers to take a more direct and active role in reducing staff costs. They were successful in showing that this could be done in many but not all cases. Thus, today one should consider labour as a factor input whose cost levels are largely determined by prevailing economic and social factors in an airline's home country but, when national labour laws and social pressures permit, wage levels and costs can also be influenced by effective management action.

While airlines have some flexibility in reducing the unit cost of labour, that is the average wage cost plus social charge per employee, they can also reduce the overall cost of labour by employing fewer employees to produce a given level of output. In other words, they can strive to increase labour productivity. However, labour productivity is not only a function of the collective agreements and work practices or of the number of staff employed. It is very much influenced by the type of aircraft being flown by the airline as well as the characteristics of the network being served.

4.6 Aircraft type and its characteristics

Many technological aspects of each aircraft type have a direct effect on that aircraft's operating costs. The most important from an economic viewpoint are likely to be the size of the aircraft, its cruising speed and the range or distance that aircraft can fly with a full payload. The significance of size, speed and range is reinforced in that, taken together, they determine an aircraft's hourly productivity, which in turn also affects costs.

4.6.1 Aircraft size

As a general rule, though there are exceptions, the larger an aircraft the more it will cost to fly per block-hour, but the lower will be cost per seat-km. This is because, other things being equal, the direct operating costs of aircraft increase less than in proportion to their size or their payload capacity.

One can illustrate this basic principle of airline economics by reference to the experience of US airlines. In 2016 Airbus A-319 aircraft flown by US carriers with on average 134 seats incurred on average direct operating costs of about $3,098 per block-hour (Airline Monitor, 2017a). The larger Airbus A-320 aircraft with 156 seats cost about $3,310 per block-hour to fly. The larger aircraft's hourly costs were 7 per cent higher than those of the Airbus A319 but its capacity in terms of seats was about 16 per cent more. The greater capacity of the Airbus A-320 more than compensated for its higher hourly cost. As a result, its unit operating cost was 5.49 US cents per available seat-mile. This was significantly less than the seat-mile cost of the smaller A319, which was 6.41 cents or 17 per cent higher.

Aircraft size influences costs in two ways. In the first instance, there are certain aerodynamic benefits from increased size. Larger aircraft have proportionally lower drag and more payload per unit of weight. At the same time larger and more efficient engines can be used. Thus, the 215–221-seater Boeing 767-300 has a maximum take-off weight nearly two-and-a-half times as great as that of the Boeing 737-800, yet its hourly fuel consumption in 2016 when flown by US airlines was less than twice as high (Airline Monitor, 2017a). It is relatively easier and cheaper per unit of weight to push a large mass through the air than a smaller one. The same applies to mass in water; hence the development of supertankers.

Second, there are other economies of size related to the use of labour. Maintenance costs, a large part of which are the costs of labour, do not increase in proportion to increases in aircraft size. One can see this clearly when comparing two aircraft from the same manufacturer. The hourly maintenance costs among United States airlines in 2016 of the larger Airbus A320 and the smaller Airbus A319 were very close yet the A320 aircraft offered 16 per cent more seats, although both aircraft were being flown by two pilots. Economies also arise in flight crew costs since larger aircraft do not require more flight crew, though the pilot and co-pilot may be paid slightly more for flying a larger aircraft.

The close relationship between aircraft size and unit costs for the major aircraft types operated by United States trunk airlines in 2016 can be seen in Figure 4.2. The upper line shows how hourly costs increase in a linear progression as aircraft size, when measured in seats, rises. However, since hourly costs increase less than proportionately to size when they are converted to costs per seat-km, there is a strongly downward-sloping curve (lower line). The relationship between increasing size or seating capacity and declining unit costs is clear, though there are deviations and outliers.

It should always be borne in mind that the aircraft illustrated are in practice flown on different average sector lengths and this, as is discussed later, influences the unit costs shown in the diagram. The diagram also highlights the very high unit operating costs of the newer generation of small regional jets such as the Embraer 145 and, to a lesser extent, the Canadair CRJ-700. This cost disadvantage is largely a function of their small size. On the other hand, their hourly costs are low so they may be suitable for thin routes provided fares are high enough to cover their higher seat-mile costs.

Finally, it is important to emphasise that while larger aircraft generally produce lower seat-km or tonne-km costs than smaller aircraft when flown on the same sectors, their total round-trip costs are in most cases higher. This creates the basic conundrum of

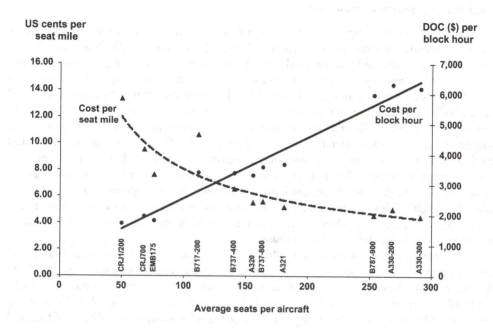

US cents per seat mile

DOC ($) per block hour

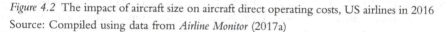

Figure 4.2 The impact of aircraft size on aircraft direct operating costs, US airlines in 2016
Source: Compiled using data from *Airline Monitor* (2017a)

airline economics and route planning. Does an airline choose the aircraft with the lower seat-km costs or the one with the lower trip costs? Clearly the choice will depend on the anticipated pattern and level of demand.

4.6.2 Aircraft speed

Apart from size, aircraft speed also affects unit costs. It does this through its effect on an aircraft's hourly productivity. Since hourly productivity is the product of the payload, measured in terms of seats or tonnes, and the speed, the greater an aircraft's cruising speed the greater will be its output per hour. If an aircraft flies at an average speed of 800 kmph and has a 20-tonne payload, its hourly capacity or output is 16,000 tonne-kms. An aircraft with a similar payload flying at 900 kmph would generate 18,000 t-kms per hour or about 12.5 per cent more than the slower aircraft.

Some elements of cost might be higher for a faster aircraft. Fuel consumption might be slightly higher unless the faster speed was due to improved aerodynamic design. But many costs, particularly those that are normally estimated on a per block-hour basis, would be similar. Flight and cabin crew costs, maintenance costs, insurance, landing fees and depreciation would certainly be fairly similar. These similar hourly costs would be spread over 12.5 per cent more tonne-kms. Therefore, assuming other things are equal, the cost per tonne-km for the faster aircraft would be lower. Since in practice the faster aircraft are frequently larger as well, the cost advantages of size and speed may reinforce each other, producing the lowest seat-km or tonne-km costs.

4.6.3 Take-off performance and range

The lower unit costs of larger and faster aircraft do not mean that airlines should always choose to operate such aircraft in preference to smaller, slower aircraft. Airlines must resolve the conundrum previously mentioned. The larger aircraft with the lower unit costs per tonne-km will have higher trip costs than smaller aircraft. In making a choice between aircraft types other factors must also be considered, such as the level and pattern of demand on the routes for which aircraft are needed and the design characteristics of the aircraft in relation to those routes. Aircraft are designed to cater for particular traffic densities and stage lengths. As a result, each aircraft type has different take-off and range characteristics and these in turn influence unit costs. An aircraft requiring particularly long runways or with engines adversely affected by high ambient airport temperatures suffers cost penalties. In either case it can overcome its design handicap by reducing its payload so as to reduce its take-off weight. This would enable it to take off despite a runway or temperature limitation. The reduced payload immediately results in higher costs per tonne-km since the same costs need to be spread over fewer units of output.

An aircraft's range performance is illustrated in payload-range diagrams such as the one in Figure 4.3. This shows the payload-range characteristics of two versions of the Airbus A-340. Aircraft are authorised to take off at a maximum take-off weight (MTOW). This weight cannot be exceeded for safety reasons. The MTOW is made up of the 'Operating Weight empty' of the aircraft, plus some combination of fuel and payload. With maximum payload, the aircraft taking off at its MTOW will be able to fly up to a certain distance for which it has been designed. This is known as the 'range at maximum payload'. To fly beyond this distance the aircraft must lift more fuel and reduce payload, always ensuring that it does not exceed its MTOW. This is why for both versions of the A340 payload is reduced if the aircraft fly beyond the 'range at maximum payload' and the payload curve declines. Initially the reduction in payload may be in terms of belly-hold freight rather than passengers, but then passenger loads must be reduced too.

The aircraft's range can be progressively increased by further uplift of fuel and a continuing reduction in payload. This process continues until the fuel tanks are full and no extra fuel can be uplifted. The range at this point is known as 'range at maximum fuel capacity'. This is the effective maximum range of the aircraft. In practice, an aircraft could fly further without more fuel by reducing its payload since a lighter aircraft consumes less fuel per hour. This is why the payload line beyond maximum payload in Figure 4.3 is not exactly vertical but very steep sloping. The shape of each aircraft's payload range line is different since aircraft have been designed to satisfy particular market needs.

Aircraft size, speed and range together determine an aircraft's productivity curve and hence its unit costs. The relationships are illustrated in Figure 4.4. The top part shows a hypothetical payload-range diagram for a certain aircraft. The middle diagram shows the impact of increasing sector distance on that aircraft's hourly productivity, that is the available or capacity tonne-kms produced per block-hour. Productivity rises with increasing sector distance because average speeds rise. The bottom diagram shows how rising hourly productivity reduces unit costs per available tonne-km as distance increases.

Hourly productivity is the product of aircraft size and speed. As sector length increases average aircraft speed rises. This is because aircraft speed is calculated on the basis of the block time for a journey. Block time is from engines on to engines off. It

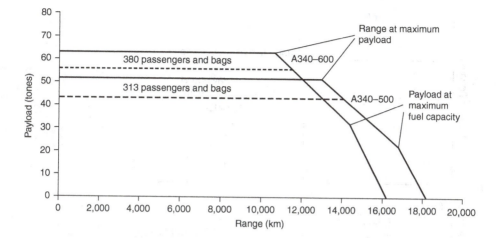

Figure 4.3 Payload – range diagrams for two versions of the Airbus A340

Note: The 500 series is an extended-range version of the A340 but this is achieved by sacrificing payload. Here both aircraft have a three-class cabin. Passenger weight is 95kg. Capacity above dotted line is available for freight.

therefore includes an amount of dead time on the ground. Ground time will vary with runway, taxiway and apron layout at each airport and with the number of aircraft movements during a given period. On departure at a very busy international airport such as London-Heathrow or Frankfurt, aircraft may spend up to 20 minutes from engine start-up to lift-off. This may be spent on being pulled out from the stand, disconnecting from the ground tractor unit; waiting further clearance from ground traffic control; taxiing to the end of the take-off runway, which may be some minutes from the stand; perhaps waiting in a queue of aircraft for clearance to taxi onto the runway and take-off. On landing the ground time is usually less, though at peak periods an aircraft may have to wait for a taxiway to be clear or even for a departing aircraft to vacate a stand. The total ground manoeuvre time at both ends of a flight may amount to 20 or 30 minutes at large and busy airports and will rarely be less than 15 minutes on any international air services.

When airborne, the aircraft may have to circle the airport of departure and it will then climb to its cruise altitude. The climb and descent speeds are relatively slow, especially if based on the horizontal distance travelled. On short sectors an aircraft may spend most of its airborne time either in climb or descent, that is at slow speeds, and may only fly at its higher cruising speed and altitude for a few minutes. As the stage distance increases more and more time is spent at the cruising speed and the ground manoeuvre, climb and descent phases become a smaller proportion of block time. Average block speed therefore increases.

Actual trip profiles of a Boeing 737-800 in 2018 flying from Manchester (UK) to Dublin and Manchester to Alicante in Spain provide a vivid illustration of the impact of sector distance on average aircraft speed (Figure 4.5). On the very short sector Manchester–Dublin the total block time with a Boeing 737-800 aircraft would be 50 minutes (assuming ground time at Manchester was at its best of 10 minutes). But of

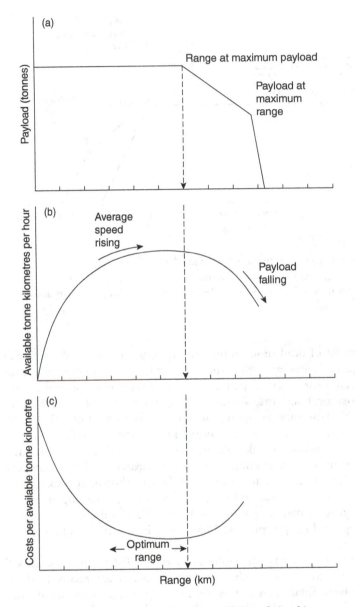

Figure 4.4 Payload – range, productivity and cost relationship

Note: (a) shows payload-range; (b) hourly productivity; (c) unit costs

this, 18 minutes was spent on the ground at either end of the route, with engines running. Nearly half the total block time, that is 23 minutes, was spent in the ascent (8 minutes) or descent (15 minutes) phases when speeds are relatively low. Only 9 minutes was spent at a cruise altitude and at close to a cruising speed.

On the much longer sector from Manchester to Alicante the time on the ground was similar, around 16 minutes (assuming only 10 minutes at Manchester). Because the

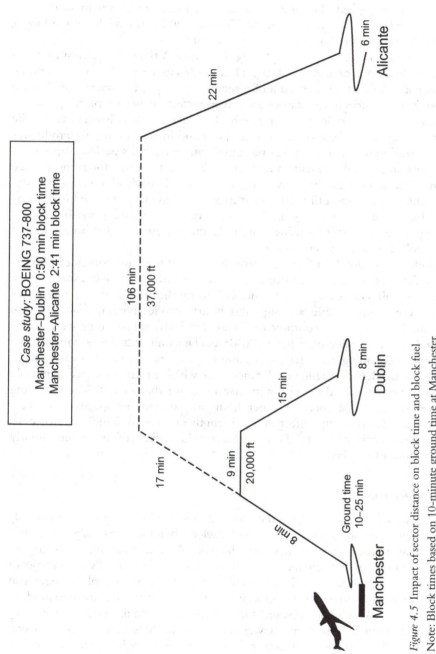

Figure 4.5 Impact of sector distance on block time and block fuel

Note: Block times based on 10-minute ground time at Manchester

cruise altitude was higher it took a few minutes longer to climb and also to descend than it did on the Dublin flight. But once the cruise altitude was reached, the aircraft spent 106 minutes or 66 per cent of the total block time of 161 minutes flying at a relatively high cruising speed. The impact on average block speed was dramatic. The average block speed on the short sector to Dublin was 320 km/hr while on the longer Alicante flight it was 630 km/hr or nearly twice as fast.

One could have used a different example, say Southwest Airlines flying from Dallas to Oklahoma City (302 kms) compared to its flight from Dallas to Miami (1,773 kms), but the block time analysis would have produced similar results. Block speed increases with distance especially and short distances have a particularly adverse effect on average block speed.

Turning back to the middle chart of Figure 4.4, one can see diagramatically the impact of increasing sector distance on average speed and in turn on hourly productivity. Initially increasing sector distance has no impact on an aircraft's payload capacity. It remains at its maximum and constant. But as sector distance increases, the rising average speed ensures that hourly productivity rises, even though payload capacity remains constant. It continues to rise until the range at maximum payload is reached (shown by the vertical dotted line in Figure 4.4). For distances beyond this, payload falls and though average speed may still be rising marginally the net effect is that hourly output (capacity multiplied by average speed) falls.

Hourly productivity directly affects unit costs because all the costs constant in hourly terms, such as flight crew costs, insurance or depreciation, are spread over more units of output. Thus, a unit cost curve can be derived from the productivity-range curve showing how unit costs decline as range and hourly productivity increase (bottom graph in Figure 4.4). Unit costs continue to decline until payload has to be sacrificed to fly further and hourly productivity begins to drop. The unit cost curve will vary for each aircraft type depending on its size, speed and range characteristics. For each aircraft type it is possible to identify a range of distance over which its unit costs are uniformly low. This might be considered the optimum cost range for that aircraft. The preceding discussion has assumed that total costs per hour are constant irrespective of sector length. The next section on the effect of stage length on costs will indicate that costs decrease relatively with distance. This reinforces the effect of increasing hourly productivity. More of this later.

4.6.4 Engine performance

A key characteristic of any aircraft type is the engine it uses. Engines are important not only because they impact on an aircraft's speed and payload but more critically on its fuel consumption. This impacts on operating costs. Increasingly, the same engines or engines with similar thrust made by different manufacturers are being used by broadly similar types of aircraft. This is because there are only a handful of manufacturers of civil jet engines in the world and competition to get their engines into the same aircraft drives them to produce similar products. This should not obscure the fact that even similar engines may have different fuel consumption. In particular newer engines are likely to be more fuel efficient. Thus, early in the 2010s two new engines were launched for new single-aisle aircraft, such as the Airbus A320 Neo and Boeing 737 Max family of aircraft as well as others. The engines were the CFM International Leap-1A and the Pratt and Whitney PW1000G geared turbofan. The engine manufacturers claimed that their new engines would reduce fuel burn per sector by 14–16 per cent and cut engine maintenance costs by up to 20 per cent.

It is clear that the type of engines in an airline's fleet and in particular whether they are new or old versions of the engine type influence operating costs. In assessing the unit costs of different airlines one needs to consider the impact not only of the type and size of aircraft being flown but also the version of engines being used.

4.6.5 Impact of aircraft type on costs

In conclusion there can be little doubt that the type of aircraft operated has a significant effect on cost levels. With this in mind the key question is how much freedom does an airline have to choose an aircraft type to minimise unit costs? Or, is the choice constrained by the sector lengths and the traffic densities on the routes concerned, or by other factors? The choice of aircraft occurs in two planning stages and management influence is critical only in the second. The first stage is short-listing the possible aircraft types with the preferred engine for a given operation. When an aircraft type can be powered by different engines, choosing the engine adds a further complication. As previously emphasised, an international airline's route structure and demand pattern is dependent on its geographical location and on economic and political factors largely beyond its control. The route structure, the airports used, in particular the runway lengths available, and the traffic density on those routes will broadly delimit the type of aircraft that is needed or can be used. For particular parts of its network, the sector lengths and traffic densities taken together will reduce the options open to the airline to perhaps only two or three aircraft types.

In some cases, only one type may fit the network characteristics and the anticipated demand levels. In the year 2017, airlines operating relatively long-haul routes of say over 8,000 to 10,000 kms but with traffic flows that were too thin to support a 400-plus-seater Airbus A380 and planning to purchase new aircraft would have been looking for a twin-engined 250–300-seater with a three-class cabin. Given these market constraints the choice would probably have been between an Airbus A350-900 or a Boeing 787-9. At another level, an airline planning to operate high density leisure flights from northern Europe into the smaller Aegean islands of Greece, such as Mykonos or Santorini, may only consider to use or buy Boeing 737-800 or Airbus A320 aircraft, or the newer Max or Neo versions of these aircraft, because of runway length limitations at the airport. This is so even if the traffic flows could support larger aircraft. In both these examples it is a combination of various external factors and traffic characteristics that produce the short-list of possible aircraft.

It is only when one moves to the second stage of fleet planning, that of choosing between the short-listed aircraft, that the role of management becomes critical. Management has to make several key and related decisions. It must not only choose between the short-listed aircraft types that both best meet its airline needs and also produce the best financial results, but it must also choose the number of aircraft and optimise the mix of aircraft in the fleet. Fleet planning is pulled in opposite directions. On the one hand an airline needs to choose the optimum aircraft in terms of size and range characteristics for each route, but at the same time it must minimise the number of different types of aircraft in its fleet so as to reduce maintenance and crewing costs (Clark, 2017). Thus, a compromise must be found between operating a different aircraft type best for each route and having only one aircraft type to serve all routes. Management must also decide on the engines that will power its aircraft, if more than one engine type is available. All these decisions will eventually affect the airline's cost levels.

Once an airline has made its choice and invested in particular aircraft types for various parts of its network then those aircraft types have to be considered as given. They cannot be changed from year to year. Because of investment in flight crew training, maintenance and ground facilities, aircraft types are unlikely to be changed except after several years. Once aircraft have been introduced into an airline's operation the most significant factor that will then affect their costs of operation, other than the level of input costs, such as the cost of fuel, is the route structure on which they will be operated.

4.7 Route structure and network characteristics

4.7.1 Stage length

Several aspects of an airline's operating pattern may influence its costs but the most critical are the stage or sector lengths over which it is operating its aircraft. The average stage lengths will vary within an airline by aircraft type since it is probable that different aircraft will have been chosen for different types of routes within the total network. For each aircraft type, nevertheless, the longer the stage length that can be flown the lower will be the direct operating costs per unit of output. This is so until sectors get so long that that payload has to be sacrificed.

The rapid decline of unit costs as stage distance increases is a fundamental characteristic of airline economics. A number of factors help to explain this relationship. One of these, the effect of stage length on block speed, has already been discussed in the previous section. It was pointed out that ground manoeuvre time and the relatively slow climb and descent phases of a flight become a decreasing proportion of the total block time as stage length increases. Consequently, the average block speed increases. In turn, since productivity is the average speed multiplied by the capacity then the hourly productivity in terms of tonne-kms or seat-kms also rises. Fixed costs, both direct and indirect, are spread over more units of output and therefore the total operating cost per available tonne-km or seat-km goes down.

The same considerations that affect block speed also influence block fuel. During ground manoeuvre time on departure or arrival aircraft are burning fuel. In 20 to 30 minutes spent on the ground they can burn a considerable amount of it (Figure 4.5). During climb and to a lesser extent during the descent phase, fuel consumption is relatively high in relation to the horizontal distance travelled. Conversely, fuel consumption is least in the cruise mode and is reduced at higher altitudes.

The earlier example of the two flights out of Manchester to Dublin and Alicante highlight the impact of sector distance on fuel burn. On the longer sector, time on the ground and time spent in ascent and descent is a much smaller proportion of the total block time. More than half the block time is spent in cruise, when fuel consumption is lowest, but it is also spent at a much higher altitude than on the shorter sector, thereby further reducing fuel burn. In short, ground manoeuvre and climb and descent fuel becomes a decreasing proportion of total fuel burn as stage distance increases. The net result is that fuel consumption does not increase in proportion to distance. Thus, if an Airbus A321 Neo or a Boeing 737 Max doubles its stage distance from, say, 500 km the fuel burned will not double. Depending on the particular circumstances of the route the fuel consumed will only increase by about 60 per cent to 70 per cent.

Looking at an actual example, the Airbus A320-200 on London to Paris with a full passenger load and no cargo consumes about 1,700 kgs of fuel. Flying to Geneva, whose distance from London is more than double or 118 per cent greater, the Airbus burns about 2,800 kgs, an increase of only 65 per cent. As a result, the fuel burned per km and the fuel cost per km drops by up to 25 per cent. This is a major saving, given that fuel may be a significant proportion of total costs. On longer sectors beyond 2,500 kms the fuel savings from additional increases in sector distance become marginal. The fuel burn in 2018 of the newer Boeing 737 MAX-9 on sectors out of London is shown in Figure 4.6 and illustrates the same principle. Fuel burn per kilometre flown drops sharply as sector distance increases.

Stage length not only affects fuel consumption but also influences aircraft and crew utilisation, and this too impacts on costs. An aircraft is a very expensive piece of capital equipment. It is only earning revenue and paying back its high initial cost when it is flying. The more flying it does the lower become its hourly ownership costs. This is because the standing annual charges, notably depreciation and insurance, can be spread over a greater number of productive hours. It is much easier to keep aircraft in the air if stage lengths are longer.

On short sectors such as New York–Boston, London–Paris or Singapore–Kuala Lumpur, where aircraft have to land after every 40–50 minutes of flight and then spend up to an hour on the ground, achieving more than six or seven block-hours per day with an aircraft becomes very difficult. This is especially so where airports ban night flights. Higher utilisation requires either a reduction in the aircraft turn-round time so as to carry out more flights within the operating day, or an extension of the operating day by scheduling very early morning or late evening departures. Low-cost airlines in

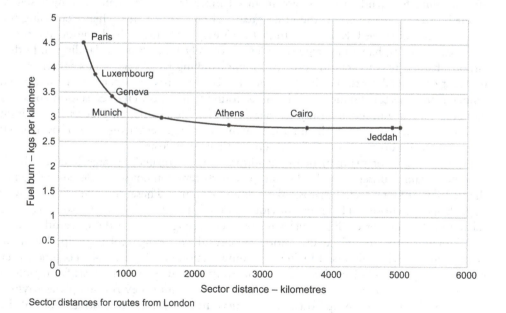

Sector distances for routes from London

Figure 4.6 Impact of sector distance on fuel burn – Boeing 737 MAX-9 on routes from London

Source: Boeing Commercial Aircraft (Copyright 2017 Boeing)

Europe and elsewhere often achieve very high utilisation on relatively short sectors by extending the operating day earlier into the day or later into the night hours, and by reducing turn-round times on the ground to 30 minutes or less. As a result, in 2016 easyJet's average daily utilisation with its Airbus A320 aircraft was 14.3 hours whereas British Airways only managed 9.

When one looks at longer sectors involving, say, five block-hours, an aircraft can fly out and back and with just two flight sectors achieve a daily utilisation of 10 block-hours while spending only a couple of hours or so on the ground. The longer the sector distances, the easier it becomes to push up daily utilisation and thereby spread the aircraft's annual fixed costs over more block-hours and more available tonne-kms. The close relationship between stage length and aircraft utilisation can be seen by examining British Airways' Airbus A321 aircraft in 2016. These A321s were flown on shorter sectors, on average around 1,300 kms, achieving a daily utilisation of 8.6 hours; but Thomas Cook, flying the same aircraft on longer sectors, averaging nearly 2,700 kms, was able to achieve 10.2 hours each day. That is one-and-a-half hours more of production each day, or, in broad terms, BA needed almost five aircraft to generate the same output as Thomas Cook produced with just four aircraft.

Flight and cabin crew, like aircraft, are a valuable and costly resource. A high proportion of crew costs are fixed and do not vary in the short term. The more flying that crews can actually do, the lower will be the crew costs per block-hour. On short sectors crews spend relatively more of their time on the ground. On one-to one-and-a-half-hour sectors, crews may actually only be flying for four to six hours during a 12–14-hour duty period. As stage lengths increase they should be able to spend more of their duty period actually flying.

A more obvious implication of short stages is that airport charges, station costs and any handling fees paid to others are incurred more frequently than on longer stages. Their impact on total costs is therefore greater. One can see this when examining the cost structure of three UK airlines. In 2014–15 easyJet, flying only domestic and intra-European services, had an average stage length of only 1,110 kms. Its landing and other airport charges, plus its station costs, including handling fees, came to a staggering 26.8 per cent of its total costs. Yet in the same year British Airways, operating with a much longer average sector distance of 2,450 kms, found that airport charges, station costs and handling fees accounted for only 11 per cent of its total operating costs. For Virgin Atlantic, an exclusively long-haul airline, with an average sector distance of over 6,800 kms, these costs drop to only 7.6 per cent of their total costs.

Some elements of maintenance expenditure are also related to stage length. This is because certain maintenance checks and spare parts replacement schedules are related to the number of flight cycles, that is, take-offs and landings. These occur less frequently as stage length increases. The most obvious part of the aircraft whose maintenance is related to the number of flight cycles is the undercarriage, though there are others too.

All these factors reinforce the more theoretical cost–range relationship, based on aircraft productivity, discussed in the preceding section and Figure 4.4. Together, they result in a typically U-shaped cost curve for every aircraft type. Unit costs fall rapidly at first as stage length increases, then gradually flatten out until they rise sharply as payload restrictions begin to push up costs. A cost curve based on a route costing study of the Boeing 737 Max-9 is shown in Figure 4.7. This study and other similar analyses indicate that the most significant economies with respect to distance occur by increasing stage lengths at the short to medium range, that is from 300–500 kms to 1,500 kms or so. The implication for airlines is clear. They must avoid short sectors, because they impose much higher costs, to should try to operate each aircraft at or near the stage distances where costs are at their lowest. This means the distances for which each aircraft has been optimised.

The relationship between sector distance and unit costs is one of the fundamental rules of airline economics. Short sectors are inherently more costly to operate, in terms of cost per seat-km or available tonne km, than longer sectors. Other things being equal, short-haul airlines will tend to have higher unit costs than airlines with longer average sector distances. This should be borne in mind when comparing airline costs.

In so far as larger aircraft tend to be used on longer stages the twin effects of aircraft size and stage length frequently reinforce each other. The result is that operating costs per tonne-km on long sectors flown by large wide-body aircraft may be as low as 20–25 per cent of the costs on short-haul sectors flown by smaller aircraft. This is vividly illustrated by comparing two Airbus aircraft on routes out of London, the 150-seat short-medium range A320 and the much larger 300-seater long-haul A340 (Figure 4.8).

The larger aircraft's direct operating costs per available seat-km (ASK) on long sectors are less than 40 per cent of those of the smaller aircraft on London–Paris.

Airlines operating primarily large aircraft over long sectors will always appear to have lower unit operating costs than airlines flying smaller aircraft on domestic and short-haul international services. But their lower costs will be primarily a function of aircraft size and sector distance rather than better managerial efficiency!

If sector distances flown have such a critical impact on unit costs, to what extent can they be influenced by management decisions? As previously pointed out, an airline's route structure and therefore its sector distances are a function of the location of its

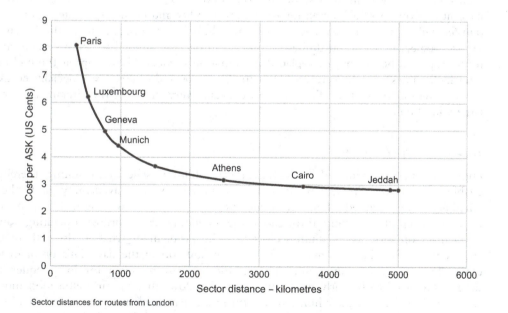

*Figure 4.*7 Impact of sector distance on unit costs for Boeing 737 MAX-9 on routes from London
Source: Boeing Commercial Aircraft (Copyright 2017 Boeing)

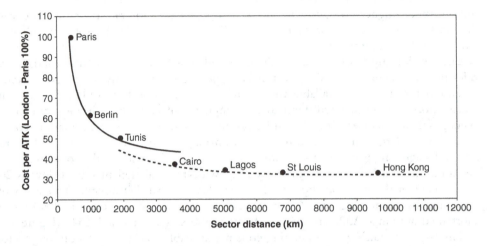

Figure 4.8 Impact of sector distance and aircraft size on unit costs on routes from London: Airbus
      A320-200 and Airbus A340-600 compared

Note: A320 is a 150-seater twin jet, A340 is four-engined and here operated with 300 seats

home base(s), the geographical location of the markets it is serving and the degree to which the regulatory regimes within which it operates allow free access to those markets. But there is some scope for action. Management must constantly assess and reassess the viability of short sectors to establish whether revenues generated exceed the high costs or at least make a sufficient contribution to fixed costs. Short sectors that have little prospect of achieving long-term profitability and do not generate significant transfer traffic onto other services at an airline's hub may be discontinued. Multi-sector services, especially those on domestic routes, can be re-examined to see if certain en-route stops can be cut out or replaced by non-stop services. Short hops at the end of long-haul routes, which were common in the 1980s and 1990s, are especially costly because the distances of the final sector are usually very short yet the aircraft used are large wide-bodies.

4.7.2 Frequency of services

High frequencies provide airlines with greater flexibility in schedules planning, thereby enabling them to increase aircraft and crew utilisation. The availability of further schedules to be operated whenever an aircraft and crew return to base makes it much easier to keep them flying throughout the operating day. Airlines operating low frequencies on short to medium sectors face the problem of what to do with their aircraft when they have completed their first round trip of the day. This problem is especially acute if for commercial reasons most departures even for low-frequency destinations need to be early in the morning. It follows that by early afternoon most aircraft will be back at their home base with insufficient further flights to absorb all of them. To avoid under-utilisation of aircraft and crews certain flights will be rescheduled to later in the day to utilise aircraft that have returned from early morning departures. But later departures may be at commercially less attractive times.

On long-haul routes high frequencies also enable airlines to reduce the length and cost of crew stop-overs. Conversely, low frequencies prove costly. In May 2018 Finnair was operating three flights each week from Helsinki to Fukuoka in Japan with an Airbus A330-300 aircraft. Low frequency meant higher costs since each complete set of flight and cabin crew had to spend two or three days and nights in relatively expensive Fukuoka hotels before flying the next schedule back.

The aircraft an airline has available, the demand patterns in the markets concerned, together with constraints imposed by bilateral air services agreements or inter-airline agreements influence or even determine the frequencies to be operated. But an airline has some scope to try to increase its frequencies by changes in the type of aircraft used or in the operating pattern or route structure. Higher frequencies also have marketing benefits.

4.7.3 Airline and fleet size

Early studies of airline economics, particularly in relation to US airlines, had suggested that there might be significant economies of scale, that is from larger company size, particularly at the lower end of the size scale. Such economies were expected to arise through the ability of larger carriers to gain the benefits of bulk buying and of spreading overhead costs over more units of output. Large carriers would also benefit from their ability to themselves undertake discrete activities such as major maintenance checks or computerised reservations systems, for which a minimum scale of operations was necessary. Increasingly during the 1970s and 1980s the view that there are cost economies of scale in airline operations began to be questioned.

Such doubts were confirmed in practice following United States domestic deregulation in 1978 and liberalisation elsewhere. During the last 40 years many small new-entrant carriers have emerged in the US, in Europe and in other deregulated markets. Many did not survive, but those that did have been able to be price competitive against very much larger and well-established airlines. Their unit costs, in many cases, have been lower because of leaner management and fewer administrative and other overheads.

There may be some limited cost benefits when an airline grows from a fleet of 10 aircraft to 20 or 30. Some overhead costs such as those of the CEO and senior executives may be spread over more units of output, that is passenger-kms. They may also get better prices from a variety of suppliers by buying in larger volumes. But such benefits of greater size are limited. When size grows from say 50 aircraft to 100 or 150 some costs may be saved but others may increase as the airline's operations become more complex. It is not clear at what stage in its growth from small to large an airline stops benefiting from limited cost economies and finds that further growth has little impact on its unit costs.

The airline industry appears to be characterised by constant returns to scale. In other words, there are no significant economies of scale on the cost side. Such a conclusion has important implications on regulatory policy and on merger and alliance strategies. It means that in the absence of entry or capacity controls new small carriers should be in a position to enter existing markets and be cost competitive with established carriers. On the cost side, the economics of the airline industry indicate a natural tendency towards competition rather than monopoly. In practice in international air transport, that tendency is distorted by bilateral agreements, by the lack of airport capacity at major airports and by other constraints discussed in earlier chapters on regulation.

If there are no significant economies of scale or size as far as costs are concerned what has been driving the tendency for consolidation; for airlines to increase their size through mergers and acquisitions? The European Commission in Brussels, among others, has argued for more consolidation between European airlines. In practice, consolidation has led to marketing benefits rather than reduction in unit costs. These benefits arise in part because competition is eliminated in those markets where previously the merging carriers were in competition. More critically, consolidation gives airlines increased market power because they have a more widespread and attractive network, one they can serve with increased frequencies and often better schedules, as a result of merging the operations of two carriers.

While cost advantages of larger size appear limited, larger airlines with a wide network spread enjoy distinct scale benefits in terms of marketing. It is primarily sales and marketing benefits that are driving consolidation, rather than cost synergies. The Air France take-over of KLM in 2004 is a good example of this. While cost benefits were being claimed, the size of each of the partners was such that most of the cost reductions could have been achieved by each independently of the other. On the other hand, the marketing benefits of joining and co-ordinating their two networks were substantial.

The same was true when British Airways merged with Iberia in early 2011. An annual cost saving of $533 million was targeted after five years. This was fairly limited given the two airlines' total annual costs of around $18 billion. It was also offset by substantial integration costs arising from the merger. In 2012 alone they amounted to $414 million. Iberia subsequently reduced its costs but this was due to internal actions rather than the merger. For BA the merger opened up eight or so new destinations in South America while BA linked its extensive Asian network to Iberia. In the United States the mergers of Delta and Northwest (2008–10), of American and US Air (2013–15) and of United and Continental (2010–12) did little to reduce the unit costs of the larger enterprises being created but they did strengthen their market power and revenue generation.

If there are no significant cost economies of scale related to airline size, what about the related question of fleet size? Varied stage lengths and differing traffic densities impose the need on many airlines to have quite mixed fleets. This in turn means that some airlines, especially smaller Third World airlines, may only operate two or three aircraft of one type. When the number of aircraft in a fleet of one type is so small there are likely to be higher costs. The cost of spares holding expressed as a proportion of the purchase price of the aircraft goes up as the number of aircraft of a particular type drops below a certain level. For instance, one spare engine may be enough whether an airline has three or 15 aircraft of the same type. Flight crew training and engineering training costs have to be spread over fewer aircraft and are therefore higher. Maintenance costs would be particularly high for small fleets if engines or aircraft have to be sent elsewhere for major overhauls. The small numbers may preclude the installation of more advanced or very specific maintenance facilities. Conversely, if maintenance or ground-handling equipment very specific for one aircraft type is installed to service only two or three aircraft it will push up the costs of maintenance or handling. Sets of flight crews per aircraft may be higher for very small mixed fleets because of the inability in emergencies to switch crews between aircraft if they are of different types. Pilots are certificated for only one aircraft type at a time. All the above considerations mean that it is relatively expensive to operate small fleets of aircraft.

It has been estimated that hourly direct operating costs go down by 5 to 10 per cent as the fleet size of aircraft of a particular type increases from two or three to 15 aircraft. Fleets larger than this do not appear to achieve further significant cost economies. This means that airlines with small and mixed fleets have a cost disadvantage.

In summer 2017 Air Madagascar operated 11 aircraft of four different types, made by four different manufacturers. No fleet had more than four aircraft of the same type. Operating four fleets of such small numbers imposed cost penalties, but the fleet mix was imposed on Air Madagascar by its geographical location and the markets it aimed to serve. In the same summer Aegean, the regional Greek airline, operated a fleet of 47 aircraft all of the Airbus A320 family. Of these 38 were A320s, eight were A321s and there was a single A319. There was some commonality of parts and all these types could be common rated for pilots so that each pilot could fly any of them. Cost economies could be achieved. The low-cost airlines have learned this lesson. Despite having large or very large fleets they aim to standardise on flying only one aircraft type or less frequently just two.

Some cost advantage of increasing airline size, through growth or mergers, may arise if as a result the size of individual type fleets increases or if the number of different aircraft types in the fleet is reduced.

4.8 Airline marketing and product policy

Produce and service quality is both an integral part of an airline's marketing strategy and a significant cost determinant. It is also an area of cost over which an airline has much greater control. However, airlines do not have complete freedom of action over marketing spend except in those few cases where an airline operates on its own, as a monopolist, on all or most of its network. This is most likely to occur in domestic operations. On their international operations, where they face direct or indirect competition and in competitive domestic markets, airlines clearly do not have an entirely free hand. The nature and strength of the competition an airline faces in its main markets, together with its own positioning in those markets, will have a major influence on its product strategy and therefore on its costs. For example, network airlines facing direct competition from low-cost carriers and wishing to be more price-competitive will be forced to reduce their costs. This may well mean simplifying and cutting back on their product and service offering, for instance, abandoning free in-flight catering and offering a trolley service from which passengers can buy snacks or drinks. British Airways adopted this strategy on its European short-haul services in spring 2017. In long-haul markets the nature of the competition will be different and more diverse, especially since some of the competitors may be offering indirect services through their own hubs.

Product and service standards are also dependent on the sector distances, or rather the trip travel times. Service standards must be different on a six-hour sector compared to a one-hour sector. They may also differ according to the time of day or night that a flight is operated. Above all, service quality must be responsive to competitive pressures from other carriers operating in the same or in parallel markets. Such pressures will even impact on routes where an airline may be the only operator, since it must offer the same consistent product throughout its network. It cannot afford to alienate customers by providing a poorer service on routes where it operates a monopoly.

Within the constraints imposed by sector times and by competitive pressures, an airline has considerable freedom to decide its marketing strategy. This means not only deciding which markets to serve, but also includes pricing policy as well as decisions on the type of products and the quality of services that the airline wishes to offer in those markets. The whole issue of marketing is discussed in a later chapter (Chapter 8). But it is important to appreciate that several aspects of marketing policy impact directly on cost levels. They can be grouped under two headings: costs associated with product and service features and those costs more directly related to sales, distribution and related promotional activities.

4.8.1 Product and service features

Airlines have to decide on the nature and quality of the product they are going to offer in the various freight and passenger markets that they serve. This must be done within certain constraints. For commercial and competitive reasons airlines may have to conform to certain minimum standards of product quality. They must also conform to a variety of international or national safety and technical regulations. These affect many aspects of the cabin layout such as the seat pitch next to emergency exits, or the minimum number of cabin staff, and so on. Within these constraints airlines enjoy considerable freedom to decide on the quality of the product they are going to offer, both in the air and on the ground, and on the costs they are prepared to incur.

In the air, three aspects of cabin service standards are particularly important for passenger services. *Cabin layout and seating density* is frequently the most significant in terms of its impact on unit costs. Each aircraft type has a maximum design seating capacity based on an all-economy layout at a given minimum seat pitch (that is the distance between the back of one seat and the back of the seat in front). The actual number of seats that an airline puts in its own aircraft of a particular type depends on a number of key decisions the airline itself takes. It must decide whether it is going to offer a one-, two-, three- or four-cabin class product in each part of its network.

A large number of airlines such as Delta, SAS, Garuda or KLM abandoned First class on their long-haul routes in the early 2000s and only offered Business or Economy cabins. More recently some have introduced a Premium Economy class on their long-haul flights. Basically, this offers three to five inches greater seat pitch than Economy class, that is more leg room, plus improved meal services.

In 2000 British Airways was the first to launch fully reclining seats in their long-haul Business cabins and other airlines gradually followed suit. By 2017 most of the larger US, European and Asian airlines were offering long-haul Business passengers seats that converted into flat or almost flat beds. It was the success of the lie-flat Business seats that led many airlines to phase out First class altogether and focus on Business class as their top premium product.

Today, airlines such as BA, Air France or Singapore only offer First class on a select number of their long-haul services, where there is a demand for such a highly priced product. They are also responding to a more recent innovation. In summer 2008 Emirates, one of two launch customers, introduced the ultra-large Airbus A380 with First class 'suites'. The suites were large enclosed areas offering total privacy and even a shower or a double bed. A few airlines such as Qatar Airways and Singapore also offer suites. In fact, Singapore Airlines currently offers Suites, First class, Business, Premium Economy and Economy on long-haul services though not necessarily all on the same flight.

In short-haul and domestic markets airlines in most parts of the world offer either a two-class cabin, Business and Economy, or a single Economy class. First class has been phased out in most shorter-haul markets. The United States is a major exception. US airlines still offer First, Business and Economy on many of their longer domestic sectors, though some airlines give them other names in an attempt to brand their products.

The distribution of space between fare classes, if there is more than one, the type of seating and the seat pitch adopted for each class and the numbers of seats abreast are the more crucial determinants of seating capacity. The distribution of cabin space between seating areas, galleys, toilets and storage is another factor. The fewer the number of seats on offer, the higher will be the cost per seat-km since the aircraft's trip costs need to be divided among the fewer seat-kms generated.

The range of seating densities offered in 2017 by international airlines in two aircraft types is illustrated in Table 4.5. Some scheduled airlines, as part of a superior product strategy, choose cabin and seating configurations that may result in a reduction in the number of seats by 20 per cent or more when compared to the seating capacity offered by other scheduled carriers in the same aircraft. The airline's product may be improved but the cost implications are serious. For example, in 2017 British Airways flew its Boeing 787-9 aircraft in a three-class configuration with only 216 seats. This meant that costs per seat were 38 per cent higher than if it had adopted Air Canada's three or Etihad's two class layout, both of which offered 298 or so seats (Table 4.5).

Clearly BA is focusing on premium products and service in its long-haul operations, so operates low density seating. In short-haul markets its focus is to compete effectively with the low-cost carriers, which are increasingly dominating intra-European markets. In its short-haul Airbus A320, therefore, BA offers more seats than most of the other legacy carriers. It averages around 166 in two-class layout, but by using convertible seats

Table 4.5 Impact of different airline seating density on costs per seat, 2017

Airline	Airbus A320		Airline	Boeing 787-9	
	No. of seats**	Index cost per seat*		No. of seats**	Index cost per seat
Scheduled airlines			**Scheduled airlines**		
British Airways (2)	166	100	Etihad (2)	299	100
Bangkok Air (1)	162	102	Air Canada (3)	298	100
Air France (1)	158	105	American (4)	285	105
American (3)	150	111	Korean (3)	271	110
Silk Air (2)	150	111	United (3)	252	119
Jet Blue (2)	150	111	ANA (3)	246	122
Air India (2)	140	119	British Airways (3)	216	138
Low-cost airlines			**Low-cost airlines**		
easyJet (1)	186	89	Scoot (3)	375	80
Spirit (2)	182	91	Norwegian (2)	344	87
Air Asia (1)	180	92			

* Assuming operating costs are the same, 'cost per seat' reflects each airline's seating density with the scheduled airline having most seats and so lowest cost per seat indexed at 100

** Number of cabin classes indicated in brackets ()

it can increase to around 180 seats and still keep a couple of rows of Business seating. The target is to reduce the cost per seat or per passenger through higher seat density and so try to match low-cost carriers such as easyJet.

A key element of the low-cost model is to reduce the cost per seat by packing more seats into the aircraft. This is clearly evident in Table 4.5. Both in short-haul and long-haul markets, most low-cost airlines offer significantly more seats in the same aircraft than their legacy competitors. The result is that their costs per seat, even assuming all other costs are similar, can be much lower.

In conclusion, airline executives can affect their unit costs by the seating density they adopt for their different aircraft or different markets.

A second aspect of cabin service standards that has important cost implications is the *number of cabin crew* used. Safety regulations impose a minimum number for each aircraft type. It is up to each airline to decide how many more than the minimum it wishes to use. This is partly a function of the number of cabin classes it decided to offer and partly a function of the sector distance. On short-to-medium-haul sectors where there is less time for meals and other in-flight services, cabin crew numbers may be close to the minimum. On long-haul sectors airlines have more scope to try to differentiate their product through their in-flight services and one aspect of this may be more cabin staff. When an airline's cabin crew wages are comparatively low then the cost of improving the in-flight product by having more cabin staff is not high. This is the case with some Asian carriers. Conversely, it is more costly for high-wage airlines to compete in terms of cabin staff numbers.

The third key element of cabin service standards is that of *in-fight catering and related cabin product features*. As a result of international liberalisation the need and the scope for management initiative in this area increased, particularly on long-haul services. Many airlines place great emphasis on trying to persuade potential customers that they offer the best meals, cooked by well-known master chefs, together with the most expensive and sought-after wines, the best spirits and the finest coffees. Turkish Airlines goes as far as having white-coated chefs on some of its long-haul flights, in addition to cabin stewards. This focus on catering standards is done despite the fact that passenger surveys repeatedly show that in-flight catering is way down in the list of factors that influence choice of airline. Moreover, competitive pressures push most carriers to more or less match what their competitors are doing. For this reason, while in-flight catering costs may vary between airlines, they are unlikely to be important in explaining difference in total unit costs between those airlines. The same is also true of the minor elements of cabin service such as the range of newspapers and journals on offer, free give-aways, toiletry bags on long-haul flights and so on.

There may be greater cost differentiation in the provision of in-flight entertainment because the options available to airlines are much greater. For instance, some long-haul carriers, such as Emirates in Dubai, have for some years offered seat-back screens for all Economy class passengers with a multiple choice of channels. This is clearly an expensive marketing decision since it means refurbishing all aircraft with complex and more expensive seats, as well as installing more expensive equipment. Such seats are likely to be heavier imposing a weight penalty. Moreover, the video and audio programmes are also expensive to buy and must be changed frequently. Individual screens and associated controls impose a weight penalty and added fuel burn.

There is also scope for product differentiation on the ground. Airlines can rent and staff more check-in and baggage drop desks to reduce passenger waiting times and they may also decide to provide more ground staff for passenger handling and assistance in general. Many international airlines go further and provide sometimes quite luxurious and costly First or even Business class lounges at airports, while their competitors may provide neither. An example is Singapore Airlines, which has decided, as a matter of product policy, to provide its own exclusive First/Business class lounges at nearly all the airports it serves irrespective of the frequency of its services or the number of First or Business class passengers handled. In this way it imprints its own brand and product style on the lounges. On the other hand, some other carriers share executive lounges with one or more different airlines in order to save costs. Airline members of the same global alliance tend to share VIP lounges especially at each other's home base.

4.8.2 Sales distribution and promotional policies

Scheduled airlines enjoy considerable discretion in the way they organise and run their sales and distribution activities. They decide on the extent to which they should sell their services through their own sales offices, telephone call centres and online through their own websites rather than through retail or online travel agents. Such decisions have cost implications. While setting up and operating its own customer-oriented website or retail sales outlets costs money, the airline saves the commissions it might otherwise have to pay to travel agents. (The impact of commission payments on costs was discussed earlier in Section 4.4.)

A major development in the 2000s was the switch to online selling through an airline's own website. The low-cost no-frills airlines such as Southwest in the US and easyJet in Europe were the first to grasp fully the value of the internet in reducing distribution costs by cutting out commissions to agents, which in the past represented between 6 and 10 per cent of total costs. Others followed. At the same time, online travel agents such as Expedia or Opodo became increasingly powerful and could be accessed directly by passengers. Though retail high street agents continued to use the global distribution systems such as Amadeus, Sable or Travelport, airlines were focusing more and more of their sales to their own websites or to online travel agencies and away from retail travel agents. This is particularly true of European and US airlines, but retail agents still play a key part in many Asian markets.

Several other important decisions have to be made in relation to sales and distribution. One consequence of the digitisation of air travel through online sales and the abandonment of printed tickets is that many airlines have closed their own in-town ticket sales offices. Many of these were in expensive key streets in the heart of major cities. In London, until the early 2000s many airlines had sales offices in or close to prestigious Regent Street in central London. They have all gone. Some airlines have moved their sales to much cheaper offices away from the centre of London, often on higher floors rather than street level. As a result, costs have been cut. Airlines that still maintain their own retail sales offices in their own country or abroad must constantly reassess whether the costs involved represent value for money.

An important issue is whether an international airline should set up offline retail sales outlets, that is, outlets in cities or countries to which it does not fly. Equally crucial may be the decision on whether it should itself staff and operate sales offices at some of its less important overseas destinations or whether to appoint a general sales agent, who may or may not be another airline. When airlines enter cross-border global alliances they may cut the costs of distribution by merging their sales offices and sales staff in a partner airline's country or in third countries to which two or more of the alliance partners operate.

Decisions on advertising and promotional activity are very much at management's discretion. It is open to airlines to decide themselves how much to spend on advertising and promoting their services and how to spend it. A key decision is how to split their efforts between a more digital-based approach using direct e-models, Facebook and other social media platforms or in the more traditional media outlets. In the latter case, numerous promotion channels are open to them from television, radio or national press advertising aimed at large numbers of potential customers at one end to promotional activities or trade press advertising targeting relatively small numbers of freight and travel agents or travel journalists at the other. Many airlines target an advertising and promotional budget equivalent to about 2 per cent of their revenue. They may spend much more than this in particular markets, especially when they are launching a new service, or in foreign countries where they are less well known than the home-based carriers. Advertising spend is also likely to be higher in markets where competition is more intense.

Different management attitudes towards advertising can be seen in Table 4.6, which shows the 2016 advertising expenditure in the UK press, radio and television for the 20 airlines spending the most. Some interesting differences emerge in airline policies. Not surprisingly, the biggest spenders are the UK's own airlines focusing on their home market, and Ryanair, an Irish airline, which sees the UK as one of its two home markets. More surprisingly the largest spender overall is Jet2, a relatively small UK airline with a fleet of only 70 single-aisle jets in 2017 compared to easyJet with almost three and a half times as many. Clearly the Jet2 management has decided that high advertising is a key element of its marketing strategy. Among the biggest non-UK airline spenders one finds Emirates, Turkish, Qatar and Etihad. They need to spend more in order to attract passengers to destinations beyond their own Middle East hubs, which is a key aim of their business models.

Table 4.6 Total airline spend in UK in all media, 2016 – print, TV, radio, etc. (excluding digital display)

UK-based	Non-UK airlines	Total spend £000
Jet2 (for flights)		20,431
easyJet		15,565
British Airways		13,514
	Emirates	9,409
Ryanair (Irish)		5,940
	Turkish	3,594
Virgin		2,643
	Air France/KLM	1,862
	Norwegian	1,587
	Qatar Airways	1,514
	Etihad	1,453
	Aer Lingus	1,248
	American	1,071
	Cathay Pacific	972
	Lufthansa	957
	Singapore Airlines	517
	Air Canada	211
	United	144
	Malaysia Airlines	51
	Thai Airways	27

N.B.: Other airlines spent less than £25,000 per annum

Interestingly, the US carriers are not big spenders despite the fact that for them the London–US market must be one of their major international markets. They all have high frequencies into London, but they may feel that the bulk of their clientele is US originating and so may be less concerned about attracting UK residents. Delta appears to rely for its UK advertising on the efforts of its partner, Virgin Atlantic. These examples show that advertising spend, while it is influenced by competition, is very much at the discretion of management.

Ticketing, sales and promotion represents around 8 per cent or less of total operating costs of scheduled airlines, but becomes more significant on short-haul markets. This is clearly a major item of expenditure, yet one very much influenced by the policies adopted by individual airlines.

4.9 Financial policies

Aircraft ownership costs, that is depreciation and or lease payments and rentals, may represent up to 10 per cent of total costs. Management can influence such costs in three ways: first through the price it negotiates when buying or leasing aircraft; second through choosing the type of financing it uses to obtain the aircraft; and third by the depreciation policy it chooses to adopt.

4.9.1 Timing and size of aircraft orders

A number of variables determine the price of new or second-hand aircraft and of lease rates too. When the industry is booming financially, the demand for aircraft is high and this pushes up both prices and lease rates. The converse is true when the airline industry is in crisis. Lease rates drop as airlines terminate or fail to renew leases. Aircraft are grounded, aircraft deliveries are delayed and options cancelled. By buying or leasing when demand for new capacity is low, airlines can significantly reduce their costs of purchase or lease. Timing is all. The size of orders is also critical. An airline ordering 30 or more aircraft at a time is bound to get a better price than if ordering just a handful. This may encourage management to delay orders until they need to replace a larger part of their fleet, perhaps even two different aircraft types.

A good example of perfect timing was easyJet's order in 2002 for 120 Airbus A319s with an option for a further 120 that could be swapped for A320s or 321s. The order was placed at a time when the airline industry was in deep crisis and orders for new aircraft had slumped. It was a very large order by an airline previously flying a small but all-Boeing fleet as all low-cost carriers were at the time. Airbus was desperate to establish its aircraft in the low-cost sector. This factor, plus the timing and size of the order, meant that easyJet was able to negotiate a substantial reduction on the then list price. The reduction was reputed to be well over a third. Years later, in September 2007, British Airways placed an order for 19 Airbus A380s, of which seven were options. This was at a time when new orders for this new aircraft had slumped, because of two-year production delays. The need to revitalise its A380 order book and also to generate business from British Airways, an airline that had never ordered Airbus aircraft previously, is thought to have induced the manufacturer to sell this aircraft at as much as 50 per cent off the list price (The Times, 28 September 2007, London).

4.9.2 Methods of finance

Having decided on fleet expansion or renewal, management then has to get the finance in place. This is so even for cash-rich airlines such as Singapore Airlines or easyJet, since they are unlikely to be able or willing to finance all their purchases from cash.

Financing aircraft purchases or leases is too complex and dynamic a process to discuss in detail in the present book, yet management has a crucial role to play in deciding between leasing and purchasing the aircraft it wishes to order and also between the alternative financial models that are available for each (see Morrell, 2013).

Interest charges on loans are often considered within the airline industry as a non-operating item. As such they do not affect operating costs or the operating results. However, they do affect each airline's overall profit or loss after inclusion of interest and other non-operating items. The bulk of interest charges relate to loans raised to finance aircraft acquisitions though some airlines may also be paying interest on bank overdrafts arising from cashflow problems or from the need to finance losses incurred in previous years.

An airline can reduce or avoid interest charges by financing part or all of its aircraft purchases internally from self-generated funds. Self-financing is clearly cheaper than borrowing, especially at a time when interest charges are high. To do this, airlines must first build up their cash reserves from accumulated profits and possibly depreciation charges. But even highly profitable airlines may only be able to self-finance part of their capital expenditure. Singapore Airlines (SIA), through a policy of rapid depreciation and as a result of its relatively high profits, has been able to build up substantial reserves. Yet even SIA has been no more than 70 per cent self-financing in most years. There are few airlines in as favourable a position as SIA. Most are dependent on external sources of finance.

Airlines would prefer to be self-financing but may be unable to generate sufficient reserves from their depreciation charges and retained profits to do so except to a limited extent. Their remaining capital requirements can be met in one of two ways. First, there may be an injection of equity capital into the airline. The advantage of equity finance is that airlines only pay interest on it in the form of dividends if they make a profit. Many of the international airlines outside the United States are partly or totally government-owned, but governments have been loath to put in more capital to finance aircraft purchases, especially as the sums involved are very large. This is one of the reasons that has been pushing governments to partially or fully privatise their airlines. By injecting some of the funds raised through the privatisation back into the airlines concerned, the latter's debts and finance charges could be reduced.

If equity finance is unavailable, airlines must borrow in one form or another. Several different forms of loan finance are available, but either directly or indirectly they all involve interest charges. This is true even of finance or operating leases. In the past, the traditional reliance of state-owned airlines on external loan finance rather than self-financing or equity capital pushed them into having very high debt:equity ratios. In other words, too many of their investment requirements were financed by loan capital and too few by equity. Many airlines have been under-capitalised and have needed an injection of capital if the interest burden was to be kept within manageable proportions, and if they were to be in a position to order new aircraft without bankrupting themselves. It is generally believed that a debt:equity ratio of 25:75 is desirable and that a ratio of up to 50:50 is acceptable. Given the very high cost of new aircraft, airlines can only stay within acceptable limits by injections of new capital.

As previously mentioned, an alternative solution for airlines with inadequate financial resources is to lease aircraft from specialist aircraft leasing companies, such as GECAS, AerCap or smaller companies such as Orix, or from finance houses that provide the same facility. During the last 20 years there has been a marked trend towards greater use of leasing among all airlines including the largest. This solution is particularly attractive for airlines that are too small to obtain the best prices from the manufacturers or airlines that are not themselves in a position to get any tax advantages from direct purchase. The leasing companies, by doing both, can provide aircraft which in theory may be cheaper in real terms. But timing is critical here too. Lease rates inevitably rise when the demand for additional aircraft capacity outstrips the supply of available aircraft.

Large airlines placing large aircraft orders may obtain such high discounts that purchase may prove cheaper than leasing. But leasing may offer other advantages, especially in terms of flexibility, which may still make it attractive despite being more costly.

4.9.3 Depreciation policy

The hourly depreciation cost of an aircraft (as discussed in Section 3.3) depends on the length of the depreciation period, the assumed residual value of the aircraft at the end of that period and the annual utilisation of the aircraft. The annual utilisation, that is, the block-hours flown during the year, is dependent on the pattern of operations, on the stage lengths flown and on the scheduling efficiency of an airline's management. The depreciation period adopted and the residual value assumed are determined by an airline's financial policy. In many countries legislation or accounting convention may require the adoption of a particular depreciation policy or may impose certain minimum requirements. Most international airlines, however, have some flexibility in deciding on the effective commercial life of their aircraft and their residual value at the end of that life. This flexibility is important. If an airline adopts the practice of depreciating its aircraft over 20 years to a 10 per cent residual value, its hourly depreciation costs (assuming the same annual utilisation) will be 32 per cent less than they would have been had it used a 12-year life for the aircraft with a 20 per cent residual value.

Both these depreciation policies are currently in use by different airlines and they show the significant variations in depreciation costs that can result from the adoption of different policies. Since, for some airlines, depreciation charges may represent around 8 to 10 per cent of their total operating costs, then the depreciation policy adopted can influence total costs by as much as 3 per cent.

Many airlines change their depreciation policy in order to increase or reduce their costs. Depreciation periods are frequently lengthened or residual values increased in periods of falling profitability in order to reduce costs and improve financial results. It is less usual for depreciation periods to be shortened when times are good. It was mentioned earlier how in the financial year 2014, Lufthansa significantly lengthened its depreciation period and thereby added US$452 million to its profits (Chapter 3).

Singapore Airlines (SIA) provides a good example of changing depreciation policies. In the 1980s it used very rapid depreciation of eight years. Then in April 1989 SIA again lengthened its depreciation period to 10 years with 20 per cent residual value so as to be more in line with industry practice. SIA's rapid depreciation was also linked to its policy of rapid fleet renewal and the investment allowances available in Singapore that could be used to offset taxation. As the crisis of 2001 began to bite into airline profits, SIA announced that it would once again change its depreciation to bring it in line with industry practice. For the financial year 2001–2 it stretched its depreciation period from 10 to 15 years and halved the residual value from 20 to 10 per cent. These changes reduced its depreciation cost for the year by US$151 million! By 2016 SIA had again changed its depreciation policy for its passenger aircraft; using straight-line depreciation over 15–20 years to 5–10 per cent residual value. For its freighters the residual value used was 5 per cent.

An additional problem when considering depreciation costs is how to treat aircraft that have been leased rather than purchased since legally the airline is not the owner. One approach is to differentiate between *finance lease agreements* that give the airline rights approximating to ownership, often involving the transfer of ownership at the end of the lease period, and so-called *operating leases* that do not give such rights and are usually of shorter duration. In the case of finance leases the aircraft can be depreciated in the normal way so that its depreciation cost appears under the airline's direct operating costs in the profit and loss account. However, while the interest element included in the lease payment is added to the other finance charges in the airline's accounts, the capital repayment element is not charged to the profit and loss account but is shown only as a liability. This is to avoid double counting since the capital cost of the asset is already covered by a depreciation charge. The lease payment covers the aircraft's depreciation cost already. Conversely, annual lease payments on operating leases would appear as a flight operating cost and there would be no separate depreciation charge. This is the approach adopted by Singapore Airlines. It follows that the type of aircraft leases that an airline negotiates will affect the absolute and relative level of its depreciation costs.

4.10 Corporate strategy

An airline's corporate strategy and objectives are likely to have major impact on its cost structure and cost levels. It is self-evident that an international airline that sees its mission as being to operate low-cost no-frills services will have lower costs than a conventional scheduled network carrier. Costs will differ because they are engaged in different business models.

A key strategic decision is the degree to which an airline focuses on the carriage of freight as well as on the passenger business. On average, IATA's scheduled airlines generate around one quarter of their total traffic, domestic plus international, from the carriage of freight (Table 1.2 in Chapter 1). Yet several airlines, as part of their corporate strategy, are much more heavily involved in freight. In 2016, 53 per cent of Korean Air's revenue tonne-kms was generated from freight. The comparable figures for other airlines whose corporate strategy was to place particular emphasis on the development of air freight were as follows: Cathay Pacific 48 per cent, Qatar Airways 42 per cent and Singapore Airlines 43 per cent. On the other hand, US carriers have more or less given up the carriage of freight as anything other than fill-up on their passenger services, especially on domestic flights, and even here they have been outsold by the integrators such as FedEx and UPS. As a result, freight is of little importance. For both American and United, in 2016 freight represented 10 per cent of total traffic carried, and for Delta only 9 per cent. Since the costs of carrying freight are significantly lower than those of carrying an equivalent amount of passengers then those airlines that focus on freight will have lower over-all unit costs.

Another strategic issue is whether an airline sets out to be a major network operator or whether it sees its role as being that of a more restricted 'niche' carrier. The 'niche' may be geographical in scope or it may be a particular type of operation such as providing feeder services into a network carrier's hub. The 'niche' carrier may be able to reduce its costs through greater specialisation. For instance, it may operate only one type of aircraft and it may also be able to increase flight crew and staff productivity through the simple pattern of its operations. Airlines that try to be all things to all men and serve every possible market end up with very mixed fleets of aircraft and pilots, complex maintenance arrangements and large over-staffed head and regional offices. Inevitably their costs are pushed up.

Airlines with domestic networks in countries where there is only one major national carrier often find that their corporate mission is heavily influenced by government policies. This is particularly so if they are government owned. Such airlines may be required to provide domestic air links whose primary objective may be the social and economic cohesion of the country or the stimulation of domestic tourism rather than the provision of commercially justified and financially self-supporting air services. Services provided with social objectives in mind are usually on thin routes, with small aircraft and often at frequencies that are too high in relation to the demand. Malaysia Airlines and Air Algerie are among the many airlines whose corporative objectives have traditionally included the provision of services to isolated and small domestic communities. By their very nature such services are inherently high cost. Since in many cases the governments that expected this of their airlines also held back increases in domestic air fares, such social services became a constant financial haemorrhage on the airlines concerned.

Airlines, like most business enterprises, will normally have several, sometimes mutually conflicting, corporate objectives. Invariably operating profitably is one of the objectives. But the key question is the degree to which profitability is pursued as the prime and key corporate objective. If it is, then airline managers will be under pressure to do all they can to reduce costs. This is the case with most privatised airlines or airlines which, though not fully privatised, such as Singapore Airlines, are nevertheless operated as fully commercial enterprises. Many government-owned airlines are expected to operate profitably. But this objective is often lost and blunted among a whole series of other corporate objectives often imposed by the government as the major or only shareholder. When profit is not clearly the prime corporate objective, then costs are likely to creep up as other objectives are pursued.

4.11 The quality of management

The analysis so far indicates that the most important variables affecting airline costs are the level of input prices, including the cost of labour, the type and size of aircraft used and the stage lengths over which these aircraft are operated. Insofar as the last two of these variables are themselves influenced by the pattern and levels of demand that an airline is trying to satisfy, then demand may also be considered an important variable. Other, though less important, variables have also been discussed. Many of the latter are particularly prone to management decision and choice. There is a further dimension of management whose importance may be absolutely crucial in establishing an airline's unit cost levels, but may be difficult to define or measure. One might broadly define it as the quality of management and it permeates through to most areas of an airline's activities.

The quality of management affects the efficiency with which the management of an airline brings together the various factors of production at its disposal in order to meet different levels and types of demand in different markets. In theory it is management's ability or the lack of it that should explain cost differences between airlines that cannot be attributed to variations in input costs, aircraft types operated, stage lengths or any of the other cost variables.

In practice no airline management is likely to be equally efficient or inefficient in all areas of management. It may well be efficient in one area, such as flight crew scheduling, but relatively inefficient in the organisation of maintenance procedures. Thus, the total unit cost of an airline may mask wide variations of performance in discrete areas of activity such as flight operations or maintenance management. Ideally, inter-airline cost comparisons should be on a disaggregate basis, looking at such discrete areas separately.

5 The economics of the low-cost model

It's the easiest thing in the world to offer low fares. The hard thing is how to make money with low fares.

(Greg Saretsky, President and CEO, WestJet, May 2017)

5.1 Emergence of low-cost airlines

In the three or four years following 2000, traffic growth in many airline markets slowed down or collapsed while yields continued to fall. It was a turbulent time for the airline industry. It was not until 2005 or 2006 that the industry as a whole began to look healthy again, and then another period of instability followed the financial crisis of 2008–9. Yet throughout both periods Southwest, the largest so-called low-cost carrier (LCC) in the United States, together with Ryanair and easyJet, Europe's largest low-cost airlines, continued to grow rapidly and profitably, as did AirAsia in Malaysia.

The low-cost no-frills airline business model is a relatively recent phenomenon whose emergence is linked directly to the spread of deregulation at first domestically in the United States and later in particular international markets.

The international airlines that grew in the decades up to the 1980s were essentially 'network' carriers. They operated radial networks centred on their main base or hub. If a national flag carrier they generally operated from one and occasionally two hubs. The major US carriers had secondary hubs as well. The international networks of the national flag carriers were relatively simple, with out and back routes radiating from their hubs. They were simple because of the constraints imposed by the bilateral regulatory regime (Chapter 2). The US majors operated hubs at their US international gateway airports but also had much more complex interconnected domestic route networks through domestic hubs. A key aim of all these network carriers was to attract traffic by providing a wide range of possible destinations and linkages. They did this by offering transfer connections at their hubs for passengers wishing to fly between points that were not served by direct flights or could not be served because of the restricted air services agreements. In order to maximise the opportunities for such connections, network airlines were forced to adopt complex and costly schedules and operating practices. Competition also drove them to provide a wide range of services and products on the ground and in the air, such as in-flight meals, airport VIP lounges and so on. Hence, network airlines are also referred to as legacy or full-service carriers. (More on hubbing in Section 10.7, Chapter 10.)

The characteristics of the traditional network model made it inherently costly and ensured that passenger fares were relatively high. In response, two other airline business models have emerged whose prime focus has been to offer lower fares. The older of the two models is that of the *charter or non-scheduled* leisure airline. Such airlines expanded rapidly in the 1960s and 1970s, especially on European holiday routes and on the North Atlantic, and spread later to a few other markets such as that between North America and the Caribbean. Their impact elsewhere in the world was very limited. Their early success arose from the fact that in certain markets they were less strictly regulated than scheduled services (Chapter 6). For the most part they catered for so-called package holidays. The charter airlines sold their seats to travel companies, who combined them together with hotel rooms or car hire and sold them to travellers as complete packages.

The second and more recent airline model is that of *low-cost no-frills* airlines also referred to as budget airlines. These have a different product and market strategy from the earlier charter carriers, but their focus is the same: to offer low-priced air travel by cutting out the costly frills offered by the network airlines. Their emergence is closely linked to the gradual liberalisation of domestic and later international regulations affecting the airline industry.

It was progressive deregulation of domestic and later international air services that offered carriers and entrepreneurs the opportunity to try out more innovative business models. One of the first to do this was Southwest Airlines. Launching services in 1971, it had operated purely within the state of Texas on short sectors offering low unrestricted fares, high point-to-point frequencies and excellent on-time performance. The essence of the model was simplicity. A simple product and simple operations. It worked. Southwest diverted passengers from other carriers and also generated new traffic by attracting travellers off the roads. It was the simplicity of the product and operating model that enabled Southwest to operate at much lower unit costs, which, in turn, meant it could offer much lower fares and use these to stimulate demand. When US deregulation came in 1978 Southwest was well placed to export its low-cost model beyond Texas. It did this slowly, focusing initially on its traditional south-western and West Coast markets. It was only in the 1990s that it expanded beyond the sun belt. Other US airlines adopted a low-cost no-frills strategy but only a few survived. The peak of low-cost new entry was between 1993 and 1999 when 12 new low-cost carriers were launched. Only three of that group survived to 2018, namely Frontier, Allegiant and JetBlue.

In Europe, the emergence of the low-cost model was dependent on the liberalisation of intra-European air services. This came with the 'Third Package' of aviation measures that came into force in January 1993. Though Ryanair had launched low-cost services between the UK and Ireland in 1992 it was not until after 1995 that Ryanair and new start-ups easyJet, Debonair, Go and Buzz launched intra-European low-cost services, which grew rapidly. Most of these early European low-cost carriers did not survive. The two that have, Ryanair and easyJet, have continued to grow very rapidly and very profitably. Being first in the field they have benefited from what economists call first mover advantage, becoming well-known brands throughout Europe. The success of Ryanair and easyJet in turn encouraged others to launch low-cost airlines in Europe. While most did not survive, some did. By 2018 Vueling, Wizz and Norwegian were also significant low-cost operators.

A crucial difference in the operations of the two models in Europe is that the network airlines base virtually all their aircraft and crews in their home country, most of them in their major base, usually the capital city, and operate a radial network. A few, such as Lufthansa or SAS, may have a second large hub. Flights radiate from their hub(s) and then back to the major hub(s).

The European LCCs operate a matrix of services; while they have one or more major bases in their home country, they have also established numerous bases with aircraft and local crews throughout Europe. Ryanair has over 30 bases in Europe, apart from its major bases in Dublin and the UK, though some have only one or two aircraft based there, with associated crews.

easyJet has fewer bases outside the UK but its largest at Milan-Malpensa in northern Italy has over 25 based aircraft with Italian pilots and cabin attendants. All this was made possible by the deregulation of air services in the European Union in 1993. This enabled EU airlines to set up bases and operations in any other EU state. The LCCs do this and can operate a matrix of services criss-crossing Europe. The network airlines have failed to do so and instead have focused on defending their home hubs with their radial short-haul services feeding their long-haul flights.

In other parts of the world the emergence of low-cost airlines was also directly linked to the progressive liberalisation of the domestic and international regulations which had hitherto constrained airline management. Thus, in the Asia-Pacific region five low-cost airlines were operating by 2001 but with purely domestic services. As governments slowly relaxed their domestic regulations and also their bilateral air services agreements many LCCs were launched in Asia and elsewhere too.

By 2018 there were over 50 low-cost carriers operating in the Asia-Pacific region, the largest being AirAsia in Malaysia and Lion Air in Indonesia. The Asian legacy carriers appreciated the potential impact of LCCs more quickly than their European counterparts and virtually all of them launched their own low-cost subsidiaries. Some, such as Singapore Airlines (SIA), Thai Airways and All Nippon Airways, actually had two such subsidiaries. In 2017 SIA merged its own two LCCs into a single carrier called Scoot. Thus, in Asia, the larger legacy airlines operate with a twin brand model – traditional and low-cost. The European airlines, with the exception of British Airways, have been slower to fully adopt this model. Lufthansa and Air France/KLM have operated small LCC subsidiaries for some years, but it was only after about 2012 that they accepted that to fight back against market erosion to Ryanair, easyJet and the other LCCs they would need to really expand and develop their own LCC subsidiaries; that is Eurowings (Lufthansa) and Transavia (Air France).

In Asia, liberalisation has not gone as far as in Europe. To bypass the nationality clauses, in the bilateral air services agreements, the larger ASEAN region LCCs set up subsidiary companies, in other countries, in which they had less than 50 per cent shareholdings but maintained effective control. This enabled them to operate matrix-type networks similar to those of the European LCCs. Thus, the Malaysian low-cost carrier AirAsia has almost ten partner subsidiaries or affiliates based in different Asian countries including Thai AirAsia, AirAsia India, Indonesia AirAsia and AirAsia Japan.

5.2 The essence of the low-cost model

The essence of the low-cost business model is twofold. First, 'keep it simple' by providing a simple no-frills product or service based on simple operations and a simple point-to-point network and thereby minimise costs. Second, 'create demand', which means do not try merely to satisfy an existing passenger demand but set out to generate and stimulate new demand both by offering very low fares and flying to and between destinations or airports not previously served.

The aim of the Southwest Airlines business model was to offer a simple, uncluttered, low-fare, point-to-point product using a single-type aircraft fleet, while achieving very high aircraft and crew utilisation by operating from secondary and uncongested airports. Ryanair, easyJet and the other low-cost airlines adopted the Southwest model, but each modified it to a lesser or greater extent to suit their own marketing needs. For example, unlike Southwest or Ryanair, easyJet from its very inception in 1995 ignored sales through travel agents and focused on 100 per cent direct sales, initially through its own telephone call centre and then increasingly through its own website. Others later followed.

The essential features of the European low-cost model are summarised in Table 5.1. Despite individual variations, low-cost airlines in other parts of the world have generally adopted most of these features, in some form or another, into their own operations. It is by adopting these features that low-cost carriers can achieve unit operating costs per seat-km that are 30 to 60 per cent lower than those of network carriers flying on the same or similar routes with similar aircraft. In the 20 years or so since the low-cost revolution began in Europe, network full-service carriers have adopted some of the low-cot features but, as is argued later, a marked unit cost difference still exists between the two models.

Table 5.1 Characteristics of the low-cost model in Europe

	Simple operations
Network	Point-to-point
	No hubbing or transfers – pax can self-connect
	Short sectors – mainly 500–1,000 kms. Maximum five hours
	No night stops
Aircraft	Single-type large fleet – maximum two types
	High daily utilisation (target 11 hrs/day on short haul)
Airports	Uncongested with capacity to grow
	Secondary or regional preferred
	Fast turn-rounds
	Outsource ground-handling
Staff	Younger, newer staff costing less
	Flexible conditions. High productivity
	Simple product
Fares	Low, simple, one way – minimal restrictions
	Unbundled – extras must be paid for
	Fares rise as departure date approaches
	No frequent flyer programme
In-flight	Single-class cabin
	High-density seating
	No free assigned seating – must be paid for
	No meals or free drinks
Distribution	Aim 100 per cent direct (online or call centre)
	No or minimal sales via travel agencies
	GDS only if no commission to be paid
	Ticket-less – no paper tickets
Cargo	None

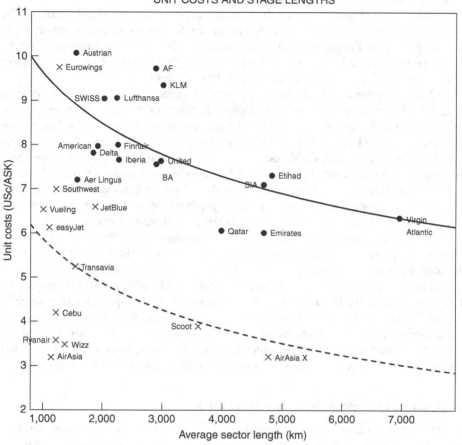

Figure 5.1 Unit costs – sample of low-cost and network airlines compared, 2016

Low-cost: X

Network airlines: •

Source: *Aviation Strategy*, December 2017

The wide unit cost differences between the two business models, the network or hub model and the point-to-point low-cost model, are quite dramatic, as can be seen in Figure 5.1. In 2016 the lowest-cost LCCs in Europe were Ryanair and Wizz with unit costs per available seat-km of US cents 3–3.50. These were 50 to 70 per cent lower than the unit costs of legacy or full-service European network carriers with broadly similar average trip length such as Austrian or Aer Lingus. easyJet's cost were about double those of Ryanair and Wizz but still 30 to 40 per cent lower than those of comparable legacy airlines.

In Asia, too, one finds that the larger and more successful LCCs, notably AirAsia, have unit costs 40 to 50 per cent lower than those of full-service airlines operating with broadly similar average stage or sector lengths. In 2016 AirAsia's cost per available seat-mile was US cents 3.15. Its main competitor, Malaysia Airlines, had a unit cost of US cents 6.81 or more than twice as high, despite operating average sector distances over 400 km longer than those of Air Asia, which should have helped reduce its unit costs.

It is noticeable (Figure 5.1) that the cost gap between Southwest, the first and by far the largest US low-cost airline, and the big three US network carriers is much narrower than is the case in Europe or Asia. Over time, Southwest's costs have risen, while the three majors were able to reduce their costs by going into Chapter 11 bankruptcy procedures. All three did this in the period 2002 to 2011.

In 2017, Southwest's unit costs per available-mile on its single-aisle fleet were marginally lower than those of the single-aisle fleets of the three majors, American, Delta and United, even though the latter benefited from average sector lengths 150 to 450 miles longer (Table 5.2 shows unit costs for single-aisle fleets). But the younger, ultra-low-cost carriers (ULCCs), especially Spirit and Frontier, show a more dramatic cost gap with the network legacies. Both had average unit costs per available seat-mile in 2017 that were 26 to 29 per cent lower than those of United Airlines, the lowest-cost operator among the legacies. The cost gap with other legacies was even greater. They also had significantly lower unit costs than Southwest (Table 5.2).

Table 5.2 compares average costs for the total single-aisle fleets of each carrier. To mitigate the possible cost impact of the very mixed fleets and different average sectors operated by the US network airlines, Table 5.3 compares network and LCC unit operating costs for just one aircraft type, the Boeing 737-800, in 2017. From Table 5.3 it is evident that the block-hour cost of Southwest when operating this aircraft was around 25 per cent lower than the block-hour costs of the three major network airlines when flying the same aircraft. Again, this was so despite the fact that the latter were flying their Boeing 737-800s on somewhat longer sectors, which should have helped reduce their costs. None of the ultra-low-cost airlines operated this aircraft.

5.3 Cost advantage of low–cost operators

It is evident that many low-cost airlines around the world achieve unit operating costs substantially lower than those of the traditional network-based airlines. Their cost advantages stem from the characteristics of the low-cost model as summarised in

Table 5.2 Average unit costs on single-aisle fleets of US legacy network and low-cost airlines, 2017 Annual 2017

	Cost per available seat-mile (US cents)	Average flight stage (miles)
Delta	6.90	894
American	6.74	1,042
United	6.29	1,217
Southwest (LCC)	6.18	754
Allegiant (ULCC)	5.99	893
Spirit (ULCC)	4.64	1,006
Frontier (ULCC)	4.44	1,106

Data is for total operations, domestic plus international, with single-aisle aircraft. 2. 'Operating' costs only (i.e. fuel, flight crew, maintenance, aircraft depreciation and rentals)
Source: Airline Monitor (August 2018) ESG Aviation Services. Ponte Vedra Beach, Florida

Table 5.3 US legacy network and low-cost block-hour costs compared – Boeing 737-800 in 2017

	Cost per block-hour US$	*Average sector miles*
Delta	4,084	1,292
United	4,007	1,200
American	3,921	1,085
Southwest (LCC)	3,025	1,038

'Operating' costs only (i.e. fuel, flight crew, maintenance, aircraft depreciation and rentals)
Source: *Airline Monitor* (August 2018) ESG Aviation Services. Ponte Vedra Beach, Florida

Table 5.1. Different LCCs all operate somewhat different models and, as a result, the ways in which they achieve their lower costs may vary, but an examination of European airline operations can identify where LCCs are most likely to achieve cost economies.

Direct operating costs are all those costs dependent on the type of aircraft being flown. The LCCs may enjoy marked cost advantages in four areas.

First, *flight and cabin crew* costs may be lower for LCCs because they may offer lower salaries or use fewer cabin crew and/or obtain higher productivity from their employees. For example, in 2015 a British Airways cabin attendant earned, on average, £37,200 per year compared to an attendant with easyJet who earned £21,800. At Monarch, another LCC then operating, their salary would be even less at £16,500. By offering only a one-class cabin, LCCs may be able to keep cabin crew numbers to the minimum required by the safety regulations. A full-service carrier may have one or two attendants above the safety minimum to cater for passengers in a First or Business class compartment and to serve in-flight catering, if any, sufficiently quickly in the Economy cabin. Pilots may also be paid less. For example, the starting salary in 2015 for a new captain at Lufthansa was €135,000 and for a new co-pilot it was €65,000. But at Eurowings, Lufthansa's low-cost subsidiary, their starting rates would have been only €78,000 and €44,000, substantially lower (Der Spiegel, 2015).

LCCs may also use their pilots and cabin attendants more efficiently, thereby increasing their productivity and reducing their costs per available seat-km. They can do this because they may have more flexible terms and conditions of employment with their staff than the older network airlines, who may still have out-dated work practices. Second, their operating model based on point-to-point services flown by a single aircraft type makes it easier to roster both flights and cabin crew to fly as close as possible to the maximum permitted monthly or annual hours. This is also made easier by the faster turn-rounds at airports and by the avoidance of night stops.

Network airlines, such as British Airways or Air France, invariably night stop their last short-haul evening flights out of their base at their destination since they need, for competitive reasons, an early morning return flight. This means lower crew productivity and additional hotel costs. While British Airways, for example, night stops a flight and its crew in Milan to get an early morning departure to London to cater for business travellers, easyJet does not need to do this since it has aircraft based permanently in Milan, which is one of its many European bases.

The second area where there may be a significant saving is in airport charges, that is *aircraft landing fees and passenger-related charges*. easyJet's airport charges per seat-km on short-haul European sector out of London are likely to be lower than those of British

Airways because it may be flying from a London airport, Gatwick, Luton or Stansted, where airport charges are lower than at Heathrow, which is British Airways' major home base. At the European end of the route, easyJet may be using a smaller and cheaper secondary airport or regional airports where it has negotiated special reduced charges.

Ryanair, by focusing much of its network on small secondary and little-used airports, many of which were desperate to attract a new airline, has made even greater savings in this area. For Ryanair airport charges per passenger have often been well below those of easyJet. In addition, Ryanair was able to persuade airports with little or no international services previously to contribute to its own costs. The airline argued that its air services to these small airports helped stimulate the local economy. This justified subsidising Ryanair's new services. An example was the airport of Verona in northern Italy. Under a five-year contract starting in 2010, Ryanair was paid €17.50 per departing passenger by the airport authority. In addition, the handling fee it should have paid per departing passenger was reduced from about €5 to €1. Following complaints to the European Commission, the airport cancelled the deal and Ryanair pulled out of Verona in September 2012, but similar kinds of deals were made with several smaller airports around Europe. Since on short-haul sectors in Europe, airport charges will normally represent 10 to 20 per cent or more of total costs, savings on such charges may impact significantly on overall costs. This is certainly an area where Ryanair enjoys a major cost advantage.

In the early days of the low-cost revolution it was easier for European LCCs to negotiate good five-to ten-year deals with airports eager to attract them. This has become increasingly difficult, especially when flying into larger established airports, except where the LCCs can use cheaper terminals. The European Commission also considers such deals as distorting competition. The degree to which LCCs can serve their target markets by flying to secondary or ex-military airfields will largely determine the cost advantage they can obtain in this area.

In March 2018, Benyamin Ismail, Chief Executive of Air Asia, stated that his airline was targeting a 40–50 per cent saving on airport charges by moving flights to smaller airports such as Avalon to serve Melbourne, Australia, instead of the main airport of Tullamarine.

The third direct operating cost where LCCs can achieve some cost saving is *maintenance cost*. This may be due to three factors: first, through operating newer, younger aircraft, which are cheaper to maintain. Rapid growth and high profits make it easier to invest in a young fleet. In 2017 the average age of easyJet or Ryanair aircraft was just over seven years and for Wizz it was less than five years. For most network airlines' short-haul fleets, however, their average age was over ten years and they operated some quite old aircraft. Second, as a result of the decision by many low-cost carriers to get the lowest possible costs by outsourcing most of their maintenance requirements, in some cases even their line maintenance, they have no top-heavy maintenance administration or costly hangars and maintenance facilities of their own. Finally, low-cost carriers can keep their facilities and spare parts costs to a minimum by operating a single aircraft type or if they operate a second type ensuring that they have sufficiently large numbers of each type to obtain scale economies and as much commonality of parts and systems between the two types as possible.

In summer 2017, easyJet operated 254 aircraft on its domestic and intra-European services. All were of the Airbus 320 family, that is A319, A320 and two A320neos with much commonality between them. Air France, competing with easyJet both domestically in France and on short-haul European services from France, had a very mixed fleet. The main Air France airline operated 123 Airbus, A320 family aircraft. However, HOP, its regional airline, operated a variety of aircraft: ATR 42s and 72s; Bombardier CRJ700 and 1000; and a range of Embraers – 145s, 175s and 190s. But Air France's low-cost subsidiary Transavia flew 29 Boeing 737-800s. Operating such a widely mixed fleet, with some types in relatively small fleet sizes, must have made it very difficult to match easyJet's low maintenance costs. Similarly, in the United States in 2017, Delta's large fleet of 800 or so single-aisle aircraft was made up of five very different types: Boeing 717s, Boeing 737s, the relatively old Boeing 757s, Airbus A320 family aircraft and another old type, the MD80s and 90s. In contrast LCC Southwest operated around 700 aircraft but they were all versions of the Boeing 737. Of these, 474 were Boeing 737-700s.

As a result of all these factors, in the 12 months to September 2017, easyJet, Europe's second largest LCC, faced maintenance and repair costs of euro cents 0.32 per ASK whereas for British Airways and Lufthansa maintenance costs came to 0.60 and 1.40 cents respectively (Ainley, 2018).

The fourth area of direct costs where LCCs may be able to achieve some savings is that of *depreciation and leases or rentals*. If they can achieve higher annual utilisation, that is total block-hours, with their aircraft they can reduce their unit costs. This is because depreciation and leases are fixed annual costs. So as annual utilisation increases the fixed cost is spread over more hours and the cost per hour and per available seat-km goes down (see Section 3.3). In the busy summer quarter of July to September 2017, British Airways was getting only 9.6 hours per day out of its Airbus A320 aircraft, while easyJet's A320s were averaging 12 hours each day. Put another way, five easyJet A320s were doing the work of six A320s operated by BA. By using its aircraft more intensively easyJet would have been able to both reduce their hourly depreciation costs and to buy or lease fewer aircraft to meet its market needs. Other European network carriers would also have achieved lower daily utilisation on their short-haul aircraft than easyJet or Ryanair.

There are two distinct categories of direct costs in which LCCs are unlikely to enjoy any marked cost advantages, namely fuel and en-route navigation charges. *Fuel* is a major cost item and for most short-haul airlines it is the single largest input cost. But airlines pay very similar prices for aviation fuel. Though larger airlines may be able to negotiate marginally lower rates because of the larger volumes uplifted, the price differences are small. There are marked variations in fuel prices between airports, so where airlines fly from or to will influence their cost of fuel, but within Europe differences will be limited.

While not being perhaps able to buy fuel more cheaply LCCs may benefit from lower fuel consumption. First, LCCs can obtain a marginally lower fuel cost per seat-km by operating newer aircraft with more fuel-efficient engines. Being younger airlines, they tend to buy and operate newer aircraft. Second, LCCs fly many of their services to smaller and less congested airports where long taxiing times on the ground or long holding patterns in the air may be rare so minimising fuel burnt. Network airlines operating on parallel routes may be flying from large hubs where congestion on the ground and in the air may be frequent, thereby pushing up fuel consumption.

The other cost area that offers no scope for savings is *en-route navigation charges*. This is because en-route charges for using air navigation facilities are non-negotiable. All airlines on a route flying the same aircraft will pay similar charges. *Insurance costs* are another item that cannot be reduced significantly by LCCs. All they can achieve is marginal reductions through higher aircraft utilisation.

While savings in *direct operating costs* may be important, LCCs achieved their most dramatic savings vis-a-vis traditional network carriers in most categories of *indirect operating costs*. But these are also the cost areas in which some legacy airlines have been able to fight back, in recent years, by learning from the LCCs.

Low-cost operators' reductions in indirect operating costs arise primarily in handling-and marketing-related costs. A significant saving can be achieved in so-called *station and ground-handling costs*, that is the costs associated with providing ground staff, check-in staff, equipment, business lounges, office space and related facilities at each of the airports served by an airline. While conventional airlines maintain significant numbers of staff and equipment and may rent considerable space for business lounges and offices, especially at their base and larger airport(s), low-cost carriers do away with much of this expenditure by outsourcing most of their passenger and aircraft handling and maintaining only very minimal numbers of their own staff. Since they have few or no online or interline connecting passengers or baggage, they do not need significant staff numbers or facilities for such handling. Nor do they have to handle freight, since most LCCs do not carry freight; and, of course, they do not require business lounges at all. In Europe, LCCs outsource the ground-handling wherever they can, and this enables them to further reduce costs through competitive bidding.

Another area of cost saving is in aircraft cleaning. Legacy network carriers in most cases have their own sub-contracted ground staff who clean the interior of the aircraft during each turn-round. This in itself lengthens the turn-round time. LCCs ask their cabin crew to clean up the interior towards the end of each flight, by collecting all rubbish from passengers, and then just tidying the cabin as passengers disembark. All this is made easier because there is no free in-flight catering. Where they need to rent space for check-in desks, offices, etc., LCCs negotiate very low rentals or at small secondary airports they may pay no rent at all. Wherever they can, they minimise the space they require in the knowledge that their passengers will accept some degree of discomfort, for instance longer check-in queues, in exchange for the low fares. As Southwest does in the United States, they argue that their entry onto a route generates so much new traffic that smaller airports have much to gain by offering them free or very cheap space.

Another area of major indirect cost savings for low-cost carriers is that of *passenger services,* which include the cost of meals, drinks and other services furnished to passengers as part of the trip experience as well as meals or accommodation for transit or delayed passengers. Since airlines such as easyJet or Ryanair do not offer any free meals or drinks on board, but only a trolley from which passengers can buy drinks or light snacks, their passenger service costs are negligible. In fact, they aim to generate additional ancillary revenue and profit from on-board food sales. Also, since they offer only point-to-point services, they do not have to cater for transfer or transit passengers or their baggage, or for connecting passengers who have missed their flight. If flights are cancelled, they may not be prepared to meet the high cost of putting passengers on other airlines' flights but will rebook them on their own flights on subsequent days. Passenger service costs are not a major item, but they are a cost LCCs can reduce very significantly.

Ticketing, sales and promotion, which basically represent the costs of distribution, is the cost area where historically LCCs have made the most significant savings both in absolute and relative terms. They have done this by being the first to introduce innovative distribution processes based on disintermediation. Disintermediation meant cutting out all intermediaries in the sales process between the low-cost airline and its customers, thereby saving all commissions and fees legacy carriers were having to pay. easyJet was the pioneer. From its launch in 1995, it was the first airline both to cut out travel agents altogether and to sell 100 per cent direct, by-passing the global distribution systems (GDS). In this way, it saved all commissions to travel agents and GDS. In 2014 British Airways' commissions paid for ticket sales by others amounted to 3.4 per cent of its total costs; easyJet had no such costs. LCCs also save money by not setting up their own retail sales offices in expensive high street locations in the towns they serve. easyJet was first in Europe to introduce internet selling direct on its own website, and by 2010 all sales were on the internet. Other LCCs such as Ryanair or Southwest did not initially focus on 100 per cent direct selling. They used travel agents, but they quickly began to follow easyJet and focused increasingly on direct sales through the internet.

At the end of 2007, easyJet allowed its seat inventory to be accessed for the first time through two of the GDSs. In this it was following the example of JetBlue in the US, which claimed at that time that its average fare sold on the GDS was $35 higher than fares sold direct by the airline. easyJet also wanted to target corporate business passengers, who are very dependent on business travel agents. But the deal made with Travelport and Amadeus did not involve any costs to easyJet. The GDS fees would be borne by the agent or the passenger. This was a breakthrough on GDS service fees and other LCCs followed.

Low-cost airlines, by focusing on direct selling and on simplifying the whole process of reservation, pricing and ticketing, enjoy substantial savings in their costs of distribution. But the gap between the low-cost and network airlines in this area is being reduced as the latter have increasingly adopted some of the former's practices such as direct on-line selling and 100 per cent e-ticketing.

Finally, by their very nature low-cost carriers are likely to have a smaller, tighter central administration partly because they outsource many activities and partly because, as new or relatively new businesses, they do not carry any of the administrative accretions that old established conventional airlines are burdened with. For instance, they do not have large numbers of planning and other staff dealing with IATA issues or bilateral air services negotiations. Their small size and flexible staff also mean that in many areas one person will be undertaking two or three functions that in a conventional airline may require two or three separate people or even departments. Low-cost carriers would expect to achieve administrative costs per seat-km half or less than those of their conventional competitors. In the search for lower costs, low-cost airlines can operate more or less as virtual airlines outsourcing many of the non-core functions to the cheapest suppliers.

This analysis identifies the cost categories where low-cost airlines have been able to make savings because of the nature of their business model. The many LCCs around the world have adapted the basic no-frills point-to-point model in their own way to meet the needs of their particular markets. As a result, the areas in which they make their most savings will differ. Nevertheless, LCCs in most short-haul markets are able to operate *aircraft trip* costs 20–50 per cent below those of network carriers when using the same aircraft. In the United States such a cost gap is only achieved by the so-called ultra-low-cost carriers, Spirit, Allegiant and Frontier (Table 5.2).

5.4 More seats and higher aircraft utilisation

The previous discussion identified areas where low-cost airlines can reduce their costs so as to cut the block-hour or aircraft trip costs when flying the same aircraft as network carriers on short- to medium-haul routes. The lower block-hour costs of the low-cost model stem from the simplicity of the product offered to passengers and from the simplicity of the operations required to generate the product.

There are two further features of the low-cost model that enable low-cost airlines to transform their low hourly costs into even lower unit costs, that is costs per available seat-km or seat-mile. Central to the economics of the model are the *higher seat densities* in the aircraft and the *higher daily utilisation* (that is block-hours per day) achieved with these aircraft when compared to network airlines. These two features are important because they increase both the hourly and the annual productivity of each aircraft measured in available seat-kms (ASK) or seat-miles.

Hourly aircraft productivity in ASKs is the average distance flown in an hour multiplied by the number of seats on offer. Thus, even if the hourly costs of the same aircraft flown on the same sector were identical, the unit cost per seat-km of the low-cost operator would be lower than those of the network operator because the former was generating more seat-kms. Stated simply, if you offer more seats in the same aircraft, the cost per seat will be less. By doing away with a two-class cabin, by reducing or removing galleys, especially hot galleys, and by reducing the seat pitch, that is the distance between seats, low-cost airlines can significantly increase the number of seats available in their aircraft. They may reduce the seat pitch to 28 or 29 inches compared to the 30–33 inches more common among conventional network carriers.

In Europe in 2017, low-cost easyJet was flying its Airbus A319 aircraft with 156 seats while its full-service competitors were operating the same aircraft with many fewer seats. British Airways had 123 seats in its A319, Lufthansa 122, while SWISS operated with only 108 though more than half of those seats were in Business class. In South-east Asia, AirAsia and its subsidiaries operated Airbus A320s with 180 seats. Yet SilkAir, a full-service airline, with which they competed on several key routes, flew the same aircraft with only 150 seats. Similarly, in the United States in 2017 American and United operated their own A320s with 150 seats while Delta had 158 on its A320s. However, the 'ultra' low-cost airlines flew this aircraft with a much higher seating density: Spirit with 179 seats and Frontier with 180.

The impact of higher seating density on unit costs can be gauged by re-examining the block-hour costs of the Boeing 737-800 in the United States in 2017 (Table 5.3). This showed that Southwest's block-hour cost was around 25 per cent lower than the hourly costs of the traditional network carriers when flying this same aircraft. Southwest, however, put more seats into their aircraft; 175 compared to the 160 or 165 seats used by their competitors. The impact of Southwest's higher seating density on unit costs can be seen in Table 5.4. It converts the 25 per cent *hourly cost* advantage into *unit costs* per available seat-mile, which are 31 to 33 per cent below those of the legacy carriers.

A second key characteristic of the low-cost operating model, as mentioned earlier, is the ability of most LCCs to fly their aircraft more hours each day and more hours in total each year. As a result, all those fixed annual costs, such as depreciation, insurance and some overheads, are spread over more hours and, therefore, the cost per hour will be less. The use, where possible, of less congested airports, the rapid cleaning of aircraft by cabin crew rather than ground staff, careful marshalling of embarking passengers, the

Table 5.4 Impact of seating density on unit costs – Boeing 737-800 in 2016

Airline	Cost/block-hour US$	Seats per aircraft	Cost/ASM US cents	Index of cost per ASM [*]
American	3,921	160	6.57	100
Delta	4.084	160	6.39	97
United	4.007	165	6.18	94
Southwest	3,025	175	4.38	66

[*] Highest unit cost (American) indexed at 100
Source: Compiled using data from *Airline Monitor* (August 2017a)

absence of catering or freight to load or off-load together enable low-cost carriers to schedule for and achieve faster turn-round of their aircraft. On short-haul sectors easyJet targets 30–35 minute turn-rounds whereas its full-service competitors schedule turn-rounds for 50–60 minutes or more. Because they spend less time on the ground aircraft can spend more time flying and so push up the daily utilisation achieved.

By avoiding these major hubs where there may be night bans, LCCs can lengthen their operating day by scheduling very early departures or late-night arrivals. This too enables them to push up aircraft utilisation. The network carriers need to schedule their short-haul flights at times most suitable for feeding other short- or long-haul services at their major hub(s). This imposes scheduling constraints and makes it more difficult to achieve high daily utilisation for their short-haul aircraft.

In the United States in 2017, Spirit Airlines, an 'ultra' low-cost airline, flew its Airbus A320 aircraft for an average of 11.40 hours each day. This was at least two hours each day more than was achieved, when flying the same aircraft, by United (9.20 hours), Delta (9.11 hours) and American (8.86 hours). As mentioned earlier, Spirit's A320s offered 179 seats while its three competitors had only 150 or 158 seats in their aircraft. High daily utilisation together with high seating density are two of the key factors that explain Spirit's ability to fly this aircraft with an operating cost per seat-mile of US cents 4.68 (operating costs include flight crew, fuel, direct/indirect maintenance, maintenance burden, depreciation and leases). This was about 32 per cent lower than Delta's (6.90 cents) and American's (6.86 cents) unit cost for the same aircraft and even lower when compared with United's unit cost of 7.49 cents (Airline Monitor, August 2018). All four airlines were flying this aircraft on average stage lengths of 950 to 1,000 miles, so stage length did not have a significant impact on these costs.

5.5 Higher seat factors

In Europe, the major low-cost carriers easyJet and Ryanair, as well as smaller ones such as Wizz, enjoy one final cost advantage, namely much higher passenger load factors, also called seat factors. On average in 2016 and 2017 they achieved passenger load factors that, year-round, were close to or above 90 per cent, whereas most European network carriers managed only around 70 to 85 per cent loads on their short-haul domestic and intra-European services. By operating their aircraft with higher seating density and then selling a higher proportion of the available seats the LCCs fly with many more passengers on each flight than do full-service carriers flying the same or similar aircraft. This has a dramatic impact on costs per passenger or per revenue passenger-km.

A comparison of an easyJet Airbus 319 with a similar flight by an assumed network carrier in 2017 clearly shows the impact of combining higher seating with higher seat factors. In 2017, European network carriers flew their Airbus 319 aircraft with a variety of seating densities from 108 to 140, as mentioned earlier. easyJet flew this aircraft with 156 seats. Assuming that the network carriers flew, on average, with 130 seats, then easyJet had 20 per cent more seats in its aircraft (Table 5.5).

In 2017 easyJet's year-round seat factor was 92 per cent. The European network carriers have difficulty matching this on their domestic and short-haul European operations for several reasons. Their short-haul flights to their major hub are scheduled to meet the requirements of their arriving and departing long-haul flights. Their timings may not be optimum for non-connecting traffic. They may continue to operate certain routes with low loads because they have a high proportion of connecting passengers who they want to keep. On some sectors, with a high business component, they may keep seat factors lower so as to have seats available for late bookings, which are a feature of business travel. In the year 2017, it is estimated that the European network airlines achieved an average seat factor of no more than 80 per cent on their intra-European operations, though the figures varied for individual airlines between 70 and 85 per cent. These seat factors were 10 per cent or so higher than the figures they had achieved ten years earlier.

Operating with more seats in the aircraft while achieving a 92 per cent seat factor on its 156-seater Airbus A319, easyJet would have carried on average 144 passengers. A network carrier with say 130 seats and achieving an 80-seat factor would have flown with only 104 passengers on board its own Airbus A319 (Table 5.5). In effect, easyJet would be carrying 42 per cent more passengers. Let us ignore the possibility that the low-cost carrier might be able to save on some costs, as indicated earlier in Section 5.3, and assume that both easyJet and a European network carrier have identical block-hour costs when flying the Airbus A319. By carrying 144 passengers, instead of 104 as the network carrier would, easyJet would have a cost per passenger 28 per cent lower. In reality, easyJet's cost per passenger would be even lower because it is able to reduce costs in a number of areas, as indicated earlier.

In short, in Europe at least, the cost savings achieved by the LCCs are magnified by their ability to fly with higher seating densities and achieve significantly higher passenger load factors. In Asia, we have already noted that there too the LCCs employ higher seating densities on their aircraft. They also tend to enjoy higher seat factor than their network competitors, but the gap in seat factors achieved is smaller than in Europe. Thus, AirAsia, the largest Asian LCC, in 2016 flew with a 78 per cent seat factor while Malaysia Airlines and SilkAir, major competitors, only achieved passenger loads of 71.5 and 70.5 per cent respectively.

Table 5.5 Impact of higher seating density and higher seat factor Airbus A319 in 2017

	easyJet	European Network Airline
Seats	156	130 (Estim. average)
	= **20% more seats**	
Seat factor	92% (actual)	80% (Estim.)
Passengers	174	104
	= **42% more passengers**	

The United States airlines are the exception to this pattern. In 2016 all airliners, low-cost and network carriers, achieved seat factors in the mid-80s, that is between 83 and 87 per cent. The LCCs do not appear to enjoy any significant advantage in terms of seat factor. Some of the highest seat factors were achieved by the large network carriers, American, Delta and United, whose domestic seat factors were 86–87 per cent.

5.6 Long-haul low-cost?

In Europe, virtually all short-haul LCCs have an average sector distance of less than 1,500 kms. In the United States, LCC average sector distances are generally below 1,700 kms, but LCCs may be flying many longer sectors. The limit of what one might categorise 'short haul' is about 3,800 kms or so, which corresponds to about five to five-and-a-half hours' flying time. This is also close to the maximum range of the Airbus A320 and Boeing 737 family of aircraft, if unmodified. Sectors longer than this would require night stopping at the destination, with associated hotel and other expenses because of regulations limiting pilot duty hours.

Until the mid-2000s low-cost airlines had focused on short-haul operations. There was considerable doubt as to whether the model would work on much longer sectors. Yet at the end of 2004 Zoom Airlines launched low-cost flights from Canada to Europe and in 2006 Oasis, a long-haul low-cost start-up, inaugurated flights from Hong Kong to London and Paris. Both collapsed in 2008 in part because of the escalating price of aviation fuel. These collapses reinforced the doubts about the viability of the long-haul model. In the meantime, two other low-cost airlines launched long-haul services and have survived. Jetstar began such services in 2006 and AirAsia X in 2007. It is significant that both were helped by each airline's own short-haul operations. Jetstar already had a network of domestic flights in Australia as well as short-haul international services. AirAsia X benefited from short-haul feeder traffic brought into its Kuala Lumpur hubs by its parent low-cost company, AirAsia, though it was not until 2016 that AirAsia X generated adequate profits.

Uncertainty remained, and it was another five years before another long-haul low-cost operator was launched. That was Scoot, set up in 2012 by Singapore Airlines. Despite the fact that Scoot did not break into profit until 2016, another 14 long-haul low-cost airlines entered the market between 2012 and the end of 2017. Most were existing short-haul LCCs, such as Cebu Pacific, Lion Air and WestJet, which launched new long-haul routes. As was the case earlier with AirAsia X and Jetstar, all the later long-haul LCCs were able to provide their own short-haul feed or associated airlines could provide such feed.

Norwegian Air, at that time one of the smaller European LCCs, launched long-haul services in the summer of 2013 from Oslo and Stockholm to New York and Bangkok. It then set about rapidly expanding its long-haul low-cost operations. By 2018 it was operating a wide range of routes from various points in Europe to east and west coast destinations in the United States as well as to Bangkok and Dubai. There was much more to come. Routes to South America and more in Asia were being planned. Norwegian would have a fleet of 32 long-haul Boeing 787-9 aircraft by the end of 2018 and was also launching transatlantic services with the 189 seater Boeing 737 MAX-8 single-aisle aircraft.

Facing the threat of long-haul LCCs and feeling especially threatened by Norwegian's rapid expansion, network carriers set up their own long-haul low-cost subsidiaries to safeguard their markets. First among these were Canada Rouge, launched by Air Canada in 2013, followed by Lufthansa's Eurowings. In 2017, IAG, the British Airways and Iberia parent company, launched 'Level' from a Barcelona base in anticipation of Norwegian starting long-haul routes from there to North and Latin America. Air France set up its own version called 'Joon' at the end of 2017.

The average sector distances flown by the long-haul aircraft of six low-cost airlines are shown in Table 5.6. Data for summer 2015 indicates that only three of the six operated really long sectors: Jetstar, Azul from Brazil and Norwegian. The others were clearly operating their long-haul aircraft on both long- and medium-haul routes, bringing their average sector distance to relatively low levels. This was true even of Scoot, which, unlike the others, was set up specifically as a long-haul operator to serve long-distance markets.

Given the launch of so many long-haul LCCs after 2012, a key issue is whether they can achieve cost savings comparable to those obtained by short-haul LCCs.

In terms of *direct costs* they can perhaps operate with lower cabin crew costs by using non-union labour or pilots on a pay-to-fly scheme or crews from low-wage economies. However, since flight crew costs are only about 5 per cent of total costs, the overall saving can only be 1–2 per cent. It is also difficult to achieve higher pilot productivity on long-haul routes than other carriers on the same routes. When it comes to cabin attendants, LCCs will fly the minimum required by safety regulations, while the full-service network airlines will have more attendants since they have to provide in-flight catering for two, three or perhaps even four different cabin classes. There are some small savings here too. Airport landing and passenger charges cannot easily be reduced unless the LCC flies to smaller airports able to offer lower charges. This is what Norwegian does on some of its transatlantic flights. It flies from UK regional and other airports to Stewart Airport, 60 miles from Manhattan, to serve New York and to Providence Airport, 50 miles from Boston. It may save on airport fees and ground-handling charges. Maintenance costs are unlikely to be lower, unless the low-cost operator is flying newer aircraft compared to the legacy network carrier, which may be the case. But again, the impact on total trip costs will be limited.

In short-haul operations, as we have seen earlier, LCCs can reduce their depreciation and insurance costs per block-hour by achieving substantially higher daily aircraft utilisation. In long-haul operations, it is unlikely that LCCs can achieve higher block-hours per day than the network carriers. In short-haul operations, LCCs saved some money by avoiding night stops, which would involve hotel expenses and possibly additional expenses and payments for crews. On long-haul flights such expenditure cannot be avoided.

Table 5.6 Average sector length of long-haul fleets of low-cost airlines – summer 2015

	Average sector distance kms
Norwegian (Boeing 787)	7,450
Azul Airbus A330)	6,637
Jetstar (A330 and Boeing 787)	6,019
AirAsia X (Airbus A330-300)	4,543
Scoot (Boeing 777 and 787)	3,354
Cebu Pacific (Airbus A330)	3,256

Source: *Airline Leader* (May–June 2017)

As with short-haul operations LCCs cannot operate long-haul flights with lower fuel costs than their competitors unless they fly newer-generation aircraft such as the Boeing 787, the Airbus A350 or even the Boeing 737 MAX-8. That is currently the case on some North Atlantic routes. Any such advantage will only last until competitors upgrade their own fleets. En-route navigation charges are obviously significant on long-haul routes, but there is no scope here for LCCs to make any savings.

In terms of direct costs, the long-haul low-cost model may enable airlines to make some cost savings but these are more limited than those achievable in short-haul operations.

In long-haul operations, *indirect costs* may account for 25–30 per cent of total trip costs. It is here that LCCs can make more significant cost savings. They can reduce passenger service costs in several ways. They provide little or no in-flight catering, unless it is paid for separately, and no lounges for premium passengers. Ground staff will be at minimum levels. Ground-handling costs can be reduced by outsourcing to specialist companies while the airline's own ground staff is kept to a minimum. They can minimise the number of check-in or baggage desks they rent from the airport. On the other hand, if they require feed from their own or a parent company's short-haul operations, LCCs operating long-haul may not be able to reduce their station costs as much as pure short-haul LCCs can. Legacy network carriers tend to have large administrative and other overhead costs. These are a function of their size, often resulting from previous mergers, and of outdated work practices and administrative structures. LCCs being newer and meaner can reduce such overheads to a minimum.

Because long-haul low-cost airlines have not been operating for very long and their models have varied, it is a sector with limited statistical data. It is difficult to be precise on the level of cost economies that low-cost operations can achieve, but they will be lower than those achieved in short-haul services. It is estimated that 10 to 25 per cent of trip costs can be saved. A cost saving of this order was confirmed in a confidential report carried out in mid-2017 by consultants '*Aviation Strategy*'. They found that an LCC operating new Boeing 787-9 aircraft across the Atlantic from London would have total trip costs 24 per cent lower than those of a legacy network carrier flying the same aircraft.

From the earlier discussion of short-haul LCCs, it was evident that their lower trip costs advantages were magnified by the higher seating densities on their aircraft and, at least in the case of European LCCs, by higher seat factors. Since many of the larger network carriers already achieve high year-round seat factors of 85 to 90 per cent, it is unlikely that LCCs operating in the same long-haul markets can operate at significantly higher seat factors. On the other hand, they operate their aircraft with many more seats, thereby reducing the cost per seat-km. The very high seating densities of low-cost airlines compared to those of network full-service airlines operating the same aircraft are shown on Table 5.7.

This table shows a huge disparity in seating density on the same aircraft for the two types of airlines. For example, Norwegian flying from various airports in the United Kingdom to the United States may be using Boeing 787-9, as it did in the autumn of 2018, with 344 seats. This would be 128 seats more than British Airways flies in the same aircraft or 59 seats more than in American Airlines' Boeing 787-9 aircraft. Such a large difference in seating capacity must minimise Norwegian's seat-km costs. Scoot based in Singapore puts even more seats than Norwegian in the same aircraft. Table 5.7 shows that Asian long-haul LCCs are particularly successful in increasing seating densities on their aircraft.

Table 5.7 Seat density on long-haul aircraft of sample airlines compared, 2018

Aircraft type	Full-service network airline	Seats	Low-cost airline	Seats
Boeing 787-8	Air India	256	Scoot	335
	Air Canada	251	Jetstar	335
	American	226	Norwegian	291
	United	219		
	British Airways	214		
	Japan Airlines	186		
Boeing 787-9	Air Canada	298	Scoot	375
	American	285	Norwegian	344
	ANA	246		
	British Airways	216		
Airbus A330-300	Delta	293	Cebu Pacific	436
	American	281	AirAsia X	377
	Malaysia	283		

The higher seating density on low-cost airline aircraft is obtained by eliminating First and Business class cabins, that is seats that take up considerable space, and by removing hot galleys and reducing food storage and preparation areas. Some LCCs may offer a premium class but with a short seat pitch. Norwegian's premium seating has 46-inch pitch compared to 78-inch flat bed offered in British Airways' Business class. Scoot's premium seat has a 38-inch pitch. Much higher seating densities is key in enabling long-haul LCCs to operate at much lower seat-km costs.

Using Norwegian's seating density of 344 seats in a Boeing 787-9 and assuming the trip cost saving of 24 per cent estimated by *'Aviation Strategy'* for an LCC transatlantic operation, one finds that the cost per seat would be around 50 per cent lower than the seat cost of flying the same aircraft with the much lower seating density of British Airways, United or American (Table 5.7).

Air Canada's Chief Financial Officer, Michael Rousseau, speaking in September 2016 claimed that Rouge, Air Canada's long-haul low-cost subsidiary, operating Boeing 767-300 ER aircraft on transatlantic leisure routes achieved seat-km costs 25 per cent lower than those of mainline aircraft. Close to half the savings were due to higher seating density, 40 per cent from lower wage costs and 10 per cent from reducing on-board services (Airline Business, November 2016).

5.7 Is the LCC's cost advantage sustainable?

The earlier analysis suggests that well-managed European short-haul low-cost operators have seat-km costs that may be 30 to 50 per cent lower than those of the European network carriers against whom they are competing. In the case of Ryanair or Wizz the cost gap may well be even greater. Where the LCCs can achieve year-round passenger load factors 5 to 20 percentage points higher than their competitors, the cost differential is magnified when expressed in terms of cost per passenger-km. In the United States, however, it is only the so-called 'ultra' low-cost airlines, such as Frontier or Allegiant, which have a cost advantage vis-a-vis the big three network carriers comparable to that enjoyed by the European LCCs. In Asia and South America the unit cost gaps are broadly similar.

A key question is whether and the degree to which such cost differentials can be sustained in the longer term. This appears to depend on two countervailing trends: on the one hand, on the ability of network airlines to cut their own costs sufficiently to appreciably reduce the cost gap; and on the other, on the degree to which LCCs can prevent their lower unit costs drifting up as they become larger and more established.

LCCs appear to be able to control or, at least, minimise any increases in their non-fuel costs. Such increases may come about as a result of new wage agreements especially for flight crew, increased airport charges or higher maintenance costs. Tremendous efforts are made to try to control the impact of any such changes. There is also a risk that increasing head-to-head competition between LCCs may force them to adopt product and service improvements in an effort to differentiate themselves. This may mean introducing a premium class cabin with more leg-room or even some in-flight catering, fast-track channels at airports, VIP lounges or even in-flight entertainment channels. Any such moves will push up unit costs but, in most cases, the effect is likely to be limited.

So, whether the gap in unit costs between the two sectors can be reduced depends very much on the network carrier's ability to cut their own costs. They have been under great pressure to do so not only because of the worldwide downturn in the airline industry in the early 2000s and after 2008 but also because the low-cost revolution has adversely impacted network carriers in two ways. In many short-haul markets they have lost passengers and market share to the rapidly growing low-cost carriers. At the same time, in most of these markets low LCC fares have forced the network airlines to change their pricing policies and to cut their own fares in order to remain competitive. This has reinforced the previously existing downward pressure on fares. In Europe and parts of Asia falling yields have undermined the economics of short-haul operations for network airlines since costs have not been falling as rapidly as fares. Network airlines in Europe, Asia and the US have been forced to act to cut costs, especially those airlines most affected by low-cost competition. They have also tried, where possible, to learn from and copy aspects of the low-cost model.

Cost reduction by traditional network carriers has focused on four areas. First, on *labour costs*. By cutting staff numbers, by improving productivity, for instance by reducing cabin crew numbers on board aircraft and by outsourcing more of their maintenance or their ground-handling at non-base airports, network airlines have been able to save on labour costs. In the United States all the major airlines and many smaller ones too filed for bankruptcy protection and operated under Chapter 11 rules for various periods between 2002 and 2013. This enabled them not only to cut staff numbers by up to a third but also to reduce wage levels significantly especially for crews. Air Canada, using Canadian bankruptcy rules, did the same thing. Lower flight and cabin crew costs at US network airlines combined with rising flight crew salaries at Southwest largely eliminated Southwest's previous advantage in flight crew labour costs. As the US majors returned to profit after 2010 labour unions agitated to recoup past wage reductions. Wages began to go up, but staff numbers have not. In Europe airlines were unable to cut wages or reduce staff numbers as dramatically as in the US so they focused much more on improving labour productivity. This was done by negotiating more flexible terms and conditions of employment.

Second, *aircraft ownership costs* have been reduced by delaying the purchase of new aircraft, especially single-aisle aircraft for short-haul sectors, at least until the Boeing MAX and Airbus A320neo became available, and also by major efforts to push up aircraft utilisation on short-haul routes. Third, *maintenance costs* have been cut through fleet rationalisation, which removed older and smaller aircraft and reduced the number of aircraft types in the fleet and through reducing maintenance staff numbers and/or outsourcing more maintenance functions.

Finally, the most significant costs savings achieved in recent years by network airlines have been in *passenger-related costs*, where they have adopted practices and procedures largely pioneered by the LCCs. These are in ground-handling, in passenger services and, above all in sales and distribution. They have increasingly focused on more direct sales, especially online, and have moved over to electronic ticketing. At the same time, they have cut or removed travel agents' commissions and renegotiated their fees with the global distribution systems. Electronic tickets removed the high cost of dealing with paper tickets and also reduced airport handling costs by allowing self-service check-in. This reduced the space, the number of check-in desks and the ground staff needed at airports. In the air, many airliners on their short-haul sectors have reduced or largely eliminated in-flight catering or, like the LCCs, they now charge for it. This is what British Airways has done since 2016. Some have moved from a double- to a single-class cabin on parts of their short-haul network. Less catering and single-class cabins both allow for a reduction in cabin crew members.

Leaving aside the cost of fuel, there is little doubt that during the last ten years traditional European and US airlines have been able to make some progress in reducing their non-fuel unit costs on short-haul operations. But have they done enough to eliminate or substantially reduce the cost gap with low-cost no-frills airlines in the markets where they compete? The figures quoted earlier suggest that this has not happened yet to any significant degree.

In essence, airlines operating a network business model are inevitably faced with higher costs because that model imposes certain cost penalties. The model aims to provide connectivity allowing passengers to fly from anywhere to anywhere through a system of connected airport hubs. The model also aims to ensure a high level of convenience and comfort for passengers. This means effective but costly processes for transferring passengers and baggage at the hubs. If incoming aircraft are delayed, departing aircraft have to be held back to pick up connecting passengers. In turn this requires good airport facilities and superior on-board and ground services. It also requires sufficient standby aircraft to deal with schedule disruption. Because they need to feed their hubs from a variety of dense or thinner short- and long-haul routes, network carriers are frequently forced to operate very mixed fleets of aircraft. Air France, mentioned earlier, is a good example as are Delta and Malaysia Airlines. Mixed fleets mean higher maintenance and pilot crewing costs. They often also mean more standby aircraft.

The hub network model depends on scheduling all arriving and departing aircraft within a short period of time. These are the so-called 'banks' whose aim is to minimise connecting times. They create intense activity peaks requiring more staff and more ground-handling to handle a large volume of aircraft, passengers and baggage within a short period of time. All are then under-utilised until the next 'bank', which may be two or three or four hours later. This is more costly than having a fairly steady traffic flow pattern throughout the day (for more on hubbing see Chapter 10, Section 10.7).

Low-cost airlines magnify their initially lower unit costs per seat-km into even lower costs per passenger-km by installing more seats in their aircraft and selling a higher proportion of them. The network carriers, with only a few exceptions, have failed to significantly increase the seating density on their short-haul aircraft. This was evident in our earlier discussion. The need to cater for business passengers, both those travelling locally point-to-point and those connecting at the hub onto premium long-haul flights, has induced European network carriers to maintain Business class cabins of varying sizes on most of their short-haul routes. Even when they have cut in-flight catering for economy passengers they have tended to keep their hot galleys thereby not liberating space for more seating, although reconfiguring the aircraft interiors would itself be costly.

It is clear that the gap in unit cost between LCC and network carriers in short-haul operations arises in part from differences in the way the two models operate. In the longer term, when competing on the same routes, well-run low-cost operators are likely to continue to have seat-km costs 15 to 25 per cent lower than those of the more efficient network carriers, even after the latter have significantly reduced their own costs. This gap could be reduced if network carriers were able to match the seating density of the LCCs. If in particular markets, the LCCs are able to continue to operate at higher seat factors, then any trip cost differential will be further widened when expressed per passenger-km.

5.8 Revenue advantages

While low-cost no-frills airlines enjoy substantial cost advantages arising from the characteristics of the low-cost model, they also benefit from more limited advantages on the revenue side.

The first of these relates to revenue management. To break even at their very low average fares, low-cost carriers need to achieve very high load factors year round. This is difficult when offering relatively high daily frequencies on a scheduled basis. Daily and seasonal variations in demand mean that passenger load factors can fluctuate. Therefore, low-cost carriers, like other scheduled carriers, need to practise yield management to try to maximise the revenue generated per flight. This is easier for them than for network carriers because low-cost airlines, with rare exceptions, only sell point-to-point single sector tickets. As a result, they do not face yield assessment problems arising from multi-sector tickets, from having two or more cabin classes and from tickets sold in a wide range of different currencies and at different values. Revenue management with multi-sector fares paid in different and at times fluctuating currencies pose difficult problems for network carriers. Because of their more limited geographical spread, most low-cost carriers in Europe or North America tend to sell the bulk of their tickets in only one or two currencies. Southwest sells virtually all its inventory in US dollars. In easyJet's case in 2016, 89 per cent of its sales were in sterling or euros. Much of the rest was in Swiss francs. Simpler fare structures make for simpler and more effective revenue management.

Because of the complexities of their fare structures, network carriers need to use up to 24 or more different booking classes in their yield management programmes. Low-cost carriers can generally manage with very few to reflect the separate fares they may offer on any individual flight. This makes effective yield management easier and cheaper to implement. Whereas network carriers have traditionally offered the same seat at any one time on a particular flight at several fares with different conditions attached and often as parts of different multi-sector trips, low-cost airlines have tended, in the past, to offer only one ticket price for each flight at the time of booking. Now some LCCs offer a second higher and more flexible fare, which may offer free seat allocation, ability to change, fast-track through security or other benefits.

This is the pricing strategy of both Ryanair and easyJet. They start selling the cheapest advertised lead-in fares when bookings for flights open and then their booking system automatically moves to higher fares triggered as seats sold at each fare level for any particular flight pass certain pre-planned numbers or as the departure date approaches. At any one time there is only one fare and possibly a 'flex' fare available for purchase on each flight, though the fares will often vary between flights on the same route on the same day or week to reflect differences in demand levels. During known or anticipated periods of high demand the early lead-in fares may start at a high level or a low fare may be available only for a few seats. Conversely, if sales are slow, existing low fares may be offered for longer than previously planned or occasionally fares may even be reduced as the departure date approaches. The overall aim is to maximise the revenue per flight. In this process, effective yield management ensures that average yield per passenger on most flights is well above the level of the lowest fare. At the same time such dynamic fast-changing pricing ensures very high seat factors.

A further advantage of LCCs is that they do not suffer yield dilution from multi-sector tickets. For instance, on a sector such as London (Luton) to Amsterdam easyJet collects the full fare at which each ticket has been sold, but KLM on its flights from London (Heathrow) will be carrying a significant proportion of passengers transferring to a wide range of destinations on other KLM flights at Schiphol or even to another airline. Because of the way multi-sector tickets are pro-rated for each sector flown, KLM may receive much less per transfer passenger on the London-Amsterdam sector than it collects from a local point-to-point passenger. Moreover, these connecting passengers may have paid their fares in a variety of different currencies. Such revenue dilution can significantly reduce the average yield per passenger on many short-haul sectors serving major hubs. Low-cost airlines do not face such revenue dilution. On the other hand, by offering a separate Business class cabin the conventional airlines can generate some very high yields.

Another revenue advantage enjoyed by low-cost airlines is that when they sell direct to the public without using agents, passengers must pay by credit card when they make the booking. They cannot make a reservation without paying. This means that airlines such as easyJet who sell most of their capacity direct generate most of their cash revenue before flights are made. This contrasts with their conventional legacy competitors who, selling much more of their capacity through various online agencies, travel companies and GDSs worldwide, may not receive all the payments for individual flights until some time after the departure date. This difference facilitates the low-cost airlines' cash flow and cash management and may enable them to generate substantial interest income from their cash deposits. This is an advantage also enjoyed by charter airlines.

A further advantage is that most bookings once made and paid for on a low-cost airline cannot be easily changed, except in some cases on payment of a surcharge, and tickets normally cannot be cancelled or refunded. This means that there are very few 'no shows' on departure. When they occur, the airline still collects the revenue from the ticket. Some lower fares on network carriers now also have no refund or change conditions that may involve additional charges. They have copied the LCC approach.

Finally, low-cost airlines were the first to make major efforts to generate additional or so-called 'ancillary' revenues from new non-ticket sources in order to supplement the low fares they were charging. Sales of on-board duty free products have long been a feature of international airline operations. But low-cost airlines explored numerous new approaches to generate ancillary income. The first was through on-board sales of food and drinks. With no free on-board catering, LCCs have been able to generate significant revenue from such sales. The provision of the food etc. is outsourced to specialist catering companies so as to minimise costs and ensure high quality.

When fuel prices rose sharply in 2007–8 and again in 2014, European network carriers imposed fuel surcharges on their ticket prices to compensate. The LCCs responded by introducing a variety of new sources of *ancillary revenue*. In Europe most began to charge for checked-in baggage, which previously had been carried free of charge, if below a certain weight. Then charges were introduced for being able to choose allocated seating in particular rows or for seats in exit rows or in the front of the cabin. Other innovative ways were found to generate revenue. In 2016 Ryanair started charging its passengers a fee for checking-in at the airport rather than online at home or office. Meanwhile, easyJet sells a premium membership card called 'easyJet Plus'. This cost £170 per annum in 2017. Subscribers to 'easyJet Plus' benefited from free choice of seating, dedicated bag drop, fast-track through security, speedy boarding and an additional carry-on bag at no extra cost. Other low-cost airlines also introduced some kind of premium product. Vueling, the Spanish LCC, was one of the first to do so, though it only allocated one or two front rows for such passengers.

Another way of generating revenue was through charges for the use of credit cards for the purchase of tickets. In Europe, all low-cost airline sales were made online or by phone, so credit cards had to be used for all ticket purchases. Low-cost carriers also make a major effort to design their websites to facilitate the sale of additional products and services such as hotel and car hire bookings and travel insurance. They are then paid commission by the providers of these services. Some, like Ryanair, also sell advertising space on their websites or provide links to other websites for which they get a fee.

Legacy network airlines have followed suit and have introduced a variety of ancillaries, such as charges for seat allocation or for checked-in bags. They also generate income from selling points on their Frequent Flyer Programmes, something most LCCs cannot do. Nevertheless, for network carriers ancillary revenues often generate a significantly lower share of their total revenues than is the case with LCCs. This is particularly so among European airlines. In 2016 most European LCCs generated more than 15 per cent of their total revenue from ancillaries (Figure 12.2, Chapter 12) and for several the share was well over 20 per cent. For Wizz Air it was 39.4 per cent, while among European network carriers it was, with the exception of Aer Lingus, less than 8 per cent. (For a more detailed exploration of ancillaries and their economic significance see Chapter 12.)

In North America, the larger low-cost airlines, Southwest and WestJet, have lagged behind their European counterparts in developing ancillary revenues as a major source of income (Table 5.8). On the other hand the 'ultra' low-cost carriers, Spirit, Frontier and Allegiant, generate both very high ancillary revenue per passenger ($48–50) and a very high proportion, over 40 per cent, of their total income from ancillaries.

The per passenger ancillary income for the US network carriers in Table 5.8 is high compared to that of most European network airlines but may be misleading. It is too high, because about half of their ancillary revenue comes from sale of frequent flyer points to banks, retailers and others. In 2017 in Delta's case, 52 per cent of its ancillary revenue came from its frequent flyer and co-branded programmes. This, however, is not net income since a proportion of points sold are used to buy seats on flights. Strictly speaking some of this could be considered as ticket revenue rather than ancillary income.

Table 5.8 North American airline ancillary revenues, 2016

Low-cost	Traditional network	As % total revenue	Per passenger $
1	2	3	4
Spirit		46.6	49.89
Allegiant		40.0	48.93
Frontier		42.4	48.60
	United	17.0	43.46
	Alaska Air	17.9	31.41
	Delta	13.1	28.15
	Air Canada	10.4	26.29
JetBlue		14.4	25.00
	American	12.2	24.66
	Hawaiian	9.7	21.41
Southwest		13.9	18.67
WestJet		9.5	13.77

Source: *Car Trawler Yearbook of Ancillary Revenue*, 2017

While some low-cost carriers have been very successful in generating revenue from ancillary sources, in general they do not carry freight, so they forfeit this revenue source some network carriers may enjoy. However, they also escape any freight-related costs.

The revenue advantages enjoyed by LCCs have been more easily eroded by the network carriers than can their cost advantages. Several network carriers, especially airlines facing the most competition from the low-cost sector, have begun to adopt many of the pricing and ancillary revenue practices of their competitors. For example, Aer Lingus was one of the first to do this. It publishes very low one-way fares well in advance on its website for intra-European markets, where it competes head-on with Ryanair. Fares then increase as departure date approaches. This is followed by a number of optional add-on charges, including a high charge for checked-in baggage in each direction. It charges varying fees for seats in different locations, the most expensive being in the two wider emergency exit rows. There was also a ticket handling charge of £4 even for those booking online. Air Canada is another airline that has adopted a similar strategy of complex charges and add-on fees, which generate substantial ancillary revenue. Network airlines around the world have now adopted various price and charging features first introduced by the low-cost airlines.

In conclusion, the cost advantages enjoyed by low-cost carriers can be reinforced by more limited advantages on the revenue side. This is especially true for those airlines selling their entire inventory online.

5.9 Conclusion – two distinct business models

While many product and service features of low-cost and network airlines are becoming increasingly similar, the fundamental difference between the two models remains. Their network structures are different.

The network airlines operate radial networks with routes radiating from and to one or more hubs. Their hub-based networks maximise the number of origins and destinations that can be connected through the hubs. However, this model imposes certain additional costs, outlined earlier, which can be reduced but not fully eradicated.

The newer low-cost model focuses on a matrix of point-to-point routes, the majority of which are short and can be flown within less than four hours or so. The network is complex, but the operations are simple and facilitate lower costs. These are achieved through the use of a single aircraft type, or occasionally two, operating at high levels of daily utilisation and with minimal number of night stops for aircraft and crews. It is the network shape that is the key differentiator between legacy network and low-cost airlines. It is not the on-board service features, or their pricing structures, or their distribution strategies, all of which may become increasingly comparable.

Both models have strengths and weaknesses. They impose different requirements in terms of fleet planning, scheduling, product features and service quality as well as pricing and marketing strategies. Characteristics of the two models will ensure that network airlines may reduce the unit cost gap with LCCs but a significant gap will remain.

Because of their lower unit costs, low-cost airlines will dominate non-hub markets and will attack dense routes to hubs wherever airport capacity at hubs is available. LCCs will capture a growing and dominant share of short- to medium-haul markets in Europe, India and South-east Asia. Already over 40 per cent of intra-European scheduled traffic travels on low-cost airlines and in some markets, such as out of Poland, it is over 50 per cent. In the United States over 30 per cent of domestic travellers fly on LCCs. Many network carriers will find it difficult to generate profits on their short-haul network and will tend to withdraw from routes not serving their hub(s) or will continue to make losses. Some will try to fight back by setting up new or expanding their own low-cost subsidiaries, as many have done. While these will operate at lower unit costs than their parent companies, experience to date suggests that many will be unable to operate at unit costs comparable to those of the better LCCs, unless they are run at arm's length as truly independent companies.

6 The economics of leisure charters

Charter – or more accurately, the package holiday – is not dead.
(Carl Denton, Managing Director, SvenCarlson Aviation Consulting, October 2014)

6.1 Charters – the first low-cost model

Charter or 'leisure' airlines had been operating low-cost and low-fare passenger services very successfully in some parts of the world long before the emergence of the so-called low-cost airlines. They grew initially in response to the restrictive regulatory environment prevailing in the 1960s and 1970s.

As controls on charter flights were relaxed earlier than those on scheduled services, charter airlines were able to expand by offering much lower costs per seat. Two types of charter flights have emerged, namely ad hoc charters, that is, one-off flights where aircraft are chartered for a specific event such as a sports fixture, a religious festival or a sales promotion, and 'series charters'. The latter are charters involving multiple flights, which may be on behalf of and paid for by tour operators, oil companies, the military or others requiring the regular systematic transfer of people. They normally have a set timetable and are operated as a regular series of flights though the series may be purely seasonal or of limited duration.

The global significance of passenger charters within the air transport industry can be gauged from the fact that in the mid-2010s around 5 per cent of the world's international passenger traffic, measured in passenger-kms, was being carried on charter flights. Interestingly, a marked proportion, about one-third, of these charters was being operated by scheduled network airlines such as Austrian, Aegean or Tunis Air or by LCCs such as Norwegian or Wizz.

The economics of the charter model enabled charter operators to sell seats on particular holiday routes to tour operators or travel agents at 40 to 70 per cent lower than the cheapest scheduled fare. It was European charter airlines' ability to offer such low seat costs that enabled them by the mid-1990s and before the emergence of low-cost carriers to capture over 40 per cent of all international passenger traffic within the European Union. The mid-1990s saw the peak penetration of charters in European short-haul international markets, before the rapid growth of low-cost carriers, especially in the early 2000s, resulted in a relative decline of charters in Europe. Charters airlines were forced to adapt and change in order to meet the new competitive pressures; several got into difficulties. Yet, still in 2016, European charter traffic accounted for one-tenth (10.6 per cent) of all passenger-kms produced by European airlines (IATA, 2017). Charter airlines are very much a European phenomenon. The two largest charter or leisure airline groups, TUI and Thomas Cook, have larger fleets than some medium- and smaller-sized European full-service legacy airlines.

In North America, there are some relatively small Canadian charter airlines, such as Air Transat and Sunwing, and also US carriers such as Omni Air and XTRA. In the United States about 2.7 per cent of passenger-kms are carried on charter flights (IATA, 2017).

On the North Atlantic the peak year for charter traffic penetration was 1977 when almost a third of transatlantic passengers travelled on charters. Today less than 4 per cent of passengers across the Atlantic are on charter flights; nevertheless, this remains an important market for charters. Another important market is that between Canada or the north-eastern seaboard of the United States to Florida and the Caribbean.

In other parts of the world the charter market is less significant and is often linked to specific events such as festivals or sports fixtures. A large niche market is that catering for the transfer of millions of pilgrims each year from countries with Moslem populations to Saudi Arabia during the Hajj season. This is served both by charter airlines and by flights chartered from scheduled network carriers. Unlike Europe and North America, a higher proportion of the charter flights in other markets are operated by aircraft leased from the conventional scheduled airlines.

6.2 The nature of leisure charters

Traditionally, within the Europe-Mediterranean area, which is the world's largest passenger charter market, the vast majority of series charter flights have been inclusive tour charters (ITCs). These are where the whole of an aircraft is chartered by one or more leisure companies, also called tour operators, who combine the round-trip seats with hotel or other accommodation into 'package' holidays. The passenger buys a holiday package from a retail or online travel agent or directly from the tour operator at a single price and is unaware of the cost of travel within that total price. Some charter packages may involve minimal accommodation or may include car hire, boat hire, cruises, camping or other services in addition to or instead of hotel accommodation. Self-catering inclusive tours do not include the hotel and meals but provide only for accommodation in houses or apartments.

Many of the larger scheduled airlines, both network and low-cost, have their own holiday companies or are linked to holiday companies, who put together inclusive tour packages using seats from their own airline. These have long been available but they represent a small share of each scheduled airline's total traffic.

In recent years inclusive tour package holidays have been declining in relative importance because travellers are increasingly demanding greater flexibility and choice when planning their holidays.

The 1993 Third Package of European Aviation liberalisation removed all restrictions on intra-EU charter flights. As a result, *seat-only sales* without a holiday package, either directly by the airline or through the tour operator(s) who have chartered the flights, have become an important element of charter economics. They enable the charter airlines to push up their load factors and their revenues. The fares for seat-only tickets are generally low but by generating additional traffic they have permitted charter airlines to fly larger and more economic aircraft on routes or at times when the demand for all-inclusive tour packages could not justify the larger aircraft.

Such was the success of seat-only sales that in the mid-2000s German charter airlines, such as Condor, designated their charter flights out of Germany as 'scheduled' flights, so they would appear in timetables and computer reservations systems. This facilitates seat-only sales but erodes the distinction between scheduled and charter airlines. Airlines in the UK and elsewhere have followed suit.

Another charter trend that emerged in Europe since the 1990s was a move away from dependence on short- or medium-haul markets between Northern Europe and the Mediterranean towards long-haul leisure markets previously the preserve of scheduled airlines. There has been above-average growth in charter flights from Europe to Florida, the Caribbean and other long-haul destinations. This change resulted in part from growing consumer demand for cheap access to new and more distant destinations and in part from the introduction of smaller long-haul twin-jet aircraft with low operating costs. Moreover, the large long-haul aircraft could also be flown to denser Mediterranean resorts in summer months. More importantly, the longer-haul routes tend to peak in the European winter and can be used to generate cash flow in what, for intra-European charter carriers, is the low season. Long-haul charters have generally developed on routes where scheduled services cannot meet the high seasonal demand for leisure travel.

Despite the spread of seat-only sales there are in essence two key features that distinguish most charter services from scheduled flights in Europe and in other parts of the world too. The first is that the majority of passengers do not buy a seat direct from the airline as scheduled passengers can do since most seats are sold as part of a holiday package. The whole package is bought through an intermediary such as a tour operator, travel agent, student union and so on. This distinction may be cosmetic rather than real, since in many cases the intermediary selling agent may be owned by the same parent company as the charter airline. Generally, only a limited proportion of the seats will be available for direct sale to the public. On some flights there may be none at all. The second distinguishing feature is that flights are put on by the charter airlines not in the hope of generating demand from individual travellers but in response to specific advance contracts from one or more holiday companies or tour operators. It is the latter and not the charter airlines themselves who determine the routes and frequencies to be served. This is true even when charter flights have been re-designated as scheduled.

6.3 Adapting to a changing market

The market share of passenger charters in Europe and North America reached a peak in the mid to late 1990s and has declined since then. A number of factors have contributed to the relative decline in charters. First, increasing use of internet booking has enabled consumers to make simple price comparisons and also to make hotel, car hire or other reservations independently of their travel arrangements. Increasingly holidaymakers have rejected the inflexibility of the 7- or 14-day 'one-size-fits-all' holiday packages traditionally offered on charter inclusive tour packages. This demand for greater flexibility has been reinforced in Europe by the tendency for people to take more, shorter three- to five-day breaks instead of, or in addition to, the traditional two-week summer holiday. Second, the rapid growth of low-cost low-fare airlines in Europe, more especially since about 2000, has undermined charter airlines' market base and reinforced the trend to more independent and self-organised holidays.

A 2006 study by the UK's Civil Aviation Authority showed the devastating impact of the low-cost challenge on charter routes from London (CAA, 2006). On those routes where charters competed head-on with low-cost carriers they lost around half of their traffic in the five years between 2000 and 2005. Surprisingly, even on routes where there was no low-cost competition, charters lost around 10 per cent of their passengers during this five-year period. The implication is clear. The low fares, the new destinations served and the flexibility offered by low-cost carriers diverted traditional charter passengers to the new low-cost sector. Passengers carried on UK charter airlines dropped from 33.5 million in 2000 to 15.6 million in 2016.

In response to their worsening market environment charter airline companies took a number of actions. First, some set out to compete more directly with their low-cost competitors by offering more capacity for seat-only sales on those European sectors where low-cost competition was most severe. Some went further and launched their own low-cost airline. For example, in the UK Britannia Airways, part of the TUI Group, launched Thomsonfly while Air Berlin switched many of its charter flights into low-cost scheduled operations. Monarch, the largest UK charter airline not linked to either of the two large groups, rebranded itself as a low-cost airline in 2016, but collapsed a year later.

Second, charter airlines and more especially their parent holiday companies realised that they had to match the flexibility demanded by their customers and clearly offered by their low-cost competitors; so they 'unbundled' their airline product. Passengers were increasingly given many more options whether booking an inclusive holiday or just a seat-only. They were offered greater flexibility on the length of their holiday package, on their choice of hotels, and were also given the ability to split their stays between hotels. They could buy one-way seat-only tickets, choose seats with longer leg-room, choose different types of in-flight meals in advance or get access to airport lounges, etc. – all at an additional cost. 'Dynamic packaging' is now the key to selling seats or holidays on charter flights. It allows consumers to bolt together a more or less complex and costly travel package based on their own choices.

Third, the earlier trend towards more distant longer-haul charter destinations has been strongly reinforced. More and more of the charter capacity both in Europe and North America is now offered to long-haul destinations, that is on sectors beyond five hours or so. For European charters these destinations include resorts in the Red Sea, East Africa, the Indian Ocean, South-east Asia, Florida and the East Coast of the United States, as well as the Caribbean islands and Central America. Capacity is offered largely in conjunction with holiday packages but in many cases also on a seat-only basis. Passenger charters became the first long-haul low-cost model.

The final response of the holiday travel companies and their associated charter airlines, when faced with so much uncertainty and market instability in the mid-2000s, was to undertake a new round of mergers and consolidation within their market sector.

6.4 Vertical integration and horizontal consolidation

Consolidation is not new in this sector of the travel industry. The European charter industry has long been characterised by a strong tendency towards *vertical integration* between travel companies or tour operators and charter airlines and in some cases with hotels or hotel groups as well. This is in marked contrast to the United States, where anti-trust regulations largely prevented this. Such vertical integration was inevitable since it was easier for a single company or organisation to order the charter seats required and tie them up with the hotel beds in each of many holiday destinations. If the same travel company owned or had long-term leases for large numbers of hotel beds or beds on cruise ships, the process of putting together holiday packages was facilitated. The travel companies also had a large number of retail travel agencies in key high street locations through which they could sell their holiday packages. Most of the larger tour operators in the major originating countries owned several travel agencies, often trading under different brand names, as well as one or more charter airlines. Frequently they also bought seats on airlines that were not their own.

The first phase of *horizontal consolidation* in Europe was in 1999–2000. The major tour operating companies were hoping through mergers with or acquisitions of smaller holiday companies to achieve economies of scale in distribution, in the provision of charter flights and in the buying of hotel beds. Greater control of the various European markets would also enable them to squeeze out over-capacity and thereby push up the charter rates. Over-capacity seems to have been endemic to the package holiday industry as the large operators fought for market share by offering more capacity. One aim of horizontal consolidation was to reduce over-capacity.

During the early 2000s the growth of the low-cost sector lead to stagnant or, in some markets, falling demand for charters and generated a second phase of horizontal consolidation in the period 2006 to 2008.

The economic drivers for this second phase of horizontal consolidation were similar to those of the earlier first phase. Large travel companies could see the need to rationalise their airline and hotel operations in order both to take capacity out of the market and to reduce competition between major players. The aim was to push up average revenues per leisure passenger. At the same time, by bringing together two or more travel companies and airlines, one could also achieve significant cost synergies, especially as some of the larger travel companies had become bloated with too many retail outlets, and were over-staffed. Cost economies would also come from bulk buying of services, hotel beds, fuel and so on. It was the large German companies that led the consolidation process.

The first to move was Thomas Cook, then Europe's second-largest leisure group, which in February 2007 announced a merger with UK-based My Travel, the third-largest leisure company. My Travel had almost collapsed in 2003 and was keen to join up with another party. The new Thomas Cook Group (TCG), which was listed on the London Stock Exchange in mid-2007, would operate a fleet of around 90 aircraft. The merger brought together Thomas Cook Airlines, My Travel Airways and Condor Flugdienst in Germany. On the cost side, TCG claimed that cost savings arising from the merger with My Travel could be as much as $200 million a year. This would arise from closing some offices, substantial staff cuts and from buying synergies and reduced distribution costs. By the end of 2017, TCG's five airlines operated 107 aircraft, the largest being Condor in Germany and Thomas Cook (UK) with 45 aircraft each.

In September 2007, the European Commission approved the merger of TUI, by far the largest leisure group in Europe in terms of revenue, with First Choice, the fourth largest. This brought together seven airlines, with a combined fleet of around 140 aircraft, including Thomsonfly, TUIfly and First Choice Airways. Interestingly, the TUI Group in 2017 had 23 of the new Boeing 787 Dreamliner aircraft on order, emphasising the continued trend to longer-haul charter destinations. By the end of 2017 the group operated over 151 aircraft. Thomson Airlines in the UK, then rebranded as TUI, with a fleet of 62 aircraft was the largest charter or leisure airline in the world. TUI owned 300 hotels worldwide as well as 14 cruise ships. The airline fleet had not grown in the previous ten years but the increasing number of hotel and cruise ships was clear evidence of the growing focus on vertical integration as a defensive strategy.

The third force driving horizontal consolidation was Air Berlin, but here consolidation took a different form. Both TUI and Thomas Cook brought together travel companies and their associated charter airlines to create even larger leisure groups. Air Berlin's aggressive acquisition strategy aimed at creating a large hybrid airline group spanning traditional scheduled, low-cost and charter operations and focusing on both the leisure and business markets. Air Berlin had started life as a charter airline in 1978. In 2002 it launched, what were in effect low-cost, services to major cities in Europe from its two major bases of Berlin and Dusseldorf. It continued operating charters for tour operators as well. In 2006 it bought dba, a Munich-based airline operating traditional and largely domestic scheduled services. Six months later, in March 2007, it bought LTU, then Germany's third-largest charter airline. In between Air Berlin had also acquired Belair, a small Swiss charter airline.

All this has made Air Berlin a true hybrid apparently operating all airline models – network, low-cost and charter – with a somewhat confused brand image or images. Strategic priorities kept changing and sustainable profits proved elusive. In December 2011, the Abu Dhabi airline Etihad increased its shareholding from 3 to 29 per cent. This provided more cash for Air Berlin and Etihad took a role in the airline's management. But problems and large annual losses continued. Despite various plans to turn the company around, Air Berlin entered into bankruptcy in August 2017 following the withdrawal of support from Etihad.

6.5 Cost advantages of charter operations

The charter airline model predates the low-cost model. Therefore, it is not surprising that the cost economies of charters are in the same areas and similar to those of the low-cost airlines (Section 5.3–5.4).

This is evident when the costs of these 'true' charter flights are analysed and compared with those of traditional scheduled network carriers. To eliminate the effect of differing aircraft types and stage lengths, any cost comparison should assume the use of similar aircraft on the same route or serving the same markets. Routes from the London area to Mediterranean points such as Barcelona and neighbouring Catalan airports, a two-hour sector, would provide a suitable example since in 2017 Airbus A320 aircraft were being flown by both charter and scheduled airlines on this route.

6.5.1 Direct operating costs

Flight operations, that is flight and cabin crew costs, fuel and airport and en-route charges, insurance and depreciation, are the largest single element of direct costs. Here charter operators may enjoy some limited advantages.

As far as *fight crew* costs are concerned, there is now little difference in most cases in the salary levels of pilots flying the same aircraft whether on charter or scheduled services. This is so unless the charter airline is based in a destination country such as Turkey or Cyprus, where pilot salaries may be appreciably lower in the charter sector.

On the other hand, charter airlines may have lower *cabin crew costs*. They will try to achieve higher productivity from their cabin crews while paying them less! In 2015 British Airways spent an average of £37,200 each year per cabin crew member. Thomson Airways spent £31,500 per crew member while Thomas Cook Airlines spent only £21,500 (CAA, 2016) (since 2015 the UK CAA has stopped publishing detailed airline financial data). At the same time the charter airlines will aim to use fewer cabin staff than a scheduled airline would have in the same aircraft type, while providing the statutory minimum required for safety. While a charter airline may offer a premium service in the front of the cabin, it is unlikely to carry the extra staff that a scheduled airline would have to cater for its Business class. Moreover, a higher proportion of the cabin staff will be seasonally employed and will not be a cost burden for the rest of the year. Some charter airlines employ up to half of their staff for a six-month peak season only. On short-haul sectors charter airlines also save money by scheduling crew rotations to avoid night stops for crew outside of their home country, thus eliminating crew overnight expenses. Fewer cabin staff and with lower expenses helps charter carriers reduce their overall cabin crew costs.

On the other hand, *fuel costs* should be similar for both charter and scheduled carriers if flying the same aircraft on the same route since they are likely to be paying very similar prices for fuel.

En-route navigation charges will be identical when charter and scheduled airlines are operating the same aircraft. On the other hand, charter operators may pay lower *airport charges* by using cheaper airports than those used by the network airlines, especially in their home country. Charters will also choose the cheaper airport at the destination when there is a choice; so charter airlines flying to Catalonia might well choose to fly to Gerona or Reus nearby rather than Barcelona's El Prat Airport.

Maintenance costs for both charter and scheduled operations would be broadly similar if using the same aircraft on the same routes. There seems to be less variation in the wages of maintenance staff between carriers than is the case with other airline employees, such as cabin crew.

Insurance costs are only a very small part of total costs but large well-established operators (whether scheduled or charter) would both tend to benefit from lower rates.

Depreciation per hour, or lease costs per hour for leased aircraft, would also be the same if both charter and scheduled airlines achieved the same annual utilisation on their aircraft. In practice this is unlikely. First, aircraft used by the scheduled network airlines will be used on different routes, many of which are relatively short. The need, for instance, to use the London–Barcelona aircraft on other shorter scheduled sectors, such as London–Amsterdam, inevitably reduces the annual utilisation that aircraft could have achieved flying only on longer sectors such as London to Barcelona, London to Canary Islands or London to Turkey, which is what the charter aircraft is likely to be doing.

Second, during the peak summer months the charter airlines will be flying their aircraft night and day. Network airline aircraft on scheduled short-to-medium-term routes have a more limited 14–16-hour operating day since scheduled passengers do not like departing much before 0700 hours or arriving after 2200 hours. Also network carriers are often flying to/from airports that have night bans or restrictions, as is the case at London's Heathrow or many German airports. As a result of these two factors, scheduled short-haul aircraft frequently spend the night hours on the ground. Not so charter aircraft. Since some leisure passengers are prepared to accept departures or arrivals during night hours, as they are often cheaper, charter airlines programme their aircraft to fly through the night during the peak months, except where constrained by night bans. By doing this, they can frequently get three rotations, that is round trips, of the aircraft on a two- to three-hour sector during a 24-hour day. A scheduled airline might plan for only two rotations.

Charter services, however, have much more marked seasonal peaks and troughs, so that in the off-peak winter months daily utilisation of aircraft may drop below that of scheduled aircraft. This can be compensated for by the very high peak utilisation achieved by using the night hours. In addition, some charter airlines are able to lease out aircraft during their own off-peak periods to airlines in other parts of the world that face peak demand at that time. Thus, in winter 2016–17 the TUI group of charter airlines leased 14 of their aircraft to Sunwing, Canada's largest holiday package company, who used them for winter charters to the Caribbean. As an alternative, airlines such as Condor or Thomsonfly, operating medium-range, wide-bodied aircraft on charters to the Mediterranean in the summer, can switch them to Caribbean, East African or Indian Ocean routes in the winter months.

The average daily aircraft utilisation in 2016 for Airbus A321s flown by Thomas Cook on charters was 10.2 hours compared to that of British Airways A321s, which was only 8.6 hours. As a result, Thomas Cook's depreciation costs or lease rentals per hour for this aircraft would have been reduced by a quarter or more. Higher aircraft utilisation can also lead to better utilisation of flight and cabin crew and therefore higher labour productivity.

In summary, a charter airline flying on the London–Barcelona market or on other short-haul markets in the Europe-Mediterranean region can achieve some limited direct cost economies compared to a scheduled operator. Through higher daily aircraft utilisation it can reduce its hourly depreciation or lease costs. By using fewer cabin crew and paying them less and employing them on a seasonal basis it can save costs here too, though this is a small cost item. If it can use cheaper airports at one or both ends of the route it can reduce the level of airport charges by half or more. Since on short-haul routes airport charges may represent 8–15 per cent of total costs, this cost saving can be important. These are the same areas in which low-cost operators save costs.

6.5.2 Indirect operating costs

The difference in direct operating costs between European scheduled carriers and charters is not large. It is in the area of *indirect operating costs* that the costs of charter and scheduled network services begin to diverge most markedly. These are station and ground expenses, passenger service costs, ticketing, sales and promotion costs and costs of administration.

Charters' *station costs* should be lower. Charter airlines can save money by sub-contracting out most of the aircraft, passenger and baggage handling activities at their destination airports. The seasonal nature of their operations means that they have no need for permanent staff or offices or other facilities at most of the out-stations they serve. At their larger destinations they may base one or a small number of their own staff to supervise local ground-handling agents. In contrast, most major scheduled airlines with daily or more frequent flights to most of their major European destinations will employ a station manager, together with assorted other station and handling staff. Even if they outsource much of the handling they will keep a small team of their own staff to supervise. They will have offices at the airport and perhaps off the airport as well, with associated rents and other costs. Year-round station costs for scheduled carriers will tend to be higher. In Europe, as in many parts of the world, scheduled airlines now provide special dedicated lounges at airports for their business or executive club members, or they may pay for access to other airlines' business lounges. This is an additional expense avoided by charter companies. As a result of all these differences, charter airlines are likely to have lower station and ground costs.

One aspect of *passenger service costs* is cabin crew costs. Charter airlines can reduce their passenger service costs by employing fewer cabin crew and, as indicated earlier, paying them less. Cabin crew numbers can be kept to the legal minimum and a high proportion will be seasonally employed for the peak months only. Thus, in the financial year 2014–15, British Airways on average spent £37,200 per cabin crew member, whereas Thomson Airways (now TUI) spent £31,500 and Thomas Cook Airlines in the UK spent only £21,500 or 42 percent less per cabin crew member than BA (CAA, 2015).

In addition, a marked saving in passenger service costs arises because it is not necessary for charter airlines to offer a Business class cabin with the more expensive Business class catering, newspapers, magazines, etc. that are a feature of the scheduled network airline's services, though some charter airlines now offer a few seat rows with more leg-room and some catering. Charter airlines will not normally have connecting passengers for whom they have responsibility. As a result, charters can escape the costs of transferring and handling passengers and baggage, which network airlines have to meet.

The greatest savings obtained by charter airlines arise in the areas of *ticketing, sales and promotion*. This is inherent in the charter model because most, and in many cases all of the seats that the charter airline offers in any market have been chartered and paid for by tour operators and travel companies. The reservation of seats, ticketing and revenue accounting is the latter's responsibility, not the task of the airline. Even if the charter airline sells seats on a seat-only basis, this may well be done either through the tour operator who chartered the flight or through the airline's own website.

A charter airline also has minimal sales costs. Since all or the vast bulk of its capacity is not sold direct to the public, it needs no retail sales offices or staff, nor does it pay commission to others for selling its tickets. Yet commissions to agents, to GDS and credit card companies are an important cost for scheduled airlines. In the financial year 2014–15, commission paid (net of commission received) represented 3.4 per cent of British Airways' operating costs. A charter airline sells most of its capacity not to passengers but to travel agents, tour organisers, or other charterers. There is no commission to be paid. Most of a European or North American charter airline's capacity may be sold to a linked tour operator(s). The balance is sold to other large travel companies or to a small number of independent tour operators. Thus, a charter airline's annual selling and promotion costs may be no more than the cost of a few meetings and lunches with the key buyers of charter capacity. But the tour company selling IT packages or seats only on the chartered aircraft may be paying commissions.

Commission payments only arise when charter airlines sell capacity to the public on a seat-only basis. Here, too, charter airlines make great efforts to avoid or minimise commission payments. Overall, enormous cost savings accrue to charter airlines from the virtual absence of ticketing, sales and promotion expenditures. This is evident when one compares the marketing costs of British Airways with those of the UK's three charter airlines. In the financial year 2014–15 BA spent £560,000 on ticketing, sales (including commissions paid) and promotion. Thomas Cook Airlines, Thomson Airways (now TUI) and Monarch Airlines together spent less than £50,000, that is less than 10 per cent of BA expenditure, yet in terms of passenger-kms together they carried half the volume of traffic transported by BA. In subsequent years the imbalance was equally striking.

Charter airlines tend to have very much lower general and administrative costs because they require fewer administrative and accounting staff. Many functions crucial to scheduled airlines and that absorb significant resources either do not exist within a charter airline at all or, because of the different nature of charter operations, require relatively few staff. A charter airline, for example, does not need a large planning department with forecasting and yield management staff or large numbers of accountants to sort out revenue and sales accounting and inter-airline ticketing debts.

A charter airline can make economies in virtually all areas of indirect costs. Its station and handling costs are lower, as are its passenger service costs. Sales, ticketing and promotion costs, which for shorter-haul international scheduled airlines average around 8 to 12 per cent of total cost, are minimal for charter carriers. Administration costs too are much lower. As a result, charter airlines' indirect costs may be up to half or less of those of scheduled airlines operating on the same routes with the same aircraft.

Major savings in indirect costs, which in short-haul operations represent one-quarter to one-third of total costs, together with slightly lower direct costs, suggest that flying similar aircraft a non-scheduled charter operator may have total round-trip costs between 15 and 20 per cent lower than those of a scheduled network operator on the same route. However, the initial 15–20 per cent operating cost advantage is magnified by two key elements in the economics of non-scheduled air services: high seating densities and very high load factors. These are two advantages also enjoyed by low-cost airlines.

6.5.3 Higher seating density

Seating densities of charter airlines are similar to those of low-cost carriers. In summer 2017 British Airways was flying many scheduled services in Europe using an Airbus A321. Typically, with a two-class cabin this had 178 seats. This is a popular aircraft with charter airlines, but they put up to 220 seats in it, as Thomas Cook Airlines did. By putting 24 per cent more seats in the aircraft Thomas Cook can reduce their seat-kilometre costs by about 19 per cent even assuming all trip costs are equal. Higher seating densities are also found on wide-bodied aircraft. Charter airlines operating Boeing 767-300 aircraft on longer sectors would normally expect to have close to 325 seats in an all-economy charter configuration, or around 290 with a two-class cabin. Yet the same aircraft flown on scheduled services by British Airways with a two-class cabin was flown with only 244 or 247 seats in 2017.

6.5.4 High load factors

Not only do non-scheduled airlines put more seats into their aircraft, but they fill substantially more of them. For reasons explained in an earlier section (Section 5.4) European scheduled airlines have difficulties achieving year-round passenger load factors on short- or medium-haul services of 75–80 per cent, especially for short-haul operations within Europe. Few get above 80 per cent. Yet the larger charter airlines are achieving seat factors of 85 per cent or more on their intra-European routes. In 2015, the German-based charter airlines Condor and TUI Fly achieved seat factors of 89.9 and 90 seat factors respectively. The following year, 2016, Thomas Cook Airlines' seat factor was 89.9 and Thomson Airways' was 94.1 per cent. Clearly, these were similar levels of occupancy to those achieved by the larger LCCs.

One can conclude that, in general, passenger seat factors are at least 10–25 per cent higher on non-scheduled charter than on comparable scheduled services, even if the charter flights are operated by network airlines. Finnair is a good example, with a seat factor of 80 per cent on its short- to medium-haul scheduled flights in 2015, but achieving a high 96 per cent on its non-scheduled operations, most of which were within Europe. It is noticeable that US charter carriers, in contrast to their European counterparts, have much lower seat factors. This is a function of the very different nature of their business, with less reliance on inclusive tour holiday packages.

The very high load factors are due not to the non-scheduled operators themselves but to the efforts of the tour operators and leisure companies, for it is they who have the responsibility for retailing the seats they have bought wholesale. By careful programming and scheduling of flights and other components of the total package such as hotel beds, self-catering apartments, ground transport and so on, the tour operators can achieve very high seat factors for the beds and other facilities they have booked. Vertical integration between tour organisers, which may be hotel owners too, and charter airlines facilitates the process of closely matching and programming the supply of and demand for hotel beds and aircraft seats. Load factors must be kept high to ensure low and competitive prices.

Ticket brokers are also used by aircraft charterers to fill up spare capacity on inclusive tour charters. Spare capacity can also be used for seat-only sales. Loads on individual flights are carefully monitored to ensure high load factors. A finely tuned and highly differentiated price structure for charter-based inclusive tours is used to induce a potential customer to travel on less popular days or times or seasons of the year.

Higher load factors further reduce the passenger-kilometre costs of charter flights as against network services. In essence, by spreading the total round-trip operating costs over many more passengers, the non-scheduled operator can significantly reduce the trip cost per passenger. The higher charter seating densities and load factors together may have a greater impact on reducing the charter costs per passenger than do the savings in trip operating costs.

The preceding cost review suggested that non-scheduled operators start with an initial round-trip cost advantage of 15–20 per cent. This arises largely because of their lower indirect operating costs. By putting more seats into their aircraft they magnify this into an even greater cost advantage per seat-kilometre. Then, by filling 85–90 per cent of a larger number of seats, the costs per passenger-kilometre become even less vis-a-vis those of traditional network operators. The net effect may be to convert the round-trip cost advantage of only 15–20 per cent into a cost advantage per passenger carried, which may range from 40 to over 50 per cent.

In practice the differential between scheduled and charter costs will depend on several factors such as the sector distance, whether night flying is allowed, the seat factors actually achieved by the scheduled as opposed to the charter carriers, and so on.

6.6 Planning and financial advantages

Apart from a straightforward operating cost advantage, charter airlines enjoy other planning and financial advantages inherent in the workings of the charter market, particularly for holiday package or inclusive tour charters (ITC). In Europe the peak for holidays is during the European summer from mid-June to mid-September. The marketing and retailing of those holidays begin one year ahead, that is the previous summer, with peak sales generally during the winter months. Because of early sales, the major tour operators have to produce their summer brochures and website displays with full details of their various package holidays the previous spring or summer. To do this they must plan and schedule their flights and 'buy' the hotel beds they need many months earlier. This planning phase is carried out at least 18 to 24 months in advance. The same pattern of charter contracts finalised a year or more in advance exists for winter inclusive tour charters to ski resorts or to long-haul destinations such as those in the Caribbean or the Indian Ocean.

The commercial pressure on tour operators and travel agents to plan and sell their holiday packages so far in advance works to the benefit of the charter airlines. They too can plan well in advance. The routes to be flown, aircraft types, frequencies, days of the week and departure times will all have been specified. From one year to the next a large part of the flying programme will be the same.

Charter operators are in an enviable position. Having negotiated contracts with their various customers they are in a position to know a year or more in advance the routes and frequencies they will be operating and the aircraft and crews they will need. They can plan their productive resources so as to ensure that supply precisely matches demand and that it does so as efficiently as possible. Knowing their total revenue in advance, charter airlines can adjust and reorganise their costs to ensure that costs do not exceed revenues. In contrast to this, network and low-cost airlines normally do not know their revenues until the costs have been incurred and it is then too late to make any significant adjustments.

The charter airline has further safeguards. The negotiated price for the series of charter flights is normally a fixed fee per round trip or per block-hour for a minimum number of trips or block-hours per season. But the price is based on the airline's input costs at a datum point and will include actual or forecast fuel prices, airport fees and navigation charges and assumed exchange rates for relevant currencies. In the case of UK airlines this would be the sterling to dollar rate. The airline is obliged to advise the charterer, which is usually a tour operator, of any net change of costs in relation to the datum costs a certain number of days before a flight. If costs have gone up there will be a surcharge to pay. If they have gone down the charterer may be entitled to a rebate. This system of surcharges on the negotiated charter price in theory insulates charter airlines against any sudden and adverse variations in their input costs. In practice, there may be limits to any surcharges.

The charter operator's cash flow is helped by the high volume of on-board sales of spirits, cigarettes, perfumes, watches and so on. On-board sales per passenger in Europe are much higher for charter than for scheduled network passengers. This may be due to the fact that many charter flights are to or from secondary airports, particularly in destination countries, with poor retail facilities of their own. Conversely, the high proportion of frequent travellers on scheduled flights may be less inclined to spend money on board. On-board sales also receive a lower priority on scheduled flights if there are more competing demands on the cabin crew's time.

While in-flight sales are a positive element for non-scheduled operations, the absence of freight revenue clearly reduces the potential revenue from any one flight. Generally, charter operators cannot top up their passenger revenue with freight revenue as their scheduled competitors can. For the latter freight can add up to 10 to 15 per cent of the revenue on a long-haul passenger flight. The price at which the charter airlines sell their passenger capacity must therefore reflect this difference.

The early negotiation of charter contracts and the ability to adjust charter rates in response to changes in input costs provide non-scheduled operators with a level of certainty and financial security that is unique in air transport. They can sell their product in advance, at a price that can be adjusted if their costs go up. They can then go out and procure the resources necessary to provide the capacity they have sold. Scheduled airlines, both network and low-cost carriers, are handicapped because they have to do the exact opposite. They first decide to provide a level of scheduled capacity they judge necessary to meet the anticipated or targeted demand level, then allocate resources to it and subsequently try to sell it. Scheduled operators must plan their output in advance, without knowing for certain how much of it they will sell. As a result, they face much greater problems in trying to match supply and demand than do the charter airlines.

6.7 Do series charters have a future?

Clearly one-off and short-series passenger charters, to meet short-term specific demand, will continue, for instance, for the transfer of pilgrims on the Hajj flights to Saudi Arabia or for major sports fixtures. The more critical question is whether leisure-based series charters in and from Europe or North America have a long-term future.

The charter business model appears to offer some competitive advantages. Charter airlines operating series charters on two- to five-hour sectors have costs per seat-km that may be as much as 40–50 per cent lower than those of traditional network airlines operating on the same or parallel routes. This cost advantage is similar to that enjoyed by low-cost airlines. On longer-haul sectors, the cost differential between charter and scheduled operators is likely to be less. The charter operators also enjoy the benefit of two unique features of the charter model. First, the bulk of their capacity is sold well in advance to tour operators or travel agents. This facilitates the close matching of supply and demand to ensure high load factors. Second, except for a limited proportion of the capacity on any flight that may be sold on a seat-only basis, the airline itself has no selling or marketing costs since it does not sell direct to passengers. Its sales effort is focused on the tour operators, who in any country are limited in number.

Passenger charters appear to be a good supply model. But what of demand? Despite these apparent advantages, both European and North American charter airlines have had a bumpy ride in the last 20 years. They have faced strong competitive pressures and attacks from both their main competitors. Network carriers using the online travel agencies and their own websites have offered short-haul passengers much greater flexibility in terms of both pricing, with much lower and one-way fares, and the offer of do-it-yourself hotel and car hire bookings. They have also become more price-competitive on long-haul leisure routes. As we have seen earlier, low-cost carriers have hit short-haul charters hard by also offering passengers greater flexibility and variety in fares, in destinations and in hotels. Above all, their very cheap one-way fares and high frequencies have diverted large numbers of passengers previously flying on charters. It is low-cost airlines that have profited most from changing consumer tastes and desire for greater flexibility. LCCs undoubtedly pose the greatest threat to short-haul charter or leisure airlines.

Some charter airlines have responded to these competitive challenges and changing market conditions by launching their own low-cost services or subsidiaries or by selling more of their seats on their charter flights on a seat-only basis or doing both, which is what Condor has done. Monarch, the UK charter airline, also did this by trying to convert itself into a low-cost airline in the early 2010s but failed and collapsed in October 2017.

Despite the flexibility offered, through the internet, by other airline and travel companies, enabling leisure travellers to make up their own holiday packages, there will be continuing demand for ready-made off-the-shelf inclusive packages. Such demand will come from the more elderly, who are growing in number, some families with children and those who are inexperienced or anxious travellers. It will be a variegated demand. At one end there will be substantial demand from families for cheap beach holidays in Mediterranean or Caribbean resorts and at the other end for up-market tours to remote destinations in Asia, Africa or Latin America. The travel companies, especially the larger ones such as Thomas Cook or TUI, will protect their presence in such markets by buying or entering into long-term rental agreements with hotels and with cruise ships. Buying beds in bulk and using series charters, often on their own aircraft, the tour operators will be able to keep down the cost of their holidays.

The longer-term survival of charter or leisure airlines will depend on their ability to offer holiday packages that are competitive in price, are good value and are attractive to different market segments. They will increasingly focus on longer short-haul destinations, that is those over three hours where LCC competition may be less acute, and on long-haul markets that are not feasible for network or low-cost airlines because they are too small or too highly seasonal. In the process of adapting to the new market conditions the distinctions between the low-cost and charter models have become increasingly blurred.

The question that then arises is whether the traditional series charter model will continue to have a future. There appears to be a future for series charters, but a more limited future. Whether operating in those short or long-haul markets suggested earlier, series charters will only survive if the larger holiday companies and the smaller specialist tour operators offer their passengers two things. First, they must diversify and differentiate their holiday products and services in such a way as to offer experiences that consumers find harder to replicate on their own by shopping online. This should also help leisure companies to push up their revenues per passenger. Second, they must continue to offer their passengers greater flexibility and choice. This means unbundling all aspects of the flight product and the holiday package so as to allow the passenger to choose what aspects of the product and service he wishes to pay for. Such 'dynamic packaging' is key to the survival of series charters.

7 Alliances as a management tool

Global alliances add value today ... but I would be surprised and question whether they will exist in ten years from now.

(Willie Walsh, CEO International Airline Group, November, 2016)

7.1 Alliance frenzy

A feature of the airline industry is the multiplicity of alliances, both bilateral and multilateral, that are entered into by all airlines especially those operating internationally. The primary aim of most airline alliances is to generate improved revenues by changing the supply conditions of the air services. Some, but only some, alliances go further and aim to generate cost savings as well as revenue increases.

Inter-airline commercial agreements are a key management tool. They play an important role in the supply of air services on most international and many domestic airline markets. The conditions of supply are determined by the nature of the alliances entered into, if any, by the airlines operating on each route. They are key to understanding how the airline industry works. This is because they can be used as a means of ensuring profitability on an airline's major routes. Inter-airline commercial agreements are not new but they have multiplied in number and grown in complexity.

The second half of the 1990s and the early 2000s were characterised by a frenzy for inter-airline alliances of various kinds. This mirrored what had happened in the United States a decade earlier. This active period of alliance-making was triggered by the deteriorating financial performance of international airlines as they were hit first by the crisis in the tiger economies of East Asia from late 1997, then by the economic slowdown in some European states in 1998, followed by the rapid escalation of fuel prices in 1999. As the global economic downturn began to bite in 2000 and the airline crisis deepened, especially after the attacks on the Twin Towers in New York in September 2001, the alliance frenzy intensified. During the difficult decade that followed, many airline managers saw alliance building as a key pillar of their survival strategy.

Alliance building was facilitated by the progressive liberalisation of both the domestic and international regulations affecting air transport in the United States, in Europe and in many other market areas. This began in the 1980s and was a particular feature of the 1990s and 2000s. Liberalisation made it easier for airlines both to enter into alliances and also to develop new and innovative approaches to alliance building. At the same time, liberalisation intensified competition, making alliances more attractive. Airline executives saw alliance building as a way of mitigating on reducing such competition. Alliances took many forms, but for most the key driver was the need to generate more revenue. Most were also bilateral in scope between pairs of airlines. This was not new. More innovative was the emergence of global alliances joining together several airlines from different regions to provide worldwide inter-connected route networks. The first such alliance to survive was the STAR Alliance launched in 1997 by United Airlines, Lufthansa, Air Canada, SAS and Thai Airways. The Oneworld alliance followed in 1999 and then the SkyTeam alliance one year later. There had been earlier global alliances such as the 'Atlantic Excellence' alliance set up in the mid-1990s and linking Swissair, Sabena, Austrian Airlines and Delta, but none survived long.

Some airline executives went further. They felt that the benefits of alliances could be maximised through mergers and acquisitions leading to greater consolidation within the airline industry. This was especially so in the United States. In 2001 American Airlines took over TWA. In 2008 Delta merged with Northwest. Then in 2010 United and Continental merged as did the two largest low-cost carriers when Southwest took over Air Tran. In 2013 American merged with US Airways, created eight years earlier by the merger of America West with US Air. Over a period of 12 years the ten major US airlines consolidated into four, of which one was the low-cost airline Southwest.

In Europe, too, there was mounting pressure for consolidation. In October 2003 the proposed acquisition of the Dutch airline KLM by Air France was announced. Finalised in 2004, this was the first significant cross-border 'merger' in Europe to be approved by regulators on both sides of the Atlantic. It represented another innovation in alliance building. Other cross-border acquisitions followed. Lufthansa led the way. By the end of 2017 the Lufthansa Group consisted of three premium network airlines – Lufthansa itself, SWISS and Austrian Airlines – as well as two point-to-point airlines – Eurowings and Brussels Airlines. Meanwhile, launched by British Airways and Iberia, the International Airline Group contained not only these two founder members but also Aer Lingus and the low-cost Spanish airline Vueling. Significantly, all the airlines in all three groupings continued to operate under their own names and brands.

Though distinct features or differences in the way they operate are not always clear cut, four types of essentially commercial alliances have emerged over the last 30 years. Since most alliances have broadly similar aims, namely to generate more revenue for the alliance members and, if possible to reduce their costs, there are many commercial features common to all or most types of alliances. For example, code-sharing plays a key part in most inter-airline alliances, irrespective of the form or structure of the alliance. It is important to bear this in mind when assessing the value of different forms of alliances:

- bilateral commercial alliances
- global alliances
- equity alliances with either minority or controlling shareholding
- metal-neutral joint ventures.

In the early 1990s Michael Porter, referring to industries in general, had written: '*Alliances are frequently transitional devices. They proliferate in industries undergoing structural change or escalating competition, where managers fear that they cannot cope. They are a response to uncertainty, and provide comfort that the firm is taking action.*' To what extent was this true of the frenzy for international airline alliances in the late 1990s and later in the 2000s? Were these alliances merely transitional devices reflecting managers' inability to cope with liberalisation and intensified competition in a period of economic downturn? Or are airline alliances and industry concentration an inevitable response to the economic characteristics of airline operations?

7.2 Bilateral commercial agreements

Over the years a very wide range of complex inter-airline agreements have grown up to meet specific airline needs. Many such agreements pre-date the period of alliance frenzy and were primarily aimed at facilitating the operation or marketing of international air services by airlines. Agreements are sometimes purely technical and might, for instance, involve provision of engineering back-up by two airlines at each other's home base or even joint maintenance of specific aircraft types in their fleets. It is common for airlines to provide ground-handling in their own home base for aircraft operated by a partner airline. VIP business lounges may also be shared.

The majority of inter-airline agreements are, however, essentially commercial in character and are primarily concerned with facilitating the marketing and selling of passenger and/or cargo services. For instance, airlines might agree for both to put their own codes on some of the partner airline's flights. This is called code-sharing. Any agreement would specify the way in which and the degree to which an airline could then sell seats on its own flights to the partner airline. These are then the seats the partner airline can sell freely using its own airline code even though it is not itself flying these seats. Partners might co-ordinate capacity and schedules, if the regulations allow, whether or not there is any code-sharing. Airlines might agree to join their frequent flyer programmes. They may agree to combine their marketing efforts for the routes or markets where they are co-operating. Some agreements might involve the joint operation of passenger or cargo flights or the operation by one airline of such flights on behalf of two or more partners. Where only one airline operates the service some kind of revenue allocation agreement has to be entered into to establish the number of seats the non-operating airline will buy from the operator and the price to be paid. Such agreements may be more or less complex. A simple formula is a block-space agreement where one airline buys a specified number of seats from the other at a specified price, irrespective of whether they are filled.

Code-share and other similar agreements may be route specific, that is covering just one or a handful of routes, or they can be more regional, that is covering many routes to and from a particular geographic region or country. The latter often arises when one airline is feeding traffic into another airline's hubs. Then the feeder airline may negotiate to put its code on some or all of the hub airline's flights out of the hub. Another kind of regional alliance may be a franchise agreement between a larger carrier and a regional or feeder operator. The latter adopts the livery, brand and service standards of the franchiser and normally only carries the franchiser's flight code and not its own. For example, British Airways has a franchise agreement with Comair, a regional airline operating a network in South Africa using a BA code and livery on its flights.

Bilateral commercial agreements may be more or less complex but the first and primary objective, in most cases, is to generate more revenue for both airlines or all airlines if more than two are involved. Rationalising schedules and/or code-sharing make the partner airline's services more attractive vis-a-vis those of airlines competing in the same market(s). If airlines are sharing codes on services beyond each other's hubs, then each gets the benefit of offering potential customers more destinations. They enjoy the marketing benefits of a larger and wider network.

A second objective of inter-airline agreements may be to reduce or weaken competition as a way of improving revenue generation. If the partner airlines are the only operators on the route(s), then a commercial agreement between them can turn the route(s) into a quasi-monopoly. Then by agreeing fare levels and/or capacity offered they can maximise revenues. If there are other competing airlines on the route(s) the latter's competitive position is weakened. The airlines in the bilateral alliance can significantly strengthen their competitive position by dominating the seat capacity available on the routes in question while also rationalising their flight times so as to offer more attractive schedules. If the partners become dominant on their routes, they may make it difficult for existing competitors to survive or for new ones to enter the market.

A good example of this was seen after Lufthansa and SAS entered into an alliance in 1995 covering the six routes from Frankfurt and Dusseldorf to each of Copenhagen, Stockholm and Oslo. Schedules were co-ordinated and fares maintained at a relatively high level. No other carriers operated. Even though the European Commission required the two airlines to make runway slots available to new entrants, these airlines were so powerful in their own markets of Germany and Scandinavia that no new entrants dared to enter these markets. There was no competition for seven years until 2002, when Ryanair started flying from Hahn, 120 kms from Frankfurt, to Torp, 120 kms from Oslo, and to Skavsta, 88 kms from Stockholm. By summer 2017, Lufthansa and SAS were still code-sharing and were still the only operators on the three Frankfurt routes to Copenhagen, Oslo and Stockholm and also on Dusseldorf to Oslo. This is because of the market power that their alliance has given them.

The most marked and adverse effect on competition is where, as a result of an alliance, two carriers previously competing on a route on which there is no third carrier decide that only one of the alliance partners should operate the route. Examples abound – one clear example is on the routes between Switzerland and Belgium. Since the late 1990s the routes from Zurich and Geneva to Brussels have been rationalised by the two airlines at either end. Originally Swissair flew all the Zurich to Brussels flights and the Belgian airline Sabena operated alone on Brussels–Geneva. All flights had both partners' codes. No one else operated on these sectors. Routes where there had been duopolistic competition were turned into monopolies. By eliminating competition, capacity growth could be held back and fares kept high. This arrangement has continued though the ownership and the names of the successors of these two airlines has changed. By early 2018, when both these airlines were owned by Lufthansa, SWISS was still the only operator on Zurich–Brussels. Brussels Airlines alone flew their code-shared Brussels–Geneva flights but with some limited competition from easyJet.

In the United States and some other countries co-ordination between airlines on capacity offered, schedules and tariffs are banned as anti-competitive unless exemptions are granted by the aviation regulators.

A third aim of a bilateral alliance may be to reduce costs, but cost synergies from bilateral commercial agreements historically have been fairly limited. There may be some arising from joint ground-handling or shared business lounges for each other's flights, possibly also from sharing check-in desks or office space. Marketing efforts may be shared, but not much else. Overall, the impact on total costs on the routes on markets concerned is likely to be less than 3 per cent or so. However, if schedule co-operation leads to a reduction in frequencies and perhaps the ability to operate with larger aircraft then there may be a greater impact on costs.

On the other hand, alliances may enable larger and often higher-cost partners to benefit from smaller partners' lower operating costs. A major factor affecting airline unit costs is the cost of labour, which can vary significantly between neighbouring countries and also between airlines in the same country if some are highly unionised and other airlines are not. Some smaller airlines with lower wage rates reinforce this cost advantage by having low administrative and overhead costs and also in some cases by judicious outsourcing of key functions such as maintenance or catering.

Substantial unit cost differences between airlines has meant that while many alliances aim at marketing benefits as a primary objective, a further objective in some cases may be to take advantage of the partner airline's lower operating costs. This is particularly true of many route-specific or regional alliances. Air Nostrum, a privately-owned Spanish regional airline with a fleet of 43 aircraft (in 2017), has long been franchised by Iberia to operate about one-third of the latter's domestic routes. The aim has been to take advantage of Air Nostrum's lower unit costs based on operating with turbo-props and smaller jets, of 100 seats or less, and on its lower staff costs. This has enabled Iberia to turn some thin, previously unprofitable routes into profit contributors. Air Nostrum flies in Iberia colours and pays a franchise fee to Iberia, which handles marketing and sales and provides ground-handling.

In the United States, all three network majors have alliances with regional carriers. The latter operate feeder services to the majors' hubs at lower unit costs than could be achieved by the majors themselves. For example, Republic, a United States regional carrier with the world's largest fleet of Embraer 170 and Embraer 175 small jets, operates services as 'American Eagle' on behalf of American Airlines. It also flies services as 'Delta Connection' for Delta and 'United Express' for United.

Bilateral alliances are essentially tactical rather than strategic. They offer only limited scope for co-operation and mutual support. For more strategic alliances, where the long-term development of the partners are intertwined, airlines turn to global alliances and especially joint ventures or equity partnerships.

7.3 Global alliances

The most significant alliances in terms of network expansion are clearly those with a *global* scope. Here the prime purpose is to achieve both the marketing benefits of scope and the cost economies from any synergies through linking the networks of two or more large airlines operating in geographically distinct markets, ideally in different continents. Global alliances would normally involve code-sharing on a very large number of routes, but ideally they aim to go much further. They may include schedule co-ordination, joint sales offices and ground-handling, combined frequent flyer pro-grammes, joint maintenance activities and so on. Such alliances may include mutual equity stakes. The individual members of a global partnership may each have a large number of route-specific and a small number of regional alliances with airlines not members of their global alliance. Thus, the network spread and influence of a global alliance may be much wider than is at first apparent. The aim of a *global alliance* is effectively linking airlines in a different geographical area so as to provide worldwide network coverage and the benefits of large size and scope.

As airlines became increasingly conscious of the marketing and revenue benefits of global alliances, joining such alliances became a key element of many airlines' survival strategy. In several cases, existing regional alliances became part of or were subsumed into global alliances. In the period 1998 to 2003, as the global economic crisis deepened, new and, in some cases, unexpected partnerships emerged, and old ones disintegrated. The major casualty was the 'Atlantic Excellence' alliance linking Swissair, Sabena, Austrian Airlines and Delta. In June 1999 Delta announced it was leaving to set up a new global alliance with Air France, an airline that had hitherto stayed aloof from major groupings.

But while the 'Atlantic Excellence' alliance was disintegrating, three other global alliances were emerging and widening their partnership base. The earliest of the larger alliances was STAR, established in May 1997 by Air Canada, Lufthansa, Thai International, United Airlines and Varig. By 2017 it had 27 member airlines. The Oneworld alliance was launched in 1998 by British Airways, American, Qantas, Cathay Pacific and Canadian Airlines, which subsequently merged with Air Canada and so left Oneworld. With only 15 member airlines it was in 2017 the smallest of the alliances in terms of airline numbers.

In 2000 a third group emerged around the Air France–Delta partnership, with Aeromexico and Korean Airlines giving the group a global dimension. This group was subsequently branded as the SkyTeam. The purchase of KLM by Air France in April 2004 ensured that KLM and its bilateral partner, Northwest, joined SkyTeam, a global alliance comparable in size to STAR and Oneworld. By 2017 SkyTeam had 20 member airlines including two of the largest Chinese airlines, China Southern and China Eastern.

Between them the member airlines of these three alliances and their associates generated 59 per cent of the world's passenger-kms in 2016 and 62 per cent of international RPKs (Table 7.1). However, most of these airlines also had separate or regional alliances with individual airlines with which they had code-share or franchisee agreements, but were not associates or formally within their global alliance. If one adds the traffic of such regional partners to that of the core members of each global alliance, the three alliance groupings together account for close to two-thirds of the world's total scheduled traffic, domestic plus international. Should this growing level of concentration be a cause for concern?

It is clear from Table 7.1 that most of the world's largest 50 or so airlines, measured in terms of total passenger-kms, belong to one of the three alliances. However, there are some notable exceptions. These include the Gulf carriers Emirates and Etihad, all the large European and North American LCCs and a handful of other carriers such as GOL and Alaska Airlines. But many of these had bilateral agreements with members of one of the global alliances. GOL, for example, in 2017 had an extensive code-share agreement with Delta, a SkyTeam member, which also held a small shareholding in GOL. Meanwhile, Etihad, one of the Gulf carriers, enjoyed a code-share agreement on routes between Europe and the Gulf with Air France/KLM.

In Asia, two small regional alliances, U-FLY and Value Alliance, were launched in 2016 bringing together low-cost airlines. The Value Alliance, the larger and more international of the two, brought together Cebu Pacific (Philippines), Jeju Air (Korea), Nok and NokScoot (both Thai airlines), Scoot (Singapore), Tigerair (Australia) and Vanilla Air (Japan).

But what generated this search for intra-continental alliances? Four major drivers appear to be behind the push towards trans-national industry concentration and possible consolidation: a search for the marketing benefits of large size and scope; the need to reduce competition wherever possible as the international airline industry became more liberalised and competitive; a desire to reduce costs; and finally the 'nationality rules', which make cross-border acquisitions and mergers virtually impossible.

Table 7.1 Global alliances ranked by scheduled passenger-km year 2016

Alliance	Share (%) international pass-kms	Share (%) domestic pass-kms	Share (%) total pass-kms
STAR Alliance: 27 members			
Adria, Aegean, Air Canada, Air China, Air India, ANA, Air New Zealand, Asiana, Austrian, Avianca, Brussels, COPA, Croatia, Egyptian, Ethiopian, EVA, LOT, Lufthansa, SAS, Shenzhen, SIA, SAA, SWISS, TAP, Thai, Turkish, United	25.6	17.2	22.6
SkyTeam: 20 members			
Aeroflot, Aerolineas Argentinas, Aeromexico, Air Europa, Air France, Alitalia, China Airlines, China Eastern, China Southern, Czech, Delta, Garuda, Kenya, KLM, Korean, MEA, Saudia, TAROM, Vietnam Airlines, Xiamen	18.0	21.9	19.4
Oneworld: 15 members			
Air Berlin, American, BA, Cathay, Finnair, Iberia, JAL, LAN, Malaysia, Qantas, Qatar, Royal Jordanian, S7, Sri Lankan, TAM	18.5	15.1	17.2
TOTAL 3 ALLIANCES	62.1	54.3	59.3
TOTAL WORLD	100.0	100.0	100.0

N.B.: Traffic data includes both alliance members and their associates
Source: World Air Transport Statistics 2017. IATA: Geneva

7.3.1 The marketing benefits of large scale and scope

During the 1980s, that is in the decade or so after deregulation in the United States, it became apparent that cost economies of scale in airline operations were limited. In other words, the very large US airlines, the so-called 'majors', were unable to achieve lower unit operating costs than much smaller airlines just because of their enormous size. In fact, the opposite was often the case. Their unit costs were actually higher than that of their smaller new entrant competitors who initially blossomed after deregulation. Yet while most of the majors survived and prospered, most lower-cost and low-fare new entrants eventually collapsed. It was the distinct marketing advantages enjoyed by the majors that enabled them to survive. In fact, as previously mentioned, the ten largest US airlines, including the two LCCs, later merged into four larger airlines, thus reinforcing their marketing advantages.

These advantages, summarised in Table 7.2, stemmed essentially from the very large scale of their operations and the wide spread of their networks. The US majors developed hub-and-spoke operations through their hub airport(s), thereby providing good online transfer connections to most points passengers would wish to travel to.

Effective hubbing also ensured higher frequencies than could be achieved by competitors' point-to-point services and the hub airlines often compensated passengers for the need to change aircraft by offering lower fares. The majors' dominance at two or more hub airports, in terms of the number of departures, made it very difficult for other airlines effectively to compete on the thicker and more lucrative routes from those hubs. Moreover, new entrants would often have great difficulty obtaining sufficient runway slots or terminal gates to mount effective competition.

If and when new entrant airlines tried to enter such routes the airline operating that particular hub could 'squeeze' new competitors through frequency increases, by rescheduling their own flights to leave shortly before those of competitors and, where necessary, through fare reductions. The larger airlines also had better and more effective distribution systems. Because of their very size they had access to more travel agencies in more markets. Large size also produced benefits in terms of advertising spend. A given amount of expenditure could promote more destinations/services because the network was so wide. With a much wider network and greater geographical spread through the use of one or more large hubs, the majors could ensure consistently high service and handling standards even when passengers had to change aircraft. Finally, airlines with very extensive networks have much more attractive frequent flyer programmes (FFP) because they offer many more opportunities both to earn points and to spend them. As loyalty schemes have become an integral part of business travel, attractiveness of those airlines with widespread networks is reinforced.

It would appear from this analysis that the marketing benefits described arise primarily from large scope, that is, geographical spread, rather than from size per se though the two are clearly linked. It was these clearly perceived advantages of larger scope that were one of the major drivers for the first wave of acquisitions and mergers in the United States in the mid-1980s. The traditional network majors were able in this way to increase the scale of their operations and their market power. As a result, only a handful of the early US low-cost carriers have survived, most notably Southwest (see Chapter 5).

The rationale and justification for the expansion and strengthening of domestic networks, seen so clearly in the case of the United States, applies equally strongly to international air services. Through code-sharing and other forms of commercial alliances with foreign airlines, the US airlines could reach into new markets and thereby dramatically increase their network spread and market power at little additional cost.

Table 7.2 Marketing benefits of large scope and network spread

- Attraction of widespread and interconnected network offering 'all' possible destinations
- Extensive network enhances attractiveness of customer loyalty scheme (FFP), especially for business and corporate travellers
- Ability to offer 'all' destinations prevents loss of passengers to other carriers at hubs (i.e. proportion of off-line transfers to other airlines falls)
- Market dominance at several hubs
- Traffic connecting through hubs supports high frequency services on spokes to and from the hubs
- Ability to maximise benefits of large advertising spend
- Ability to ensure consistently high service standard through worldwide network despite change of aircraft/airline
- Ability to squeeze competitors on particular routes through price leadership, frequency increases and/or rescheduling of flights

It is not surprising that the first two US majors to enter into cross-border global alliances in 1989 were Northwest and Delta, airlines with the weakest international networks, especially on the North Atlantic.

International cross-border alliances offer two additional marketing advantages. They enable airlines to expand their existing markets through the extra traffic generated by the feed to and from the foreign airline partner and to do this at little extra cost. But, in addition, such cross-border alliances enable airlines to expand into and develop new markets previously inaccessible to them. Thus, the alliance between United and Lufthansa, initially launched in October 1993, enabled United to access and develop new markets in Eastern Europe, via Lufthansa's Frankfurt hub, markets previously either unavailable in terms of traffic rights or non-viable economically in terms of direct flights. Alliances are seen as a way of both developing existing markets and expanding into new ones.

To summarise: alliances have a twofold beneficial impact. By increasing each airline's scope and network spread they produce marketing benefits that ultimately mean more passengers and freight for each airline member on their existing routes. At the same time the alliance itself extends each airline's total market by extending its geographical reach into new markets and it does this with little extra cost.

In the early days of alliance building, a senior Delta executive summed up the key role of marketing benefits in alliance formation as follows:

> *The reason that alliances are so critical is simple – they allow carriers to place more of their products on more shelves, to expand the scope and reach of networks more efficiently. But we are also in the business to make money and alliances allow us to generate additional revenue with minimal capital outlay.*

(Lobbenberg, 2001)

7.3.2 Reducing competition

Bilateral alliances, as mentioned earlier, may reduce competition by turning competitive point-to-point routes or markets, where there are two, three or more airlines, into monopolies or oligopolies if two airlines working together have strong market power. This tendency is reinforced when powerful hub-based airlines join together in global alliances. This is because of the increased market power of such alliance partners especially on long-haul routes dependent on traffic feed to their hubs at either end of the routes. This makes it very difficult for non-alliance airlines to compete effectively in such markets.

The experience of American Airlines on the North Atlantic clearly illustrates the impact of alliances on competition. In the mid-1990s American was competing effectively on New York to Zurich, with a 38 per cent share of passengers on direct flights in 1995, and New York to Brussels with a 43 per cent share. On Chicago–Dusseldorf it was the only operator while on Miami–Frankfurt it had a 32 per cent share. But once it had to face competition on these routes from other US airlines, operating as alliance partners with European carriers, its market share collapsed, and by 1998 it had withdrawn from all these markets. Traffic on these four routes grew but still by autumn 2017 American was flying again on only one of these four routes, namely New York to Zurich, where it offered a daily service. Delta also flew once daily on this route. But American and Delta were competing against four daily code-shared flights by STAR members SWISS and United Airlines. These four flights were scheduled through the day offering more competitive timings. Moreover, they could be fed in Zurich by a wide range of European flights operated by SWISS as well as its European STAR alliance partners, such as Aegean Airlines flying in from Athens.

The wider impact of global alliances on the competitive environment can be gauged from Table 7.3. This shows the market share, in terms of flight frequencies, of global alliance partners on key transatlantic routes in 2017. On routes from Frankfurt, Munich and Zurich the STAR partners, Lufthansa, SWISS and United Airlines, totally dominated the frequencies offered on routes to New York, Chicago, Washington, Los Angeles and San Francisco. These are among the busiest transatlantic routes in terms of passenger numbers. On thinner routes such dominance is likely too. On the majority of German routes shown the STAR airlines enjoy a monopoly. They are the only operators and face only limited and weaker competition in that passengers do not have the option to travel with other airlines transiting via points such as Paris or London. Many do this but may need to be attracted by Air France or British Airways with lower fares. Nevertheless, it is evident that the market power of the STAR partners on the majority of routes shown is such that no major airlines are prepared to enter and fight for market share. Clearly the STAR airlines should be able to benefit from such market power. This was particularly so since the STAR airlines operating on these routes operated them as joint ventures (see Section 7.4).

On the SkyTeam cross-Atlantic routes from Paris and Amsterdam, the dominance of the alliance partners was not as overwhelming as on the STAR alliance routes (Table 7.3). This was particularly true of Paris routes, but on many routes from Amsterdam, KLM and Delta, SkyTeam partners, operated as a monopoly.

Further market power arises from the control of runway slots that alliance partners may have at their hubs but also at other large airports. Competitors, current or new, may find it difficult to get slots at attractive times to compete effectively with alliance members. Many European and some Asian airports are operating at close to full capacity

Table 7.3 Alliance joint ventures' share (%) of total frequencies – key transatlantic routes, 2017

STAR Alliance						
From/to	EWR	JFK	ORD	IAD	LAX	SFO
Frankfurt	100	75	100	100	100	100
Munich	100	100	100	100	50	100
Zurich	100	33	100	100	100	100

SkyTeam Alliance						
From/to	EWR	JFK	ORD	IAD	LAX	SFO
Paris-CDG	25	40	33	67	65	53
Amsterdm	50	100	50	100	100	100

N.B.: Share of non-stop frequencies only
EWR = Newark/New York
JFK = New York
ORD = Chicago
IAD = Washington
LAX = Los Angeles
SFO = San Francisco

and frequently are full at peak demand times. Any airline aiming to compete more effectively with the dominant alliance airline will have difficulties getting sufficient slots and at attractive times. This is the case at Frankfurt Airport. In June 2017 Lufthansa operated 65 per cent of the runway slots while its STAR partners together used another 12.2 per cent of the slots. Thus, Lufthansa and its partners controlled three-quarters of the airport's slots and virtually all the peak-hour slots. Little room for any real competition.

The anti-competitive impact of alliances is likely to be much greater on short-haul routes of less than four hours or so than on medium- or long-haul routes. This is because on short routes alternative routings via other transfer hubs are unlikely to provide a competitive alternative, especially for time-sensitive passengers. The inherent risks of creating dominance on short routes, following the creation of bilateral or global alliances or mergers, are well recognised by the regulatory authorities. The European Commission has long considered that without appropriate remedies many alliances would create competition concerns. Repeatedly in a number of cases during the last 15 years, the Commission has asked new alliance members to give up slots on specific routes and make them available to potential competitors. It did this in 2003 on some routes between Paris and Italy when Air France and Alitalia entered into an alliance and again much later when Lufthansa bought Swissair on routes from Zurich to Germany. There are other examples too. But the market power of alliances has been such that in many cases competitors have failed to fully make use of the slots available.

7.3.3 Alliance cost synergies

Larger size and scope do not in themselves necessarily lead to lower unit costs. In the airline industry there are cost economies of scale, but only at the lower end of the size range. As airlines increase in size from two or three aircraft to about 15–20 the unit costs tend to decline as certain fixed and overhead costs are spread over more units of output. This is particularly true if the fleet is composed of a single aircraft type. But as airline size increases beyond 15–20 aircraft any further significant cost economies arising purely from greater size appear to be more limited. Other factors such as size of aircraft used, average length of sectors flown, the level of wages and so on become the key cost drivers (Chapter 4).

While increased market power rather than cost reduction was and continues to be the major driver for alliance formation, there is now little doubt that alliances can have a beneficial impact on costs in three ways: first, because the greater network spread and scope and the increased market power created by an alliance should generate higher traffic volumes. This is, after all, the prime objective. Higher traffic levels in turn can produce economies of traffic density. In other words, the ability of alliance partners to build up traffic levels on many routes more rapidly than would otherwise be the case means that there is scope for reducing unit costs through increased frequencies, higher load factors, and switching to larger aircraft. Also, increased traffic can push up utilisation of fixed assets such as terminal facilities, sales offices and so on, further reducing costs.

Second, cost economies may arise from possible synergies between the alliance partners. The synergies in operations or marketing enable alliance members to share some costs or reduce costs through route rationalisation. Partner airlines can share sales offices, airport facilities such as dedicated passenger lounges and reservations/ticketing or ground staff. Fleet standardisation can also produce lower costs through interchange of aircraft and crews, centralised or common maintenance facilities, standardised handling equipment and so on. As alliances become more strategic rather than purely commercial the scope for cost-sharing and cost reduction increases as airlines begin to co-mingle their assets.

Finally, the greatest potential for cost savings can come from joint procurement of externally supplied goods and services such as ground-handling, catering, maintenance, fuel and, of course, aircraft. The STAR airline members purchase over US$20 billion of goods and services each year, so even a 5 per cent saving through joint purchasing of major items would save US$1 billion annually. The most significant savings could come through the joint purchase of aircraft by several airlines. By buying in bulk they could achieve a better price per aircraft than if each was ordered separately. Cost savings are magnified if airlines could agree on common technical specifications for an aircraft including engine type. Apart from common interior layout and design of seating, galleys, toilets, etc. could also be standardised. The problem has been that the global alliances have too many airline members scattered geographically and with different and often diverging interests. Reaching agreement on big issues such as joint specifications for aircraft has, therefore, been virtually impossible except between small groups of airlines that have common interests and operate in the same region. Thus, the Lufthansa Group of airlines, Lufthansa, Austrian, SWISS and Brussels, can achieve significant cost saving because they are jointly owned, not because they belong to the same global alliance.

Some STAR members buy fuel in bulk jointly and may save marginally as a result. They share Business lounges, have joint check-in desks, undertake each other's line maintenance or ground-handling at some airports; but the overall cost reductions are limited. This is why in November 2013 Willie Walsh, then CEO of the International Airline Group, stated *'global alliances do nothing to reduce your costs . . . We can achieve better synergies through joint equity links.'* (See Section 7.4.)

However, alliances may have a down-side too. Costs may actually rise through increased overheads, or greater redemption of frequent flyer points. The costs of the integration necessary to achieve the hoped-for synergies may be higher than anticipated – for instance, the cost of IT integration. Key decisions may be slowed down by the need to reach a joint agreement between different airlines, some of whose managers may be loath to give up their cherished independence. Union problems may spread from one member of an alliance to its partners. Poor service standards by one partner may dilute the brand strength of the others. To reduce or mitigate the impact of such risks global alliance partners need to set up a strong and powerful central co-ordinating unit to ensure operational and commercial standardisation. This is crucial, and all three global alliances have done so. But the problems of co-ordinating decisions and actions of so many diverse airlines remain.

While multi-airline alliances offer scope for cost reduction there is a considerable time lag before any significant reductions can be achieved. Some cost savings related to selling and marketing can be made fairly quickly; for instance, through sharing of sales offices in particular markets, joint use of alliance lounges at airports, joint ground-handling and so on. But the more significant cost benefits such as those from bulk purchasing of aircraft with common specifications or from the creation of a joint IT platform are more difficult to agree on and take much longer to put in place. Oneworld claimed early on in 2003 that its partners saved around $300 million through joint purchasing in the previous three years since the creation of the alliance (Airline Business, July 2003). Spread over eight member airlines and three years the sum does not seem very large.

7.3.4 Bypassing regulatory barriers

The preceding discussion has indicated that in the airline industry there are substantial revenue benefits and, possibly, some lesser cost advantages in achieving greater size and larger geographical scope. In other words, there are economic forces pushing the industry towards consolidation into fewer larger units. In other industries and even in other travel sectors, the economic pressures towards larger size, wider marketing spread and globalisation have resulted in acquisitions and mergers of companies across national boundaries. One has seen this in the hotel industry, with global chains such as Marriott, which in 2016 bought the Starwood group of hotels and now controls about 5,500 hotels, the Inter-Continental Hotels group with 5,000 plus hotels or the French Accor group. There has been consolidation too in the European holiday industry around two major groups, Tui and Thomas Cook (see Section 6.4).

Consolidation of airlines within borders has taken place in the United States, within individual countries in Europe and to a lesser extent elsewhere. But consolidation across borders through mergers or acquisitions has been constrained by the framework of international airline regulations. Airlines have used alliances, global and bilateral, to circumvent these regulations and obtain at least some of the benefits of consolidation.

As discussed earlier (Chapter 2 Section 2.4), under bilateral air services agreements airlines must be 'substantially owned and effectively controlled' by nationals of their own country in order to be designated by their governments to operate on international routes where their own country has traffic rights. An airline cannot operate on those routes if it is owned by citizens or companies from outside its own country. The United States and many other countries interpret the nationality rule to mean that foreign ownership should be no more than 25 per cent. Among a few states, including those of the European Union, a figure close to 50 per cent is acceptable, that is without majority control. Of course, within the European Union ownership and control is open to citizens or companies of any other European country.

While the nationality rule allows cross-border acquisition of shares in other airlines it prohibits full mergers or the acquisition of a controlling interest. Without the ability to exercise control, there has been less incentive to buy into foreign airlines. Instead, the industry has used alliances as a way of achieving some of the benefits of industry concentration while by-passing the nationality rule.

Apart from the nationality or ownership rules there are many other regulatory barriers to airline acquisitions and mergers. These arise primarily from attempts by governments to avoid anti-competitive behaviour or the abuse of dominant market position. Regulations exist in most developed countries aimed at ensuring that competition is not distorted. Such regulations may be enforced directly by governments and/or by special competition authorities such as the Bundeskatellamt in Germany or the Competition and Markets Authority in the United Kingdom. In the United States both the Department of Justice and the Department of Transport have a say in domestic airline mergers and may become involved in issues related to co-operative agreements between US airlines and foreign carriers. The European Commission has its own regulations on mergers and competition. Moreover, many past decisions of the

Commission's Competition Directorate (DG Comp) have related directly to co-operative agreements and alliances not only between airlines of EU member states but also to those between EU and non-EU airlines.

It is the nationality or ownership rules, together with various national and extra-territorial regulations, that have forced the airline industry to move towards complex inter-airline alliances, which take many forms from purely marketing agreements to more strategic partnerships. Except within the European Union, rarely do such alliances involve true cross-border acquisitions and mergers, with one company gaining control of another, which would be natural in other industries. Where cross-border share acquisitions have taken place they inevitably involve only a minority of shares without full control, so as not to contravene the nationality rule in bilateral agreements and so jeopardise an airline's designation on international routes. The Air France–KLM merger in April 2004 marks the first real cross-border merger of any significance. But even here the complex deal was structured in such a way as to ensure that KLM continued as an operating company and brand. Also, the Dutch government was granted an option allowing it to obtain 50.1 per cent of KLM's voting rights if its traffic rights were challenged by a third country because of the nationality of KLM shareholders.

In effect, there is a fundamental contradiction in the growth of alliances. The gradual liberalisation of international regulations made cross-border airline alliances both necessary and possible, yet the remaining vestiges of international regulation, especially the ownership and nationality rules, constrained the form such alliances would take.

7.4 Equity alliances and mergers

Equity alliances, in which one airline buys a shareholding in another, have been a common feature of the airline industry for a long time. In the early 1990s, British Airways had a 24.9 per cent holding in USAir, Scandinavian Airlines owned 16.8 per cent of Continental in the United States and Iberia was part of a consortium that controlled Aerolineas Argentinas. Swissair owned 4.6 per cent of Delta, who in turn held 4.5 per cent of Swissair shares. But all these partnerships broke up. The dowries paid were not enough to ensure the marriages' survival.

During the last 20 years the use of minority equity shareholdings as a way of developing and strengthening airline bilateral or even global alliances has spread. There are numerous examples. Singapore Airlines for many years held 49 per cent of Virgin Atlantic, eventually selling its stake to Delta Airlines in December 2012. But it also still has a 20 per cent stake in Virgin Australia as well as a 49 per cent shareholding in the new Indian airline Vistara. In 2015 Delta also bought 3.55 per cent of China Eastern Airlines for US$450 million. KLM owns 26.7 per cent of Kenya Airways. There are many, many more similar cross-border airline equity holdings in other airlines. Their prime objective, in most cases, is to co-ordinate schedules of the two partners and for them to team up on marketing, on ground- and passenger-handling in each other's airports and possibly in some areas of maintenance. The focus is very much on revenue generation and market development. There may be some cost synergies but they are of less importance in the decision to invest in the other airline.

The airlines concerned normally enter into a bilateral commercial agreement prior to or after the equity investment or equity swap is made. The purchase of an equity share is normally to strengthen what might otherwise be little more than a traditional commercial agreement. It ensures longevity to the links between the partners and keeps out any competing airlines from making a commercial agreement with either of the equity partners. Shareholdings have been less than 50 per cent so as not to breach the nationality rule in international aviation regulation (Section 7.3.4).

Despite the apparent benefits when entered into, minority equity shareholdings may also be problematic. British Airways for a long time held a 25 per cent shareholding in Qantas, but according to BA executives this created more problems than benefits in the two airlines' relationship since it restricted their freedom of action. At the end of 2004 BA sold its shares and the relations between the two companies improved. Freed from the equity link to BA, Qantas was able in 2012 to announce a new deal with Emirates to channel traffic to European destinations via Dubai rather than London. In 2000 Singapore Airlines (SIA) bought a 49 per cent share of Virgin Atlantic for £600 million. This substantial investment appeared to generate few revenue benefits for SIA. It was sold to Delta in 2012 for only £224 million, marking a substantial loss on the original investment.

Some airlines have tried to combine a series of share purchases in other airlines to build their own global alliance. The first to do this was Swissair in the late 1990s when it built up the so-called European Qualiflyer alliance. By early 2000 it had a 49.5 per cent share in Belgian airline Sabena; 70 per cent in Swiss airline Crossair; 49 per cent in the French Air Littoral and 49 per cent in AOM, another French carrier; 89 per cent in the Italian airline Air Europe; 20 per cent in South African Airways; 42 per cent in Portugalia; and 10 per cent in the Polish airline LOT. But buying such substantial shareholdings did not ensure either alliance cohesion or survival. The high investments needed, both to buy the shares and to underpin heavy losses at several of these airlines, had by the end of 2001 destroyed both the Qualiflyer alliance and Swissair.

Despite this, a decade later Etihad launched a similar strategy. By 2017 it had created a global equity alliance stretching from Europe to Australasia with the following six shareholdings: Alitalia (49 per cent), Air Serbia (49 per cent), Air Seychelles (40 per cent), Air Berlin (29.21 per cent), Virgin Australia (24.2 per cent) and Jet Airways in India (24 per cent). Several of these were loss-making. Air Berlin and Alitalia were in dire financial straits. Etihad pumped hundreds of millions of US dollars into both and put in some of its own managers, but to no avail. Both effectively collapsed in 2017 after Etihad removed support. Air Berlin was sold off in pieces while the Italian government started looking for a buyer for Alitalia. Etihad changed its chief executive and abandoned this approach. The implications are clear. Buying equity shares in weak or loss-making airlines as a way of developing new markets and increased revenues is a high-risk strategy.

Despite the setbacks suffered by other equity-based alliances, Delta has embarked on a similar strategy of developing overseas equity partnerships carefully targeted to develop access to and development of new markets. Thus, in Latin America, where Delta already had a small equity share in GOL, the Brazilian carrier, it increased its shareholding in Aeromexico to 32 per cent. In March 2017 on the North Atlantic, it bought SIA's 49 per cent holding in Virgin, as already mentioned. It also had 3.55 per cent share of China Eastern Airlines. Delta is likely to make more equity investments.

Minority equity investments may help generate additional revenue but do little to reduce costs. More significant cost savings can only be achieved through majority shareholdings or full mergers. Only then does it become possible to rationalise the fleets of the two carriers, to reduce the number of different aircraft types being flown and to reduce aircraft purchase costs by buying in bulk. Maintenance facilities can also be rationalised by undertaking maintenance where costs are lowest. Facilities at airports such as check-in desks, lounges and ground-handling can be shared more effectively. Overhead and administration costs in areas such as planning, marketing revenue management, operations control and so on can be cut. A single IT platform can be used instead of two or more. Staff numbers can be cut in most areas. Such cost savings combined with revenue enhancements from wider network spread and greater market dominance, in some markets, are the benefits of greater consolidation.

United States airlines clearly understood the potential benefits of consolidation and in a series of mergers between 2001 to 2013 the ten largest US airlines became four. For some, this was after going through Chapter 11 bankruptcy procedures, which also enabled them to significantly cut costs, especially labour costs. Consolidation together with Chapter 11 has transformed the US airline industry from one beset by problems and losses for many carriers in the period 2001 to 2008 to one of the most profitable sectors of the global airline industry after 2012. In each year from 2013 to 2017 the US and Canadian airlines together generated close to or more than half the worldwide airline industry's net profits!

European airlines also understood the potential revenue and cost benefits of consolidation. One of the first to move was Air France, which announced the purchase of KLM in September 2003. The emphasis was on the cost synergies that would be generated while the revenue benefits were downplayed. The two airlines' networks are complementary rather than competitive. As a result of their 'merger', KLM customers would have access to over 90 new destinations of which 43 would be long-haul destinations, half of them in Africa. Air France customers would be offered an additional 40 new points flying via Amsterdam, many again being long-haul routes. Clearly a revenue generation impact would be expected, especially as Air France and KLM together would, at that time, be by far the largest airline in Europe. Yet, in the detailed analysis produced by the two airlines of the synergies arising from the mergers, increased revenues were not separated out. There was merely a bland statement that 'approximately 60 per cent of potential synergies are derived from cost saving' (Air France press release, 2003). Presumably the balance was due to revenue benefits. By 2017 the two airlines owned a number of regional airline subsidiaries and an LCC, Transavia.

Lufthansa and, later, British Airways also moved to acquire or merge with other European airlines. By the end of 2017 Lufthansa Group owned Lufthansa, SWISS, Austrian Airlines and two low-cost point-to-point airlines, Brussels and Eurowings. The International Airlines Group (IAG) owned British Airways, Iberia, Aer Lingus and the low-cost Spanish airline Vueling.

These large airline groups clearly enjoyed some cost synergies. For example, Air France and KLM merged their two planning departments into one. IAG rationalised aircraft specification, procurement and fleet planning for all the airlines in its group. But European airlines were unable to go as far as their US counterparts in reducing costs and maximising revenue benefits because of the nationality rule mentioned earlier. Rather than being able to fully merge they were required to operate as separate companies, in order to be able to operate any international flights beyond the European Union. For instance, SWISS, though 'substantially owned and effectively controlled' by Lufthansa, had to maintain the facade of being a Swiss rather than a German airline in order to be allowed to use Swiss traffic rights to Kenya or Japan. This meant operating as a separate company with its own logo and branding.

The disadvantages of keeping these jointly owned European airlines as separate operating companies are summarised in Table 7.4. Separate branding and marketing makes these network carriers less effective in competing in short-haul markets against the large European LCCs, such as Ryanair or easyJet, that enjoy unique pan-European brands and marketing. Also keeping airlines separate reduces the opportunities for cost reduction.

In South America the cross-border merger of Chile's LAN Airlines with Brazilian airline TAM in 2012 went further than did the European mergers. Unlike the latter, LAN and TAM from 2015 progressively moved to using LATAM as a single brand and livery for all their operations. This included their subsidiaries in Colombia, Ecuador, Paraguay, Argentina and Peru. By consolidating two of the largest South American airlines and their subsidiaries under one holding company, LATAM has become a global player. The process was not easy especially as it coincided with economic recession in Brazil. One benefit of consolidation was to rationalise capacity growth, to defer aircraft orders and reduce fleet expenditure. But it was not till 2016 that LATAM produced an annual net profit.

7.5 Metal-neutral joint ventures

Apart from a full merger, the most intensive form of co-operation in an airline is a metal-neutral joint venture. Over the last 15 years or so, such joint ventures (JVs) between two or more airlines have sprung up on many of the busiest long-haul routes 'around' the world. They are called metal-neutral JVs because the partner airlines share revenues on the routes involved irrespective of which airline is actually flying. All revenues are placed in a pot and shared by the joint venture partners broadly in proportion to the seat capacity each has put into the market. Since revenue is shared, each airline is indifferent or neutral as to whether a passenger flies in its own aircraft or its partner's aircraft or metal. Hence the term metal-neutral!

In effect the joint venture is almost like a separate company operating all the routes and services within the joint venture agreement. The overall strategy of the JV is decided between the chief executives of the participating airlines, but the day-to-day management is delegated to joint working groups that plan and manage the network and operations, the product, all aspects of marketing including pricing, revenue management, advertising, branding and sales.

Table 7.4 Two different merger models

Domestic mergers	Cross-border European
e.g. USA, Canada, UK	*e.g. Lufthansa buys SWISS, Austrian and Brussels airlines*
Focus single brand	Keep separate brands
Single marketing	Separate marketing – at times competing
Single flight code	Separate codes and code-sharing
Single revenue management system	Usually separate RMS
Optimise sales across network	
Costs harmonised	Different cost structures
Cost savings more effective	Separate companies reduce ability to save costs

N.B.: European mergers keep separate brands to bypass 'nationality rule'

By bundling their resources, the partners can co-ordinate the capacity offered and their schedules as well as their pricing. As a result, costs can be reduced; for instance, by optimising the schedule to fit demand patterns one can maximise load factors. Airport facilities and ground-handling services can be more closely integrated and costs cut. By combining each partner's traffic flows, it may be possible to operate larger aircraft and so reduce seat-km costs.

Marketing is also improved through a joint venture. The working group on pricing can ensure that fares offered by the partners on the JV routes are aligned and combinable. The distribution strategy for various media channels can be rationalised and some costs may be saved. The JV can take advantage of each partner's sales strength and brand in their home markets.

Frequent flyer programmes can be aligned and made more attractive by jointly marketing flights, and the partner airlines can reduce the economic risk of developing new routes. Thus, the JV between American, British Airways and Iberia allowed them to launch a number of new transatlantic routes, such as London–San Diego, which might not have been profitable if served by one airline alone.

JVs clearly reduce competition between the partner airlines but also more widely in the markets they serve. As a consequence, they need approval from the regulatory authority at each end of the routes covered. The US Department of Transportation has been prepared to approve JVs and give them immunity from prosecution under anti-trust legislation provided there was an 'open skies' or liberalised air services agreement with the country or countries involved. It is thought that an 'open skies' regime would allow new entrants to enter the routes affected by any immunised joint venture. To further ensure that this is possible, regulators may impose conditions before approving a JV. Thus, in December 2016, when approving and giving anti-trust immunity to a joint venture between Delta and Aeromexico, the Department of Transportation required these airlines to relinquish four airport slots at New York JFK and 24 at Mexico City to be used for trans-border services by competing airlines.

The 'open skies' agreement between the European Union and the United States, which came into force in 2008, facilitated the granting of approval for metal-neutral JVs across the North Atlantic. Three major JVs sprang up, each linked to one of the three global alliances. By 2016, 76 per cent of seat-kms flown across the North Atlantic were being offered by the three major JVs. The largest in terms of the number of airlines involved is that between United, Air Canada, Lufthansa, SWISS, Austrian Airlines and Brussels Airlines; thus, JVs cover all of these airlines' North Atlantic routes and associated connecting flights. These airlines are all members of the STAR global alliance. But, it is noticeable that other STAR alliance members, such as LOT, the Polish airline, or SAS, who also operate across the Atlantic, are not in the JV.

In addition to the North Atlantic there are also JVs on routes across the Pacific and several on routes between Europe and East and South-east Asia. All Nippon Airways (ANA) entered into a JV with United Airlines on routes between Japan and the United States in 2011. The ANA President and CEO, Shinya Katanozaka, claimed in 2016 that as a result of the JV connecting traffic through each airline's hub doubled in five years, clearly showing the marketing benefits of JVs (Airlines International, 2016).

The importance of JVs for the major global airlines can be gauged from the claim by the Lufthansa Group that 70 per cent of its long-haul revenues in 2016 were generated through its commercial JVs (Lufthansa, 2016). Apart from the North Atlantic JV the group (Lufthansa, Austrian and SWISS) has a JV with All Nippon Airways covering 11 routes between Japan and Europe. Another JV brings together Lufthansa, SWISS and Singapore Airlines on routes between Europe and Singapore and opens up points in South-east Asia and Australasia to the European carriers. More recently in 2017 the Lufthansa Group launched a JV with Air China.

While most JVs are between airlines in the same global alliance, that need not always be the case. For instance, in 2011 Delta launched a JV with Virgin Australia on the US–Australia market even though the latter was not a member of Delta's SkyTeam alliance or any other alliance. Early in 2018 Delta was negotiating a new JV with the Canadian low-cost Westjet, showing that JVs can also involve airlines with different business models. At the same time early in 2018, Delta as part of a strategy based on developing JVs across the world was concluding a JV with Korean Air.

The relatively rapid and continuing expansion of JVs in many long-haul markets and a few shorter markets, such as US–Mexico, and their significance for the airlines involved suggests that they generate significant marketing and revenue benefits. They appear to be of greater value to these airlines than their membership in the global alliances. This was clearly the view of Juha Jarvinen, Chief Commercial Officer of Finnair, when he stated: '*Real value for Finnair comes from the joint venture with BA and JAL on Europe to Japan and the joint venture with BA, American and Iberia on the North Atlantic rather than the Oneworld alliance*' (speaking at CAPA World Aviation Conference, Helsinki, October 2015).

7.6 Alliance strategies

Inter-airline commercial alliances can play a key role in extending an airline's network and so generate greater revenue but may also be a way of reducing costs. They must be part of any airline's strategic planning. The right alliance strategy will depend on the size of the airline, whether it is primarily a long-haul or short-haul operator or both, and whether it is essentially a network or a low-cost airline. A further complexity in choosing an alliance is whether it should be one covering the whole of an airline network or it should encompass only one part of the airline's operations, as metal-neutral joint ventures do.

For smaller network carriers, bilateral alliances can undoubtedly help them in generating more traffic on many of their routes while at the same time making allies of airlines that were competitors. Yields may increase as a result of reduced competition. It is not clear that joining a global alliance offers significantly more benefits. Alliance membership has to be paid for and may be costly. In any case, even if it joins an alliance, a small airline will only interface with a small number of the alliance members and then only on relatively few routes. Rather than join a global alliance, such an airline may be better off entering into a series of bilateral agreements covering its various routes with a variety of airlines irrespective of which alliance they may belong to.

In 2015, Martin Gauss, CEO of Air Baltic, stated: '*We focus on 19 bilateral code-sharing alliances with carriers such as British Airways, SAS or Air France/KLM. Joining a global alliance might mean sacrificing some of these*' (speaking at CAPA Conference, Helsinki, October 2015). With a small fleet of 30 aircraft, all with less than 150 seats, this appears to be the correct strategy. The global alliances often have protocols restricting how far partners can go in entering code-shares with non-members. For example, only a certain percentage of an airline's capacity may have non-alliance code-shares or the alliance may need to approve an outside code-share. But such restrictions appear to impact more on the smaller alliance members rather than the big players.

Airlines with substantially larger fleets may find joining a global alliance more attractive. All the evidence suggests that wider network spread generates increased revenues especially when airlines can operate to and from more major hubs. This is the economic logic for global alliances. They may also reduce competition on some routes or even create a duopoly or a monopoly in certain markets. There was an expectation that such alliances might help airlines reduce costs though any cost reductions have been more limited and less easy to quantify than the revenue and network benefits.

In the late 1990s and the decade that followed the economic imperative to join a global alliance was strong, especially for airlines in markets becoming increasingly competitive. But it is also the case that some airline executives joined an alliance at times when their airlines were facing difficulties in the expectation both that alliance membership would help them through the crisis periods and that membership would show that they were taking action. Air Berlin, which collapsed in 2017, was in this group, as was Mexicana. In fact, Mexicana became a member of the STAR alliance from 2000 to 2004 only and then joined the Oneworld alliance in 2009 but collapsed a year later. Joining two global alliances in succession failed to save Mexicana!

In 2017 over 60 international airlines were full members of the three global alliances though several smaller carriers were linked to one or other of the alliances as associated members. As mentioned earlier, global alliance members generated almost 60 per cent of global passenger-kms in 2016, but there was growing concern about the longer-term sustainability of the global alliance model. Several factors appeared to be weakening the value of this model.

- The number of airlines in each of the three global alliances appears too large, with disparate interests, so it is becoming difficult for the alliance to adequately reflect the needs of all carriers. Moreover, the commercial interests and strategies of airlines that joined 15–20 years ago may have changed and deviated over time.
- A two- or even three-tier membership structure appears to have emerged within each alliance with the larger global airlines dominating the decision-making process. Smaller airlines may feel they have little influence. To paraphrase from George Orwell's novel *Animal Farm*, it seems that 'all alliance members are equal but some are more equal than others'!
- The metal-neutral joint ventures create tighter and smaller alliances within the larger global alliances. Some member airlines feel excluded from this smaller 'club'. Thus, LOT is not included in the transatlantic STAR-led JV operated by Lufthansa, United, Air Canada, SWISS, Austrian and Brussels, yet LOT is also a STAR alliance member and undoubtedly feels that it is facing unfair competition from its partners since it too flies across the Atlantic. The same is true for SAS and TAP, also members of the STAR alliance. An even worse example of inequality within the global alliances was evident when LOT opened its Warsaw–Tokyo service. It needed code-shares with its global alliance partner All Nippon Airways (ANA) on ANA's flights beyond Tokyo to make the route more viable. These were refused because ANA's JV with Lufthansa forbade ANA from co-operating with any other European airline without Lufthansa's approval, which was not forthcoming.
- Global alliance members appear to undermine their own alliances by making bilateral code-share agreements with members of other alliances. For instance,

China Eastern (SkyTeam) has code-share agreements with both Japan Air Lines (STAR) and British Airways (Oneworld). Meanwhile, early in 2017 as part of a new expansion strategy to partner with non-STAR alliance members, the Lufthansa Group signed a major code-share agreement with Cathay Pacific, a Oneworld member, covering routes from Europe to Australasia. Also early in 2017, American Airlines, a Oneworld member, bought a 2.76 per cent stake in China Southern, a member of SkyTeam. This was linked to a commercial co-operation agreement covering sales, code-sharing and airport facilities.

All of these developments appear to weaken the significance of global alliances. Larger airlines operating long-haul or medium-haul routes appear to benefit most from entering into joint ventures with other airlines operating on the same routes or markets. These generate significant marketing benefits; competitive pressures are reduced and there may be some cost synergies. JVs will increase in number and become more dominant in major markets.

This trend was highlighted by Georgeo Callegari, Executive VP Strategy and Alliances, Aeroflot. Speaking at the European Aviation Club in Brussels in October 2016 he argued: '*Global alliances are part of the past. Partners in alliances may not have closely allied interests anymore. It is Joint Ventures which ensure close co-operation and benefits.*'

Alliances are a key tool for airline executives. Several alliance options may be available at any one time. Choosing who to ally with and the nature of such an alliance can have a major impact on an airline's profitability.

Airline alliances are proliferating in response to regulatory changes and growing competitive pressures within the airline industry. The examples and analyses covered suggest that airline alliances are driven by the significant marketing advantages and the somewhat lesser cost savings they generate but also by the need to reduce competition. The benefits of large size and wide network spread mean that the airline industry has a natural tendency towards oligopoly. Alliances are a transient phase in the process of true industry consolidation. This will only come when international deregulation permits true cross-border mergers with full control to replace many of today's alliances.

8 Airline marketing – the role of passenger demand

Marketing ... view(s) the entire business process as consisting of a tightly integrated effort to discover, create, arouse and satisfy customer needs.

(Theodore Levitt)

8.1 The interaction of supply and demand

As emphasised in the opening chapter, airline management is about matching the supply of air services, which management can largely control, with the demand for such services, which management can influence but cannot control. To be successful in this an airline can be a low-cost operator or a high-cost operator. What determines profitability is the airline's ability to produce unit revenues higher than its unit costs. Low unit costs are no guarantees of profit if an airline is unable to generate even the low unit revenues necessary to cover such costs.

In fact, profitability depends on the interplay of three key performance variables: unit cost, unit revenue and load factor (Chapter 1, Section 1.6). Unit cost is usually measured *per available tonne-km* (ATK), that is per unit of passenger and cargo capacity, or as *cost per available seat-km* (CASK); unit revenues or yields are measured *per revenue tonne-km* (RTK), *per available seat-km* (RASK) or *per passenger-km* (RPK), that is, per unit of output sold.[1] Load factor indicates how much of the capacity produced has actually been sold (it is the revenue tonne-kms expressed as a percentage of available tonne-kms) while the seat factor is the passenger-kms as a percentage of the seat-kms. Clearly, if yields are low they can be compensated for by higher seat or load factors. But high or very high load factors, in themselves, do not ensure profitability if yields are too low in relation to costs. Conversely, low load factors may not be critical if yields per unit sold are high (see Section 11.1).

To achieve a profitable matching of supply and demand, airlines need to get the balance between unit costs, unit revenues and load factor right. For this, it is crucial for airline managers to have a thorough understanding of the demand they are trying to satisfy. Such an understanding is fundamental to every aspect of airline planning. Aircraft selection, network planning, scheduling, product planning, pricing and advertising are just some of the many decision areas ultimately dependent on an analysis of demand for the transport of both passengers and freight.

As in all industries, supply and demand for air services are not independent of each other. On the contrary, each affects the other. Aircraft types and speeds, departure and arrival times, frequency of service, the level of air fares, in-flight service, the quality of ground-handling and other features of supply will influence demand for an airline's services. Conversely, the demand will itself affect those supply features. The density of passenger demand, its seasonality, the purpose of travel, the distance to be travelled, and other demand aspects should influence the way in which air services are supplied and will impact on costs. (The impact of demand patterns on costs has been discussed briefly in Section 4.2.) Thus, airline planning and management is a dynamic and iterative process.

An understanding and evaluation of the demand for air transport leads to the provision of services which themselves then affect the demand. New adjustments to the supply then take place to meet changes in the demand and this interactive process continues. The more competitive and unregulated the market, the more dynamic the interaction becomes and the greater are the headaches for airline managers. Marketing is concerned with this dynamic and interactive process of matching supply and demand in a manner that generates an adequate profit.

8.2 Key stages of airline marketing

There is a widely-held misconception that marketing is about selling what is being produced. It is much more than that. Marketing is involved in deciding what should be produced as well as how it should be sold; as such, it is the lynchpin of any industry. It is all-pervasive. It is important to recognise that virtually everyone within the airline can contribute to the marketing process.

The essence of marketing is to identify and satisfy customer needs; to be consumer or market oriented rather than production or supply oriented. If an airline concentrates on merely selling what is produced before identifying what customers want and are prepared to pay for, it is doomed to failure. A good example is supersonic air services. The supersonic Concorde aircraft was produced largely because it was technically feasible, with little reference to whether passengers would ultimately be prepared to pay the excessively high cost of travelling in the aircraft or whether people were prepared to pay the full cost of supersonic air travel to save two or three hours. A few were, but not enough to make the aircraft a commercial success. Launched in the mid-1970s, British Airways' and Air France's Concorde services survived only because they were not expected to cover their full costs since the capital costs were written off by their respective governments. No more Concorde aircraft were built after the initial batch of 16. After 27 years the last scheduled Concorde flight landed at London's Heathrow on 23 October 2003.

Marketing should involve four logical steps. The first step is to *identify markets* and market segments that can be served profitably. To do this one can use the whole range of market research methods, from desk-based statistical analyses to surveys of current and prospective users of air services. The aim is to gain an understanding of the needs of different market segments and also the degree to which such needs are not currently being satisfied. This leads on naturally to the production of traffic forecasts, which should be as detailed and segmented as possible. But the low-cost carriers have sometimes used an alternative approach. They have looked at the capacity and fares offered by network carriers on particular routes and concluded that the market is under-served and would expand rapidly with significantly lower fares. Their forecasting is intuitive rather than being based on statistical research.

The second stage of marketing is to decide, in the light of the preceding market analyses or assessments, the air services that should be offered in the market and their product features both in the air and on the ground. This is *product planning*. Price is the most critical of the product features but, as discussed later in Chapter 10, there are many other aspects of the airline's product and service provision that must also be decided on. Product planning is related to three key factors: the market needs that have been identified, the current and expected product features of competing airlines and the costs of different product or service features. In assessing the costs of proposed products, the supply and demand sides of the industry are brought together, for there is a trade-off between the two. The product planners must balance the costs of alternative product and service features against what they believe customers are prepared to pay for.

The third stage of marketing is to plan and organise the *distribution and selling* of the products on the basis of a marketing plan. This involves setting up and operating sales and distribution outlets both airline-owned, such as sales offices and telephone call centres as well as in-house on outsourced web sites, and indirect outlets involving a range of agents, sub-agents and online travel agencies. In order to attract potential customers, the marketing plan will also include a detailed programme of advertising and promotion activities in all media and increasingly using social media. The focus in distribution will be on the effective use of e-commerce wherever possible.

Finally, marketing is concerned with *reviewing and monitoring* both the degree to which the airline has been able consistently to meet the service standards and product features planned and customers' responses to them. Such monitoring through weekly sales figures, customer surveys, analyses of computer data from online sales, reviews of complaints and other market research techniques should enable airlines to take short-term corrective action, where possible, and also to make longer-term changes in their service and product features.

The aim of this book is to assess the role of marketing in the process of matching supply of air services with the demand. Marketing starts with an understanding of demand. This chapter considers certain characteristics of the demand for air travel and examines the various factors that affect the level and growth of demand in any given market. This understanding of demand leads on naturally to an examination of the forecasting techniques most widely used by airlines (Chapter 9). This is followed by an assessment of product planning and distribution (Chapter 10), of which a key element is pricing (Chapter 11).

8.3 The motivation for air travel

The bulk of air travel is either for business or for leisure. Business travel involves a journey necessitated by one's employment and paid for by the employer. The business traveller and the employer may in some cases be the same person especially if they are self-employed; but even then the traveller will not be paying directly out of their own pocket but out of the firm's. The leisure market contains two broad categories, holiday or leisure travel and travel whose primary purpose is visiting friends or relatives (often referred to as VFR). Each of these can be further sub-divided. For instance, holiday travel can be for short- or long-stay holidays and can be further split between those flying on inclusive holiday packages and those who pay for travel and accommodation separately. Another distinct and growing category is travel to/from second homes, which is often for weekend trips. Some categorise this as VFR travel. Whatever the nature of their holiday, leisure travellers, unlike those travelling for business-related purposes, invariably pay their own fares out of their own pockets. A number of important differences between the business and leisure markets stem from the fact that in the former case the passengers are not paying for their own travel whereas in the latter they are. These are discussed later.

There is, finally, a small proportion of air passengers who do not fit into the business, holiday or VFR categories. These include students travelling to or from their place of study, those travelling for medical reasons, and migrants moving to another country. They may be grouped together as a miscellaneous or 'other' category.

Of the 60 million UK residents who flew abroad in 2016, 9.9 per cent were travelling on business, 24 per cent to visit friends and relatives while two-thirds, 64 per cent, were flying for holidays (ONS, 2016). The remaining 2 per cent were travelling for a variety of other reasons. These are very global figures. In any market or on any route the mix of passengers by purpose of travel will vary by country and also on whether it is a domestic or international route. Generally, the proportion of business passengers is higher on domestic routes than on international because domestic distances are shorter and leisure passengers may find it cheaper to go by car, bus or train, especially if there are several people in the party. Thus in 2016, more than one-third (37 per cent) of domestic passengers from the UK's largest airports were travelling on business (CAA, 2017).

Several other factors affect the passenger mix. These include whether the airline service is a network scheduled, a charter or a low-cost flight, the country of residence of the passengers, the nature of economic activities at each end of the route, the airports concerned, and so on.

While as many as a quarter or so of UK residents flying abroad do so to visit friends or relatives, in some markets such VFR traffic can be even more important. On routes to Canada, to the Caribbean or to South-east Asia and Australia, the proportion of the UK originating traffic visiting friends or relatives rises significantly. For example, exactly half of all UK residents flying to Canada in 2016 went to visit friends and relatives. To Australia, 60 per cent of UK residents went for the same purpose. In the reverse flow, around 40 per cent or so of visitors from these two countries to the UK came to see friends or relatives (CAA, 2017). Clearly, airline marketing product planning and pricing in these markets must reflect that VFR is the dominant purpose of travel.

In other regions of the world the split between business, holiday, VFR and other trips will vary. As a general rule, the higher the personal disposable income of the population in a country, the greater is the proportion of holiday trips in the total international air travel generated by that country (unless, of course, travel or foreign exchange restrictions are imposed on its citizens). Low incomes in most countries of Africa mean that business trips dominate on many international air routes within the continent. Conversely, rapidly rising personal incomes in China and the industrialised countries of East Asia during recent years generated a rapid growth of leisure travel, which partly explains the unusually high growth rates enjoyed by airlines in the region during the last two decades. VFR traffic tends to be significant on air routes joining countries between which there have been earlier population movements. Apart from the UK examples previously cited, there are many other air routes with an important VFR component. These include France to Algeria or Morocco, United States to the Philippines, and Singapore to Southern India.

The variation in passenger motivation and mix airline marketing managers have to deal with is illustrated by examining air travellers flying between the United Kingdom and Europe in 2016 (Table 8.1). A close examination of Table 8.1 leads to the following broad conclusions:

- There are two and a half times as many UK air visitors flying to European countries as visitors from these countries flying to the UK. A stark imbalance.
- Purpose of travel for air passengers varies significantly between UK residents going abroad and visitors to the UK.
- While two-thirds or 67.8 per cent of UK residents who fly to Europe do so on holiday, only one-third, 34.9 per cent, of European air visitors to the UK come for a holiday.
- On the other hand, a much higher proportion of European visitors (35.2 per cent) fly to the UK to visit friends and relatives compared to UK residents travelling for the same purpose (20.8 per cent).
- Whereas less than one in ten or 9.4 per cent of UK residents fly to Europe on business, 22.1 per cent of visitors, or one in five, come to the UK for business reasons.
- Finally, one notes the high proportion of UK air passengers, 26.6 per cent or one in four, who flew to Europe in 2016 on inclusive tour packages. These are the ones who generate the substantial volumes of UK charter traffic (Chapter 6). Though many also flew on inclusive tours with network carriers or LCCs, very few Europeans visiting the UK decide to travel on inclusive packages.

Directional imbalances in traffic volumes and marked variations in journey purpose from each end of the route clearly must impact on where and how airlines flying between the UK and Europe market and advertise their services. Such marked variations are a common feature of most markets or individual routes.

The preceding examples have illustrated the wide diversity in traffic mix between different markets and routes and also between different directions on the same route. In any market or route, the mix of passengers between business and leisure or VFR has important implications on marketing and pricing strategies and also on the average yield per passenger. While this breakdown of purpose of travel into four broad categories – leisure,

Table 8.1 Purpose of travel for air passengers between UK and Europe in 2016

Purpose of visit	Visits to Europe by UK residents %	Visits to UK from Europe %
Business	9.4	22.2
Holiday	67.8	34.9
(of which inclusive tour)	(26.6)	(2.7)
Visiting friends/relatives	20.8	35.2
Miscellaneous	2.0	7.8
All visits	100.0	100.0
Visitors	**46.0 million**	**19.4 million**

Source: compiled using ONS, 2017

business, VFR and miscellaneous – is useful, it hides the fact that within each of these categories there are numerous further sub-groups. For instance, leisure passengers can be further sub-divided between long-stay or weekend travellers and between those on beach holidays, visiting mountains or going to historic cities. A rapidly growing sub-set is leisure travellers flying to ports to embark on cruise ship holidays. Among business travellers one can distinguish emergency trips as opposed to routine regular business trips, and so on. Clearly a detailed knowledge and understanding of the passenger mix, in terms of purpose of travel from each end of each route, is crucially important for airline managers.

It is also important to be aware that the air travel market is smaller than the number of passenger trips recorded since each individual traveller will normally make more than one flight. The relationship between the number of travellers and the passenger trips recorded varies on a route-by-route basis. It is greatly influenced by the proportion of business travellers on the route, since they are the most likely to be frequent users of air services. On many inclusive tour charter airline routes, the number of travellers is probably close to half the number of passengers recorded on the route since each traveller will make both an outward and a return trip, while it is unlikely that they will make that round trip more than once a year. In scheduled markets, the position is more complex, with a small proportion of frequent travellers generating a high proportion of the total passenger trips recorded. Such frequent travellers will usually be flying on business, but some may also be on leisure or VFR trips. For example, New Yorkers with vacation apartments in Florida or Singaporeans with flats in Penang may make five or more holiday trips a year.

It is also important to be aware that the number of 'bookers' is substantially smaller than the number of passengers since one person may often be buying tickets for several passengers. In 2017 easyJet carried about 80 million passengers but only 13 million bookers. It is this smaller number that is important in marketing for repeat sales.

Travel motivation has an impact on frequency of travel but also on the duration of the trip. While business travellers fly more frequently, they also take trips of shorter duration. Among leisure passengers, those on inclusive tour holidays have the longest trips since such holidays are normally of fixed duration, often in multiples of a week. As the journey distance increases so does the duration of the trip, whatever its purpose. A 2016 survey of Heathrow passengers (CAA, 2017) showed that, while 64 per cent of UK leisure passengers on international flights out of Heathrow stayed away for over one week, only 19 per cent of UK business travellers stayed away that long. In fact 22 per cent of business travellers on international routes returned within two days. On domestic flights nearly two-thirds of UK business travellers were away for two days or less. In other words, purpose of travel directly impacts on length of trip. This too has important implications for marketing of air services. Such figures also emphasise why high frequencies are important for business passengers.

8.4 Socio-economic characteristics of air travellers

Travel motivation and aspects of travel behaviour, such as frequency of travel, the number of people travelling together or the time when bookings are made, are linked to the socio-economic characteristics of the individual traveller. Sex, age, income level, stage in the life cycle, size of family and occupation are some of the many socio-economic variables that impact on travel patterns. The key variables affecting behaviour will clearly be different if one is travelling for business, or leisure, or visiting friends and relatives. They will also differ for the separate market segments within each of these categories. For an airline, the more it knows about its current or potential customers the easier it is to plan and target its services and products to meet the specific needs of each market segment. Surveys both of air passengers and those not currently using its services as well as more general surveys and market research are used to build up this understanding of what each marketplace needs. Airlines that fail to use and take account of surveys and market research are frequently the ones who lose their way. While an in-depth analysis of the socio-economic characteristics of different types of air travellers would need to be lengthy and is not appropriate here, it is nevertheless interesting to highlight some of these.

One would expect male passengers to make up the bulk of the business market, but the extent to which males still dominate is perhaps surprising. In the UK in 2016 about one-quarter of business air travellers going abroad were women (ONS, 2016). This is also indicative of the pattern elsewhere in Europe. In the United States, the proportion of women among business air travellers is higher, approaching 45 per cent.

As one would expect, the leisure market manifests a more even split of passengers between the two sexes, but there are variations and in some European and North American leisure markets women if anything predominate. The proportion of women is even higher among international VFR passengers and may reach two-thirds or more in some markets. In the United States, women are dominant in the leisure market, generating well over half the total air trips.

Traditionally, business travellers have been thought to be primarily middle and senior managers and executives and established lawyers, architects, consultants or other professionals. Their seniority inevitably meant that they would be in the middle to upper age groups. However, the business market has been undergoing a fundamental change. The internationalisation of the world's trade and industry and the fall in the real cost of air travel, together with the speed advantage offered, have resulted in recent years in a growth of business travel by more junior staff and skilled workers. Such passengers would tend to be younger and on lower incomes than the more traditional business passenger.

The most significant socio-economic variable affecting the demand for leisure travel is personal or household income, since leisure trips are paid for by the passenger, who may also be paying for a spouse and one or more children. As a result, those with higher incomes generate a disproportionately large share of the leisure market. A major UK survey of travel experiences found that of those respondents in managerial and professional occupations, 71 per cent had made at least one flight in the previous twelve months compared with 50 per cent of those in intermediate occupations and only 36 per cent of respondents in manual trades (DfT, 2014).

The UK experience is mirrored in other European countries and in the United States. A small proportion of the population, the high earners, account for a disproportionately large share of international passenger travel and in most cases of domestic travel too. In many Third World countries with low average disposable incomes, international air travel may be limited entirely to the 5–10 per cent of the population with the highest incomes. Elsewhere, international leisure travel may be more widespread but still with a predominance of higher-income earners.

In the UK air travel market, a key social variable is house ownership abroad. Those who own homes abroad undertake one-and-a-half to two times as many international air trips for leisure as those without. This was found to be true of people in all income bands (CAA, 2008).

An appreciation of the socio-economic characteristics of passenger demand in each market is helpful to airlines in planning their advertising, promotion and sales activity. It can help them in deciding which media or social channels to advertise in and what features of their services to emphasise in their advertising campaigns. Such knowledge of the market may also assist in product planning and in determining tariff policies, and possibly even in forecasting.

8.5   Market segmentation

Traditionally airlines segmented their markets on each route by trip purpose or motivation. As suggested earlier, they made a three- or fourfold division into business, holiday, VFR and other. They then used socio-economic variables such as sex, age or household income to further sub-divide these broad market segments. Market segmentation in this way is invaluable since the separate market segments have varied growth rates and respond differently to internal supply variables such as frequencies of flights, departure times and fare changes or to external factors such as exchange rate fluctuations or economic recession. Understanding the size and the characteristics of each market segment on each route is essential for forecasting demand, for many aspects of product planning such as scheduling or in-flight service, and especially for pricing. Airlines without such detailed knowledge of their markets are likely to get into difficulties when trying to match supply and demand.

In recent years there has been a growing awareness among airline managers that this traditional and simple approach to market segmentation based on trip purpose has some shortcomings. First, it tends to place too much emphasis on the demographic and socio-economic features of the passengers. Age, sex or social class are perhaps less important than appreciating passenger needs and requirements when travelling by air. Surely it is more important for an airline to know whether a passenger will cancel their reservation at the last moment or whether they are prepared to pay a lower fare for an inconvenient departure than it is to know their sex or age. Except, of course, if age or sex affects booking behaviour or attitudes to price. Second, air trips may increasingly be multi-purpose. A business trip is combined with a holiday, or a wife accompanies a husband on a business trip, while many visits to friends and relatives are considered as holidays. Third, traditional market segmentation oversimplifies the motivational factors involved in travel decisions. A senior manager or engineer required to go to another country immediately because of an unexpected crisis has different transport needs from a salesman who plans his regular overseas sales trips months in advance. A businessperson travelling to meet customers or a government official going to a conference are both considered business passengers, yet may have quite different travel requirements. Equally, the family holiday-maker buying an annual two-week inclusive tour package holiday at a sunshine resort places different demands on air services from the holidaymaker going independently and making his or her own accommodation arrangements or the couple going for a weekend break from Montreal to New York or from Singapore to Hong Kong.

Most airline planners now believe that market segmentation should be based on a more complex division related not just to journey purpose and age or sex but partly also to passenger needs and behaviour patterns. Thus, the business segment may be further subdivided into routine business, emergency business, conference or trade fair travel, overseas employment, home leave, and so on. The holiday segment of the leisure market could be split initially by length of stay, but also into an inclusive tour segment, a multi-destination touring segment and a weekender segment. But each of these segments can be subdivided further; for instance, holiday packages may be to hotels, self-catering or on cruise ships. Other ways of segmenting the market can also be used depending on each airline's appreciation of what are the key segments of its own market. The point about more complex market segmentation is that each segment is likely to have distinctive needs and expectations, such as the freedom to change reservations or routings, the need to make stop-overs, or the ability to pay particular fare levels, or varying expectations in terms of in-flight service and comfort, and so on. Buying behaviour patterns are also important. Some passengers such as elderly leisure travellers book very early, while others leave it to the last minute or may tend to change the day of travel.

Variations in needs for four of the many possible market segments on a medium-haul route such as London–Athens or Singapore–Hong Kong are shown in Figure 8.1. The contrasting needs of the emergency business traveller with those of the two-week holidaymaker stand out starkly. For the latter a low fare is critical. For the former, high service quality – seat availability, frequent flights and so on – is crucial and price is relatively unimportant. It can also be seen by comparing weekend and two-week holidaymakers that even in the leisure market there may be quite distinct segments with their own needs and expectations. It may well be that each of these groups also has different socio-economic characteristics that may help in targeting specific marketing efforts at them. But the key is their needs and expectations. What service and product features do they want or need?

The significance of this more sophisticated approach to market segmentation is that it can help airlines in their forecasting, but it can be especially helpful in product planning and pricing. It can help them in planning specific price and product combinations to attract each segment or at least those segments they wish to cater for. It can also be useful in relating fares more closely to the costs imposed by the different segments and also in working out the various conditions attached to different fares to prevent slippage of passengers from high- to low-fare categories.

The development of electronic online sales and ticketing has enabled airlines to build up a data bank about each of their customers – whether they travel alone or as a couple or as a larger family group; their frequency of trips; their preferred destinations; the most frequent times of the year for their travel; their preferred airport; where they live (which may be an indicator of socio-economic level); who makes and pays for their flight reservations; and much more. The low-cost airlines have been particularly successful in doing this as they were the first to focus exclusively on direct online sales. This data can be used to identify particular market segments and then use marketing and selling efforts, including various social media outlets, to target and attract these segments.

8.6 The seasonality problem

Like many transport industries, particularly those dealing with passengers, the airline industry is characterised by marked daily, weekly and seasonal peaks and troughs of demand. The pattern and intensity of the peaks and troughs vary by route and geographical area. Peak flows become a serious problem when they begin to impose cost penalties on the airlines involved. In meeting demand at peak periods an airline may have to provide extra capacity not only in terms of aircraft and flight crews or cabin staff but also in terms of staff, equipment and facilities in areas such as ground-handling or sales. Such extra capacity will be under-utilised during the off-peak periods.

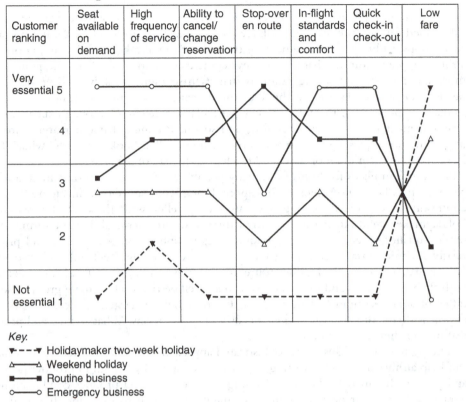

Customer ranking	Seat available on demand	High frequency of service	Ability to cancel/ change reservation	Stop-over en route	In-flight standards and comfort	Quick check-in check-out	Low fare

Figure 8.1 Market segmentation by trip purpose and passenger needs: a sample of possible segments on three- to four-hour sector

The greater the ratio of peak to trough traffic, the more difficult it becomes to ensure utilisation of peak capacity in off-peak periods. Such peak capacity then becomes very costly to operate since it must cover all its fixed and overhead costs during the short period that it is actually in use. Expressed another way, one finds costly equipment and staff required for the peak sitting around virtually unused or, at best, under-utilised in periods of low demand.

Where the peak traffic season corresponds with the school holiday period in an airline's home country even more extra staff are needed, since many airline staff with children want to take their own holidays during the same periods and are away from work. It may be possible in some areas to overcome the peak problem by using seasonal staff employed for three to six months during the peak period. Many airlines do this, notably for cabin crew.

Seasonal peaks in demand for air services to and from each country or on particular routes arise as a result of either institutional or climatic factors. The distribution and length of school holidays, the patterns of annual holidays for factories and offices, religious festivals such as Christmas, the Chinese New Year or the Hajj pilgrimage, and the distribution of major cultural and sporting events are the main institutional factors creating seasonal traffic peaks. Climatic factors are important through their effect on holiday patterns or by disrupting surface modes of travel.

Where institutional and climatic factors coalesce, then seasonal peaks become very marked. In the European area, traditional summer holidays for schoolchildren and employees coincide with climatic conditions in the Mediterranean basin which are ideal for seaside holidays and are markedly better than those in northern Europe. As a result, during the summer months there is an outpouring of people moving southwards from northern Europe. The effect on airline peaks is dramatic, particularly for those scheduled network, low-cost or charter operators who focus on catering for this demand. In North America, the Christmas holiday season coincides with very cold winter weather in Canada and parts of the United States while Florida and the Caribbean bask in warm sunshine. These conditions create a very marked peak of demand for air services to the Caribbean area in late December and early January.

Daily or weekly peaks are related to the pattern of working times and days during the week. Business travel creates daily demand peaks usually in the early morning and early evening and weekly peaks on Sunday evening or Monday morning and on Fridays. In those Muslim countries that have Thursdays and/or Fridays as days of rest, the business peaks will be different. On the other hand, leisure traffic is responsible for a peaking of demand at weekends, particularly during the holiday seasons. Inevitably, the split of traffic on any route between business and leisure influences the nature of the daily, weekly and seasonal variations in demand.

The daily and weekly peaks in demand generally pose a less severe handicap than the seasonal peaks. If airlines have a mixed network, where peaks occur at different times, they can switch aircraft around the network to keep them busy at all times. There is also enough flexibility in most airlines' operations to enable them to make sensible use of spare capacity during particular periods of the day or the week. Maintenance and training flights can be programmed for such slack periods. Many international airlines find that, on scheduled routes with a high business component, demand falls off at the weekend and they can reduce their frequencies on Saturdays and Sundays. A few use this spare weekend capacity on flights to meet the needs of the leisure market, which prefers weekend travel. Thus, BA City Flyer, which operates from London City Airport to mainly European business centres during the week, switches its aircraft during summer months to leisure holiday destinations at the weekends.

It is the seasonal peaks of demand which create more problems and impose the greatest costs. The monthly variations in demand levels vary considerably between different types of international routes. As a consequence, they pose varying problems for the airlines operating each type of route and may require somewhat different responses. The passenger traffic in the peak and trough months in the year 2017 for a small sample of six routes radiating from London are shown in Table 8.2. Three are long-haul routes and the other three are European short- to medium-haul routes.

As expected, really problematic traffic flows manifesting the most acute seasonal peaking problem are found on routes to major holiday destinations. Traffic from London Gatwick to Faro in Portugal was almost four times as high in August as in February 2017. From Gatwick to Orlando passenger traffic was nearly three times as great in August as in February. This is symptomatic of demand pattern on holiday routes with a clearly defined peak season related to climate. Many routes from northern Europe to the Mediterranean and also from Canada to the Caribbean fall into this pattern though in the latter case the peak is during the northern winter months.

Table 8.2 Seasonality problems – peak month versus low month for sample London routes, 2017

Route	Feb 2017 pax (000)	Aug 2017 pax (000)	Increase high over low month
Short-haul			
Heathrow–Athens	46	74	+ 61%
Heathrow–Munich	81	107	+ 16%
Gatwick–Faro	30	116	+ 287%
Long-haul			
Heathrow–Singapore	90	111	+ 23%
Heathrow–Washington	45	82	+ 82%
Gatwick–Orlando	35	103	+ 186%

Source: compiled by author from CAA data

In other markets, the seasonal variations may be less extreme but may still be very marked. Heathrow–Athens is an example (Table 8.2). In 2017 traffic was uniformly high during the Mediterranean summer months from May to October but these levels were generally 50–60 per cent higher than in the weakest winter month, February. This contrasts with Heathrow–Munich, which also peaks in the summer holiday season but the peak–trough variation is much lower. The peak month was only 16 per cent higher than the lowest month. This is because of the higher business component on the Munich route and because leisure traffic on this route is less dependent on the search for good seaside weather!

Airlines operating in markets with very marked seasonal variations in traffic face a major strategic dilemma. If they try to offer the full capacity needed during the peak months, they may find much of their productive capacity (aircraft and crews) is under-utilised in off-peak months and therefore costly. If, on the other hand, they limit the extra capacity they need to offer in the busiest months when demand is greatest, they may lose some high-yield passengers to competitors and also lose market share. But by limiting their own capacity they may be able to push up fares. Different sectors of the airline industry deal with this dilemma differently.

Low-cost airlines have tried to limit the degree to which they cut back on the capacity they offer in shoulder or off-peak periods compared to their offer in the peaks. This inevitably means that off-peak capacity may be too high, in relation to anticipated demand, but the response of low-cost carriers has been to try to fill these extra low-season seats by marketing very low fares and through successive low-fare promotions.

At the very least, pricing can help lengthen the period of peak or shoulder demand.

They also try to get higher daily utilisation of their aircraft in peak months by lengthening the flying day through much earlier morning and later evening departures. The network carriers may be unable to do this as their major hubs often have noise constraints. The daily utilisation can also be increased by operating with very rapid aircraft turn-rounds. Higher aircraft utilisation in peak months may partly alleviate lower utilisation in the off-peak months when schedules are reduced. The British LCCs can switch aircraft, flying to the Mediterranean summer resorts, to serve winter ski destinations. But all this may not be enough. They may still be forced to ground some aircraft during periods of low demand and release seasonally employed staff or put them on minimum-hour contracts, if that is possible. Thus, in winter 2015–16 Ryanair grounded around one-quarter of its aircraft for some months as it cut back on its summer schedule.

The legacy or traditional scheduled carriers have been less successful at dealing with marked season traffic peaks. A scheduled legacy airline operating on routes with different peak periods can try to shift aircraft and other resources between routes according to the season so as to ensure high utilisation. However, Table 8.2 shows that an airline such as British Airways operating a range of services out of Heathrow, its home base, would have only limited scope to do this since on so many London routes peaks and troughs of demand fall at the same time of the year. Many other airlines face the same problem. Nevertheless, competitive pressures and the need to target the higher yields that can be generated at peak periods generally push airlines to increase their flight frequencies during the peak seasons. As a result, the capacity provided by most scheduled airlines on international services in the peak season is substantially higher than in the low season.

Peak problems also exist in the movement of freight by air, but they are frequently less of a problem than peaks on passenger services. The use on longer sectors of the wide-bodied passenger jets, which have considerable freight capacity in their holds, means that peaks in the flow of air cargo can be met on many routes without the provision of extra peak capacity. The much more serious problem in air freighting is the directional imbalance of flows that arises because freight travels only one way, unlike passengers, who generally make a round trip (see Chapter 13).

Coping with the seasonal variations in demand is a major headache for some airline managements since they affect so many aspects of airline operations. Pricing policies, operating schedules, maintenance and overhaul checks and advertising campaigns all need to be carefully manipulated in order to minimise the adverse effect of traffic peaks and troughs on aircraft and crew utilisation and on load factors, and through these on unit costs. (Peak pricing is discussed in Chapter 11.) To mitigate the adverse impact of highly peaked demand, airlines may also lease in aircraft or try to use seasonally employed labour during peak periods. Whatever techniques are used to diminish its impact, the seasonality of demand remains a problem to a greater or lesser extent for all airlines and is an underlying constraint in many aspects of airline planning and marketing.

8.7 Drivers of passenger demand

The demand for passenger services arises from the complex interaction of a large number of factors which affect the different market segments differentially. Those factors fall broadly into two groups, summarised in Table 8.3: the general economic and supply-related factors that influence demand in all markets and the more particular factors that may influence demand on some routes but may be totally absent on others.

Of the *general factors* affecting demand, the price of air transport and the level and distribution of personal income in the markets served are perhaps the most important. Much of the growth of air travel during the last 40 years can be explained by the falling real price of air transport (as discussed in Chapter 1) and more especially by growth in the world's economies and rising personal incomes. A more detailed discussion of the impact of price changes follows in the next section.

As far as the impact of economic growth is concerned, there appears to be a very strong correlation between the annual rates of growth in the world's gross domestic product over the last 40 years and the growth rates in air travel, measured in revenue

Table 8.3 Factors affecting levels and growth of passenger demand

General factors affecting all markets	Local factors affecting particular routes
Level of personal disposable income	Level of tourist attraction: Scenic/climatic/historical/ religious attributes Adequacy of tourist infrastructure Comparative prices
Supply conditions: Fare levels Speed of air travel Convenience of air travel	
Level of economic activity/trade	Exchange rate fluctuations
Population size and growth rate	Travel restrictions
Social environment: Length of paid holidays Attitudes to travel	Historical/cultural links
	Earlier population movements
	Current labour flows
	Nature of economic activity

passenger-kms. Broadly speaking, air travel grew each year by, on average, one-and-a-half to two times as fast as world GDP.

Traffic growth is influenced not only by the more general economic climate but also by more localised factors. Accelerated rates of traffic growth in particular markets at particular times have usually been due either to rapid growth in personal incomes at either end of the route(s) or to falling air fares. The world economic climate and the rate of economic growth in particular countries or regions of the world influence demand in a variety of complex ways. They determine the level of industrial and economic activity in each country and more generally the level and nature of international trade. The level of economic activity and trade directly influences the growth of demand for business travel. Indirectly, it also influences leisure demand since it affects the level and growth of personal incomes.

Economic factors such as personal incomes or industrial activity have to be understood within a demographic context. The size and the distribution of the populations served by a route impose a major constraint on the level of potential demand. Thus, despite rapidly rising personal incomes in Singapore, the potential demand for Singapore-originating air travel is strictly limited by the small size of the island's population of only 5.6 million. This explains Singapore Airlines' critical need to develop Fifth and Sixth Freedom traffic if it is to remain a big player in international air transport. Conversely, Japan-originating leisure traffic has barely scratched the surface of the potential demand, given Japan's population of about 125 million and its rapid economic growth up to the mid-1990s. While rapid population growth may in theory increase the size of the air market, in practice it may have an adverse effect if it results in lower per capita incomes or in a larger population but one with a disproportionate share of young children who are unlikely to be air travellers. Both these phenomena have been evident in Morocco and Algeria, countries with birth rates well above average.

The social environment is also important in all markets since it determines the number of days of holiday available for travel or leisure and social attitudes towards travel. Thus, one finds in Japan that workers do not take all the holidays they are entitled to but stay at work. In the same country, though there are many working women with relatively high disposable incomes, it is only in the last 20 years or so that social attitudes have begun to accept the idea of women holidaymaking on their own, though it is acceptable for men. For both these reasons, and given its high wage levels, Japan represents a huge potential market for air travel, which will boom as social attitudes change and people start taking more of their holiday entitlement and as the notion that women can travel on their own becomes more widely accepted. At the other extreme, in much of western Europe two long holidays away from home, one in the summer and a shorter one in winter, have traditionally been the social expectation of the middle- and upper-income groups. However, in recent years this too is changing with a trend to take more, shorter leisure breaks. This has been stimulated by the very low and simple fares offered by low-cost carriers.

Demand and supply do not interact only through the price mechanism. As previously mentioned, various supply conditions other than price affect demand. In the short term, frequency, seat availability, departure and arrival times, number of en-route stops and other supply features influence the level of demand and the distribution of that demand between competing carriers.

In addition to the general considerations affecting all markets, several *other localised factors*, which may be particular to individual routes, also influence demand levels. These are factors that may explain growth on some routes but not on others (Table 8.3). Demand for holiday trips is related to the tourist attractiveness of particular destinations. In order to be attractive and have tourist potential, resort areas or towns need two things: they must enjoy certain attractive and preferably unique scenic, climatic, historical or cultural advantages; they must also have the right infrastructure to cater for tourist needs such as sufficient hotel beds of the required standard, adequate ground transport, restaurants, entertainments, shopping facilities and so on. An attractive tourist location without the necessary infrastructure is not enough to generate a significant volume of demand for holiday travel, as many countries in the developing world have found. The two must go hand in hand.

Tourist facilities in themselves may not be enough. They must be priced correctly for the market they hope to attract and in relation to competing destinations. Changes in the relative price levels of hotels and other facilities in a tourist resort area may accelerate or retard traffic growth on particular air routes. Changes in the relative costs of holidays in a country may come about as a result of internal economic conditions or even government decisions, but they may also be generated by fluctuations in the exchange rates. Often, switching of tourist demand from one destination to another or the acceleration of outward-bound tourists from a particular country can be related to changes in the relevant exchange rates. In late 2016, as the value of sterling fell in relation to the euro, some European destinations became less attractive to British tourists. Conversely, travel to Britain appeared much cheaper for many in Europe.

Exchange rate fluctuations or even political factors may induce governments to impose travel restrictions on their own citizens. These may take the form of bans on external travel, the imposition of travel taxes for outgoing travellers or restrictions on the amount of foreign exchange that can be taken out for travel purposes. Following the economic crisis that hit several East Asian countries in late 1997, South Korea, the

Philippines, Indonesia and Thailand all restricted travel for some time by one or more of these measures.

Ultimately, of course, leisure travel is also related to taste. Tourist destinations can inexplicably fall into or out of favour. Countries may become more attractive as a result of adverse developments elsewhere. In-coming tourism to Greece accelerated in 2016 and 2017 because of political and security problems affecting other leisure destinations in the eastern Mediterranean.

Visiting friends and relatives (VFR) demand is clearly affected by earlier population movements and migrations, which are very specific to particular routes. The heavy volume of demand on routes between France and Morocco, Algeria or Tunisia is related to the large number of emigrants from these countries living and working in France. Conversely, there is little VFR traffic on routes between North Africa and the UK. On the other hand, traffic demand between the UK and Canada, the West Indies, Pakistan or Australia and from Singapore to southern India or Sri Lanka can be explained only by earlier population movements. The same is true of the demand between the United States and Israel or the United States and Ireland. Many earlier migrations of population were related to the colonial period of history. Colonial ties have also resulted in linguistic and cultural links between particular pairs of countries, which generate certain types of leisure travel but also considerable student travel. Large numbers of Singaporean, Malaysian or Hong Kong students go to English-speaking countries such as Australia, the UK or the United States to study. Students are an important component of demand on the air routes between their home countries and their place of study.

Population migrations for work or settlement impact on travel patterns. Since the 1980s relatively dense traffic flows have been generated by movements of migrant labour, such as those from the Philippines, India or Pakistan to Saudi Arabia and other Middle East states. More recently the migration of large numbers of Polish workers to the UK and Ireland has stimulated dense air passenger flows often catered for by low-cost carriers.

The demand for business travel is related to several factors, not just the level of trade and commercial interaction between two city pairs. It would seem that the nature of industrial, commercial and other activities in an airport's hinterland is an important determinant of the level of business travel demand. Certain activities appear to generate more business trips than others. At the London airports, banking and finance generate a disproportionately high level, around 25 per cent or more, of UK-originating business travel but account for well below 10 per cent of employment. This reflects London's role as a global financial centre. Administrative capitals obviously generate a great deal of government-related travel. Equally there is some evidence that major international ports generate a disproportionate amount of business air travel. Then there are very specific industrial situations that may stimulate, often for a short term, a rapid growth in demand for air services. The exploration and development of a new oil field or the construction and commissioning of a new industrial complex would be two such examples.

The pattern and growth of demand on any route can be understood only by reference to the economic and demographic characteristics of the markets at either end of the route and to the supply features of the air services provided, of which price is the most important. However, when examining traffic growth on an individual route one must also consider any particular or localised factors such as those mentioned earlier that may affect demand on that route. These may include the tourist attractiveness of one or both ends of the route, the historical and cultural ties between the two markets served, the impact of exchange rate fluctuations, earlier or current population movements, and so on. These various factors provide an explanation of the growth and current level of demand on a route. Changes in any of them will affect the growth of traffic in the future. Nonetheless, the overall demand for air travel, like that for most goods or services, seems ultimately to be most closely related to its price and to the income levels of its potential consumers. The impact of changes in income level and prices on demand are therefore worthy of more detailed consideration.

8.8 Income and price elasticities of demand

Forecasting both the growth in total demand and changes in its distribution requires an understanding of the impact of changes in national and personal income. Historically, leisure travel has shown a marked responsiveness to personal income levels. Surveys of air passengers have established that two things happen as people's personal incomes rise. First, they spend more on all non-essentials. This includes greater expenditure on travel by all modes. Second, air transport, which is the high-cost but more comfortable and convenient mode for longer journeys, becomes more competitive with surface travel and there is a shift of demand from surface modes to air. In other words, higher incomes result in greater expenditure on longer-distance leisure and VFR travel, and at the same time a higher proportion of that expenditure goes on travel by air rather than surface modes.

The relationship between income changes and demand for air travel can be measured by what economists call the income elasticity. This is arrived at quite simply by dividing the percentage change in demand generated by an income change by the percentage change in personal income which brought about that shift in demand:

$$\text{income elasticity} = \frac{\% \text{ change in demand}}{\% \text{ change in income}}$$

Thus, if a 3 per cent increase in personal income results in a 6 per cent growth in demand for air travel then the income elasticity is 6 per cent divided by 3 per cent, which is +2.0. This means that every 1 per cent variation in income will induce a 2 per cent change in demand. A comparison of annual changes in world GDP and air travel over the 20 or so years to 2008 suggested a global GDP elasticity of demand of around +1.4 (IATA, 2008). This will, of course, differ by country and by market.

Multiple regression models are used to establish income elasticities of demand for air travel in different countries or markets. Using historical time-series data, showing air passenger numbers, personal or national income or GDP levels and one or more other variables, the models aim to establish how demand responds to changes of income.

A number of problems arise. The first is how to isolate or exclude the impact of other variables, such as fare changes, on demand. This is the aim of multiple regression techniques, which in turn pose certain methodological problems discussed in the next chapter. Second, there is the question of how to measure personal income. Ideally one would like to use a measure of the per capita personal disposable income (after adjustment for inflation) of the population in a market or of the populations served at either end of a route. But disposable income data are not always available, and countries tend to calculate it differently. Proxy measures have to be used for disposable income. Gross national product (GNP) or gross domestic product (GDP) are frequently used but they may be converted into per capita GDP. The latter is itself problematical in that it assumes a fairly even distribution of income among a country's population, which frequently is not the case. In the past the UK's Civil Aviation Authority (CAA) in their forecasts have used an index of consumer expenditure as a readily accessible measure of the income available to consumers in different countries. Third, since air travel for leisure is a relatively new form of expenditure, one can assume a higher rate of growth in the early stages of increasing incomes and then a gradual saturation as people on high incomes get to the stage where they cannot easily consume more leisure travel. But how do we know when a saturation level is being reached?

One would not expect the demand for business travel to be closely related to per capita income since business travellers' expenditure patterns are related not to their own personal incomes but to the needs of their employers. On the other hand, several studies have found that gross domestic product or some other measure of a country's national income or wealth correlates with the volume of business traffic generated. It is not difficult to accept that business activity and travel will increase as a nation's total wealth grows. Thus, it has proved possible to establish income elasticities for business travel but based on changes in national rather than in per capita income.

In the United Kingdom most demand studies have produced results indicating income elasticities, for various categories of passengers, which were usually between +1.0 and +1.5. As one would expect, these studies indicated lower income elasticities for business as opposed to leisure travel.

This is the case in one of the more recent analyses, that of the UK Department for Transport in its 2017 forecasts (Table 8.4). This found the UK leisure sector to have an income elasticity of +1.4 with regard to international air travel while the UK business sector's elasticity is only +1.2. For foreign visitors flying to the UK, the elasticities for both business and leisure demand were lower (Table 8.4, column 2).

But these are only global figures. At a disaggregate level income elasticities were found to vary by market area as well as purpose of travel. Thus, UK leisure travel to less developed countries, primarily Saharan and Sub-Saharan Africa but not South Africa, showed the highest elasticity among overseas markets at +1.84.

An earlier and more global study carried out by IATA found broadly similar results. Income elasticities of passenger demand in developed countries was +1.3 for short–haul travel but higher at +1.5 for long–haul travel (IATA, 2008). Elasticities were higher in

Table 8.4 Income and price elasticities used for UK aviation forecasts, 2017

Market sector 1	Income elasticity 2	Price elasticity 3
UK business	+1.2	−0.2
UK leisure	+1.4	−0.7
Foreign business	+1.0	−0.2
Foreign leisure	+1.0	−0.7
Domestic business	+1.0	−0.5

Source: UK Aviation Forecasts. Department for Transport, October 2017

the United States at +1.6 for short-haul and +1.8 for long-haul. These figures suggest that long-haul travel becomes progressively more attractive as incomes rise. In this they mirror the results of the UK Department for Transport study.

Apart from income, price is the other variable that has, historically, had a major impact on the growth of air travel. The responsiveness of demand or fare changes can also be measured in terms of coefficient:

$$\text{income elasticity} = \frac{\%\ \text{change in demand}}{\%\ \text{change in price/fare}}$$

Unlike income elasticity, price elasticity is always negative since price and demand must move in opposite directions. If the fare goes up, demand is expected to fall and vice versa; so there is invariably a negative sign in the equation. If fares go up 3 per cent and demand drops 6 per cent, then the price elasticity is $(-6\%) \div (3\%) = -2.0$.

Normally, some form of time-series regression modelling is used to identify fare or price elasticities in different markets. Most of the problems previously mentioned which have to be faced when estimating income elasticities also arise in price elasticity studies, but there are some additional ones too. In examining traffic and fare data, for a route or several routes over a period of time, which fare should one choose to indicate price changes? Not only will there be several fares on each route, but the fare levels often may change rapidly over time, sometimes from day to day. Some analysts have overcome this problem by establishing different price elasticities for different fare groups or classes. It is the real level of the fare, in constant value terms, that is significant, not the current level. Therefore, fares have to be adjusted for price inflation so as to establish the real cost of air travel in relation to the cost of other goods and services. On international routes this means making different adjustments at each end of the route. An additional problem in establishing fare elasticities in leisure markets is posed by the inclusive tour (IT) passengers, who have no knowledge of the cost of the fare within their total holiday package price. Moreover, fare changes within an IT package will have a disproportionately small impact on the total holiday price paid by the prospective IT consumer.

In so far as business travellers do not pay for their own travel, one would expect them to be relatively insensitive to fare changes. This should be reflected in lower price elasticities for business travellers compared to leisure or VFR passengers. An examination of price elasticities in most studies shows this to be true. An example is the UK Department for Transport report mentioned earlier (Table 8.4, column 3). This indicates relatively low fare elasticities for both UK and foreign-based air travellers on routes to the UK. Interestingly, the most price-sensitive market segments are often those at the lower end of the market, that is those travelling on highly discounted fares such as those offered by low-cost airlines when entering new markets.

It is the high elasticity of demand to price changes at the bottom end of the leisure market that appears to explain the very rapid growth of demand for low-cost airlines such as Southwest in the United States and Ryanair and easyJet in Europe. But another factor has also played a part. This is the so-called price cross-elasticity of demand. This measures the responsiveness of demand for product A (say a low-cost airline) to the price of product B (say the fares of a legacy network carrier). In other words, very low LCC fares diverted passengers from higher-fare airlines, but also surface modes such as rail, bus or private cars.

Economics textbooks deal at length with the concept and the mathematics of elasticity. It is not opportune to discuss the complexities of the concept here. Suffice it to say that, in order to make pricing and other marketing decisions, airline managers need to have a feel for the price elasticity of the various market segments on the route or routes they are dealing with. Without such a feel, they may make major planning and pricing errors. They basically need to know whether their markets, or rather different segments of each market, are price elastic or inelastic. They also need to have an awareness of the fare cross-elasticities affecting these markets.

If the price elasticity of demand in a particular market is greater than -1.0, that is, if it is -1.1, -1.2 or more, the market is considered to be elastic. This means that a change in the price or fare has a more than proportional impact on demand. If the fare is reduced, demand will grow more than in proportion. Though each passenger will be paying less than before, many more passengers will be travelling, with the result that the total revenue generated will go up. Conversely, a fare increase in an elastic market has such an adverse effect on demand that total revenue will decline despite the fare increase. When the price elasticity is less than -1.0, as in the case of many business markets, demand is inelastic. Fare changes have a proportionally smaller impact on demand levels. In such market conditions, fare increases will generate greater total revenue because demand will not fall off very much. On the other hand, fare reductions will stimulate some traffic growth, but it will be proportionately less than the drop in fare, so total revenue will decline.

The easiest way of appreciating the pricing and revenue implications of different price elasticities is to consider a simple hypothetical example. Let us assume that on a short-haul international route an airline is flying a daily return service with a 200-seater aircraft. It is the only operator and there is a single fare of $100 one way. The daily traffic and revenue on the route can be summarised as in Table 8.5.

Because of an unexpected increase in jet fuel prices, the airline needs to increase revenue on the route by about 4 per cent. In the short term, costs cannot be reduced in other areas, so the marketing manager is required to generate the additional revenue through tariff changes. The instinctive reaction would be to increase fares to cover the increase in costs. However, earlier market research had established that, while business demand is relatively inelastic to fare changes, with an elasticity of -0.5, the leisure market is very price elastic with an elasticity of -2.0. Using these price elasticities the marketing manager estimates the traffic and revenue impact of a 10 per cent increase in the fare from $100 to $110.

The business price elasticity of -0.5 tells him that, for every 1 per cent increase in the fare, the airline will lose 0.5 per cent of its market. Thus, a 10 per cent fare rise results in a 5 per cent loss of business travellers (i.e. change in demand $= +10\% \times -0.5 = -5\%$). Therefore, their daily number will decline by 5 per cent, from 100 to 95. Leisure

Table 8.5 Case study: short-haul international return flight $100 single fare

Total seats offered per day (200 each way)	= 400
Business passengers (approx. 50 each way)	= 100
Leisure passengers (approx. 50 each way)	= 100
Daily seat factor (200 pax in 400 seats)	50%
Revenue from business market (100x$100)	= $10,000
Revenue from leisure market (100x$100)	= $10,000
Total revenue per day	= $20,000

traffic, being more elastic to price changes, will drop more, by 20 per cent (or −2.0 per cent for each 1 per cent increase in fare), to 80 passengers on average each day.

Surprisingly, in this example, even a 10 per cent fare increase results in a drop in revenue, not an increase (Table 8.6). Revenue from business travellers would go up because, though fewer would travel, the drop in traffic is more than compensated for by the higher fare they are all paying. But leisure passengers react in larger numbers to the higher fare and total revenue from this segment of the market would go down markedly. The net result is that, if the airline followed an instinctive reaction and increased the fare by, say, 10 per cent, it would end up with a significant fall in traffic, and a collapse of the seat factor from 50 per cent to 44 per cent. This in turn would lead to a drop in total revenue. Too often airlines fail to appreciate that increasing fares may reduce rather than increase their total revenues.

What would be the effect of reducing the fare by 10 per cent to $90? Both business and leisure demand would increase – the former by 5 per cent (i.e. −10% x 0.5 = +5%) and the latter by 20 per cent. Using the price elasticities as before, the traffic and revenue implications can be calculated (Table 8.7).

The lower fare would generate 25 more passengers each day and the seat factor would jump to 56 per cent, a creditable improvement from the current 50 per cent. Most of the additional passengers would be leisure passengers, who are more price elastic, and revenue from this sector of the market would increase. While there would also be more business travellers, business revenue would decline because the 5 per cent increase in passenger numbers would not be sufficient to compensate for the 10 per cent drop in fare paid. However, total revenue would increase by only $250. This might do little more than cover any additional costs imposed by the extra 25 passengers. Cutting fares would produce a better revenue result than increasing the fares, by increasing total revenue by 1.25 per cent. But this is still less than the 4 per cent required.

Examination of these figures suggests that revenue could be maximised by a two-fare price structure (Table 8.8). The airline should charge the business travellers more because their demand is relatively inelastic to price, but it should charge less to the price-elastic leisure market, knowing that lower fares will generate proportionally more demand and thereby increase total revenue from this market segment.

By introducing separate fares for each market segment, the airline can increase its total revenue by $1,250 or 6.25 per cent and its seat factor by four points to 5.4 per

Table 8.6 Impact of $10 increase from $100 to $110 single fare

95 business passengers at $110 = $10,450
80 leisure passengers at $110 = $ 8,800
175   = $19,250
Seat factor: 175 as percentage of 400 seats = 44%

Table 8.7 Impact of $10 cut from $100 to $90 single fare

105 business passengers at $90 = $ 9,450
120 leisure passengers at $90 = $10,800
225 passengers Total revenue = $ 20,250
Seat factor: 225 as percentage of 400 seats = 56%

Table 8.8 Impact of two-fare price structure – $90 and $110 fares

95 business passengers at $110 = $10,450
120 leisure passengers at $ 90 = $10,800
215 passengers Total revenue = $21,250
Seat factor: 215 as percentage of 400 seats = 54%

cent. The net revenue gain might be less because there may be some extra costs involved in carrying 15 more passengers. This solution also presupposes that the airline can create effective tariff 'fences' to prevent slippage of business passengers into the low-fare market. Simply put, the above example illustrates the principle that, in price-elastic markets, low fares may increase total revenue and that conversely, where demand is price inelastic, higher fares will generate higher total revenue.

It must be emphasised that even on a simple route the best pricing solution is dependent on two variables, the price elasticities of the different market segments, and those may be more than two, and the market mix, that is the proportion of the total market represented by each segment. In the example, the pricing policy recommended might be different if business travellers represented 90 per cent of the market or if the price elasticity of leisure demand was −2.4 instead of −2.0.

8.9 Are fare/price elasticities low?

The UK Department for Transport study of air travellers found, as mentioned earlier, that the demand for air travel to and from the UK was relatively inelastic to changes in air fares (Table 8.4, column 3). Price elasticity of demand was −0.7 for leisure and even lower at −0.2 for business. Most studies have found, as one might expect, that businesspeople are even less responsive to fare changes on long-haul international routes than on shorter routes. This may reflect the fact that while on short sectors travellers may switch to surface modes in response to fare changes, they cannot do this on long sectors.

An IATA review of price elasticities found similar results. It suggested that falling real air fares have not been the main driver of the growth of air travel demand in the last 30 or more years. Changes in fares affect choice of airline or may lead to switching destinations. But long-term growth in demand for air travel has been driven by rising incomes. This is evidenced by the numerous studies that show income elasticities to be higher than price elasticities in most markets. One reason for this may be that for leisure travel the air fare is only one part of the total holiday cost.

Low price or fare elasticities suggest that demand is unresponsive to fare changes, but this assumes relatively small or marginal changes in fares. Southwest and later the European low-cost carriers realised that dramatic deep fare cuts of the order of 50–70 per cent or more could generate an explosion of demand even if the fare elasticity was −0.8 or even less. In Europe in the late 1990s and early 2000s Ryanair and easyJet were growing their traffic by 20 to 30 per cent each year by entering new markets and slashing the prevailing fare levels. Not only would much lower fares generate new demand, but the price cross-elasticity, which was strongly in their favour, would divert passengers away from traditional network carriers who continued to offer higher inflexible fares. In Europe, the LCCs also diverted traffic from charter airlines whose package holidays were not flexible enough. Ryanair and easyJet, like Southwest before them, clearly understood the concept of price elasticity. Perhaps the fact that very large price decreases were needed to stimulate significant increases in traffic itself suggests that the basic price elasticities were low.

The concept of demand elasticity can be taken further to establish the reaction of passenger demand to changes in other variables. For instance, it is possible to calculate the demand elasticities of service elements such as frequency or journey time. Journey time elasticities would show that business travel is the most responsive to reductions in journey time and VFR demand probably least responsive. There is also the concept of price cross-elasticity mentioned earlier. This measures the impact on the demand for air travel of changes in the price of competing goods or services.

Different studies even of the same markets seem to produce different income and price elasticities. Airlines may have difficulties in choosing between them. Larger ones may carry out their own studies to establish elasticities on the routes they are most interested in. If they can overcome the data and methodological problems, they must still face up to the fact that the elasticities are based on historical traffic data, which may be influenced by particular variables other than fare or income that have not been included in their analysis. There is the additional problem that price, income or other elasticities are changing over time. This is inherent and inevitable. Since elasticities are based on proportional changes in demand, such proportions change as the total demand changes. In the simple example used here, once the fares have changed from the $100 starting level to a new fare generating a different level of demand, then the price elasticities at that new demand level will have changed too, though the change may be a relatively small one.

The pragmatic and methodological problems involved in establishing elasticities should not induce airlines to abandon the concept. Some understanding of elasticities is so crucial for pricing, marketing and forecasting that they cannot be ignored. Even an approximate appreciation of price and income elasticities for the major market segments will help airlines make more soundly-based decisions.

Note

1 Yield or revenue per seat-km (RASK) is a measure of revenue per unit of capacity rather than per passenger or seat sold. As such it is a revenue measure independent of the seat or load factor. By measuring revenue per unit of capacity one can compare it directly with the cost per seat-km (i.e. the CASK) on any route or with any other airline, while leaving aside the passenger load factor achieved.

9 Forecasting demand

9.1 The need for forecasts

Forecasting is the most critical area of airline management. An airline forecasts demand in order to plan the supply of services required to meet that demand. Broadly speaking, tactical or operational decisions stem from short-term traffic forecasts covering the next 6–18 months or so and are included in the airline's operating plan and budget for the current and the coming financial year. Aircraft scheduling decisions, maintenance planning, advertising and sales campaigns and the opening of new sales offices are among the many decisions ultimately dependent on these shorter-term forecasts.

There are in addition a range of strategic decisions, many related to an airline's corporate plan and objectives, which stem from long-term forecasts. Decisions on aircraft procurement and the airline's future fleet plan, the opening-up of new routes or markets, the training of additional flight crews, investment in new maintenance facilities and similar strategic decisions all stem from longer-term forecasts of up to five years or longer. Almost every tactical or strategic decision taken within an airline stems ultimately from a forecast. At the same time, forecasting is the area in which mistakes are most frequently made and the one about which there is least certainty. There is no absolute truth in forecasting, no optimum method that can guarantee accuracy. Instead, airline forecasters use any one of a range of forecasting techniques, of varying mathematical complexity, each of which has advantages, none of which can ensure consistent accuracy. Yet forecasts have to be made since so many decisions flow from them.

The annual budgets and the longer-term plans on which so many supply decisions hinge start with forecasts of passenger and freight traffic. Forecasting involves different types of forecasts, each of which pose different methodological problems. In the first instance, airlines need to forecast traffic growth assuming a continuation of current operating conditions with no dramatic changes in fares or in other supply factors. They may forecast the total growth of passenger and/or freight traffic on a route, group of routes or geographical region. Such forecasts represent the total demand, from which the airline then has to predict its own share and its own traffic. Essentially, they involve an assumption that, all other things being equal, traffic growth will continue in the future very much as it has done in the past.

But frequently 'all other things' are not equal. They do not remain unchanged. The economic climate, exchange rates, and changing tourism trends are among the many external factors that impact on demand and may change over time or very quickly, as is the case after terrorist attacks. Many external factors that impact directly on the demand for air travel or air freight are unforeseeable. Their impact may be local or much wider. Because external factors are unpredictable they create much of the uncertainty in airline forecasting.

Demand is also dependent on numerous internal factors and changes. Airlines need to be able to forecast the response of demand to a change in the conditions of supply. Such changes may include an increase or reduction in the real level of fares, a change from narrow- to wide-bodied aircraft, a marked increase in frequencies or a change in departure times. A significant change in supply conditions may be under consideration by the airline itself or change may be imposed by one or more of its competitors. In either case, an airline must be in a position to forecast traffic reaction to such changes in the supply conditions.

A somewhat different forecasting problem exists when an airline is trying to forecast demand on a new route under evaluation. This may frequently be a route on which there have been no direct air services at all previously, or it may be a route on which the airline concerned is a new entrant. In either case the airline has no experience and there may be little or no historical traffic data on which to base its forecasts. This is particularly so if the route has had no previous air services at all. Forecasting in such circumstances is clearly very difficult, with a high risk of error, and may require different forecasting techniques from those normally used.

Finally, there is the question of segmental forecasting. Passenger traffic on a route is composed of identifiable market segments related partly to purpose of travel and partly to service requirements. Such segments may be further categorised by point of origin. The earlier analysis of demand factors indicated that each market segment is likely to have differing demand elasticities and to be growing at different rates (Chapter 8). It should therefore be possible to produce more accurate forecasts by forecasting the growth in each market segment separately and then aggregating them, rather than by forecasting the total traffic from the start. Many traditional network airlines already produce forecasts using two market segments, business and leisure, or possibly three or more based on fare types. Only a small number of airlines have the resources to carry out more extensive segmental forecasting. In the future, however, planning requirements and the need to improve the accuracy of forecasts may push more airlines to consider this disaggregate forecasting. In many airlines there is a dichotomy in forecasting methods. If an airline has a yield management system, its revenue planners may be using very detailed forecasts disaggregated by fare type but with a very short time horizon of a year or two; yet, in the same airline, route and fleet planners will be basing their own three-to-ten-year forecasts on less detailed models with fewer market segments.

The aim of this chapter is not to suggest the best way of forecasting but to review and assess some of the problems of forecasting and the alternative techniques most commonly used in the international airline industry, without going too deeply into their mathematics. As a result, this is not an exhaustive review, since some forecasting tools, little used by airlines, are not examined. The forecasting methods more widely used by airlines, often in combination, fall broadly into three groups of growing complexity: qualitative methods, time-series projections and causal or econometric methods.

9.2 Qualitative methods

9.2.1 Executive judgement

Of the numerous forecasting techniques available to airlines, executive judgement is one of the most widely used, often to modify and adapt other more mathematical forecasts. Such judgement is based on the insight and assessment of a person, who often may not be a forecaster, but who has special knowledge of the route or market in question. For instance, the country or area managers of an airline are frequently asked to predict traffic growth on their existing or new routes. Their knowledge will include an understanding of recent and current traffic levels and growth and an awareness of competitors' plans. They will also be aware of economic and other developments likely to affect future demand, as well as first-hand knowledge of their own market and its peculiarities. They weigh up the factors involved and therefore their judgement and their predictions may be quite soundly based, but the approach is basically simple and unscientific. The more detailed and the more long-term the forecast, the more likely it is that executive judgement will prove inadequate. On the other hand, executive judgement as a forecasting tool has two distinct advantages. It is quick. Forecasts can be made almost instantaneously and do not require any detailed assessment or working out of data. In addition, the person or persons making the forecast may be aware of extraneous and particular factors that may affect future demand on a route, which the more data-based techniques would not pick up. It is for this reason that many airlines subject their data-based forecasts, if they do such forecasts, to assessment and possible modification by certain key managers and executives.

9.2.2 Market research

A wide range of market research techniques can be used by airlines in order to analyse the characteristics of demand for both passengers and freight. These techniques will include attitudinal and behavioural surveys of passengers and, it is hoped, those not travelling by air. They will also involve studies of hotel and tourism facilities, surveys of travel agents and business houses, analyses of trade flows and other business interaction, and so on. Analyses of existing traffic flows from airports or government statistics can be used to analyse traffic flows and patterns and hopefully traveller profiles. Using specialist companies that monitor ticket sales, it may even be possible to access data on passengers flying indirectly via hubs to identify their true origin and destination. Any such studies might be commissioned from specialist market research companies or they might be carried out by the airlines themselves.

Many larger airlines in any case carry out regular and systematic surveys of their own passengers so as to build up a profile of their needs and characteristics. Others carry out such surveys on an ad hoc basis when a specific question needs to be resolved. Airlines also build up market knowledge through data collected from their reservation systems, especially from direct online bookings, and from their frequent flyer programmes. The aim of all this is to derive empirically an understanding of how demand for air transport varies between different sectors of the population or, in the case of air freight, between different industrial sectors. This knowledge can then be used in combination with forecasts, done by others, of sociological, demographic or economic changes to predict future levels of demand.

In many circumstances such an empirical approach to forecasting may be more appropriate than the more econometric methods. On an air route where the demand for air travel is suppressed by the inadequate number of hotel beds at the destination, a study of hotel and tourism infrastructure projects at that destination may produce a better indication of future travel flows than would an analysis of past traffic trends. Equally, the forecasting of air freight demand often lends itself to the use of market research studies, especially on routes where freight flows are relatively thin.

On many routes the erratic and irregular growth of air freight makes time-series analyses or other econometric techniques difficult to use. Air freight forecasting models have generally been less successful than models for forecasting passenger demand. On most air routes, the goods freighted by air fall into a limited number of clearly-defined commodities. Exports by air from many developing countries are usually confined to one or two commodities, while imports are quite different and cover a wider, though still limited, range of goods. As a result, air freight forecasts may often fruitfully be based on market research analysis of trade developments in a few key commodities.

Market studies are particularly useful as a forecasting tool when past traffic data is inadequate or non-existent, thereby prohibiting the use of time-series and possibly of econometric forecasts too. This happens on many routes from developing countries and is obviously the case on entirely new routes. In these circumstances market research may be the only way of evaluating future demand. Market research also helps airlines to forecast demand reaction to changes in supply conditions, such as a change of timing, and to gain an appreciation of their different market segments if they wish to get involved in segmental forecasting.

9.2.3 Delphi techniques

The Delphi approach requires the building up of a consensus forecast based on the views of individuals who are considered to have sufficient expertise to be able to anticipate future trends. The process is an iterative one, possibly involving several rounds of consultation. In simple terms, a group of experts may be asked to give their forecasts of growth in a region or market. These forecasts are used to build up a composite forecast. This can then be communicated to each expert, who may wish to revise his own original forecast in the light of what other experts are predicting. The individual forecast from this second round of consultations can be used to arrive at an agreed or consensus forecast. This is the principle of the Delphi method. In practice, the consultative process can be more or less complex depending on the amount of information exchanged between the experts.

The Delphi technique is more suitable for aggregate forecasts of growth in major markets or regions than for individual route forecasts. As a result, it is little used internally by airlines, but until 2014 it was the basis of the industry-wide forecasts produced annually by the International Air Transport Association (IATA). These were regional forecasts for nearly 20 route areas such as Europe–Middle East or Middle East–Far East. Forecasts by direction were produced for freight traffic too. Individual airlines submitted their own forecasts for individual routes or markets. A consensus forecast based on a compilation of individual airline forecasts was then prepared by IATA. It was in essence a Delphi forecast based on a consensus of expert opinion. The IATA annual forecasts were used by smaller airlines as inputs into their own forecasting processes and by larger airlines as a counter-check to their own internal forecasts. After 2014 IATA moved to using more econometric-based models for its forecasts.

9.3 Time-series projections

Time-series or trend projections represent the forecasting technique most widely used by airlines. Many smaller airlines do little else. Essentially the technique involves a projection into the future of what has happened in the past. It assumes that whatever factors affected air traffic in the past will continue to operate in the same manner in the future. The only independent variable affecting traffic is time, and as time progresses so will traffic.

To establish the relationship between traffic (the dependent variable) and time (the independent variable), it is essential to have accurate and detailed traffic statistics for the route in question. Without such data, trend projections cannot be used. The first step in the forecasting process is to plot the time-series data on a graph so as to show monthly or annual traffic totals against the appropriate month or year. Drawing a freehand curve through the points should indicate whether the traffic trend on the route is exponential or linear (Figure 9.1). An exponential trend is one where traffic seems to grow by a constant percentage with each unit of time. This means that the absolute increase in each time period in passenger numbers or freight tonnes is greater than in the previous period. This is because each successive growth is a constant percentage but of a larger preceding total. The equation of the exponential curve is given by

$$\text{traffic}(y) = a(1+b)^t,$$

where a is a constant and b is the rate of growth and t is time. A linear or straight-line trend is one where the traffic increases by a constant absolute amount with each unit of time. It is expressed in the form

$$\text{traffic}(y) = a + bt,$$

where a and b are constants and t is again time. Because changes for each unit of time are by a constant amount and the total traffic is growing, the percentage growth is gradually declining.

There is therefore a fundamental difference between the impact of exponential as opposed to a linear growth trend on forecasts of traffic growth. Exponential growth means ever greater annual or monthly traffic increments, though the percentage change may be more or less constant. Linear growth would indicate constant increments in terms of numbers but declining percentage changes. Deciding which trend best represents developments of a route will therefore have a major impact on forecasts, especially longer-term ones. There is also the possibility that growth on a route may be linear in its early stages and then become exponential or vice versa. An added problem is that at times it might be difficult to decide whether an exponential or linear trend fits the data best, yet choosing between them will produce quite different forecasts.

It has been observed that some air routes or markets, after achieving very rapid growth for a number of years, reach a plateau where traffic growth flattens off. It is frequently assumed that this plateau level is reached when the market has matured and is in some sense saturated. If this has happened or is happening on a route, the trend of past traffic data may best be described by growth curves that asymptotically approach an upper limit such as a logistic curve or a Gompertz curve. Both of these are S-shaped and indicate declining absolute and relative growth as markets reach maturity. In practice, international airlines tend not to use logistic or Gompertz trend curves for forecasting. Most time-series forecasting is either exponential or linear. Of these, the former is probably more widely used both because of its simplicity and also because past air traffic trends often appear to be exponential.

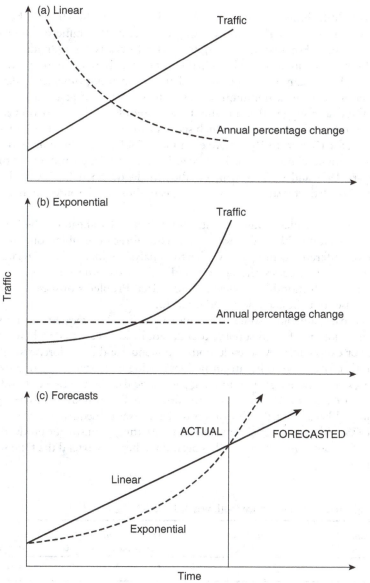

Figure 9.1 Types of traffic growth
(a) Linear: $y = a + bt$, (b) Exponential: $y = a(1+b)^t$, (c) Forecasts: linear and exponential

Most published forecasts, whether for individual routes or markets, are shown as being exponential; that is, the forecast is given as a percentage growth rate, though the rate may decline over time.

The workings and implications of different time-series techniques can best be appreciated by using them to make forecasts for an actual route. The historic case study chosen is London (all airports) to Nice on the French Mediterranean, a short-haul scheduled route with little indirect traffic transiting via Paris or elsewhere. The case study assumes that one is living in 1984 and wishing to forecast the traffic on the route for 1988, five years hence. For reasons of simplicity the forecasts for individual years from 1984 to 1988 are not discussed. Though the data used is old, London–Nice is used because it exemplifies many of the problems that arise in using time-series data.

To make time-series forecasts, a minimum of seven to ten years of past traffic data is required and some forecasters suggest that one should not forecast for a longer period ahead than about half the number of past years for which statistics are available. For the London–Nice route, traffic data for 12 years to 1983 were examined (Table 9.1). This indicated that, though passenger movements almost doubled between 1972 and 1983, growth was at times erratic, with two years, 1974 and 1977, in which traffic actually declined. Such volatility in traffic growth was also characteristic of many European short-haul routes in the two decades after 2000.

In practice, many larger airlines would hesitate to forecast so far ahead on the basis of time-series projections alone. Nevertheless, a five-year forecast enables one to see clearly the impact of different techniques. While the analysis which follows relates to annual traffic volumes and forecasts the annual traffic for 1988, the same forecasting methods could be used with monthly or weekly traffic data. Problems of seasonal traffic fluctuations would arise, but these could be adjusted for.

The London–Nice data underlines some of the difficulties faced in forecasting. To start with, examination and plotting of the past traffic data do not make it easy to decide whether past growth is linear or exponential. As a result, both exponential and linear forecasts will be made in the analysis that follows. Another major problem facing forecasters using time-series analysis is how far back they should go in examining past traffic data. In the case of London–Nice, ten-year data to 1983 meant 1974 would be the first year. This was known to be a year in which traffic slumped because of the first oil crisis. There was subsequently a very large jump in traffic in 1975. Using a maverick low year as the starting point might produce less accurate forecasts, so forecasters may decide, as has been done here, to extend the time series back by two years to 1972.

Table 9.1 Total passenger traffic, London–Nice (both ways), 1972–83

Year	Terminal passengers '000	Annual change %	Three-year moving average passengers '000	Annual change %
	1	2	3	4
1972	140.6			
1973	148.5	+ 5.6	143.8	
1974	142.4	− 4.1	151.6	+ 5.4
1975	163.8	+15.0	158.6	+ 4.6
1976	169.6	+ 3.5	166.9	+ 5.2
1977	167.4	− 1.3	174.0	+ 4.3
1978	185.0	+10.5	187.4	+ 7.7
1979	209.9	+13.5	206.7	+10.3
1980	225.1	+ 7.2	225.4	+ 9.0
1981	241.2	+ 7.2	245.0	+ 8.7
1982	268.8	+11.4	259.3	+ 5.8
1983	268.0	− 0.3		

Source: *UK airports: Annual statements of movements, passengers and cargo*, UK Civil Aviation Authority

This then raises a different question. Are data and traffic so far in the past a good reflection of what will happen five years in the future? Would it not be logical to take a shorter time series? Is the recent past a better indicator of the future than the more distant past? There is no absolute answer to this enigma. Forecasters must choose the time series they feel in each case will best allow them to make a realistic forecast. To do this they must ensure that their stream of data embodies the underlying trends and encompasses complete cyclical variations if any exist.

9.3.1 Exponential forecasts

9.3.1.1 Average rate of growth

Many airlines, especially the smaller ones and those that have relatively new routes with only a short stream of data, base their forecasts on the average of the past rates of growth. This approach has the advantage of simplicity. In the London–Nice case, adding up the annual percentage change each year from 1972 to 1983 and dividing by 11, which is the number of observations, produced an average annual growth of +6.2 per cent. Using the formula

$$y = a(1 + b)^{t},$$

where a is the actual traffic in 1983, b is the growth rate and t is the number of years forecast, then

$$1988 \text{ traffic} = 268 \times (1.062)^{5} = 362.0$$

In this and subsequent equations, traffic volumes are in thousands.

In the London–Nice case, the number of observations is relatively small, and only 12; this is so with many airline forecasts, but it raises some doubt about whether +6.2 per cent is the true average growth rate. It is possible to estimate mathematically what the possible range of values for the true growth rate might be. The true growth rate at a 95 per cent level of confidence would be 6.2 ± 4.2. If one were to adjust the 1988 forecast accordingly, the range would be very wide. It is for this reason that most airline forecasters tend to ignore the implications of having a relatively small number of observations.

9.3.1.2 Moving average growth

The use of annual average growth rates should be based, in theory, on data series that are long enough to show what are the random variations and what are shifts in underlying trends. Where the time series is not very long and where there are very marked fluctuations in traffic growth from year to year, as in the case of the London–Nice data (Table 9.1), some forecasters will use moving averages as a way of flattening out wild traffic variations so as to understand the underlying trends.

In order to do this, normally three (or more) observations are added together and the average calculated. This is then given as the actual observation for the middle of the three years (or months if one is using monthly data). For London–Nice the actual traffics for 1972, 1973 and 1974 were added together and divided by three. This produced a three-year moving average of 143,800, which was the traffic attributed to 1973, the middle year (column 3 of Table 9.1). Then 1972 was dropped and the average for 1973, 1974 and 1975 calculated and attributed to 1974 and so on, the final moving average being for 1982. The choice of the number of observations for the moving average is up to the forecaster, whose aim is to eliminate sudden short-term traffic variations without losing sight of longer-term changes.

Moving averages cannot be used with small data sets since one effectively loses data at each end. Examination of the moving average data for London–Nice in Table 9.1 (columns 3 and 4) shows a flattening out effect. Traffic does not decline in any single year and the growth in the good years is not as high as the unadjusted annual figure would suggest. The highest growth was 10.3 per cent in 1979, following which there seems to have been a downward trend in the underlying growth rate.

The annual average rate of growth can be calculated from the annual changes in the moving average figures (column 4 in Table 9.1). In this case it was 6.8 per cent. Using this to forecast 1988 traffic, then

$$1988 \text{ traffic} = 259.3 \times (1.068)^6 = 384.8$$

The use of a moving average here seems to have identified a faster underlying growth than was evident previously.

9.3.1.3 Exponential smoothing

Some forecasters believe that the recent past is a better pointer to the future than the more distant past. It follows that, in projecting past traffic growth into the future, greater weight should be given to the more recent observations. Mathematically, the technique for doing this is similar to the moving average but adjusted to give a particular weighting to recent as opposed to more distant observations. In a simple form,

$$y + 1 = \alpha y + \alpha(1 - \alpha)y_{-1} + \alpha(1 - \alpha)^2 y_{-2} + \alpha(1 - \alpha)^3 y_{-3} \ldots$$

where α is a smoothing factor ($10 < \alpha < 1$), y is the number of passengers in year y, and $y + 1$ is the first-year forecast.

The greater the value given to α, the greater will be the weight given to the more recent observations. The forecaster can decide the value of α. The above formulation is relatively simple, but some smoothing techniques can be quite complex. The best known is the Box-Jenkins model. This is a sophisticated and complex model requiring a large number of observations. Though airline forecasters make reference to Box-Jenkins (Nguyen Dai, 1982), few actually use it.

Simpler formulations are available. One of these is Brown's double exponential smoothing model and another the Holt-Winters model. Both use a smoothing technique to deal with time-series data containing a trend variation. Since the London–Nice traffic data showed a clear trend pattern, the Holt-Winters model was used. The 1988 forecast produced on this basis was 326,200 passengers. This is much lower than the other exponential forecasts because the effect of the smoothing technique is to give much greater weight to the fact that in 1983, the most recent year, traffic declined marginally. While exponential smoothing techniques have been widely used in some other industries, their use is still fairly limited within the airline industry. There is, however, a growing awareness that, by giving greater weight to the more recent observations, forecasters may be in a position to improve the accuracy of time-series projections.

9.3.2 Linear trend projections

9.3.2.1 Simple trend

The underlying assumption is that a straight line best represents the trend of the traffic over time and that traffic increases by a constant amount with each unit of time. The technique involves drawing a straight line through the time series so as to produce a best fit. This is normally done by the least squares method, though other mathematical techniques are also available. The least squares criterion requires that the line fitted to the data should be the one which minimises the sum of the squares of the vertical deviations of the individual data points from the line. Some of the points are likely to be above the line, and therefore positive, and some below the line, and so negative. These would cancel each other out if one were merely trying to minimise the sum of the deviations. By using the squares of the deviations this problem is avoided.

In fitting a line of the form $y = a + bt$ to the time-series data so as to satisfy the least squares criterion, there remains the problem of how closely the straight line corresponds to those data. The goodness of fit is measured by an index known as the coefficient of correlation (R), or the square of this quantity (R^2), which is strictly speaking the coefficient of determination. In practice the R^2 coefficient is used most frequently. If the fit of the straight line to the data is very poor, the value of R^2 approaches zero. If the fit is very good, the value of R^2 will be close to 1.0. Within the airline industry, experience suggests that accurate predictions using linear trend lines require very high coefficients of determination. They should be above 0.90 and preferably higher.

Fitting a trend line to the London–Nice data produced the following result:

$$y = 111.9 + 12.7t, \qquad R^2 = 0.939$$

This indicates that a trend line starting at 111,900 passengers and growing by 12,700 passengers per year (t) produces a good fit with the actual traffic in each year since the coefficient of determination at 0.939 is high. To forecast traffic in 1988 one needs to add 12,700 passengers for each year of the 17 years from 1972 to 1988 to the starting figure of 111,900:

$$1988 \text{ traffic} = 111.9 + (12.7 \times 17) = 327.8$$

Trend projections are simple and easy to use, but they can be used only if the data exhibit some regularity without wide fluctuations. Many air routes, however, exhibit very pronounced traffic variations, with large jumps in traffic followed inexplicably by sudden slumps. In such conditions, fitting trend lines with an adequately high coefficient of determination may prove difficult. One possible solution is to use moving averages.

9.3.2.2 Moving average trend

Unusually large variations in the past traffic volumes can be reduced by calculating moving averages and establishing a new time series. This should now contain only the trend component in the traffic and it should be easier to fit a trend line. Using the moving average data for London–Nice (as previously given in column 3 of Table 9.1), the following trend line and forecast were calculated:

$$y = 119.9 + 13.1t, \qquad R^2 = 0.961$$

$$1988 \text{ traffic} = 119.9 + (13.1 \times 16) = 329.5$$

On London–Nice, the use of a moving average trend produces a forecast very close to the one based on the unadjusted trend. This is because the London–Nice traffic did not exhibit wide fluctuations and therefore using a moving average trend has relatively little impact. It has been done here only for illustrative purposes.

If one working in 1984 was forecasting the London–Nice traffic five years later, that is for 1988, and using alternative time-series techniques, five differing forecasts could have been produced. They are summarised in Table 9.2. The difference between the highest and the lowest forecast is around 58,000 passengers a year, equivalent to five round-trip flights a week in an Airbus A320 at about a 65 per cent seat factor. The range is very wide and could play havoc with any airline's strategic fleet planning decisions. Which forecast should the forecasters and planners go for? As a group, the exponential techniques in this particular case produced higher forecasts than the linear trends. This seems to be frequently so in airline forecasts and may be an additional reason why airlines prefer working with exponential rather than linear projections. They prefer to be optimistic in their forecasts.

What happened on the London–Nice market by 1988? The year-by-year growth after 1983 seems to have been relatively rapid, averaging close to 8 per cent per annum. By 1988, 392,800 passengers were travelling on the route. Comparison with the summary of forecasts (Table 9.2) suggests that growth in this market was clearly

Table 9.2 Alternative time-series forecasts (made in 1984) for London–Nice traffic in 1988

Forecasting method	Number of passengers forecast
Exponential forecasts:	
Average annual rate of growth	362,000
Moving average	384,800
Exponential smoothing (Holt–Winters)	326,200
Linear trend projections:	
Simple trend	327,800
Moving average trend	329,500
Difference between highest and lowest forecast	58,600

Table 9.3 Alternative time-series forecasts (made in 1994) for London–Nice scheduled traffic in 1999

Forecasting method	Number of passengers forecast
Exponential forecasts:	
Average annual rate of growth	859,700
Moving average	920,700
Exponential smoothing (Holt–Winters)	743,400
Linear trend projections:	
Simple trend	764,200
Moving average trend	745,800
Actual traffic in 1999	*980,300*

exponential rather than linear. The linear forecasts were much too low, while two of the exponential forecasts, based on the annual or the three-year moving annual rates of growth, were relatively close to the 1988 outcome. Despite the very high values of R^2 obtained for the linear trends they proved poor predictors of future traffic. This suggests that one should not accept very high values of R^2 uncritically when forecasting.

The exponential smoothing forecast was not very accurate, but this was no doubt due to the fact that 1983 had been a year of slight decline. Had one used 1982 as the final year, when traffic grew 11.4 per cent, then an exponentially smoothed forecast, which places greater weight on the most recent years, would have produced a much higher forecast. This suggests that exponential smoothing may be too dependent on what has happened most recently and may distort the longer-term trend. Moreover, this technique, though called *exponential* smoothing, is mathematically more akin to linear forecasting. This may explain its low 1988 forecast of only 326,200 passengers.

A similar exercise for the London–Nice route carried out ten years later in 1995 to forecast passenger numbers for 1999 produced similar conclusions (Table 9.3). The forecasts were based on annual traffic volumes for the period 1983 to 1994. Most forecasts were way off the actual traffic, especially the linear projections. The exponential forecast, using a moving average, was the closest. This predicted traffic of around 921,000 passengers in 1999 compared to the actual traffic of 980,300, so it was still 60,000 short of the actual traffic. In 1996, however, there occurred a significant change in the supply conditions. In that year, easyJet, a low-cost carrier, launched services from Luton, one of the London area airports, to Nice, offering very low fares. This had a dramatic impact on demand levels. In 1998, by which time easyJet was well established on the route, passenger numbers grew nearly 30 per cent in that year alone. All carriers between London and Nice increased their traffic that year, though growth rates in following years were lower.

The dramatic impact of the entry of a low-cost carrier on London–Nice traffic highlights one of the problems of forecasting based on time-series data. Such forecasts cannot predict and allow for sudden and significant changes in supply or demand conditions. They often need to be modified by executive judgement or the findings of market research. These may be better able to forecast any future changes in the market environment that will impact on traffic volumes.

As markets mature it is likely that annual growth will slow down and as a result exponential forecasts will over time need to reflect this maturity. The London–Nice market shows the onset of maturity very clearly. In the 11 years from 1988, when passengers on this route numbered 392,800, to 1999 traffic grew by 150 per cent to 980,300. Growth rates averaged around 13–14 per cent per annum, due largely to the impact of low-cost carrier easyJet and much lower fares. Forecasts made in 1999 or 2000 using the very high growth rates experienced in the 1990s would have been seriously over-optimistic. In the following ten years to 2009 traffic grew by only 37 per cent to about 1.35 million and annual growth averaged only 3–4 per cent. The market had clearly matured and low fares were no longer stimulating demand as previously. In fact, traffic stopped growing after 2009. Traffic levels fluctuated but by 2016 traffic numbers on this route were little higher than they had been in 2009.

Executive judgement may be needed to assess when markets are maturing and to adjust exponential forecasts downward. Not always easy.

The London–Nice case study supports the view of many airlines that traffic growth is more likely to be exponential than linear. But there will be routes where linear trend projections may produce more reliable forecasts. In practice, every airline's forecasting group has developed, in the light of its own experience, a preference for a particular approach to forecasting involving only one or two of the methods proposed here.

Throughout the world the majority of airlines use time-series projections as the starting point for their forecasting exercises. They are simple to use provided that adequate statistical information on past traffic flows is available. They require little else. They are also likely to be reasonably accurate for short-term forecasts. It is relatively easy to forecast next week's traffic if you know the average traffic handled in recent weeks. Beyond 18 months or so, the risk of error with time-series forecasts increases as various external factors begin to impact on demand. Time-series projections allow airlines to make individual forecasts for each route. Annual forecasts can be disaggregated into monthly forecasts reflecting seasonal variations without too much difficulty. Alternatively, time-series forecasts can be built up using monthly rather than annual data.

Although they are widely used, time-series forecasting methods have a fundamental underlying weakness: they are based on the assumption that traffic growth and development are merely functions of time. As time changes, so does demand. Yet our earlier analysis of demand showed that many factors affect the level of demand, such as the level of trade or of personal income, and that these factors are themselves changing over time. Even if these did not do so, there are numerous supply factors, of which the most critical are the fare levels, which are invariably changing and affecting demand in the process. It is clearly an over-simplification to relate demand purely to changes in time. Time can be only a very poor proxy for a host of other critical variables. The longer ahead the time-series projection, the less likely it is to be accurate, as there is more time and scope for demand to have been influenced by changes in one or more of the many independent variables or to be simply maturing.

There are two ways in which airline forecasters can try to overcome this underlying weakness. Most airlines start by making time-series projections. They then modify these projections on the basis of market research findings and executive judgement and turn them into forecasts. In this way they can allow for the impact of the expected changes in demand factors and of planned changes in supply they themselves control. As an alternative, a few airlines, usually larger ones, may try to use econometric or causal forecasting techniques, which relate traffic growth not to time but to a series of assumed causal factors.

9.4 Econometric or causal methods

The underlying principle of all such models is that the demand for passenger transport or for air freight services is related to and affected by one or more economic, social or supply factors. Economic theory suggests that the demand for any product or service depends primarily on its price, on the prices of competing products or services, on the nature of the product and the degree to which it is essential for consumers, on levels of personal income and on consumers' taste. Changes in any one of these variables will affect demand. Econometric models attempt to measure that causal relationship so that by forecasting or even implementing change in any one of the variables one can predict the consequent impact on demand levels.

The starting point in causal modelling must be to identify and select the factors, known as the independent variables, which must be assessed in order to forecast the dependent variable, which is the level of passenger or possibly freight traffic. The second step is to determine the functional relationship between the dependent variables and the independent variables selected. This means specifying the form of the model to be used. Normally for airline forecasting it will be a regression model. Other model forms such as gravity-type models are used in other areas of transport but less frequently in air transport. The third step in the forecasting process involves the calibration of the model and the testing of the mathematical expression for the relationship between the dependent and the independent variables. Should the tests show that the relationship established through the model is significant and statistically robust then one can move on to the final step. This involves forecasting the independent variables or using other people's forecasts in order to derive from them the forecasts of air traffic.

9.4.1 Regression models

Most econometric forecasts of air traffic tend to be based on simple or multiple regression models, where traffic is a function of one or more independent variables. The two variables most frequently used are the average air fare and some measure of per capita income. Thus, for a route such as London to Nice, one might consider a model of the form:

$$T = f(F, Y, t), \tag{9.1}$$

where T is the annual number of passengers travelling between London and Nice; F is the average fare in real terms; Y is an income measure such as gross domestic product or consumer expenditure per head; and t is some underlying time trend. Fare level, income levels or other economic variables have to be adjusted for inflation and expressed in constant value or real terms. The choice of fare is critical. Ideally only change in the lowest fare should be considered, as only this should affect the total market; changes in other fares would affect only the market mix. On many routes it is not as clear-cut as that, since the number of seats for sale at the lowest fare may be strictly limited in number. Also, many fares including the lowest may be constantly changing, even over a short period of time.

Many analyses will choose the average yield rather than the lowest fare as the fare variable. Income levels pose the additional problem of identifying those whose income one considers to be the variable affecting demand. In the given case, should one use a global figure of UK per capita income and another for French income or should one try to establish the income levels in London and those in Nice? If one adjusts the fare level for inflation, one would have to make adjustments to the fare in euros for Nice-originating traffic and a different adjustment to express the sterling fare in constant terms. This kind of problem would induce many forecasters to develop two separate directional models for the route based on origin of travel. For London-originating passenger traffic going to Nice the formulation would be

$$T_L = f(F_L, Y_{UK}, t_L), \qquad (9.2)$$

where T_L is the London-originating passenger traffic on London–Nice; F_L is the real sterling air fare from London; Y_{UK} is the per capita income in the UK; and t_L is the time trend for London-originating traffic.

In order to convert fares, income or other independent variables into number of passengers, a constant (K) has to be incorporated into the equation:

$$T_L = Kf(F_L, Y_{UK}, t_L), \qquad (9.3)$$

Most airline forecasting models assume that the relationship between the independent variables is multiplicative, that is to say, the effects of each of the variables on traffic tend to multiply rather than to add up. The independent variables must represent quite different influences on demand, otherwise the multiplicative relationship may not apply. Expressing the multiplicative relationship between the dependent and the independent variables in logarithmic form turns the relationship between the logarithms into a linear one:

$$Log T_L = K + a \log F_L + b \log Y_{UK} + c \log t_L + u, \qquad (9.4)$$

where u is an error term and a, b and c are model parameters, and the higher their value the more impact changes in the corresponding variables will have on the traffic level.

It is not essential for the model to be log-linear, but many empirical studies of demand have found this to be a useful and relevant form.

Many forecasters may decide to go further and relate the percentage change of traffic from one year to the next to the corresponding percentage change in the independent variables, in this case fare and income. The model is then expressed as follows:

$$\Delta \log T_L = K + a \, \Delta \log F_L + b \, \Delta \log Y_{UK} + c \log t_L + u, \qquad (9.5)$$

where Δ is the logarithm of the percentage change in the variable in question over the previous year. Effectively a and b are now the demand or traffic elasticities. The value of a is, in fact, the fare elasticity of UK-originating traffic on the London to Nice route, and b is the income elasticity of that traffic. It is through regression models of this kind that the price and income elasticities discussed in the preceding chapter are derived.

Having specified the regression model and the independent variables to be initially included, the model is calibrated to past traffic levels and changes in the independent variables. It is usual for time-series data to be used, that is, past data over a period of time. Less frequently a model may be calibrated using cross-sectional data, that is, data at one point in time but covering many routes. Using an iterative process based on the estimation of ordinary least squares, the regression model establishes the value of the constant term (K) and of the coefficients a, b and c.

It is normal for several model formulations to be tested before the independent variables to be used for forecasting are finally selected. While fare and income levels are the most frequently used, many others have also been found to give good results on particular routes or markets. Models for forecasting business travel may well use trade or an index of industrial production instead of income as a variable. Models on routes where holiday traffic is dominant may include hotel prices, currency exchange rates or some other variable that is especially relevant to tourism flows. Quality of service variables may also be introduced into the model. The simplest of these is a speed or journey time variable, though a few more complex models have included frequency, load factor or some other service variable.

Having fitted the data and established the value of the constant (K) and of the coefficients, forecasters need to find out how statistically sound their model is. They can use it as a forecasting tool only if they are convinced of the reliability of the relationships the model purports to have established. A number of statistical tests can be used for this purpose. The most straightforward is the coefficient of multiple determination (R^{-2}), which measures the closeness of fit of the time-series data to the regression model. A very close fit will produce a coefficient approaching 1.0, whereas a low coefficient of, say, 0.5 or less would indicate a poor fit. Using time-series data one would ideally expect to obtain a coefficient of 0.9 or more if one wanted to use the model for forecasting with some degree of confidence. The R^{-2} coefficient may also be used to choose between models with different combinations of independent variables.

While the R^{-2} value tells forecasters how well traffic variations fit variations in the independent variable, it does not tell them how traffic is related statistically to each of the independent variables separately. This is done by partial correlation coefficients. These measure how closely traffic is related to any one of the independent variables when all other variables are held constant.

Other tests to establish the validity of the model and the significance of the relationships it purports to measure include Student's t test and the F statistic. The latter is an alternative to the coefficient of multiple determination and is found by comparing the explained variance of the data with the unexplained variance. It is not the aim of the present book to deal in detail with the conduct and significance of the various statistical tests which can be carried out. These are covered adequately in many statistics textbooks and in one or two specialist air transport texts (Vasigh et al., 2008).

While academic economists have developed quite sophisticated and apparently robust econometric models for forecasting air traffic, airlines tend to use fairly simple models, which often may not be as statistically sound as, in theory, one might wish. Some airlines undertaking long-term route forecasts may use the econometric-based forecasts produced by bodies such as IATA or the aircraft manufacturers. These all produce route or country-pair forecasts that can be used by airlines as a basis for their own forecasts.

While simpler models may be useful for specific route forecasts, econometric models are used to forecast traffic development in wider country-to-country or inter-regional markets. For example, the UK Department for Transport, in its 2017 long-term forecast of air traffic for the whole of the UK, divides the traffic flows to, from and within the UK into 16 discrete international and two domestic market segments based on purpose of travel, place of residence of passengers, that is UK or foreign, and by geographical area. There are four distinct areas of travel: from the UK to Europe; to newly industrialised countries; to OECD member states; and to less developed countries. There is a separate market segment for transfer passengers. Each market segment had its own causal model and its traffic was forecast separately. This was done because the strength of the independent variables affecting air traffic differs between markets. For all 19 sectors, elasticities were developed on the basis of past data for air fares, exchange rates, GDP, trade volumes on other variables. Using these elasticities and forecast changes in the level of the independent variables, forecasts of air traffic in each segment were produced up to the year 2050. The segmental forecasts were then aggregated to generate the total air traffic for the UK year by year (DfT, 2017). A separate model was then used to allocate this total traffic to individual UK airports.

Econometric models can become very detailed and complex, especially if the forecaster splits the market into numerous discrete segments. Another good example is provided by the forecasts prepared by the International Air Transport Association (IATA). As previously mentioned, after 2014 it moved away from using a Delphi approach to developing a complex econometric forecasting methodology. Short- and long-term passenger forecasts are produced for individual countries and for 4,000 or so country pairs. Key model relationships and elasticities have been drawn from prior studies and models using IATA's historical database. The country pair forecasts are aggregated to produce region-to-region flows and global forecasts (IATA/Tourism Economics, 2017)

For its short-run forecasts, IATA uses four key independent variables. First, GDP growth is used as a composite indicator for business and leisure travel in each country. Second, unemployment levels, compared to their long-run average, are seen as an indicator of consumer confidence and likelihood to spend on air travel. Third, exchange rates affect both destinations visited and outward travel from each country. The final variable is the price of air travel.

The longer term 20-year forecasts use a different mix of independent variables. First, GDP per capita is used as a measure of living standards and is linked to changing propensities to travel as living standards rise. Second, the population size of each country and its demographic structure and predicted changes are important. Older generations travel less, so an ageing population will impact on future demand. Third, a high correlation has been observed between a nation's openness to trade and its propensity to travel by air. Exports and imports as a percentage of a nation's total output measures its trade openness. The final factor is the future level of air fares. IATA believes that the downward trend in average fares or yield will continue at a rate of 1 to 1.5 per cent each year. This will be a result of falling airline costs arising from continuing efficiency improvements and the progressive introduction of new technology aircraft.

Using their own and their consultants' forecasts of changes in the independent variables, IATA generate forecasts of future levels of passenger traffic by country pairs or regions or total traffic for an individual country. The final step is to be able to adjust these forecasts in the light of known or expected developments that might impact on specific country pairs, or different scenarios can be tested. IATA uses two scenarios to adjust its long-term forecasts. The pessimistic scenario tested is that there will be growing protectionism in international aviation. This contrasts with a more favourable scenario that further relaxation of international regulation will stimulate traffic growth beyond the base case especially in regions such as East Asia.

The aircraft manufacturers Embraer, Airbus and Boeing also use complex econometric models to produce long-term passenger and freight forecasts. Airbus, for example, believes that while changes in gross domestic product remain an important driver of demand for air transport, GDP is not the only factor. Airbus uses as many as 15 different explanatory factors (Airbus, 2017). Interestingly, the three aircraft manufacturers' 2018 forecasts were optimistic and predicted long-term annual compound rates of 4.4 to 4.7 per cent, markedly higher than IATA's 3.5 per cent (Table 9.4).

Econometric models pose several methodological problems. Forecasters must bear in mind that very high coefficients of multiple determination are not in themselves a guarantee of causality or even of a close relationship between the independent and the dependent variables. A high coefficient of determination may be produced if the error terms produced by the regression equation fall into a pattern. This is called autocorrelation, and may occur either when a significant independent variable has been left out or when there is a marked cyclical variation in the dependent variable. One can test for autocorrelation using the Durbin-Watson d statistic. The values of d which will enable one to assess whether autocorrelation is present are related to the number of observations and the number of independent variables. As a general rule, if the Durbin-Watson statistics are below 1.5 or above 2.5 the forecaster will be concerned with the possibility of autocorrelation.

Another problem that might exist despite high coefficients of determination is that of multicollinearity. This occurs if the independent variables are not statistically independent of each other. For example, air fares and fuel prices may move more or less in unison and often do. Therefore, including both as independent variables would result in multicollinearity and would pose difficulties in interpreting the regression coefficients. In particular, they could no longer be strictly considered as elasticities. One can test for multicollinearity by using a matrix showing the correlation between the independent variables. Independent variables showing a high correlation, say 0.86 or higher, should not really be included in the same model. The possibility of autocorrelation and multicollinearity are two key problems for the airline forecaster using econometric models. There are other more obscure ones, such as heteroscedasticity, which are dealt with in detail in the specialist texts.

Having developed and tested models such as those described here, anyone forecasting air travel demand needs to obtain forecasts of the independent variables used in order to be able to derive from them forecasts of future air traffic. In doing this, particularly for longer-term forecasts, one should not necessarily assume that the elasticities remain constant over time. It is inherent in the way that elasticity is measured that it must

Table 9.4 Long-term world passenger forecasts compared

Forecaster	Unit used	Period	Compound annual growth (%)
IATA	Passengers	2017–2037	+ 3.5
Airbus	RPK	2017–2036	+ 4.4
Embraer	RPK	2016–2036	+ 4.5
Boeing	RPK	2017–2036	+ 4.7

Source: World Air Transport Statistics 2018, Geneva: International Air Transport Association

change over time as total traffic grows. Because of this, many forecasters build changing elasticities into their predictive processes. Changes in elasticity values can be derived mathematically or they can be assumed. The UK Department for Transport 2017 forecasts, mentioned earlier, use declining income elasticities to allow for growing market maturity (DfT, 2017). In the base year, 2016, income elasticity for UK leisure passengers is +1.4 and for business travellers it is +1.2. By 2050 they have declined to +1.0 and +0.8 respectively.

It is while forecasting the independent variables that some form of sensitivity test may be introduced into the forecasting process. Airlines might consider what would happen to the economy of a particular country and its per capita income if industrial growth did not turn out to be as fast as predicted by the government concerned. Alternatively, they might evaluate the impact of a disruption of oil production in the Middle East on the price of fuel and ultimately on economic growth or on the future level of air fares. These sensitivity tests may produce band forecasts suggesting a range of possible traffic outcomes rather than point forecasts. Another way of dealing with uncertainty is to use different scenarios of, say, GDP growth or future airline regulation to produce different forecasts as IATA does.

For decisions dependent on forecasts over a two-year time span or less, airline managers tend to prefer point rather than band forecasts. Decisions have to be taken and giving a range of forecasts is no help to the decision-makers. They need precise traffic estimates to plan for the immediate future. They expect the forecasters to have assessed the risks and the sensitivity of the forecasts to external variables and to have made the point forecasts in the light of such assessment. When it comes to strategic decisions for the longer term, band forecasts become useful. They should force the airline to maintain flexibility in its long-term planning decisions. An airline must avoid taking decisions that lock it into a size and level of production it cannot easily vary. This is particularly true of aircraft purchase or other major investments. Band forecasts also emphasise the uncertainty inherent in forecasting.

9.4.2 Air freight models

The factors affecting the growth of air freight are complex and often fickle. The tonnage of freight moving on any route is subject to sudden and unexplained variations. There is the added complication that, unlike passengers, who tend to return to their point of origin, freight movements are unidirectional. Also, freight is indifferent to the routeing it uses, unless it is very time sensitive. Therefore, the available cargo flow data may not show the true origin of the freight landed at an airport.

There is a multitude of commodity freight rates on any route and such rates have also tended to be less stable than passenger fares. Much freight capacity is produced as a by-product of passenger capacity, and as a consequence there is frequently an over-provision of freight capacity with a strong downward pressure on freight rates. Tariffs charged often bear little relationship to the published tariff, so that even establishing average tariff levels is difficult. Freight flows are also volatile subject to sudden changes. As a result of all these complexities, it has often been difficult to relate past freight growth on individual routes or country pairs to one or more independent variables.

As a result of such difficulties, airlines wishing to forecast freight growth tend to rely on projecting past trends and then modify such trends on the basis of market research and executive judgement. Such forecasts, in any case, tend to be short term.

Causal freight models tend to be dependent on two independent variables: some measure of world trade such as volumes of exports and an indicator of the average air freight tariffs. The few causal freight models developed have tended to be used for forecasting global air freight demand or demand in large markets rather than on individual routes. Both Boeing and Airbus have used such models. In 2008 Airbus Industrie derived its long-term forecasts of global air freight traffic, measured in freight tonne-kms, primarily from econometric analyses of 144 directional air freight flows. Independent variables driving air freight include economic growth, international trade, air freight yields and industrial production. However, traffic in each direction on every market was analysed separately because freight movements in opposite directions are often imbalanced and involve different types of goods. The Airbus forecast therefore included an extensive analysis of the type of goods traded (Airbus, 2008).

The International Civil Aviation Organization (ICAO) has used econometric models for its long-term forecasts of the world's scheduled air traffic (ICAO, 1997). For instance, using data for the period 1960–91, ICAO developed two separate models, one for passenger traffic and one for air freight. The freight model took the form:

$$\log FTK = -0.41 + 1.58 \log EXP - 0.37 \log FYIELD \tag{9.6}$$
$$ (20.3) (5.1)$$

where *FTK* is freight tonne-kilometres, *EXP* is world exports in real terms, *FYIELD* is freight revenue per freight tonne-kilometre in real terms, and figures in brackets are the *t*-statistics and the $R^2 = 0.996$. This clearly suggested that air freight was much more responsive to growth in world trade than to changes in freight tariffs.

Most route-by-route forecasts for freight are based on a combination of executive judgement, market research and, where appropriate, time-series projections. Frequently such forecasts are on a commodity-by-commodity basis since the number of separate commodities being freighted by air on any route is usually fairly limited. The development of causal models of individual commodity flows may ultimately prove more rewarding than attempts to model total freight flows on particular routes.

9.4.3 Gravity models

Time-series analyses or regression models are of little use when trying to forecast traffic on new routes, where there is no historic traffic data, or on routes where traffic records are inadequate or non-existent. Traditionally, this problem has been overcome by using a combination of market research or executive judgement. Another possible approach is to use a gravity model. This was the earliest of the causal models developed for traffic forecasting. It has been relatively little used in aviation, even though gravity formulations have played a crucial part in many road traffic forecasting and assignment models.

The gravity model concept has a long history. It was in 1858 that Henry Carey first formulated what has become known as the 'gravity concept of human interaction'. He suggested that social phenomena are based on the same fundamental law as physical phenomena and that 'gravitation is here, as everywhere else in the material world, in the direct ratio of the mass and in the inverse one of the distance' (Carey, 1858). One of the first applications to transport was by Lill (1889), studying movements on the Austrian state railways in 1889. Subsequently the concept was taken over by highway engineers who developed gravity models for forecasting road traffic. The first recorded use for aviation was in 1951, when D'Arcy Harvey, working for the US Civil Aeronautics Administration, developed the gravity concept to evaluate the air traffic flow between two communities (D'Arcy Harvey, 1951).

Translating the concept into aviation terms, one starts with the simple formulation that the air traffic between two points is proportional to the product of their populations and inversely proportional to the distance between them:

$$T_{ij} = K \, \frac{P_i \, P_j}{D_{ij}} \qquad (9.7)$$

where T_{ij} is the traffic between two towns i and j, K is a constant, P_i and P_j are the populations of the two towns, and D_{ij} is the distance between them.

The top half of the equation, namely the populations, contains the generative variables while the bottom half contains the impedance variables, in this case distance. This is a simple causal model with population size and distance as the independent variables affecting traffic flow. As the concept has been developed, both generative and impedance factors have been modified and the model has become more complex. For instance, the level of air fares has often been considered a better measure of impedance than distance. It has also been thought necessary to modify crude population numbers to take account of purchasing power, nature of economic activity of that population, and so on.

An early study in 1966 involved replacing the population in the interactive formula by the product of the total air traffic of each of the cities concerned (Doganis, 1966). Total airport traffic was thought to provide a good measure of a region's income levels, of the type of economic activities within it and of the effective catchment area of its airport. Using airport traffic obviated the need to incorporate other economic variables into the model. It was also found that raising the distance term to a power other than unity improved the correlation of the model when tested against actual traffic levels. This model took the form:

$$T_{ij} = K \, \frac{A_i \, A_j}{D_{ij}^p} \qquad (9.8)$$

where T_{ij}, K and D_{ij} are as before, but A_i and A_j are the total passenger traffics of the two airports at either end of the route and P is distance raised to a power of between 1 and 1.5.

Subsequent studies using gravity models to predict traffic on new or potential routes include one in 1989 carried out for the European Commission, which involved forecasts of air traffic between airports in the southern regions of the European Community, some of which did not already have direct air links (Westminster, 1989). Various model formulations were calibrated on 47 existing air services for 1987. The one that produced the highest correlation of 0.97 took the following form:

$$T_{ij} = K \, \frac{(A_i \, A_j) \, Q^{3/4}}{F^{1/2}} \qquad (9.9)$$

where K is a constant, A_i and A_j are the scheduled passenger traffics at each of the two airports, $Q^{3/4}$ is a service quality variable raised to the power of three-quarters, and $F^{1/2}$ is the normal economy fare raised to the power of half. The quality of service variable (Q) was a measure of equivalent weekly frequencies that makes allowance for intermediate stops and type of aircraft. Whereas a weekly non-stop jet service is given a Q value of 1.0, a one-stop service is valued at 0.5 and a turbo-prop service at 0.7. Services involving two or more en-route stops are ignored.

The great advantage of gravity models is their ability to forecast traffic between airports that have not been served by air links previously. Consultants frequently use such models. Lufthansa Consulting, for example, developed a complex gravity model for forecasting passenger traffic for new air services in Europe. It's a complex model in which the generative variables are the populations, the gross domestic product and the tourist numbers of the two regions, and the total passenger traffic of the airports to be served (Solomko, 2009). Other studies have used various combinations of generative and impedence factors (Grosche et al., 2007).

Over the last 20 years, in Europe it has been above all the low-cost airlines that have launched new air services between numerous airports, often very small ones, not previously served. In the case of Ryanair the strategy has been described as one of flying from 'nowhere to nowhere'. But the LCCs did not use gravity models to assess the potential demand on the new routes they were launching. Nor did they use other models. They used a combination of executive judgement and limited market research, for instance to establish the number of migrant workers from one end of the route who were working at the other, or patterns of holiday home ownership. But above all they relied on the impact of extremely low fares in generating demand and new travel patterns. When evaluating the launch of services on routes already served by others, low-cost carriers, while examining historical traffic data on the route, focused on the impact their very low fares would have on diverting traffic from existing carriers.

Michael O'Leary, Chief Executive of Ryanair, summed up this approach by saying, 'We don't set up to meet demand, our aim is to create it'. With a strategy of very low fares, low-cost budget airlines had less need for sophisticated forecasting tools. But they were flexible. If they got it wrong, they were quick to pull out of a new route if it did not meet their traffic targets.

9.4.4 Assessment of economic models

The strength of causal forecasting models is that they are logical. They relate demand to changes in factors one would expect to have an impact on demand. The models chosen must therefore be logical too, despite the findings of any statistical tests. A model with a high coefficient of determination should not be used if the independent variables are intuitively wrong. The forecaster's direct experience of market conditions and knowledge gained through market research can provide an insight into demand behaviour, which may ultimately be more useful than that obtained through statistical analysis and mathematical correlation.

The models used must be logically consistent. If they are, it follows that, if one can forecast the independent variables for three or more years, then one should be able to derive longer-term traffic forecasts with a lower risk of error than if one were using time-series projections where demand is related purely to changes in time. Herein lies the strength of causal forecasting but also its weakness: by using a causal model in the interests of logical consistency and greater accuracy, airline forecasters transpose their problem. Instead of having to forecast air traffic, they must now use someone else's forecasts of the independent variables and, if these are not available, they must make their own. Many governments, central banks and other institutions make forecasts of gross domestic product, consumer expenditure, trade and other economic indicators that might be used as independent variables. Such economic forecasts are not always reliable, nor are they necessarily long term. No forecasters in 2006 or 2007 were predicting the melt-down of key economies in 2009 nor the sudden collapse of the oil price in mid-2014. Where more than one institution is forecasting a particular variable, the forecasts do not always agree. If the air fare is one of the independent variables used, then this should in theory be easy for an airline to forecast since it is under airline control. In practice it is difficult for the airlines to predict fare levels more than two or three years hence, without getting embroiled in forecasting oil prices or changes in other factors that may affect future fare levels.

Causal techniques pose some further problems too. Like time-series analyses they also depend on the availability of historical data. Clearly, to calibrate regression models in particular one needs not only good air traffic data but also adequate and accurate statistics going back many years of independent variables being used in the model. In most developed countries these should be available. In many Third World countries, adequate data is either unavailable or possibly unreliable. Where data is available, the complexity of the modelling work is daunting and time-consuming, especially if an airline wishes to develop separate forecasts for key markets or major routes, each requiring separate models.

It should be borne in mind that econometric forecasting, despite its inherent logic and mathematical complexity, is not a mechanistic exercise. Judgement is involved at all stages, from the model specification to the choice of independent variables, and more especially in the choice between alternative forecasts of those independent variables.

9.5 Choice of forecasting technique

It is clear from the preceding analysis that there is no certainty in forecasting; no forecasting tool that can guarantee the accuracy of its predictions. Even very similar forecasting methods may produce widely diverging forecasts. Whatever the uncertainties, however, airlines cannot avoid making forecasts because so many other decisions stem from them. Their forecasters and planners must make a choice between the numerous forecasting techniques open to them. Several factors will determine that choice.

The starting point is to determine the prime objective of the forecast. Is it to forecast traffic growth; is it to predict the reaction of demand to some new development such as a fare increase or frequency change; or is it to forecast the traffic on a new route? While all techniques enable one to make a forecast of traffic growth under normal conditions, only a few are suitable for forecasting traffic reaction or demand on a new route (Table 9.5). If an airline is planning to open up an entirely new route, it has little choice but to use a qualitative technique or a gravity model.

Having determined the forecasting techniques suitable for the type of forecast being undertaken, then speed and data availability become important criteria. A quick forecast means either executive judgement or a straightforward time-series projection. Data availability is crucial for certain of the techniques. Time-series projections need accurate and detailed traffic data over a reasonable period of time. Regression models need all that but also adequate data on the independent variables included in the model. If either traffic data or data on the various socio-economic variables are unavailable and unobtainable, then the forecaster is obliged to turn to qualitative methods. Cost may be an important consideration too. Smaller international airlines may not be prepared to meet the high costs of market research, while sophisticated causal forecasting for them would mean using consultants, and consultants do not come cheaply. In fact, some smaller airlines are dependent on aircraft manufacturers for their long-term forecasts or use IATA forecasts combined with their own executive judgement for shorter-term planning.

If speed, data availability and cost are not a constraint, then airlines might choose between the forecasting techniques open to them on the basis of their predictive accuracy. This is a difficult judgement to make. The various techniques are listed in Table 9.5 and their accuracy for short-, medium- and long-term forecasts is indicated on a three-point grading of poor, fair and good. However, the gradings are to a certain extent subjective and influenced by one's personal experience and judgement. Different forecasters would use different gradings. Inevitably, most techniques are fairly accurate for short-term forecasts and some are also reasonable for two-year forecasts. Beyond that time span there is some doubt, but it is likely that qualitative or causal techniques will produce the more accurate forecasts. These techniques are also the most likely to be able to identify and predict turning points in the underlying growth trends. In theory, causal models should produce the better results, but some aviation experts suggest that there is no compelling evidence that econometric techniques produce more accurate air traffic forecasts than do the simpler and more straightforward approaches.

Within most international airlines a range of forecasting techniques is used. Faced with differing planning requirements, airlines carry out both short- to medium- and longer-term forecasts. The former tend to be based on time-series projections, frequently modified by executive judgement and by market research findings. The precise time-series technique or techniques used by each airline will depend on its experience and the judgement of its forecasters. Where new routes are being evaluated, the airline's preference may well be to use market research methods to forecast potential demand. For longer-term forecasts beyond a couple of years or so, many smaller airlines continue to use time-series projections, despite doubts about the accuracy of such methods for longer time spans. Some of the larger airlines switch to causal models for long-term forecasts often using forecasts prepared by others such as those of IATA, ICAO or the aircraft manufacturer. But, ultimately, so many exogenous and unpredictable factors may affect air transport demand that forecasts beyond three to five years ahead must be thought of as being very tentative.

Table 9.5 Attributes of airline passenger forecasting techniques

	Qualitative methods			Time-series projections				Causal models	
	Executive judgement	Market research	Delphi	Annual average growth	Exponential smoothing	Linear trend	Linear trend on moving average	Regression analysis	Gravity model
Accuracy:									
0–6 months	Good	Good	Fair/good	Fair/good	Good	Fair/good	Good	Good	Good
6–24 months	Fair	Good	Fair/good	Poor/fair	Fair/good	Poor/fair	Fair	Fair/good	Fair/good
5 years	Poor	Poor/fair	Fair	Poor	Poor/fair	Poor	Poor/fair	Poor/fair	Poor/fair
Suitability for forecasting:									
Traffic growth	Good	Good	Good	Good	Good	Good	Good	Good	Good
Traffic reaction	Fair	Good	Fair	n.a.	n.a.	n.a.	n.a.	Good	Poor
Traffic new routes	Poor	Fair	Poor	n.a.	n.a.	n.a.	n.a.	Fair	Good
Ability to identify turning points	Poor/fair	Fair/good	Fair/good	Poor	Fair	Poor	Poor/fair	Good	Poor
Ready availability of input data	Good	Poor/fair	Poor	Good	Good	Good	Good	Poor/fair	Fair
Days required to produce forecast	1–2	90+	30–180	1–2	1–2	1–2	1–2	30–90	20–60
Cost	Very low	Very high	Moderate	Low	Low	Low	Low	High	High

Note: n.a. = not applicable

10 Product planning

Our product needs to be at least as much better than it is more expensive.
(Lufthansa Roadshow Presentation, January 2018)

10.1 Key product features

Product planning is about deciding what product and service features an airline should offer in each of its markets. It is also about ensuring their delivery. For each airline, product planning is crucial in two respects. First, it is the key tool in the process of matching potential demand for air services with the actual supply of services it offers in the markets it serves. Each airline controls its own supply of services but can influence the demand only through its product planning. Much, therefore, depends on product planning. Second, as previously mentioned, product planning has a direct impact on operating costs (Sections 4.6 and 4.8).

In deciding what products to offer in the different markets it has entered, an airline has to bear in mind a number of objectives. It must consider its overall marketing strategy, which will have emerged as a result of its demand analyses and forecasts (Chapters 8 and 9). It must set out to attract and satisfy potential customers in the different market segments it has identified. This means using its understanding of the needs and requirements of these different market segments. Such understanding will have been acquired through a range of market research activities, including passenger and other surveys, the monitoring of its own and its competitors' past performance in each market or route, and so on. Finally, an airline will want to maximise its revenues and profits, not always in the short term but certainly in the long run. In brief, the ultimate aim of product planning is to attract and hold customers from the market segments that an airline is targeting and to do this in such a way as to generate adequate profits.

Experience suggests that passengers, when making travel decisions and when choosing between airlines, are influenced by numerous factors or product features. These fall broadly into five groups, which are summarised in Table 10.1. Clearly some features could be included in more than one group or category.

An airline must decide how to combine these various product features to meet customer needs and stimulate demand in different markets. This is a complex process because customer requirements will vary not only between different market segments on the same route but also between neighbouring routes and geographical areas. In

Table 10.1 Key product features affecting travel decisions and choice of airline – but also operating costs

	Product group	Product feature
1	Price	Fare levels and conditions
2	Schedule based	Network size – no. of points served Frequency Timings Non-stop flights Connections Punctuality
3	Comfort based	Type of aircraft Interior configuration Individual space Boarding experience On-board service Ground/terminal service Airline lounges In-flight entertainment (IFE)
4	Convenience	Distribution/ease of reservations Baggage allowance policy Capacity management policy Seat availability Ability to change reservations
5	Reputation	Reputation for safety Branding Use of digital technology Frequent flyer loyalty schemes Promotion and advertising Market positioning

N.B.: Some product features might be considered as falling into more than one product group

different parts of its network an airline may offer different combinations of these five product features. To a certain extent there may even be a trade-off between them. Greater comfort can be offered, for instance, by reducing the number of seats in an aircraft, but this may necessitate selling at higher fares. One would expect that the fare level or price is the most critical product feature for many market segments, especially in many price-sensitive leisure or VFR markets. It may be less important for business markets that are relatively price inelastic, though even here marked fare differentials between airlines or between different fares on the same airline may have an impact. Fares are also the most dynamic product feature in that they can be changed rapidly, often daily, at least in deregulated markets. Moreover, in those short-haul markets and routes where low-cost airlines have made a major impact, air travel has begun to resemble a commodity, in that price or fare has become the dominant product variable.

This has been confirmed by many passenger surveys including a 2017 worldwide survey of 10,675 passengers conducted by International Air Transport Association. This asked respondents to name the three most important factors that influenced their airline choice. The results are shown in Table 10.2. Clearly price or fare is the dominant factor, mentioned by nearly two-thirds (63 per cent) of respondents as being one of their three important choice factors. This is why the question of pricing and revenue generation justifies the more detailed investigation provided in Chapter 11.

It is frequently suggested that air travel has been commoditised. There is not much to choose between airlines and as a consequence price and price alone is the dominant factor when travellers choose between carriers. Certainly the 2017 IATA survey confirms the dominance of price as a choice factor. But the surprising result of this survey was the importance afforded to 'airline reputation' by 39 per cent of respondents. 'Reputation' in this survey also embraced safety record and perceived punctuality. It was all-embracing. This may explain why it was ranked higher in this IATA survey than in earlier surveys. The significance attributed to 'reputation' perhaps suggests that air travel is more than just a commodity.

In markets that are price inelastic or those where fares of competing carriers are very similar, product features other than price become relatively more important in determining the market penetration of different airlines. They also tend to become relatively more important in medium- and especially long-haul routes. The results of the 2017 IATA survey suggest that schedule-based factors and image are relatively more important than comfort or convenience factors (Table 10.2). But in different regions of the world and for differing market segments the critical product features will vary.

Interestingly, membership of a frequent flyer programme seems to be declining in importance. In a 2008 IATA survey of business passengers, FFP membership was the single most important factor in choice of airline. It remains important but as Table 10.2 indicates it is less significant than some other factors. The 2017 survey suggests that this is so even among passengers travelling in First or Business class. It may well be that the attraction of FFPs has declined as virtually all airlines now offer them and business travellers are likely to belong to more than one programme.

Table 10.2 Three most important factors influencing choice of airline

Decision factors mentioned	Mentioned by:	Factors other than price by grouping			
	%	Schedule	Comfort	Convenience	Reputation
Price	63				
Flight schedule	45	✓			
Airline reputation (inc. safety and punctuality)	39				✓
Frequent flyer programme	26				✓
On-board comfort	23		✓		
Flight duration	14	✓			
Connection at convenient airport	13	✓			
Baggage allowance	11			✓	
Competent, friendly cabin crew	11		✓		
Easy booking on computer	8			✓	
Responsive customer service	7			✓	
Food and beverage	6		✓		
In-flight entertainment	5		✓		

Source: 2017 Global Passenger Survey, Geneva: IATA
Note: Respondents asked to name three factors so percentages add up to over 100. Seven factors mentioned by less than 5 per cent of respondents not included above

As one would expect, the factors influencing choice of airline are different if passengers are going on short- as opposed to long-haul flights (Table 10.3). For both types of flights by far the most important factors are the 'price' of the ticket, the 'flight schedule' and the 'airline's reputation'. For short-haul flights, the air fare is relatively more important, mentioned by 73 per cent of respondents, while for long-haul flights 62 per cent mentioned price as one of their three key decision factors. The flight schedule is also more significant when deciding on short-haul flights than on longer trips. The success and growth of low-cost airlines in the last 20 years or so is clearly linked to their product offering of faster point-to-point schedules, bypassing the hubs, and much lower fares.

When looking at those product features mentioned less frequently, it is clear that for long-haul travellers comfort features, as expected, are generally more important in their choice of airline than they are for those travelling shorter distances. 'On-board comfort', 'competent and friendly cabin crew', 'food and beverage' and 'in-flight entertainment' are all mentioned by a higher proportion of long as opposed to short-haul passengers. Interestingly 'easy booking on computer' is mentioned by 19 per cent of short-haul passengers but by only 7 per cent of those travelling further. This suggests that a much higher proportion of the former make their own bookings. It also emphasises why a user-friendly and interactive website is so critical for airline distribution.

10.2 Schedule-based features

Most surveys, including the 2017 IATA survey, show that for many airline passengers schedule features are, after price, the most frequently mentioned decision factor (Tables 10.2 and 10.3). From a consumer viewpoint, the critical schedule-based features in any market are the number of frequencies operated, the convenience of departure

Table 10.3 Three most important factors influencing airline choice by flight length

Decision factors mentioned	Nature of flight	
	Long-haul %	Short-haul %
Price of ticket	62	73
Flight schedule	39	51
Airline reputation (inc. safety and punctuality)	41	42
On-board comfort	22	18
Frequent flyer programme	17	16
Flight duration	20	12
Competent/friendly cabin crew	17	10
Easy booking on computer	7	19
Baggage allowance	13	15
Connection at convenient airport	10	11
Food and beverage	9	6
Responsive customer service	8	8
In-flight entertainment	7	2

Note: Respondents asked to name three factors so percentages add up to over 100. Seven factors mentioned by less than 5 per cent of respondents not included above
Source: Global Passenger Survey 2017, Geneva: IATA

and arrival times, the total journey times, the points served and in particular whether flights are direct or involve one or more stops or a change of aircraft en-route. For long-haul flights an important schedule feature may be whether the flights are during daylight hours or overnight. Interestingly, aircraft type is not seen as important, though on some short-haul routes a jet may well be preferred to a turbo-prop.

Different market segments will have differing schedule requirements. Short-haul business markets generally require at least an early morning and an early evening flight in each direction on weekdays so as to allow business trips to be completed in a day. But the ideal is several flights each day. Weekend flights may be less important for business travellers but crucial for short-stay weekend holiday markets. Frequency requirements will also vary depending on the type of market, the length of haul and the level of competition. For instance, offering a once-daily service when a competitor has 10 flights a day is unlikely to make much impact on the market.

Passenger surveys frequently highlight the importance of punctuality. Numerous surveys, especially in the United States, have emphasised growing passenger concern with poor on-time performance. This is why United States airlines are required to submit on-time performance records to the Department of Transportation. These are publicly available so that they can be seen, if required, by passengers when booking flights. The second leading cause of consumer complaints in the United States has been lost or delayed baggage. Here, too, airlines are required to provide comparative statistics on how often they lose, delay or damage baggage. The UK Civil Aviation Authority (CAA) has followed the US lead on punctuality but not on baggage, which is less of a problem in European markets. Currently, UK airlines have to submit punctuality data to the CAA, which is then published. Punctuality is a schedule-related feature but because data is publicly available and often in the media, an airline's punctuality record clearly impacts on its image and brand.

The main reason why schedule-based features together with the fare are generally the most important factors affecting airline choice for many market segments is that they can be seen and quantified objectively. They are explicit and precise: one can compare one scheduled departure time with another, or the total journey time of a direct as opposed to a one-stop service. By comparison, assessment of comfort, convenience or image-based product features, such as the quality of an airline's in-flight entertainment or of its distribution system, is more subjective. Customer perception of these product features will vary for each trip and between different customers on the same flight. They cannot easily be quantified or compared between different airlines.

10.3 Comfort-based product features

The schedule-related features of an air service are important in all markets, while in short-haul markets they appear to be more significant than comfort-based features. But schedule features cannot always be adjusted rapidly. In many cases they cannot be changed at all, either because an airline does not have enough aircraft or aircraft of the right age or because of external constraints such as the bilateral air services agreements or possibly an absence of available runway slots. Yet, as markets become more competitive, the need for product innovation has intensified. Since schedules, in most cases, can be changed only in the medium term, if at all, airline product development has often concentrated on improving comfort-based features, which may be changed more readily and relatively quickly. Three aspects of the airline product are important in determining passenger perceptions of comfort.

The first is the *interior layout and configuration* of the aircraft, which affects the width and pitch of each seat and thereby determines the space available for each passenger. Individual space seems to be the key comfort variable, but so too is the quality of the seating provided. Comfort is particularly important for long-haul passengers both for those flying on business, and those on leisure trips. But, there is a trade-off between seating density and unit costs in that the more seats that can be put into the aircraft the lower are the operating costs per seat. Thus, deciding on cabin layout and seating density has major cost implications (see Table 4.5 in Chapter 4). Many options are available, and the choices made will reflect each airline's marketing strategy.

A key aspect of comfort relates to the width and pitch of each seat. Pitch is the distance between the back of one seat and the same point on the seat in front, and is a measure of the leg-room available. Seat pitch and width and the type of seat in each cabin class has a major impact on perceived comfort, especially on long-haul services. It also affects the total number of seats offered. More spacious seats will mean fewer seats per aircraft.

Seating density and, in particular, the number of seats allocated to each class are a key element of an airline's product offering. This also reflects its marketing strategy and positioning. Contrasting approaches can be seen when comparing the seating densities used by four airlines early in 2018 on their Boeing 787-9 long-haul aircraft (Table 10.4).

Clearly Air China and Air France were focused on attracting lower-fare Economy passengers. On the same aircraft they offered nearly twice as many Economy class seats as did United or British Airways. They achieved this not by giving less space to Economy passengers – seat pitch and wide was broadly similar for all four airlines – but by offering significantly fewer seats in Premium Economy and Business. Additionally, they offered less space to their Business passengers. The business seat pitch in Air France was 42 inches and for Air China 60 inches compared to 72 and 78 inches for BA and United respectively. All this reflected a clear marketing strategy. The net result was that the total number of seats available was very high, 293 on Air China's aircraft and 276 on Air France.

British Airways shows a contrasting approach. It positioned itself as offering a superior overall product. It was the only carrier of the four to offer First class, even if only eight seats, and it also offered a substantial number of Business and Premium Economy seats while its normal Economy seating was down to only 127. As a result, total seats were only 216, or 26 per cent less than those offered by Air China. Relatively low total seating seems to have been a feature on all BA's long-haul aircraft. Willie Walsh, CEO of IAG, British Airways' parent company, speaking at the World

Table 10.4 Alternative seating strategies of four airlines on Boeing 787-9 aircraft in 2018

Airline	First class	Business class	Premium Economy	Economy	Total
Air China	–	30	34	229	293
Air France	–	30	21	225	276
United Airlines	–	48	88	116	252
British Airways	8	42	39	127	216

Routes conference in September 2017 revealed that BA's First class offering was used primarily as a marketing tool: '*We are using it to upgrade customers and even sell it as Club class where there is strong business demand.*' BA chose carefully in which markets it offered First class since paid First class occupancy was less than 50 per cent (HSBC, 2017).

United Airlines again has had a slightly different strategy focusing on offering more than half its total seats on its Boeing 787-9 aircraft in Business or Premium Economy. In fact, it offered 88 seats in Premium Economy, which was more than double that of any of the other three airlines in the sample. United was clearly targeting this particular market segment on the routes where it was flying this aircraft.

Some innovative customer-focused airlines use interior cabin layout and seat design as a marketing tool to gain a competitive edge. Thus in 2000 British Airways was the first airline to introduce fully flat seats for its long-haul Business class and it also created a new World Traveller Plus cabin area. This was effectively a new class for Economy passengers paying the full fare. It is now called Premium Economy. Many of BA's competitors such as Air France or Delta were slow to follow and did not offer something similar to a Premium Economy class in long-haul until the mid-2010s.

The introduction of the spacious Airbus A380 in 2007 allowed airlines that bought this aircraft to experiment with innovative cabin design. Singapore Airlines, the launch customer, was the first to introduce First class 'suites'. Emirates followed with suites on its own A380s large enough to contain double beds and even showers. The concept of suites, that is fully enclosed private spaces, has slowly been adopted and used in smaller aircraft. Thus, in December 2017, Emirates launched services with Boeing 777-300ER aircraft offering six First class suites. Each is 40 sq. feet in area and fully enclosed, and they are three abreast in a 1–1–1 configuration. In December 2017 Singapore Airlines launched a new configuration for its A380s with six 'suites', each resembling a well-appointed bedroom and each with 'two stylishly furnished lavatories'!

In the United States, in late 2017, JetBlue introduced Airbus A321 aircraft for its transcontinental services, which offered four suites in the Business cabin, two abreast, as well as another 12 lie-flat beds in the same cabin. The net effect was the total number of seats in this version of the A321 was 159 compared to the version without Business class, also flown by JetBlue, which offered 201 seats for sale.

Other aspects of the interior layout an airline must decide on, since they affect the nature of the product it is offering, include the number and location of food galleys, the number of toilets, interior design and colour schemes, the size and suitability of overhead lockers, and so on.

The second important area where decisions have to be made is that of *in-flight service and catering standards*. This covers the nature and quality of food and beverages provided, the number of cabin staff for each class of cabin, if there is more than one cabin, the availability and range of newspapers and magazines, in-flight entertainment and communications, give-aways for premium passengers or children, and so on.

A great deal of effort goes into planning airline meals and meeting target catering standards. Again, there are cost implications and as a result the composition of meals is planned down to the precise weight in milligrams of a pat of butter or the weight of the sauce going on a meat dish. While airlines place much emphasis in their advertising on the quality of their food and wines, there is little evidence that gastronomic preferences determine choice of airline for a journey. In the large 2017 IATA survey, discussed earlier, only 6 per cent of passengers mentioned food and beverages as being among the top three factors influencing their choice of airline, though it was more important for long-haul flights (Tables 10.3 and 10.2). Nevertheless, catering standards together with the quality and attentiveness of the cabin staff may create a certain image for a particular airline, which may be important in marketing or branding terms.

During recent years, in an effort to cut costs and in response to the challenge of low-cost no-frills airlines, many legacy network carriers reduced or cut altogether their free in-flight catering in the Economy cabin on short-haul sectors. The US legacy carriers have done this on most of their domestic services as have many European airlines. Many of the latter, such as British Airways, have replaced free food and drinks in their Economy cabin on short-haul sectors by trolleys selling a range of hot snacks, sandwiches and alcoholic and soft drinks while continuing to offer a meal service in the Business cabin. But some smaller legacy carriers have maintained a full meal service for their Economy passengers as a way of competing against larger and more powerful legacy competitors. Thus, in 2018, on the three-and-a-half-hour flights between London and Athens, British Airways, like easyJet and other LCCs, did not provide any free catering for Economy passengers, but Aegean, the Greek airline, offered a good meal service. Regular travellers on this route were certainly aware of this and it gave Aegean a competitive edge.

In recent years much effort has gone into improving the quality and range of in-fight entertainment (IFE) facilities in all cabins on long-haul flights. Aircraft seats are now expected to provide interactive multi-channel music and films, as well as sockets for computers, in-flight telephones and electronic games. Increasingly passengers will be looking to have live TV or radio as JetBlue provides in the United States. But all this costs money to install in the seat, and also creates substantial running costs to buy and prepare film and sound programmes, which often need to be changed monthly. Seats also become more costly in order to incorporate all the electronic gadgetry. By 2010 it cost around $20,000 per seat to install IFE, the final cost depending on the range of facilities offered. This figure may have doubled since. IFE may add up to 2 per cent to the total purchase price of a new wide-body aircraft. Pro-active, innovative airlines, such as Emirates, which was one of the first to introduce seat-back screens and multi-channel films in Economy class, gained some initial marketing benefit. But it is a short-term benefit. IFE improvements can be introduced fairly quickly and as more airlines do this any competitive advantage is soon lost, but the high costs remain.

Currently, all long-haul airlines have personal IFE systems in First and Business class and most now have them in their Economy cabins too. Therefore, it has become an expected airline feature by passengers travelling in these cabins. This is why, despite the high spend on IFE, most surveys show that it is not an important factor in choosing between airlines. In the 2017 IATA passenger survey, mentioned earlier, only 7 per cent of long-haul passengers mentioned 'in-flight entertainment' as one of the three key factors affecting their choice of airline (Table 10.3).

The third key comfort component of an airline's product is the *services offered to passengers on the ground*. An airline has to consider whether to provide its own check-in and handling staff at out-stations or to use another airline or handling agent. It must decide what is an acceptable average waiting time for check-in for its passengers, since this will determine how many check-in desks and staff it needs for each flight. More desks cost more money. Despite increasing use of online check-in, 46 per cent of airport passengers in 2017 were still using check-in desks and another 15 per cent airport self-service kiosks (IATA, 2017). Then the airline must determine the nature of any special ground facilities for First and Business class passengers, such as special departure lounges, office services, car parking valets or the provision of limousine service to collect and deliver passengers from their homes or offices. If they offer lounges for premium passengers should they rent and equip their own lounges or share lounges with other airlines, possibly alliance partners? Surveys suggest that many business travellers are primarily concerned with speed through the terminal rather than comfort as such. This means they want separate, fast-track channels through security.

To speed up the check-in process, particularly when baggage is involved, airlines have in recent years progressively introduced online check-in and self-service kiosks at the airport as well as off-airport check-in at hotels (as SAS does) or at railway stations (Lufthansa). Some airlines, such as Ryanair, penalise passengers for not checking in online and doing so at the airport. To further reduce staffing costs some have introduced automatic labelling systems so that passengers can themselves check-in their bags at unmanned desks. Airlines have also started to introduce arrival lounges for First or Business class passengers on long-haul flights.

The ground environment and quality of service provided can have an important influence on a passenger's perception of an airline, but they are inevitably also affected by the actions and efficiency of the airport authority. This is why more and more airlines now wish to operate and possibly own the terminals they use. This is fairly common in the United States but rare elsewhere.

A non-measurable and intangible aspect of comfort which underpins all the areas mentioned is the efficiency, helpfulness and friendliness of staff, both the cabin crew in the air and also the ground staff at check-in, in the airline lounges and at the boarding gates. This appears to be dependent on three factors. First, the quality of the training received by all staff in contact with the public, but also the degree to which they are constantly being retrained.

The second factor is the success of management in motivating and empowering staff at all levels. Staff need to feel that they 'own' any problems that arise and are empowered to deal with them, rather than pass them on to someone else higher up the management chain. Motivating staff may become a problem whenever an airline outsources passenger ground-handling to other airline staff or to specialist ground-handling companies. Such staff may feel little loyalty to the client airline and the latter may have difficulty motivating them to perform as friendly, efficient and helpful customer-oriented service providers. This was a serious problem faced by easyJet in the late 2010s at London's Gatwick Airport, where its ground-handling was out-sourced to a specialist company.

Finally, the number of staff employed in each functional area is important. Cabin crew normally represent the largest group of staff. Safety regulations require that there should be one cabin crew member on a flight per 50 seats whether or not they are filled. Especially on long-haul flights with two or more cabin classes, airlines use their discretion to go above the legal minimum and many put two or three more stewards on board. But some airlines, such as Emirates, go much further in using even more crew, so as to ensure higher service in all cabins, though at a higher cost. Similarly, decisions have to be made for the ground staff. The motivation and quality of staff in contact with clients is crucial. Poor staff attitudes can destroy the best-planned product. On the other hand, friendly, warm, welcoming staff, who are obviously trying hard, can overcome shortcomings in the product and win over customer support. Singapore Airlines at one time had a small poster pinned to check-in desks which could be seen by check-in staff but not by passengers, which simply said: '*If you see someone without a smile, give them one.*'

Product and service planning is a complex task. Product planners must work in two dimensions. They must ensure that their product and service standards match or are better than those of their key competitors. But they must also try to differentiate the products offered in their own aircraft in such a way that passengers in each class feel that they are getting value for money.

It is primarily in the comfort-based aspects of the airline product that distinctions between the products offered to different cabin classes by the same airline become most apparent to passengers. This means that airline product planners have a complex task. They must specify differing comfort-based features for the different market segments they are trying to attract. Not only may product features have to be varied by class of cabin and type of ticket, but the same cabin class may require different product features on different routes, different sector lengths, or in various geographical areas. Thus, Business class in Europe does not have the same product specification as Business class on Europe to Asia services.

Because they can be more easily changed and more readily advertised, comfort-based product features are continuously being monitored and revised. There is a constant requirement to respond to product changes introduced by competitors and an even greater need for an airline to be the first to introduce innovative changes. Airlines that are innovative can enjoy a competitive advantage until their new product is copied by others.

In planning new product or service improvements airlines have to balance three factors – the cost of the innovation, its marketing benefits in terms of revenue generation and the speed with which it can be copied. It is not an easy balance to calculate.

10.4 Convenience features

Convenience as a product feature is multi-faceted. It is not only about the quality and user-friendliness of an airline's website and reservation system, but also about speed and frequency of information exchange between the airline and its current or potential customers. It is about the ease with which services and products can be assessed through the airline's website. It is about the availability of seats when requested by potential customers and the ease of changing or cancelling bookings. Frequent flyer programmes may also play a role both in enhancing convenience and accessibility as well as in improving an airline's image. Airline managers need to be aware that various 'convenience' features can play an important role in marketing airline services.

Inventory or capacity management is one aspect of convenience. Each airline has considerable freedom of action in deciding its capacity management policy, though it will be influenced by what its competitors are doing. Capacity management is a key tool for airline executives. There are two broad challenges. The first is how to plan capacity, that is frequencies and seats offered on a year-round basis, so as to deal with seasonal variations in demand (see Chapter 8, Section 8.6). The traditional approach of legacy network airlines has been to offer more capacity by increasing frequencies in the peak holiday periods, which are usually the summer and/or religious festivals. They hope that the higher fares and greater passenger volumes generated during periods of peak demand will more than compensate for the fact that some assets, such as aircraft and crews, may be under-utilised and therefore more costly in the off-peak periods when frequencies are reduced or some services cut altogether.

The low-cost carriers have generally adopted a different approach. To ensure high utilisation of all assets on a year-round basis, they try not to vary their capacity or frequencies so much between seasons. Instead they use the pricing mechanism to stimulate demand in the periods of low demand to fill up their capacity. In other words, very low fares and seat sale campaigns in shoulder and off seasons are used to fill up what would otherwise be empty seats. But the revenue per flight flown declines. If the revenue falls below direct operating costs, then LCCs will also reduce frequencies or cut some sectors altogether.

The second challenge is how to manage the seats that have been put on each route so as to ensure passenger convenience in terms of seat availability at short notice, especially for customers who are willing to pay higher or premium fares. Moreover, such seat availability must not prevent the airline maximising the potential revenue per flight. Airlines must use their inventory management system and the efficiency of their revenue managers to ensure that passengers wishing to enjoy the benefits of booking at or near the last minute pay a much higher fare. It is the higher fare that will prevent the last few seats being sold too soon.

A key aspect of capacity management is the degree to which over-booking is practised and, more especially, the airline's success in accurately predicting the pattern and number of 'no-show' passengers and cancellations so as to end up with a very high load factor without the need to deny boarding to any passenger. A high level of expertise is required to plan and implement over-booking profiles on individual flights or sectors. If an airline's predictions are consistently wrong it may end up paying costly denied boarding compensation to its over-booked passengers. Its image inevitably suffers too, especially if over-booking situations are mishandled and get into the media. This happened to United Airlines in April 2017 when film of one of its passengers being violently manhandled off one of its aircraft went viral.

From a passenger's point of view, especially if travelling for business or some kind of emergency, availability of a seat when required is an important convenience factor that may well differentiate one airline from another.

Another aspect of convenience is the ability of passengers to change or cancel their reservations once made. From the airline's point of view a cancelled or changed booking may mean that particular seat on the flight concerned may not be sold later. This means lost revenue. This must be balanced against the need to attract bookings by not imposing too many onerous conditions, which requires a fine balance. On network carriers the cheapest fares offer the least flexibility and impose the highest penalties if changes are required. Many will be non-changeable and non-refundable in the event of cancellation, while others will allow changes but at a cost to the passenger. Total flexibility requires paying the highest fares; this applies to all classes. Many airlines including British Airways, Lufthansa and others now offer two or more fares in Business class on most routes, one offering total flexibility including a refund for cancellation and a cheaper Business fare with severe restrictions that might include paying a charge to change the booking or no refund in the event of cancellation.

Initially in Europe fares on low-cost airlines allowed for little flexibility. But some airlines, such as easyJet, soon realised that the convenience of having more flexible booking conditions was an important product feature. Though European LCCs generally do not give refunds for cancelled tickets or a missed flight most now allow passengers to change flights, by paying a small fee and any increase in the fare, and may even allow them to change the name of the person booked, so someone else can use the booking. In some cases passengers may also be able to get on an earlier flight on the day of their booking at no extra cost if seats are available. Both network and LCCs have introduced a so-called 'Flex' category of fares, which gives passengers greater flexibility when changing some aspect of their flight.

A key decision area in any airline's marketing is how to distribute and sell its products and, in particular, how far it should use its own website and sales outlets in addition to independent travel agents including online agents such as Opodo, Orbitz, Kyak, Trivago, ebookers or Expedia. Since traditionally airlines paid commission on sales through travel agents, they had a vested interest in trying to sell directly through their own sales offices, through their own telephone call centres or their own website. But airlines also relied heavily on smaller travel agents and they still do in some markets, especially in Asia. The major benefit of travel agents was that they were and still are very numerous and widely scattered, giving airlines a much wider distribution network at relatively lower cost than they could achieve themselves. But high commissions paid to agents, together with the extensive spread of online selling, has undermined and changed the role of high street travel agents. Online distribution has also led to a reduction in airlines' own high street sales outlets and many such outlets have been closed. In the mid-2000s IATA mounted a major drive to get its members to switch from paper to electronic ticketing by the end of 2007 and had achieved this by mid-2008. The death of paper tickets not only reduced costs but further undermined the need for travel agents or airline sales offices.

Easy online access to schedules, routings and price information as well as reservations, combined with tickets that can be issued electronically, have significantly improved the accessibility and convenience of air travel to both business and leisure passengers. Airlines now compete through the speed, quality and user-friendliness of their own online websites. They also compete in terms of the speed and quality of ancillary services, such as hotel booking, car hire, car parking, duty free on-board sales and so on, that can be accessed through their websites. It is the low-cost carriers who have led the field. EasyJet was the front runner because, from its launch in 1995, it insisted on selling 100 per cent of its seats direct to passengers and did not use travel agents or other intermediaries at all. Initially it focused on its telephone call centre and then switched rapidly to selling entirely online through its own website. It was not until late 2007 that it also began to sell through the Travelport and Sabre global distribution systems (GDS) with the aim of attracting business and corporate passengers. But it did not pay a commission on such sales.

Network airlines were slower in switching to direct online selling. It was the financial losses of the early 2000s and the competitive pressures from low-cost competitors that forced them to focus on online selling. The quickest way to cut distribution costs was to develop direct online selling, which provided an improved level of service, while at the same time reducing the high commission payments being paid to travel agencies and GDSs.

Airlines face a major dilemma. Through the use of third-party agents airlines can maximise their access to different markets and thereby generate higher sales but at a cost. They may have to pay a commission to the selling agent, possibly a fixed charge to the GDS used by an agent for the booking. So for the last two decades, airlines – especially network airlines – have focused both on selling more of their seats through their own websites, to avoid commission payments, and on reducing or eradicating commissions paid for bookings made through the GDS systems. These are used by virtually all independent and online travel agents. The key strategic decision is how far should an airline go in reducing sales through third-party agents.

In mid-2015 the Lufthansa Group took a bold pioneering decision. As from 1 September that year all bookings made through a GDS portal would have to pay a fee of €16 (almost US$18). Travellers booking direct with Lufthansa or through an agent using Lufthansa's online agent booking portal would avoid this 'Distribution Cost Surcharge' (DCS). The aim was clearly to make it more attractive to book flights directly with Lufthansa or agents using its portal. This was a high-risk strategy as, at the time, it was estimated that about 70 per cent of Lufthansa Group global sales were through the GDS portals. Lufthansa subsequently claimed that the DCS had no effect on total revenues but sales through the GDS dropped to 60 per cent within two years as direct sales via Lufthansa's website increased.

Two years later, in summer 2017 Lufthansa introduced a further penalty for those using the GDS. Travellers paying for 'Lite' fares and not booking direct would be required to pay a surcharge of €5 (US$6) for checking in their first bag on top of the normal charge of €25 (US$30). Both these extra charges applied to bookings on all Lufthansa Group airlines, namely Lufthansa, SWISS, Austrian and Brussels Airlines.

British Airways and its partners followed Lufthansa's bold move. From November 2017 all fares booked on BA or Iberia through a GDS and not on BA's website carried a surcharge of €9.50 (US$11.40) on each fare component, meaning €19 (US$23) for a return ticket. Exceptions were made for travel companies such as American Express who agreed to work with BA in delivering IATA's New Distribution Capability (NDC) standard aimed at helping airlines to retail and market all their various products through indirect channels. Such companies continued to sell BA/Iberia tickets without the need to charge customers the surcharge.

Other airlines were expected to follow the Lufthansa and BA approach of penalising clients who book through the GDS, but for the present, the dilemma continues. What is the optimum balance between direct sales on an airline's own website or portal and indirect sales through airline travel service providers such as ebookers, Kyak, Orbitz or Expedia using GDS portals on which commission may have to be paid?

As a result of airline efforts to focus on direct online sales, bypassing agents, while at the same time reducing commission rates, especially in their home markets, airline distribution costs have also been reduced. In the financial year 1996–97, British Airways' commission payments of all kinds absorbed 14 per cent of sales revenue. Twenty years later this figure was 3 per cent.

The various aspects of convenience, discussed previously, are a key element of any airline's marketing strategy; but they need to be communicated to potential clients and current customers. Airlines must use to the full multiple opportunities offered by the digital world for interaction with customers. This means having a user-friendly website that is informative, fast and easy to navigate. It also means airlines using various forms of social media both to advertise what they have on offer and to learn more about what different market segments want and are prepared to pay for or what they are unhappy about. Many airlines now offer customers their own app: this enables them to book directly on that airline and receive an e-ticket. It provides information on flight status, on the airline's lounges and on airports. It can also be used to make special offers not only on flights and holidays but a variety of other non-airline products and services.

Social media can provide important channels of communication between airlines and various market segments. The aim of e-commerce (Section 10.6) is to make it easy and convenient for passengers to find out what an airline has to offer in terms of destinations, fares, schedules, ancillaries and add-ons such as hotels, car hire, et cetera.

10.5 Airline reputation and brand

All surveys show that an airline's reputation is an all-important factor when consumers are choosing between airlines. In the 2017 IATA passenger survey, discussed earlier, reputation was the third most frequently mentioned factor influencing airline choice (Tables 10.2 and 10.3). Reputation depends, in part, on very tangible and transparent features, notably safety record and punctuality. Total safety and excellent punctuality are top priorities for all airlines. But an airline's reputation is also dependent on the image and branding that an airline can create about its product and services.

A final group of product features are those associated with the image and brand that an airline wishes to create, both among its own customers and among the public at large. This is done in a variety of ways: through the nature of its advertising, its promotions and its use of social media. Additionally, this is achieved through the airline's logo, its colour schemes and the design of its aircraft interiors, sales offices and airport lounges, and through the quality of service provided by its staff in the air and on the ground. Ensuring an excellent safety record is also an important consideration.

The success of Singapore Airlines' (SIA) 'Singapore Girl' advertising campaigns during the 1980s created the image not only of helpful, smiling, attentive cabin staff but also of an airline that took care of its passengers. This image was an important factor in enabling SIA to maintain unusually high passenger load factors throughout the period and up to the present day.

In developing a brand, airlines need to identify those features of their product or service which differentiate them from other carriers. Such unique features may be product related, such as the type of network or the geographical area served, or service oriented such as the quality of in-flight catering and cabin crew. For instance, Turkish Airlines has white-suited real chefs serving meals in First and Business class on its long-haul flights. Ideally, brand features should be distinctive and difficult for others to copy. While branding may focus on one or two aspects of an airline's product it should permeate and impact on everything the airline does. Thus, as part of Emirates' overall branding as an airline offering top-of-class service in the air and on the ground, it provides free limousines to collect and deliver Business class passengers before and after their flights.

A key element in brand building is to ensure that what is promised before the flight actually materialises and meets passenger expectations when the flight takes place. SIA's ability to do this has been crucial for its success. In other words, an eye-catching logo and an attractive colour scheme in themselves are not enough to establish an attractive brand. The airline has to offer an excellent product and service standards that reflect the brand and are delivered consistently in all aspects of its operation. This is why marketing and product planning must be all-embracing, covering what is offered and how it is delivered as well as how it is sold.

In order to establish an image, an airline needs to first identify its market position and marketing strategy. Clearly Southwest Airlines in the US or easyJet in Europe position themselves quite differently to, say, United Airlines or British Airways. The former are low-cost no-frills airlines who would need to project a different image from the latter. But even within the same sector airlines may adopt a different market position and brand.

easyJet and Ryanair offer contrasting examples. They were the first successful and fast growing LCCs in Europe. From the early days easyJet was more customer responsive and friendly. On-board service was relaxed and fun even though there were no freebies. It dealt better with delays and cancellations and developed a user-friendly website. It flies not just to holiday destinations but offers high frequencies between major European cities so attracting business traffic It has managed to brand itself as a quality and customer-friendly LCC. In many markets, this superior branding enables easyJet to sell at higher fares than competing airlines. This more than compensates for unit costs that are higher than some other LCCs.

Ryanair, on the other hand, has branded itself as the lowest-fare airline. It believed that its rather indifferent service standards were counterbalanced by very low fares. Passengers know this and many, many millions of them choose to fly with Ryanair. As a result, Ryanair is highly profitable and very successful, but its brand image had suffered – especially in comparison to easyJet. This is why in June 2014 the airline announced that it was reinventing itself as a family-friendly airline.

Airline services have been commoditised. An airline seat from point A to point B on a scheduled airline is perceived by the passenger as being very similar irrespective of which airline actually flies the service. Fares may differ, but otherwise the essential product is very much a commodity. Product planning as discussed earlier tries to differentiate an airline's product from that of its competitors, but it can only be partially successful since so many service elements, such as the quality of in-flight catering or of ground-handling, are subjective. This is where the concept of branding comes in.

Through product and service improvements, combined with targeted and effective advertising and promotion, airlines attempt to change their product from being a common commodity to being a 'brand'. As a unique brand it becomes more attractive and may even, on certain routes, attract a higher fare than that prevailing in the market. A brand is exemplified not only by service and product standards but also by designs and colours used in the aircraft interior and exterior and on the ground, as well as in more mundane aspects such as crockery, cutlery and so on. A distinctive logo and colour scheme may differentiate an airline product, but to establish a successful brand one needs to deliver what is promised. Employees are crucial in this process and in conveying the brand image to customers.

A key step in this process of branding on international flights was seen in the mid-1980s when airlines began to give their Business class distinctive names, even though the product offered in terms of space and comfort was broadly similar. As previously mentioned, long-haul airline Virgin Atlantic called its Business class 'Upper' class and was successful in creating a high-quality brand image, which it still maintains. Many passengers still think of it as a First class product at Business class fares. In 2000 British Airways introduced lie-flat bed seats in its long-haul Business class to sustain the Club World brand. In this it succeeded for a time as some of its long-haul competitors, such as Air France, were slow to adopt fully-flat beds.

Many airlines have now followed in trying to brand their long-haul Business class product as something special by giving it a distinctive name. This was especially true of airlines that over the last two decades have abandoned First class on long-haul routes and need to market their Business class as a superior product approaching First class. Thus, Air France has 'l'Espace Affaires', Delta Airlines has 'Delta 1' and United's Business class in long-haul is named 'Polaris'. Even airlines still operating a separate

First class cabin, often with 'suites', give fancy brand names to their Business product. Singapore Airlines has 'Raffles' class while Etihad offers 'Pearl' class. But merely giving fancy names to Business class will not in itself create an attractive brand.

Changing the brand or mixing brands within the same airline can be problematic. Aer Lingus in recent years overcame such problems. It managed successfully to rebrand itself as a superior low-fare and low-cost airline for its short-haul intra-European services while maintaining a more traditional legacy airline brand for its long-haul services. On the other hand, Air Berlin, having bought a disparate group of scheduled and charter airlines in the mid-2000s, had great difficulty in sorting out its brand or brands and collapsed in 2017.

The ever-growing global alliances pose a particular branding and image problem. That is, how to try to create an alliance brand, which can be an effective marketing tool, while not diluting the strength of any existing strong airline brands. The problem becomes especially acute when there are many airlines within an alliance since they are then less likely to all have the same high service standards and an equally good image. The STAR alliance has faced exactly this problem in recent years because it has 25 or so members with very differing service qualities. This is evident from Table 10.5, which shows how UK passengers rated four of the larger STAR airlines for their most recent long-haul trips (Which, 2018). While the best, Singapore Airlines, achieved very high customer satisfaction scores and ratings, for boarding experience, customer service, quality and range of food and drink and value for money, the other three were rated as relatively poor in all these categories, especially United Airways. They also earned very low overall satisfaction scores. The very different service standards of STAR alliance members clearly pose a problem when trying to develop a STAR brand. Other global alliances face similar difficulties because their member airlines have products and services of varying quality.

The challenges of successful branding are compounded when airline companies adopt a twin brand strategy operating two or more separate companies, of which one or more may be a low-cost carrier. Difficulties arise in ensuring that the different brands are distinct and well thought of and are not confusing for potential customers. The difficulties involved in multi-branding forced Singapore Airlines to announce in mid-2018 that it would merge its two full-service airlines – the regional carrier SilkAir with the parent SIA. It had earlier decided to merge its short-haul LCC, Tiger Airways, with its long-haul LCC, Scoot, under the Scoot brand.

Frequent flyer programmes (FFPs), originally developed by airlines as a way of ensuring passenger loyalty, also play a key role in improving their image. Under such schemes, passengers are awarded points for each flight with the airline whose FFP they have joined. The number of points earned in most FFPs depends on the length of the flight and the class of travel. A few airlines now link the number of points awarded to the price paid for the ticket. As the points built up, passengers can redeem them for free flights for themselves or family members, for upgrades to a higher class when they buy a paid ticket or for a variety of other travel or related benefits. However, there may be strict conditions as to when and on which flights such redemptions can be made. This minimises the costs of redemption in terms of lost revenues.

The FFPs are normally operated as clubs, giving higher grades of membership and more privileges as the number of points earned or journeys made with the parent airline within a year climbs above certain thresholds. In theory it is the combination of more points and greater potential awards, together with increased privileges associated with higher grades of club membership, such as access to an airline's airport lounges, that ensure passenger loyalty. The efficiency of the FP and especially the ease with which awarded points can be used to obtain flights or other services together with the various benefits of membership are an integral part of an airline's brand and image creation.

Certainly, as mentioned earlier (Section 10.2 and Table 10.3), FFP membership has become one of the key factors in airline choice especially for business travel despite the fact that most business travellers normally belong to three or four separate FFPs. Airlines used to target the frequent flyers who are primarily those flying on business, though many leisure and VFR passengers also fly frequently and belong to FFPs. The main objective of all loyalty schemes has been to sell more seats. Airlines appreciate that it is much more expensive in marketing terms to attract a new customer than to obtain repeat business from an existing one. As a result, the efficiency, flexibility and user-friendliness of FFPs are key marketing tools.

In recent years airlines have been focusing increasingly on a further objective of FFPs. Loyalty schemes can provide the database on which airlines can build effective customer relationship management (CRM) while the internet provides the means for communicating with customers. Airlines with long-established FFPs have considerable data on their customers' travel patterns and preferences, family, residence, place of work and so on. This data can be leveraged either to prevent defections or to encourage repeat business. The latter can be done by developing an interactive relationship with FFP members by offering them discounted fares to their favourite destinations, special fares for family members, and so on. By using the internet to question customers about needs and preferences, by setting up customer panels and through other survey techniques airlines can develop customer bonding and loyalty. Customer relationship management plays an important part in airline marketing.

As competition has intensified, brand and customer loyalty have become key product features. With the strengthening of airline alliances and joint ventures they will become even more important.

10.6 E-commerce is key

Effective use of e-commerce is essential for many aspects of an airline's operations but for marketing and distribution it is crucial. Airlines need to communicate to potential customers the advantages of their products and services and their various fares and other charges. They must also make it easy and convenient for customers both to purchase and to use their products. To do all this, airlines must maximise the opportunities

Table 10.5 UK passenger's rating of four STAR Alliance long-haul airlines in 2017

STAR Airline	Punctuality %	Boarding process	Customer service	Quality food/drink	Value for money	Customer score
Singapore Airlines	78	*****	*****	****	****	88
South African Airways	74	***	***	***		59
Air Canada	63	***	***	**	**	50
United Airlines	74	**	**	**		39

N.B.: Survey of over 7,500 passengers. Blank means too few responses
Source: Which? January 2018, London

offered by the digital world and cyberspace to interact with potential, current and former passengers.

The electronic marketplace offers consumers both fast and efficient access to information on airline services, on timings, on product features and prices and also the ability to make rapid and effortless reservations and payments. In terms of economic theory, greater knowledge among consumers or purchasers means greater market power. It also means greater freedom of choice. To capture consumers' choices, airlines must switch from being supply focused and focus on the customer. It is the customer who decides when, where and how to access information on flight options and the product features he wants. The airline must try to develop a one-to-one relationship with customers. E-commerce, in all its forms, can be the key to effective marketing, distribution and customer relations management.

But e-commerce is about much more than getting the technology right to sell tickets online. It is about putting e-commerce at the core of an airline's business model. Carolyn McCall, then Chief Executive of easyJet, summed up this approach:

> *We don't see ourselves as an airline when it comes to digital. I always see ourselves as an e-commerce platform ... We have a billion visits to our digital channels, which gives enormous amount of data; e-mail contact, text contact, etc. We can do an enormous amount with what we have, but our core proposition is always about making it the easiest it can be for our customers.*

(Airline Leader, November–December 2016)

All airlines use e-commerce in some form or other to market and distribute their products, but not all of them maximise the opportunities and potential offered by e-commerce. This is clearly borne out by a major wide-ranging study of airline e-commerce carried out in 2016 by Dr Michael Hanke. This examined the key requirements for effective use of e-commerce and reviewed a large sample of airlines to assess their use of e-commerce. The assessment of individual airlines was based on six groups of digital attributes. Some were more technical in nature, such as the range of digital platforms used, the digital performance in terms of speed, the design and quality of an airline's website and so on. Others were more qualitative and included the quality of service provided to web customers or the way tariff information is presented (Hanke, 2016).

Later in 2017, in an updated assessment, airlines were again given scores for their digital performance in six areas. These scores were aggregated into a total 'Digital Airline Score' (DAS) showing how advanced each airline was in terms of using e-commerce. On the basis of their scores, airlines were then characterised as being 'Constrained', 'Emerging', 'Transitional' or 'Advanced' e-commerce carriers (Figure 10.1).

'Constrained' airlines have begun to engage in e-commerce but their adoption and use of the internet and digital applications is limited. 'Emerging' airlines have made significant progress in adopting and using e-commerce but are still not optimising its use. 'Transitional' carriers have an above-average adoption and use of e-commerce and are constantly expanding their cyberspace capabilities. E-commerce plays a key role in all aspects of their business. 'Advanced' airlines are highly sophisticated and advanced in the use of e-commerce and are innovative in deploying new digital applications. E-commerce for them is a key corporate strategic priority.

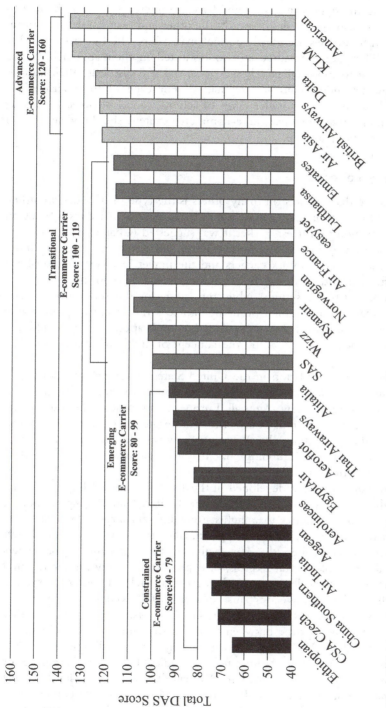

Figure 10.1 Measuring airlines' digital capabilities: Digital Airline Score, 2017

Source: Michael Hanke, SkaiBlue. Santa Monika 2017

It is evident from Figure 10.1 that airlines vary significantly in their effective use of e-commerce. Some, such as Ethiopian Airlines, Air India or Aegean, are not yet engaged in maximising the opportunities offered by e-commerce. This may be due to a lack of vision or to an inadequate talent base. At the other end of the scale, American, KLM, Delta and British Airways are clearly airlines maximising the opportunities that e-commerce offers. They are innovative and sophisticated in their approach. These airlines use e-commerce to more effectively advertise, sell and distribute their various products and to develop their brand and reputation. For each of these airlines, e-commerce is at the heart of a much wider range of activities and functions. Designing and implementing an effective and advanced e-commerce strategy should be an integral part of any airline's product planning.

10.7 The 'hubbing' concept

A major product feature that impacts on many others is the type of network an airline offers to customers. Does it primarily operate a hub-based network or does it focus on offering direct point-to-point services? Earlier it was suggested (Chapter 1, Section 1.2 and Chapter 5, Section 5.9) that the most distinctive difference between the more traditional, so-called legacy or network carriers and the newer low-cost or ultra-low-cost carriers arises from the structure of their route networks. The former build their networks around hub-and-spoke systems while the latter, for the most part, operate networks more like matrices and which primarily aim to satisfy point-to-point traffic demand by offering direct flights. To appreciate the implications of these differing network strategies, one needs to understand the concept of 'hubbing' and the benefits and costs involved.

In the 1980s, following deregulation in the United States, 'hubbing' was developed by most major airlines as a crucial schedule-based product feature. Hub-and-spoke networks in themselves were not new. After all, European and most airlines outside the United States had always operated radial networks because the international regulations prevented them from doing anything else. What was new was the way in which radial networks came to be operated. 'Hubbing' has major implications both for airline economics and for competition policy.

The concept of hubbing was first developed in the 1970s by Federal Express for the carriage of overnight express parcels throughout the United States, using its hub at Memphis. Effective hubbing requires that flights from different airports, which are at the spokes of a network, arrive at the hub at approximately the same time. The aircraft then wait on the ground simultaneously. This facilitates the interchange of passengers and baggage or, in the case of Federal Express, of express parcels between aircraft in a short period of time before they depart in quick succession back out along the spokes. This process, which involves a wave or 'bank' of arrivals followed shortly after by a wave of departures, is described as a complex. In simple terms, flights arrive together and leave together. The transfer time between flights in the same complex should be close to the best attainable. A US airline with a major hub will operate several complexes during the day. American Airlines now schedules about eight complexes or banks daily at Dallas-Fort Worth. Air France in 2018 had five at Paris Charles de Gaulle and Lufthansa operated four complexes at Frankfurt. KLM operated five complexes at Amsterdam centred approximately at 09:00 hours, 12:00 hours, 15:00 hours, 17:00 hours and 20:00 hours.

An airline able to develop and operate a hub-and-spoke system with a series of complexes enjoys numerous potential advantages. The increase in city-pair coverage that can be obtained as a result of hubbing is much more dramatic than is often realised. If three point-to-point direct links from cities A to B, C to D and E to F, where each city only has a link to one other city, are replaced by six direct services from each of these six airports to a new connecting hub at an intermediate point G, the number of city-pair markets that can be served jumps from three to 21. This advantage increases in proportion of the *square* of the number of routes or spokes radiating from the hub. Thus, if a hub has n spokes, or radial routes, the number of direct links is n to which must be added $n(n - 1) \div 2$ indirect links connecting via the hub.

The progressively greater impact of adding more links through a hub can be seen in Table 10.6. The ability to reach a large number of destinations from any one origin gives the airline operating the hub system considerable market appeal. Effective hubbing generates substantial volumes of additional traffic, and revenue, but most of it is transferring through the hub airport.

A number of further marketing advantages flow from the increase in the number of city-pairs linked via the hub. By channelling what may be a large number of separate but thin city-pair flows originating at an outlying airport but going to different final destinations onto a service going into the hub airport, the density of traffic on that particular spoke may be built up. The additional traffic generated by the connecting passengers may allow an airline to use larger and more economical aircraft, but also to operate more frequent flights along each of the spokes. As this will happen on many spokes, the frequencies of possible connecting services via the hub linking two distant spokes, with low traffic between them, increases. Not only does this stimulate traffic but it also inhibits potential competitors from starting a direct service between the two spokes, since they may be unable to compete in terms of frequencies or departure times.

The hub operator may also drop its fares on connecting services if it needs to undermine any new competition from an airline offering direct point-to-point services bypassing a hub. It can do this easily by cross-subsidising this service from other routes where it faces no direct competition. Moreover, once traffic between two airports at the periphery of a hub-and-spoke system builds up, the hub airline may itself offer a direct service between them to pre-empt a new entrant.

Table 10.6 Impact of hubbing on the number of city pairs served

Number of spokes from the hub n	Number of points connected via the hub $n(n - 1) \div 2$	Number of points linked to the hub by direct flights n	Total city pairs served $n(n + 1) \div 2$
2	1	2	3
6	15	6	21
10	45	10	55
50	1,225	50	1,275
75	2,775	75	2,850
100	4,950	100	5,050

The power of an effective hub to build up dense traffic flows on key routes by attracting passengers from a wide range of origins linked to the hub is well illustrated by the case study of a Lufthansa Boeing 747 flight from Frankfurt to Hong Kong in September 2015 (Table 10.7). Nearly two-thirds of the capacity of the aircraft (364 seats) was filled by the 237 passengers who came into Frankfurt on feeder flights from 51 different mainly European airports, but also from North and South American points. Without such volumes of feed Lufthansa would have had difficulty supporting a once-daily Boeing 747 flight to Hong Kong. It would have been forced to reduce frequencies, cut them altogether or fly daily with a smaller aircraft, with possibly higher unit costs.

One of the most important benefits to arise from effective hub-and-spoke operations is the extent to which individual airline networks can become self-sufficient in meeting demand, enabling operators to keep passengers on their own services rather than lose them at the hub to interline connections to another airline. This has been illustrated clearly since deregulation in the US. The proportion of all passengers making an online

Table 10.7 Power of hubbing – connecting passengers on Lufthansa LH-796 Frankfurt–Hong Kong on 17 September 2015

Origins to Frankfurt	Flight LH796		Final destination
No. of transfer pax from:	*FRA. to Hong Kong Boeing 747*		*No. of pax going to:*
34 Paris CDG			
32 Prague			
27 Munich			
14 Hanover			
14 Berlin-Tegel			
13 Brussels			
10 Caracas			
7 Hamburg			
6 Barcelona			
6 Dubrovnik	Seats		
5 Aberdeen			
4 Zurich	First	8	30 Manila
4 Milan Linate	Business	80	16 Taipei
3 St Petersburg	Premium Economy	32	9 Auckland
3 Rome	Economy	244	5 Kaohsiung
3 Dusseldorf			1 Wellington
3 Bogota	**Total**	**364**	1 Brisbane
2 Bremen			
2 Copenhagen			
2 Oporto			
2 Gothenburg			
2 London LHR			
2 New York-JFK			
28 various other origins with 1 or 2 pax			
Total feed: 237 pax from 51 origins	**Total FRA-HKG: 311 pax**		**Total onward feed: 62 pax to 6 destinations**

Source: Lufthansa

transfer connection with the same carrier or regional affiliates has risen from 25 per cent in 1977 to over 90 per cent of all transfer passengers. In 1984 at London's Heathrow Airport 27 per cent of transfer passengers were British Airways to British Airways. By 2017 this had grown to over 75 per cent.

The scheduling of 'banks' or complexes of arriving and departing flights ensures that the probability of the first outgoing service to any particular destination being by the same airline as the delivering flight is disproportionately high. Interlineable fares, involving transfer from one airline to another, therefore no longer become necessary. Even if a parallel journey from a competitor exists on one leg of a connecting journey, there will now usually be a severe financial penalty for using it. In other words, the hub carrier will offer a lower through fare on its own service than can be obtained by transferring to or from another carrier at the hub. The passenger also gains in terms of convenience and reliability from single airline service. Frequent flyer incentive programmes further encourage the use of online connections with the same airline rather than interlining onto a different carrier.

Certain pairs of links created by hubbing will generate substantially more traffic than others. Such demand can be stimulated by offering through services. Unlike traditional scheduling methods, whereby aircraft return on the same route from which they originated, they can now proceed on through the hub to the location with which there is most market potential. This is often done in the United States but rarely in Europe.

The result of all this is to ensure that a major airline at a particular hub in terms of routes and frequencies will become even more dominant in its share of transfer passengers, as its operations develop. In the early 1980s as 'hubbing' began to be implemented in the US, there were only a couple of the 15 or so larger airports where a single operator had more than 50 per cent market share in terms of flights. By the late 2010s many of these airports had a dominant hub carrier who, together with an owned or contracted regional airline, generated 70 per cent or more of the flights. They had become fortress hubs. Thus, in 2017 American Airlines operated 85 per cent of flights at Dallas-Fort Worth and 90 per cent at Charlotte. United offered 81 per cent of flights at Houston. Delta operated 79 per cent of flights at Atlanta, 76 per cent at Detroit and 73 per cent at Minneapolis-St Paul (Anker, 2018). The dominance was least marked at major international gateways such as Los Angeles and New York-JFK. This is inevitable as many foreign carriers also operate into these airports.

The European airlines, despite operating radial networks, were much slower than their US counterparts in developing schedules to provide effective hubbing. The European experience in developing powerful hubs contrasts with that of US airlines in three respects.

First, the hub dominance is not so marked. In 2017, at only a handful of the major European hubs did the base airline operate around 60 per cent or more of the total flights. This was the case at Frankfurt where Lufthansa and its subsidiaries had 64 per cent of the departures while it also offered 59 per cent of departures at Munich. At Amsterdam KLM and various subsidiaries operated 52 per cent of all flights. At London-Heathrow British Airways' share of flights was 53 per cent (Anker, 2018). This is partly due to the fact that all the European airports are also international gateways with many foreign airlines flying in.

Second, European airlines have generally operated only one hub. Those with two such as the former Swissair (Zurich and Geneva) or Alitalia (Rome and Milan) faced serious problems and downgraded their secondary hub. Lufthansa has developed a second hub at Munich, but this is in part because Frankfurt was previously full due to lack of runway slots. The US majors tend to operate multi-hub networks with two or more hubs each. For instance, as a result of its earlier merger with Northwest, Delta now operates major hubs at Atlanta, Minneapolis-St Paul, Detroit and Salt Lake City with a smaller one in Seattle, Los Angeles, Boston and Cincinnati. Partly to overcome their focus on single hubs, European airlines have embarked on acquisitions of other European carriers in order to develop multi-hub systems. For instance, Air France by buying KLM now has two major hubs, Paris and Amsterdam, while the Lufthansa Group of airlines have five hubs in central Europe of varying size – Frankfurt, Munich, Zurich, Vienna and a smaller one at Brussels. Perhaps too many!

Finally, Europe has no shared hubs with two carriers each having a significant market share at the same airport. This is what American and United do at Chicago O'Hare, while United Airlines and Southwest share Phoenix airport.

If an airline operating a hub can establish dominance at its hub through control of a disproportionate share of the flights offered and traffic uplifted, it is very difficult for another airline to set up a rival hub at the same airport, because it is unlikely to get enough runway slots to offer a similar range of destinations with good frequencies. In the United States the hub operator will also control most of the terminal gates. If the new entrant chooses to compete on just a few direct routes from the hub airport, it will face a competitive disadvantage vis-a-vis the hub airline in terms of ensuring adequate feed for its own services; hence, the notion of the 'fortress hub'.

Consumers clearly benefit from hub-and-spoke systems in that they can fly to many more points with higher frequencies and, where necessary, shorter connecting times than was the case before hubbing became so finely developed. On the other hand, passengers who as a result of hubbing are deprived of direct services that might otherwise be operated, possibly by another airline, are clearly worse off. Moreover, their journey times may be longer and their fares may be higher if there is no alternative routing. There may be other disadvantages too. Hubbing is very dependent on excellent punctuality, and delays anywhere can throw whole 'complexes' into disarray, with serious knock-on effects. This is because a delayed flight may be carrying passengers transferring to a dozen or more departing flights, all of which may have to be held back. The short transit time between arriving and departing flights can create havoc in trying to handle large volumes of connecting baggage. It is not surprising that passenger awareness of and concern with punctuality and misdirected baggage increased significantly in the United States as hubbing spread.

10.8 The economics of hubbing

Hubbing can be an effective schedule-based marketing tool providing wider market spread, generating increased revenues and resulting in market dominance on many routes. The economics of hubbing are quite complex, however, since it imposes certain cost penalties on the operating airlines. These are largely of two kinds: those associated with the extra flying required and those arising from the extra passenger handling that is involved compared with direct flights.

An example of the extra flying involved can be seen in the efforts of SWISS to sell London to Rome services via its Zurich hub in the London market. This involves carrying passengers on two sectors, London–Zurich, with an aircraft block time of one hour 40 minutes, and Zurich–Rome with a block time of one hour 35 minutes, making a total block time of three hours 15 minutes. Yet a direct flight London–Rome requires a block time of only two hours 30 minutes. In other words, 40 minutes of extra block time is required for the passenger hubbing through Zurich. Carrying online transfer passengers through a hub as opposed to a direct flight creates higher costs in a number of areas. Fuel costs will be higher both because of the longer flight time and the extra landing and take-off when fuel consumption is highest. In fact, all direct operating costs will be higher, including airport landing charges since landings will be more frequent. In a European context, where airport charges are especially high, this may be a severe cost penalty. En-route navigation charges will also be higher. In order to provide feeder traffic for the first bank of departures from the hub airlines must night-stop aircraft and crews at the outer end of the shorter spoke routes and schedule early morning departures to the hub. Such night stops are expensive.

Each passenger making a transfer connection at the hub is involved in two boardings and disembarkations, a transfer of baggage at the hub and the use of two or three departure or arrival lounges. The costs of handling must be high. The airline may also have to pay two airport passenger departure charges. Moreover, the complexing of flights at the hub and the need to transfer passengers and baggage in the shortest possible time create tremendous peak pressure on staff and facilities as large volumes of passengers have to be handled in a very short period of time. This contrasts with a normal operation where demand is spread through the day. To meet such peaks of demand, extra staff will be needed, who may be underused between complexes. Additional and also more sophisticated baggage- and passenger-handling equipment and facilities are required.

The cost disadvantages of hubbing are particularly severe if one is trying to operate a short to medium-haul hub such as one linking European points. On gateway hub services connecting short- to long-haul services the cost penalties are less marked because the increase in total flight distances as a result of hubbing may be less pronounced.

The economics of hubbing hinges on whether the increased flying and passenger-related costs of indirect services via a hub are off-set by the ability to operate larger aircraft with lower unit costs, as in the case of the Lufthansa Frankfurt–Hong Kong services cited earlier. Larger aircraft should result from combining several thin flows to various destinations onto a single radial service going to the hub. It may also be possible to increase aircraft utilisation because of the higher frequencies resulting from the denser traffic flows. On the cost side it is a fine balance. The emergence of small regional jets able to offer low-cost point-to-point services on thin routes joining the spokes of a radial network has made the cost economies of hubbing for short-haul services more precarious.

To what extent can increased revenues through improved passenger loads and/or higher yields per passenger counter-balance the higher costs? Certainly, airlines have tried to off-set the diseconomies of hubbing by trying to increase their fares on services through the hub. They can do this in two ways; first, by charging a premium for purely local traffic travelling only between a spoke and the hub, and not connecting, especially if they are the only operator on the spoke. For instance, following its purchase of SWISS in 2006, Lufthansa has had an effective monopoly on the local feeder routes from Zurich to its hubs at Frankfurt and Munich and from Geneva to Frankfurt. It can, and does, charge high fares for local traffic on these routes. The second way is, by trying to exact high fares when offering hub services between two points that have no direct links. There may be many of those.

Conversely, there may be a downside to revenue generation when a hubbing airline has to offer low through fares for online connecting passengers to attract them away from competitor airlines offering direct services between two points or better connections through their own hub. For example, early in January 2018, British Airways was selling its lowest Economy class return for London–Singapore for a flight one month later, out on Friday 9 February and return one week later, for £939, but Lufthansa was offering the same route via their Frankfurt hub for only £802. This £802 revenue had to be split between the two sectors London–Frankfurt and Frankfurt–Singapore, diluting the average yield on both. In fact, Lufthansa's separate lowest Economy fares for the relevant sectors were £215 and £854 respectively, making a total of £1,069. Selling these seats for only £802 to connecting passengers meant substantial yield dilution.

The economies of hubbing depend largely on having sufficient local traffic from each spoke to the hub, paying a premium price to compensate for the lower yield on hub transfer traffic. This means that a hub which is itself a major traffic generator or attractor has a distinct advantage. It also means that the proportion of transfer traffic on each spoke route should ideally not rise more than 55–60 per cent.

US experience, and more recent experience in Europe and at long-haul hubs such as Singapore or Dubai, suggests that for an airport to become an effective hub it must possess five attributes: (1) a central geographical location in relation to the markets it aims to serve, whether these are purely short-medium haul or intercontinental; (2) ample runway and apron parking capacity; (3) a single terminal building or a well-connected complex for the hub airline and, ideally, (4) strong local demand to and from the hub. Many airports satisfy these criteria. Where strong local demand does not exist, one may try to create it by building up local industry, business or tourist infrastructure as both Singapore and Dubai have done. The fifth and most critical requirement is to have (5) a strong hub-based airline prepared to develop effective hubbing by operating banks of arriving flights followed by banks of departures.

Following the downturn in the fortunes of the airline industry in the early 2000s United States airlines reduced their secondary hubs, as Delta did with its Cincinnati hub, or de-complexed their schedules and moved to operating 'continuous' or 'rolling hubs'. The aim was to reduce the costs of handling very marked passenger peaks during complexes. Over time, however, it became apparent that the revenue lost because some connecting times were no longer convenient was greater than any cost savings. Delta and United therefore soon rescheduled their flights into complexes of arrivals and departures. The last of the majors to do so was American, which did not reinstate complexes until the summer of 2014 following its merger with US Airways the previous December. Doug Parker, its Chief Executive, summed up the reasons for the change: '*Instead of being scheduled to maximise connections, the (rolling hub) was scheduled to lower costs – better asset utilisation, better pilot and flight attendant utilisation. It is lower cost … but you lose all that revenue and it overwhelms the cost saving*' (Dallas News, 22 December 2013).

In Europe, after 2002, SWISS downgraded its Geneva hub where it had offered 25 domestic and European services to just a handful, plus a few where it code-shared on foreign carriers. But as competition with easyJet at Geneva intensified in the late 2000s, SWISS set out to rebuild its secondary hub. Alitalia in 2008 more or less abandoned its Milan–Malpensa hub and focused on Rome. Of growing concern, in North America, Europe and elsewhere, is the impact of low-cost airlines on hub feeder routes. As network carriers lose traffic to low-cost competitors on routes feeding their major hubs some of these routes will become less viable once higher-yielding local point-to-point traffic is lost. Some routes may have to be abandoned, making their hubs even more dependent on locally generated traffic.

11 Pricing for profit?

We have been doing à-la-carte pricing for six years and it is popular with our customers ... About 47 per cent of our customers choose a higher fare product for its attributes – even with lower fares available.

(Montie Brewer, CEO, Air Canada, April 2009)

11.1 Varying objectives of airline pricing

Pricing is a crucial element in airline management. It is only one of several product and service features that are planned and combined together in order to generate demand, but it is the key mechanism whereby the demand for air services is matched with the supply. An airline's primary aim must be to sell the capacity it is prepared and able to offer at prices that will generate sufficient demand to ensure an adequate level of profit. A great deal hinges on what each airline considers an adequate profit. For some state-owned airlines it may mean little more than breaking even. For others it may be measured in terms of an adequate rate of return to shareholders or a target rate of return on the value of the assets employed. Some airlines may go further and set out not only to produce a target rate of return on their current assets but also to generate an adequate reserve fund to self-finance, as far as possible, the acquisition of new assets such as aircraft. Singapore Airlines appears in recent years to have followed this latter objective. Thus, even the profit objective in airline pricing may have different implications for different airlines.

There is also a temporal dimension to the profit objective. While some airlines may be concerned more with current profits, others may place the emphasis on longer-term profitability. They may be prepared to forego profits in the short term to ensure their longer-term objective. When launching new services or entering fresh markets airlines will often accept losses in the short term, in the expectation of long-term profits. Short-term losses may be exacerbated by the need to offer low fares in order to capture market share and get established.

For many government-owned airlines, particularly in their early years, profit has been less important than achieving other indirect benefits such as stimulating incoming tourism and related employment or ensuring adequate international air connections. Profit may be seen as a desirable longer-term objective rather than a short-term priority. This was certainly the case with the newer Gulf area airlines such as Qatar Airways, established 1993, and Etihad Airways, launched by Abu Dhabi in 2003.

Most international airlines will normally have a clear profit objective, but it will only be one of a number of corporate objectives. These other objectives may also impinge on pricing policy. Expansion into new routes and new markets figures large in many airlines' corporate objectives. Expansion may be an objective in its own right or the ultimate aim may be rapid growth or the attainment of a particular size of operation. Many airlines want to be big! There may be cost advantages from growth but ultimately the purpose of growth seems to be more akin to a revenue-maximising objective. However, revenue-maximising may not be the same as profit-maximising, as Air Berlin found out in the late 2000s. After floating on the stock market in 2006 it expanded rapidly. Total revenues doubled in the next two years, but profits disappeared. To stem continuing losses Etihad Airlines was brought in as 29 per cent shareholders in 2012, but restructuring failed and the airline collapsed in 2017. If development of new markets or rapid growth are objectives of an airline's pricing policy then the pricing strategies it adopts must be coloured by this fact.

The adverse cost impact of large seasonal or even daily variations in demand may induce airlines to use the pricing mechanism as a way of reducing those fluctuations. This might be done by using high tariffs at peak periods both to increase revenues but also to restrain or dampen peak demand and lower tariffs to stimulate off-peak traffic. Such a policy may reduce the total revenue that could be generated by a policy of expanding the supply of services at the peak periods so as to carry all the potential demand. But revenue maximisation may be less important in the short term than restraining peak-period demand in order to reduce unit costs by not over-providing capacity at the peak that remains under-utilised in the off-peak periods.

Pricing has a further role: it should in theory be a guide to new investment. Where the number of consumers who are prepared to pay the full cost, including a reasonable profit, of the goods or services they consume exceeds the supply, then the producers have a clear indication that if they can supply more at the same or a lower price, demand will be sufficient to generate further profits. Conversely, if consumers in total do not generate sufficient revenue to cover the full costs of particular services then it would be foolhardy to invest in the expansion of such services. If pricing is to be used as a guide to further investment, then the prices of different services should broadly reflect their costs of production. If not, demand may be artificially high or it may be suppressed. On two or three occasions falling tariffs on the North Atlantic have generated a surge in demand, which pushed up load factors to high levels. Some airlines misread the signs and increased the capacity on offer. Here, as on numerous other occasions, airlines have found that adding more seats, which can only be filled at very low fares, proved a recipe for financial distress! The low tariffs were only feasible if mixed with a certain proportion of high-fare Business and First class traffic. Putting on extra services to cater exclusively for the low-yield traffic could prove ruinous since the revenue generated may be insufficient to cover the costs. The pricing mechanism, if used as a guide to further investment, must be used with care.

In short, few international airlines have a single overriding objective in their pricing policy, though the attainment of profitability looms large, especially for privately owned airlines. Most want their pricing policy to achieve a number of internal objectives, but they may also have externally imposed objectives. Some national airlines are required by their governments to stimulate incoming tourism. This may well require a low-fare policy irrespective of its repercussions on the financial fortunes of the airline itself. The attempt to attain different pricing objectives simultaneously may produce conflicts and contradictions in pricing policy. Such conflicts and complexities in pricing are further increased because the same airline may be pursuing different objectives on different parts of its network. It may be trying to maximise profits on some routes, especially those on which there is little or no tariff competition, while on other routes its prime objective may be increasing its market share or its rate of growth. Inevitably within any airline different pricing objectives will prevail at different times and in different parts of their operations.

11.2 Three key variables

The theme of the present book is that airline management is about matching the supply of air services, which airline executives can largely control, with the demand for such services, which executives can influence but cannot control, in a way that generates adequate levels of profit. Profitability, which appears to be an important objective for most airlines, depends in turn on the interplay of three variables, the unit costs, which are a function of supply conditions, the unit revenues or yields and the load factors achieved, both of which are related to demand. The interplay of these three variables can be illustrated by reference to a simple hypothetical case study.

Let us assume that in the late 2010s a European low-cost airline flying a high-density Airbus A330-300 with 400 seats, and operating three times weekly to New York, may have incurred a total one-way operating cost of, say, $80,000. On this basis it would be possible to draw a break-even load factor curve (Figure 11.1). This sloping line shows the load factor the airline would have needed to achieve to break even at different average fare levels or yields (the average being the weighted average of all fares paid). At any point along the curve, the average fare shown (on the vertical scale) times the number of passengers carried or the load factor (horizontal scale) equals $80,000. By plotting on the graph the average fare and the average load achieved on each day's flight in each month or season it is possible to see whether the flight is profitable or not. The plots for just three days in the first month of the summer season are shown in the diagram. On both Mondays and Saturdays the combination of average fare and passenger load were clearly above the break-even curve. These flights are profitable. The Thursday flight was problematic! Average yields were low and so were loads, averaging close to 40 per cent.

What could be done? Two obvious strategies come to mind immediately – push up the loads or increase the fares. At the then existing one-way fares, which on Thursdays were averaging just over $200, the average load factor would need to be pushed up to more than 85 per cent to cross the break-even load factor curve. This seems unrealistic. On the other hand, to break even at the current 40 per cent load factor, the average fare would have to more than double to $500 to achieve a profitable operation. But if fares went up so much there would be a passenger reaction and it would be difficult to maintain the same volume of passenger traffic. Clearly the easiest task for Thursday flights would be to try to cross the break-even curve at the nearest point. In other words, to try to increase both average yields and average loads. This could be done by targeting high-yield Business class passengers, thereby improving the traffic mix, by focused advertising and so on. There is a further solution: to try to move the break-even curve downward and to the left by reducing total operating costs, through tighter cost control or, if available, by operating the Thursday service with a smaller 260–300-seater aircraft, such as a Boeing 777-200, with lower trip costs. The airline's planners have three variables to play with in order to achieve profitability – unit costs, fares and load factors.

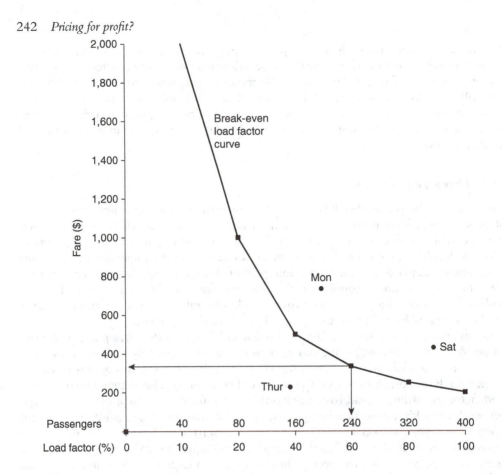

Figure 11.1 Unit cost, yield and load factor trade-off (total operating cost Europe to New York – one way = US $80,000)

11.3 Inherent instability of airline fares

As in the simple case above, airline managers must juggle with costs, fares and load factors to produce a profitable combination. This is a very dynamic and interactive process, made more difficult by the pricing instability inherent in the airline industry. The industry is characterised by short-run marginal costs close to zero. In other words, the marginal cost of carrying an extra passenger on a flight due to leave with empty seats is no more than the cost of an additional meal, an airport passenger charge, the cost of ground-handling and a few pounds of fuel burnt as a result of the extra weight. The problem is that even when operating with high load factors of 70 per cent or more there will be many empty seats. These cannot be stored or sold later. If they are not sold at the moment of production, the seats and the seat-kms generated are lost forever. The same considerations apply to unsold freight capacity.

An airline committed to operating a published schedule of services for a particular season finds that its short-run total costs are fixed and cannot be varied. Therefore, it makes business sense to try to maximise revenues. Having sold as much capacity as possible at normal tariffs, the airline or tour operator is tempted to sell any remaining empty seats at virtually any price above the very low marginal cost of carrying the additional passengers.

The problem is how to prevent slippage or diversion of passengers, prepared to book early and pay the normal tariffs, into paying the lower tariffs. If that happens then the total revenue generated may decline. Historically in markets where tariff rules were regulated and enforced, diversion was prevented or minimised by the conditions, the so-called 'fences', which circumscribed the availability of the very low tariffs (see Section 11.5). However, most markets are no longer regulated or, if regulated, regulations are not enforced. As a result, the low marginal cost of carrying an additional passenger (or freight consignment) has a strong downward pressure on all tariffs, including the normal Economy, Business or First class fares. It is in conditions of over-capacity that airlines are most likely to resort to marginal cost pricing.

In international markets the price instability is aggravated by a number of additional factors. One of these has already been mentioned and that is the tendency of new airlines entering established markets to try to capture market share by undercutting prevailing tariffs. The most significant factor and the most widespread, even affecting regulated markets, is the availability of Sixth Freedom capacity. While the point-to-point, Third and Fourth Freedom carriers on a route may be trying to maintain an adequate mix and level of different tariffs, Sixth Freedom carriers operating via their own hubs may be prepared to charge almost anything to fill empty seats with traffic that they would otherwise not have had. The Sixth Freedom operators' tariffs will be particularly low if they want to compensate passengers for having a lengthy stop-over at their hub en-route to their final destination. The development of hubbing (Section 10.7, Chapter 10) has aggravated this problem as it has increased the number of convenient routings and timings available for many longer-haul journeys. This, together with so much additional capacity being available, has intensified competition. In most long-haul international markets there is a great amount of spare indirect capacity slushing around and depressing tariffs. On some routes there may be the additional problem of the marginal carrier, that is an airline for whom the route is marginal to its total operation. It may therefore be unconcerned by low fares on the route, particularly if it sees them as a way of attracting traffic onto the rest of its network.

Examples of the various pressures on fares from Sixth Freedom indirect carriers could be found on the London–Singapore route in April 2018 (Table 11.1). In Economy class, Singapore Airlines (SIA) offered a high fare of £1,366 return while BA's fare at £714 was almost half. British Airways was clearly trying to match the fares of some of the Sixth Freedom operators listed in the table. These were undercutting the SIA Economy fare by several hundred pounds, though if purchased much earlier the SIA fare itself would have been lower. When it came to Business class, it is SIA which is trying to match the fares of indirect competitors. The SIA fare of £3,549 is close to the fares of Emirates (£3,654) and Etihad (£3,257) while BA's fare is somewhat lower. In both Economy and Business class the lowest fares by far are those offered by Finnair and Turkish! In their pricing and their revenue management SIA and BA must be constantly watching what these and other competitors are offering in the market.

In 2018 there was a new entrant on the London–Singapore route with the potential to further destabilise pricing. In April 2018 Norwegian, the low-cost airline, was offering four non-stop services each week from London-Gatwick to Singapore. Its lowest return fare was £552 with no meals or £652 with two meals in each direction. These were close to or lower than those offered by Finnair and Turkish (Table 11.1), but were a greater threat for both SIA and BA because Norwegian would also be operating non-stop on this sector.

Table 11.1 Sample of lowest return Economy and Business class fares: London–Singapore, April 2018

Economy (£)		Business (£)	
Singapore Airlines	1,366	British Airways	4,120
British Airways	714	Singapore Airlines	3,549
Air France	835	Air France	4,004
Etihad	846	Etihad	3,654
Emirates	802	Emirates	3,257
Lufthansa	758	Lufthansa	2,836
Finnair	630	Finnair	2,622
Turkish	606	Turkish	2,347

Note: Fares offered by airlines' websites early February 2018 for travel 7–15 April 2018. Only BA and Singapore Airlines flew non-stop until early 2018 when low-cost airline Norwegian launched non-stop flights

Many but not all Sixth Freedom operators generally had lower fares than those of BA or SIA. In the case of the European carriers this was despite the fact that they had to carry passengers on high-cost, short sectors from London to their European hubs. These very low Sixth Freedom fares were to encourage passengers despite the inconvenience of changing aircraft at an intermediate hub on the way to Singapore.

While Table 11.1 shows the apparent price structure, the availability of so many low fares and so much capacity inevitably meant that all carriers, but especially the home carriers BA and SIA, were under tremendous pressure to cut fares, especially on flights when loads were poor. They did this by offering lower fares through internet travel agencies and/or by frequent price changes on their own websites.

On other routes, price instability may be increased by the actions of financially weak or government-supported carriers. Surprisingly it is often the weak or loss-making airlines that drop their prices most in competitive markets in order to generate sufficient cash flow to meet their day-to-day payments.

Some state-owned airlines may continue operating on certain routes at yields and load factors that are uneconomic because of government pressure or because they can rely on subsidies to cover their losses. In the process, however, they depress the market for other carriers.

The low marginal cost of carrying additional traffic, together with the other factors that undermine price stability, means international airlines are often under pressure to reduce tariffs often to very low levels especially in very competitive markets. The inherent instability of air transport markets may well push tariffs to levels at which no operator can make a profit except for short periods. It is this fear above all else that pushes airlines to try to reach a tacit understanding or an explicit agreement between themselves on tariff levels. One way of removing real price competition on routes where there are only two competitors, or where two airlines carry most of the traffic, is for these two airlines to enter into a code-share agreement or even a full alliance. They may still compete on price but within limits. The optimum solution is for airlines to be able to fix the fares in the markets they jointly operate. This is possible if they operate metal-neutral joint ventures, approved by the regulatory authorities (Section 7.5).

11.4 Impact of the internet on airline pricing

The inherent instability in airline pricing was been made worse by the spread of the internet over the last 20 years or so. Its impact has been twofold: first, by giving potential travellers, who have online access, easy and immediate knowledge of all airlines' fares. In by-passing the traditional travel agents, the internet has shifted market power from the suppliers, the airlines, to the consumer. Using airline websites and online travel agencies the consumer can quickly obtain nearly perfect knowledge of what different airlines can offer in terms of fares, schedules, seat availability and service offers. There is full transparency. This gives the consumer considerable power. He can make his choice of airline with all the knowledge of the various options at his fingertips. Since on most routes service standards of different airlines are fairly similar or unimportant, if on short sectors, consumer awareness of all the fare options has reinforced price as a differentiator between airlines. In fact, in many short-haul markets the internet has turned air travel into a commodity where price is the key variable on which consumers make their choice. All this has made it more critical for airlines to get their pricing levels and strategies right.

The second impact of the internet is that it has made airline pricing much more dynamic in real time. The development of computerised reservation systems and later automated revenue management programmes working in real time has given airline revenue controllers instant knowledge of fare changes introduced by their competitors. They can also monitor how well different fares are selling. The internet has given them the ability to respond immediately with new or matching fares, which can be communicated worldwide in seconds through their website and those of the GDSs. The speed with which new fares can be introduced but also matched in many markets is a more recent and additional cause of instability in airline fares. The more truly competitive the market, the greater the inherent instability.

In markets with several competitors and where product and service standards are not that different, attempts by any one or more carriers to gain competitive advantage by dropping fares will inevitably be matched by all the others. They all end up with similar fares but at a lower level and no one airline is better off in competitive terms. The internet facilitates this downward drift in fare levels.

11.5 Cost–related or market pricing?

In developing their pricing strategies international airlines must bear in mind both their pricing objectives and the inherent instability of airline tariffs. Broadly speaking, two alternative strategies have been open to them. The first is to relate each tariff to the costs incurred in providing the services used by those paying that tariff. This is 'cost of service' pricing, more frequently referred to as cost-related pricing. The alternative is to base tariffs for different categories of service not on costs but on what consumers are able and willing to pay. This is market pricing or demand-related pricing. Market pricing does not ignore costs, but the aim is to ensure revenues in total cover costs rather than attempting to ensure that individual customers or groups cover their own particular costs.

In the four decades up to the mid-1980s most international and domestic fares around the world were regulated by IATA or governments to a greater or lesser extent (see Section 2.7). If fares were to be controlled the only logical and quantifiable basis on which this could be done appeared to be by linking approved fare levels to costs. In the 1980s several regulatory authorities, European governments (CEC, 1983) and the Commission of the European Communities (CEC, 1984) argued most strongly in favour of cost-related pricing.

The arguments in favour of cost-related pricing in utilities and transport services hinge on the twin issues of equity and economic efficiency. It was considered inequitable that some consumers of air services should be charged more than the cost of providing those services either to generate excess profits or in order to cross-subsidise consumers who are paying less than the full cost of the services they consume. If tariffs are not cost-related then they may well be discriminatory. That means that certain consumers will be discriminated against not on the basis of costs they impose but on the basis of their age, their marital status or, for instance, because they want to spend less than six nights at their destination.

There are efficiency implications as well. If fares are above cost for some services, then demand for those services will be suppressed even though it might be profitable to supply that demand at prices that were cost-related. Conversely, fares below cost may generate excess demand for particular services and induce airlines to expand such services even though consumers are not meeting their full costs. This would clearly be a misallocation of resources. Cost-related pricing was supported both on social grounds, in order to reduce discrimination between consumers, and on economic grounds, in the belief that it created pressures towards improved airline efficiency and a sounder allocation of productive resources.

On the other hand, several arguments can be used to question the principle of cost pricing. The first of these is that there is no satisfactory way for transport industries to allocate costs to particular users because of the incidence of joint costs. This means that a high proportion of fixed costs have to be allocated arbitrarily. Joint costs arise when in producing one service another is inadvertently provided. A daily scheduled flight aimed at a business market generates freight capacity whether or not there is an adequate demand for freight services. Its operations will also inevitably result in vacant seats, which might be sold off to meet tourism demand. How is one to allocate the costs of that flight between business passengers who were the prime objective in setting up the flight, and freight or holiday travellers? Any allocation of joint costs must have an element of arbitrariness in it. Airlines pursuing cost-based pricing would end up calculating what is more akin to an average cost for all users rather than a separate cost specific to different categories of users.

Another argument against cost-related pricing is that on some routes such a pricing strategy would not generate sufficient revenue to cover costs and would therefore fail to ensure the continued operation of services. On a simple route with one fare and one class of service a cost-related fare may not generate sufficient demand to ensure profitability. On the other hand, if two market segments with different price elasticities can be identified, then the airline concerned may generate higher revenue by charging two separate fares to the two market groups even though there may be no significant difference in the cost of transporting them. Without discriminatory but market-related tariffs the services might be abandoned, and all consumers would be worse off. Such a hypothetical case was illustrated earlier (Chapter 8, Section 8.8) when discussing the concept of price elasticity.

It is important to bear in mind that demand or market pricing does not ignore costs, but its focus is to try to ensure that total costs of a route or a flight are covered, rather than to try to ensure that every user pay their own identifiable costs. From an airline viewpoint, demand-related pricing strategies make sense. A scheduled airline that is committed to a published timetable of flights and has brought together the productive resources to operate that timetable finds that its short-run total costs are more or less fixed. In those circumstances it needs the freedom to price its services in such a way as to be able to generate sufficient revenues to cover its costs. This may mean charging more than cost to price-inelastic segments of the market and perhaps less than cost to elastic market segments. In liberalised competitive markets, competition between carriers should ensure that market-related pricing is not abused to produce excessive profit for the airline.

Where effective competition does not exist and market entry of new airlines is difficult, then there may well be a danger of excessive profits being made through discriminatory pricing. In such situations regulatory or government intervention to monitor costs, tariffs and airline profits may be necessary to prevent this happening, though there must be some doubt as to how effective such intervention can be. Deregulation of tariffs, of capacity controls and of market access would be the most effective way of minimising the likelihood of excessive profits.

As liberalisation of prices, traffic rights and market access spread, first domestically in the United States after 1978 and subsequently in a growing number of international markets, the airline industry moved increasingly from cost-based to market- or demand-related pricing. In the United States and Europe this switch was accelerated by the rapid growth of low-cost airlines with their innovatory pricing policies. Today in most liberalised markets demand-related pricing prevails, though this does not mean that airlines do not constantly monitor the profitability of different market segments such as that of First or Business class passengers in long-haul aircraft. It is only in countries or markets where governments wish to control fares that attempts may be made to link fares with costs.

A simple, hypothetical example illustrates the basic differences in approach between cost-based and market-based pricing. The daily demand for air services between Athens and a small but important Greek island is shown in the first column of Table 11.2. This shows how much each potential passenger is prepared to pay to be able to fly to the island. It is a measure of the value or benefit to each passenger of this service. Some wealthy Athenians have holiday homes on the island and two of them (as shown) would be prepared to pay $300 or more to fly in 35 minutes and so avoid the five-hour boat services. Effectively column 1 is the hypothetical downward sloping demand curve and shows how the demand increases as the cost or fare goes down.

The total one-way operating cost of this service with a small ten-seater twin is $1,200 for a 35-minute sector. This means that the average cost per seat is $120. If a cost-based fare of $120 is charged, there would be seven passengers daily, that is, all those who, based on their willingness to pay (as shown in column 1), value the trip more than $120. The seat factor is good, 70 per cent, but the service would make a loss (column 2) of $360 per trip.

Clearly another option for the airlines' planners would be to base the fare not on the cost per seat but on the cost per passenger. If they target a 60 per cent seat factor, then the cost per passenger would be $200 (that is, $1,200 divided by six passengers). The airline could build in a profit margin of $10 per passenger and charge $210. The demand curve shows that six passengers would be prepared to pay this price and total revenue would rise to $1,260, producing a small profit. However, it is clear by

Table 11.2 Pricing alternatives: Athens to Greek island case study

10-seater aircraft
Total operating cost = $1,200 (one way)

Passengers' willingness to pay, i.e. the demand curve	Average cost pricing		Market pricing
	Fare based on cost per seat = $120	Fare based on cost per pax at 60% Seat factor = $210*	Three separate fares: $300, $150 and $90
(1)	*(2)*	*(3)*	*(4)*
	Fares paid by passengers willing to travel		
$	$	$	$
1	310	120	210	300
2	310	120	210	300
3	280	120	210	150
4	260	120	210	150
5	230	120	210	150
6	210	120	210	150
7	160	120		150
8	110			90
9	90			90
10	55			
11	55			
12	50			
13	40			
	etc			
TOTAL REVENUE		$840	$1,260	$1,530
SURPLUS-DEFICIT		− $360	+$ 60	+$ 330
Seat factor		70%	60%	90%

* Cost per pax based on 60% load is $200 plus $10 profit margin

comparing columns 3 and 1 of Table 11.2 that several passengers are paying a lot less than the value to them of the service. What economists call the 'consumers surplus', which they enjoy, is substantial. Two who are prepared to pay $310 for the flight are getting it for only $210.

Market-related pricing aims at ensuring that producers do not lose out in this way. One might introduce a three-tier fare structure, with fares of $90, $150 and $300 as indicated in the final column (4), to ensure that fares are more closely aligned to market demand rather than to costs. Then seat factor and revenue can be pushed up markedly (Table 11.2). In this case study a significant surplus of $330 per flight and a seat factor of 90 per cent would result from the proposed three-level fare structure.

In practice, pricing is not as simple as the example would suggest. But the basic principle still applies. Market-related pricing may, in most but not all markets, enable airlines to generate higher revenues. The complexities of implementing such pricing are discussed later. For instance, in the case study above barriers or fare fences would need to be devised to prevent high-fare passengers using the lower fares.

While, in the short term, a strategy of market-oriented tariffs makes sense as a way of maximising revenues, it does not in itself guarantee profitability, especially in price-competitive markets. Because of the inherent instability in airline tariffs, discussed earlier, which is due to very low short-run marginal costs, market-related tariffs may reach such low levels that the total revenue generated is insufficient to cover total costs. This is particularly so if extra capacity is provided to cater for the demand generated by the low tariffs. While revenue maximising might be a short-term pricing objective, in the longer term airlines are likely to adopt a profit-generating or loss-minimising objective. This means they should abandon routes where revenues do not cover costs or change their pricing policies to ensure that they do.

In order to achieve such objectives through their pricing strategies airlines must be in a position to do three things. First, they must have a fundamental understanding of the different market segments in each of their markets and of customer needs and requirements, both in terms of product features and price (as discussed earlier in Chapter 8, Section 8.5). Second, in markets where airlines offer fares that are market-related rather than cost-based, they must implement effective yield- or revenue management. This is needed to ensure both that revenue dilution does not occur through slippage of high-fare passengers into lower-fare categories and that their total revenues are maximised.

Finally, where market segments are fairly distinct, they should monitor the degree to which each major market category or traffic group covers the costs it imposes on the airline. This, together with the need to evaluate the feasibility of aircraft investments, of new routes and of different products, pushes airlines to consider carefully the costs of the different services they provide. Whatever pricing strategy they are forced to adopt by the market conditions on each route, the starting point for their pricing procedures should be and normally is an evaluation of the costs of the different services they provide. Even market-related pricing cannot ignore costs. Understanding the relationship between pricing and costs is fundamental to effective airline management. In brief, the key to successful revenue generation is market knowledge, effective revenue management and cost awareness.

11.6 Choice of price and product strategies

The fare charged is only one aspect of the product or service provided by an airline to different classes of passenger. Other product features include frequency, timings, seat comfort, the quality and nature of ground and in-flight services and so on. These have been analysed in Chapter 10, though price is often the most important, particularly for leisure and VFR travel. In planning the supply of services on each route it serves, an airline must also decide on the various price and product mixes it feels will generate the level of demand it requires. In markets that are less regulated and where there is a high degree of price competition the pricing options available are much wider but the choice between them more difficult to make.

The starting point for deciding on a pricing strategy, that is the structure and level of tariffs and the product features associated with them, must be an assessment of demand and of the airline's pricing objectives. Is an airline setting out to meet a particular profit target, to expand rapidly, to capture market share, or does it have some other objective it wishes to achieve? Given the objectives of its pricing policy, an airline must examine the costs of the different products it can put into the market in relation to its assessment of what potential consumers want and are prepared to pay for. It must also consider its own positioning within each market. Is it setting out to meet the needs of all market segments or is it trying to attract only certain segments? How does it position and brand itself? By going for the top end of the market airlines can aim for high-yield traffic and accept that this may mean lower load factors and a loss of market share.

In those international markets where there is still some government oversight of tariffs, a pricing strategy must also be acceptable to the airline's own government and, on international routes, to the government at the other end of the route. The other government's response will be dependent on the interests of its own airline and in particular on the relationship of the tariffs proposed to its own airline's costs and objectives.

In price-competitive markets, the pricing strategy may need to be dynamic and changing in response to price or product changes introduced by competing airlines. Airlines have many difficult decisions to make. Should they match a competitor's lower fares when they know the competitor has lower unit costs, or is prepared to face a loss or may be heavily subsidised by his government? What proportion of its capacity should an airline offer at price-competitive fares? Is there any point in undercutting a competitor's tariff if the latter is going to match one's own new, lower tariffs? These and other considerations will affect the pricing strategy and tariff levels that airlines adopt in each of their markets. The ultimate aim must not be forgotten, however: that is to bring supply and demand together in such a way that the airline achieves its corporate objectives.

11.7 Traditional structure of international passenger fares

In many international markets, especially long-haul markets, the traditional structure of fares, with complex rules, based on cabin classes was originally developed through the IATA tariff machinery and traffic conferences (see Chapter 2, Section 2.7). Since 2000, as domestic and international markets were progressively liberalised, more flexible fare structures have emerged, driven, in large part, by the innovatory pricing policies of the low-cost airlines. (These new pricing structures are discussed in the following section (11.8).) At the same time, the markets in which the IATA tariff machinery was used progressively shrank. Finally, in November 2018 IATA abandoned its role in setting tariffs. Nevertheless, the widespread adoption of IATA tariffs on international air routes in the past means that there is today considerable uniformity in the structure of the air fares of network airlines, though not in the levels of such fares.

The complexity of traditional international tariffs was of two kinds. First, there was a multiplicity of fare types. These include First, Business, Premium Economy and Economy fares linked to different cabins as well as preferential fares plus a range of promotional fares.

Traditionally on most international routes legacy or network airlines offered fare types corresponding to the separate cabin classes, that is First, Business and Economy. On European routes and some long-haul routes there may no longer be any First class services. While normally there will only be a single First class or Business fare, or in some cases a couple of such fares, there were frequently several different fares available for the Economy cabin. It was the full Economy fare that was considered as the basic 'normal' fare for the Economy cabin, but there were in addition numerous promotional Economy class fares, discussed below. On long-haul routes several airlines have progressively introduced an additional but small improved Economy cabin, which is generally referred to as Premium Economy and was first launched by British Airways in

2000. But some have been slow to do so. United Airlines did not introduce its own 'Premium Plus' cabin until the second half of 2018.

Preferential fares are those which are available only to passengers who meet certain requirements in terms of age, family kinship or occupation. They were usually expressed as a percentage discount on the normal fares and are generally applicable over large geographical areas. The most widely accepted and used were the 33 or sometimes 50 per cent discount, on the Economy or more expensive fares, for children under 12 years of age and the 90 per cent discount for infants under two but without the right to a seat. In particular regions there might be discounts for students travelling to or from their place of study, or discounts for military personnel or ships' crews. Traditionally, the aim of preferential fares has been partly developmental to encourage demand from particular groups within the community and partly social through the choice of groups to be encouraged, that is families with young children or students.

Promotional fares, sometimes referred to as discount fares, were various low fares, usually with one or more restrictions on their availability, which offered passengers significant savings on the normal fares. Such fares were not of general application, as most preferential fares tended to be, but were separately negotiated and agreed for particular market areas or routes.

The early development of promotional fares was aimed at stimulating particular market segments, such as off-peak demand or the demand for inclusive tours, while taking advantage of the low marginal cost of scheduled air services once airlines were committed to a published timetable. Off-peak fares, weekend fares, night fares and group (GTX) or individual inclusive tour (ITX) fares have been the most common of a wide range of promotional fares that have been developed. Fundamentally there could be only one justification for them: they must increase an airline's net revenue and hopefully its profits too. They can only do this by increasing traffic by a greater amount than is needed to overcome both the revenue loss arising from the lower fares and the possible diversion of higher-fare traffic to these lower fares.

To minimise the risk of diversion '*fences*' or conditions were often attached to promotional fares. A promotional fare tended to have one or more '*fences*' built into its conditions. '*Fences*' tended to be of four kinds. First, there may be a limit on the *trip duration*. Most promotional fares had a minimum and maximum stay limitation. Second, there may be *departure time limitations*. It was common to limit the availability of many promotional fares to particular times of the day, or days of the week or seasons. The aim here was to generate off-peak demand or to try to fill up seats that otherwise were expected to remain empty because of the timing or day of particular flights. Third, some of the lowest promotional fares entailed *purchase time restrictions*. Their aim was to direct demand more effectively than could be done with departure time limitations. Such restrictions required either advance reservation a minimum number of days before departure or late purchase, normally within 24 hours before time of departure. The aim was to use them to push traffic into days where projected demand was expected to be low.

Finally, there have also been a range of *inclusive tour fares,* which were not publicly available but could be purchased by tour operators and used to package into inclusive tour (IT) holidays. Such packaged holidays normally included accommodation but might involve some other element such as car hire or tickets for a cultural or sports event instead of or in addition to the accommodation.

While in many markets the need for promotional fares has been overtaken by the new more flexible pricing structures, inclusive tour fares are still widely used especially in Europe but in Asia and North America too. They are basically non-public fares for seats sold to tour or holiday companies by both network carriers and LCCs. IT fares have allowed legacy network carriers to compete more effectively against charter carriers (Chapter 6).

Thus, the traditional fare structure was a mix of cost-based and market-related pricing. The attempts of regulators to balance the need to protect airlines, many of whom were financially weak, with the interests of consumers, who hungered for easier and cheaper access to air travel, created a pricing framework that was rigid, inflexible and not responsive enough to the changing needs of the market. The fare structure that emerged was extremely complex. On any one flight there would often be a dozen or more separate fares, some publicly available, others only available through agents, each with complicated fare conditions that at times ran to several pages. The longer the routes, the more complex the fares available and the conditions attached to them.

In the late 1990s and early 2000s the explosive growth of short-haul low-cost carriers, especially in Europe, using a much simpler and lower fare structure forced many legacy network carriers to rethink their own pricing, at least for short-haul routes. Deregulation within the European Union and further liberalisation elsewhere in both domestic and in international markets made this easier. By the mid-2000s, airlines such as Air Canada and Aer Lingus had introduced simpler, more flexible market-oriented pricing. Other legacy airlines followed and adopted the new pricing strategies to a greater or lesser extent.

11.8 Low-cost airlines' new pricing strategies

A key feature of the low-cost model has been the use of very low and simple fares in order to divert passengers from existing carriers, both airlines and ground transporters, and also to generate new traffic from passengers who would not otherwise be travelling. Southwest in the United States, Ryanair and easyJet in Europe, Gol in Brazil and Air Asia in Malaysia have based their rapid growth and success on low, simple fares with the minimum of conditions or constraints. Fares are transparent and easy to understand. The focus is on generating demand by market-related pricing that is flexible and changed frequently in response to changing demand patterns. The fact that LCCs are operating in short-haul primarily point-to-point markets has made it easier to simplify pricing.

All low-cost carriers' fares policies are not identical, but they exhibit certain features, common to most but not all LCCs, which differentiate their pricing from the traditional fare structures outlined previously:

*   Passengers can buy a single one-way fare. There is no obligation to buy a return fare. Historically network carriers were unlikely to offer single one-way fares on short-haul routes. In fact, their single fares, if available, were often more than half the return fares. Therefore, there were strong incentives to purchase only return fares. Certainly, the cheaper promotional fares were only available as round-trip fares.
*   At time of booking on a low-cost carrier, there is normally only one, or less frequently two or three fares available for a particular flight. The simplicity of the fare structure contrasts with traditional pricing on network carriers where numerous separate fares may be available, with varying conditions, for any one flight at time of booking. The fact that most LCCs have only one cabin class has made it easier to simplify pricing.

- While there may be only one (or two) fares available for each LCC flight, different flights on the same route and on the same day may have a different fare on offer. This reflects different demand patterns during the day on each route. Again, this contrasts with traditional pricing, where fares generally have not varied between flights on the same day and on the same route.
- LCC fares change rapidly. LCC pricing entails the offer of very low fares well in advance of the departure date. As the departure day approaches or as the number of seats at the low initial fare fill up, the single fare available for each flight moves up in a series of steps. It may also move down if a flight is not selling well. In other words, the fare for each flight is very responsive to the day-by-day demand for that particular flight. Traditionally, short-haul fares on network airlines have tended to be much less flexible. Some fare types were closed off or others opened but generally fare levels were not responsive to demand. In some markets fares might be cut at the last minute if a large number of seats was left unsold. This was the opposite of the LCC pricing philosophy, which is to raise last-minute fares.
- Fare conditions on LCCs are few and simple, and uniformly applied to all fares and flights. This is made easier if there are only one or two fare types available. The fare conditions may be tough, for instance no refund if a ticket is not used, but they tend to be uniform. Conditions are not complex or difficult for passengers to understand, as was often the case with the different fare types traditionally offered by network carriers.

The key elements of low-cost airlines' pricing strategy outlined here can be seen in the example of easyJet's fares between London-Gatwick and Athens, Greece, in May 2018 well before the peak of the holiday season (Table 11.3). The fares are for easyJet's only two daily flights and include a UK government passenger duty as well as airport charges. The fares available for a flight out on Monday 9 May 2018 and back on Friday 13 May were monitored at roughly two-weekly intervals starting on 10 February 2018, that is three months before the planned departure. From an examination (Table 11.3) of the fare changes as the departure date approached, the following features stand out:

- At any one time there is only one basic fare available on each flight. There was also a very much more expensive 'Flexi' fare.
- Fares vary between flights on the same day despite being on the same route.
- Fares can be bought at the prices shown for a one-way trip.
- Fares increase, sometimes day by day, in response to demand as departure day approaches but may also go down if sales are below target. For instance, fares for the afternoon flight London to Athens fluctuate widely up and down.
- The fares are lower and less volatile on the very early morning flight from London – 5.45 am departure – indicating it is less popular than the afternoon flight.
- Close to the day of departure the fares may be at their highest to reflect the scarcity of seats.
- Frequent fare changes are responses to both changing booking levels (i.e. demand), but also to fare levels of other competitors on the London–Athens route – British Airways, Aegean and Ryanair.

The fares shown in Table 11.3 were the basic unbundled fares. Passengers could buy a number of additional services or product features. If checking in luggage for the

Table 11.3 Changing easyJet fares London-Gatwick to Athens, for flights out Monday 9 May and return 13 May 2018

	Date of fare quotation on easyJet website in 2018						
	Feb 10	Feb 25	Mar 10	Mar 24	Apr 10	Apr 25	May 5
	£	£	£	£	£	£	£
Gatwick–Athens							
Dept. 05.45	57	71	77	77	77	77	120
Dept. 14.40	67	125	87	150	95	95	150
Athens–Gatwick							
Dept. 12.20	45	123	123	93	93	93	123
Dept. 21.05	37	93	74	68	107	107	140

N.B.: Fares are one-way inclusive of airport charges and government taxes, but exclude any ancillary charges, such as priority boarding, seat selection, etc., which are at passengers' discretion.
Flexi fares that include most ancillaries are £100–£350 above the basic fares shown

aircraft hold they would need to pay £42 each way for a bag of up to 15kgs, rising to £73 for bags up to 26kgs. If a passenger wanted an allocated seat before departure day, they would need to pay £4 for an ordinary seat, £18.50 for seats in the front of the cabin and exit row and £20 for a front-row seat. Thus, a large bag and a preferred seat might cost more than the seat price, when booking two to three months in advance.

Alternatively, a passenger could opt to pay the much higher 'Flexi' fare, which would give the passenger free hold baggage and free choice of seat as well as the following benefits:

- a second cabin bag free
- speedy boarding
- special bag drop
- fast-track security
- unlimited date changes
- free route changes
- on-board voucher of £7.

However, one had to pay a high price for this; for example, while the cheapest London–Athens flight in May 2018 if booked in early February 2018 would have cost £57, the Flexi fare for the same flight would have cost £354. A huge increase! Instead a passenger could have bought an annual *easyJet Plus* card for £200. This would have given them most of the benefits of a Flexi fare, except date and route changes, whenever travelling with easyJet even if paying just the basic fare.

Charges for bags checked in, and seat allocation, as in the case of easyJet, quickly became fairly common. Among European LCCs other charges introduced include a 'service' fee for issuing a ticket, a charge for checking in at the airport as opposed to online check-in as well as charges which mirror those imposed historically by network carriers, such as fees for changing a flight, for sports equipment, etc.

While some US low-cost carriers have followed similar pricing policies to their European counterparts, Southwest has adopted a slightly different approach. It offers three distinct fares but without 'a la carte' add-ons. In 2018 Southwest was selling a very low '*Wanna Get Away*' fare, which was non-refundable, as well as a much higher '*Anytime*' fare, which was both changeable on day of travel at no extra fare and refundable. On many routes, the 'Anytime' fare might be three or four times as high as the 'Wanna Get Away' fare, except at peak times when 'Anytime' fares often rose sharply. But instead of offering a series of optional services with add-on charges, Southwest offers a '*Business Select*' fare, which is essentially the 'Anytime' fare with a small $20 to $30 fare increase, for which passengers get priority boarding, a priority security line, an alcoholic drink and bonus miles. By incorporating its 'add-ons' in this enhanced higher fare, Southwest can then claim and advertise that it has no add-on charges. It just offers three separate fares with distinct product features. A simple pricing strategy!

The pricing philosophy inherent in the low-cost business model is to offer very low simple fares, with few but easy-to-understand restrictions. Fares vary between flights on the same day, on the same route (Table 11.3) and change over time in response to changing levels of demand as departure day approaches. Fare yields can be supplemented by 'dynamic' or 'a la carte' pricing, that is, by charging for a variety of service add-ons such as seat allocation or checked baggage. There is little attempt to relate fares to the costs imposed by particular users. Even though some of the add-on charges, such as baggage fees, are claimed to be cost-related, any link to additional costs imposed is conceptual rather than real. Low-cost pricing is market-driven. Costs are not ignored when fixing fares, but the aim is to ensure that the total costs of a flight or route are covered, not the individual costs of particular passengers. Therefore, revenue management is crucial; but, as will be argued later, the simplicity of their fare structure makes revenue management much easier for low-cost carriers.

In summary, the emergence of low-cost carriers has had a three-fold impact on airline pricing. First, LCCs have simplified fares with fewer and simpler restrictions, and made them more responsive to demand. Second, they have deconstructed fares and made them more transparent. Passengers can purchase a simple fare and then buy a variety of 'add-on' services or products of their choosing. Third, the LCCs have proved that these 'add-on' charges can generate substantial ancillary revenues in addition to those from more traditional ancillaries such as on-board duty free, excess baggage charges, etc. The LCCs have shown that ancillary revenues could become a much more significant part of an airline's total revenues. In 2016, 27 per cent of Ryanair's total revenue was generated by ancillaries!

11.9 Network airlines adopt 'a la carte' pricing

In the early 2000s, network airlines became very conscious of the success of low-cost carriers such as Southwest or Ryanair who continued to operate profitably at a time when the industry as a whole was in crisis and many airlines were losing money. This happened again after 2008. Moreover, the LCCs were constantly increasing their market shares on short-haul routes at the expense of the traditional network carriers. So progressively from the mid-2000s on network carriers adopted the LCC pricing strategy of simplifying and unbundling their fares.

In Europe, one of the first to do so was Aer Lingus. This was in response to the fact that Europe's largest LCC, Ryanair, ran a huge operation from Aer Lingus' hub, Dublin airport. Aer Lingus went further than most other European airlines; it abandoned Business class altogether on its short-haul operations only and operated a single-class cabin. But within that cabin it offered three distinct fares with different attributes. In 2018, the three economy fares were: '*Economy Saver*', '*Economy Plus*' and '*Economy Advantage*'.

The price for each of these includes a different number of additional product or service features for no extra cost. These are listed in Table 11.4. Purchasers of 'Saver' tickets get the least additional product features but can buy most of them as and if required. Thus, in 2018, lounge access could be bought for €30, priority boarding for €5, checked bags for a price depending on their weight, and seat selection prior to boarding would cost between €10 and €16.

As LCCs do, Aer Lingus offers different fares on the same day for different flights on the same route and these fares can change as departure day approaches. They start at low levels several months out and gradually increase, reaching their highest levels a day or two before departure. The fares for different flights on the same day do not move in unison but fares move in response to demand for each particular flight time.

Other European network airlines, such as British Airways or Lufthansa, have also adopted a similar approach of offering a limited number of separate fare classes, each with different product or service features. Most have two or three separate fares in their Economy cabin plus two fare categories for their Business cabin. They also offer a number of add-on products or services that can be bought by passengers if these are not included in the fare category they have purchased. But there are differences between airlines. For instance, some try to keep all fares on the same day on the same route more or less similar rather than having wide differences. The speed or frequency with which fare levels change over time also varies between airlines.

In North America it is perhaps Air Canada who, responding in 2003 to strong competition from Canadian low-cost carrier Westjet, was one of the first to switch and adopt the new pricing practices. For its longer domestic flights Air Canada offered four fare categories or classes. In the economy cabin fares increased from the lowest *Tango* fare to *Tango Plus* and then *Latitude*. Then there was the executive fare for the *Business* class cabin. The fares in the same category often differed between the various flights on

Table 11.4 Aer Lingus European Economy fare categories and associated benefits, 2018

	Economy Saver	*Economy Plus*	*Economy Advantage*
Avios FFP Points	Yes	Yes	Yes
Checked bag (20kgs)		Yes	Yes
Advanced seat selection		Yes	Yes
Priority boarding		Yes	Yes
Stand-by for earlier flight		Yes	Yes
Lounge access			Yes
Free change and refunds			Yes
Security fast-track – Dublin			Yes

N.B.: Some services not included could be bought on payment of a fee.
Aer Lingus has no Business class on short-haul routes

that day depending on the level of demand. Air Canada, like most LCCs, introduced a wide range of add-on charges, especially for the Tango and Tango Plus fare classes. In 2009 the airline's then Chief Executive Montie Brewer summed their pricing strategy as follows:

> *We have been doing à-la-carte pricing for six years and it is popular with our customers. We offer four basic fare products, the benefits of which are transparent.*
>
> *About 47 per cent choose a higher fare product for its attributes – even with lower fares available. Then we offer options to either opt out of discounts or to select for purchase – such as checked baggage or lounge access.*

(Airlines International, April–May 2009)

The airline claims that it is this pricing strategy that has enabled its domestic operations to compete effectively and profitably with Westjet, an LCC with low costs and aggressive pricing. On longer domestic routes, by 2018, Air Canada had up to six fare products, four in Economy, including Premium Economy, and two in Business class.

Unlike Air Canada, United States network carriers while adopting 'a la carte' or dynamic pricing have generally adopted fewer fare products. Thus in 2018, Delta Airlines on its domestic routes generally offered no more than two or three separate fares – two in Economy and one in First. On some routes there was an ultra-cheap Basic Economy fare too. Individual fares increased as departure approached but it seemed less rapidly and in smaller steps than did Air Canada fares. Even on its transatlantic services Delta only offered two Economy fares and a First class fare that was for a product more akin to Business class. It did not have Premium Economy on its own aircraft though this was available on code-shared flights operated by Virgin, Air France or KLM. Also, unlike Air Canada, Delta offered its domestic passengers fewer key add-ons, namely only priority booking and on-board wi-fi. The adoption of LCC pricing principles appears to have been less whole-hearted among United States than European airlines.

In contrast to US airlines many other long-haul international airlines have adopted a strategy of numerous fare products or categories. Thus, in 2018 Singapore Airlines had eight different fare products, apart from First class, on its services to Europe. It offered three separate fares in its Economy cabin, two fares in Premium Economy and, surprisingly, three in Business class. These all had quite different conditions, including penalties if passengers did not follow the rules linked to their particular fare class. The rights and possible penalties associated with the different Singapore Airlines Economy and Premium Economy fares are shown in Table 11.5. The three Business class fare categories had their own different conditions. SIA's numerous fare products are of course linked to offering three or four separate cabins on long-haul flights.

Low-cost carriers have basically two simple pricing models. Ryanair and easyJet have basically a single fare available for each flight, which changes as departure approaches. Passengers can add various additional products and services by paying a fee.

easyJet has a second much higher fare that includes all these add-ons but is priced at an unattractive level and, in fact, it's cheaper to purchase the easyJet Plus loyalty card to get the same benefits. In contrast to this model, Southwest packages the various additional product features into three separate fares and offers no add-ons. Both models are simple and consumer friendly.

Table 11.5 Conditions and charges attached to Singapore Airlines Economy and Premium Economy fares, 2018

	Economy			Premium Economy	
	Lite	Standard	Flexi	Standard	Flexi
Seat selection	$15	Free standard seat only	Free standard seat only	Free except extra legroom seat	Free except extra legroom seat
Cancellation	No	$200	$100	$200	$100
Booking change	$200	$50	FREE	$50	FREE
No show penalty	$300	$100	$100	$200	$200
FFP air miles	50%	75%	75%	200%	200%

N.B.: Fees/penalties are in US dollars.
SIA also offers three long-haul Business class fares: Business Lite, Business Standard and Business Flexi.
Also First class in some markets

Legacy airlines in adopting the low-cost approach of simplifying airline pricing seem in many cases to have created complex fare structures with varying conditions that may be difficult for prospective passengers to disentangle and appraise. Singapore Airlines' numerous fare products and fare conditions shown in Table 11.5 and Air Canada's numerous fare categories mentioned earlier epitomise this growing complexity in airline pricing.

The role of the tariffs manager and their team has become more critical but also more difficult as fares become more volatile and dynamic. Moreover, as fares become increasingly demand or market oriented, tariffs managers become totally dependent on effective revenue management tools to ensure that revenues generated cover costs. This is equally true for network or low-cost carriers.

11.10 The theory of revenue management

Revenue management involves the control of fare levels and the seat capacity available at different fares through an airline's reservations control system in order to maximise total passenger revenue per flight. This is not the same as ensuring the highest load factor or the highest average yield. In fact, maximising revenue may in many cases mean that neither of these is achieved. Revenue management is equally crucial for both the network and the low-cost business models.

Yield management is based on the simple economic concept of utility as expressed through the demand curve. There is a maximum price each consumer is willing to pay for a good or service. That price is equivalent to the utility or benefit they get from consuming it. They will happily pay less for it but will not pay more. Different consumers gain varying levels of utility from a particular good or service and therefore each will only buy it if the price is no greater than that utility or benefit. For air services as for most products the lower the price the greater the demand. By summing up the demand for a service at different price levels we can draw a demand curve. On a simple diagram showing air fare on the vertical axis and seats demanded on the horizontal axis one could draw the demand curve for an air service between two cities. This has been done for a hypothetical short-haul route in Figure 11.2(a). It shows a downward sloping demand curve, indicating the number of seats that would be bought at different fares.

An airline wishing to provide this service with a 100-seater aircraft has estimated a one-way total operating cost of, say, $3,500. It sets a target seat factor of 70 per cent, which means carrying 70 passengers. If pricing were purely cost-based then the airline

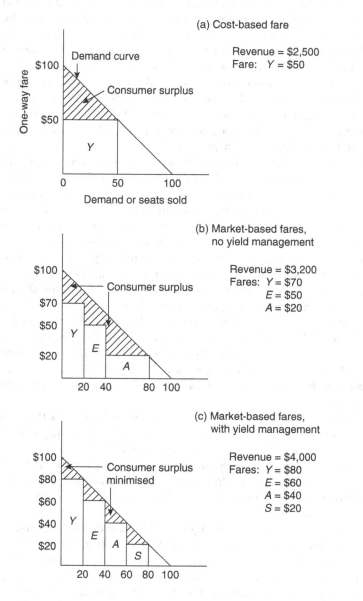

Figure 11.2 Interplay of demand curve and pricing strategies: (a) cost-based fare, (b) market-based fare with no yield management, (c) market-based fare with yield management

Fare types: Y = Economy Flexi, E = Standard Economy, A = Economy Lite, S = Super Saver

would charge a $50 one-way Economy fare (that is, $3,500 divided by the target of 70 passengers). But at that fare the demand curve tells us that the airline would only get 50 passengers, thereby generating an income of only $2,500, which would result in a substantial loss (Figure 11.2 part a). The load factor achieved would be 50 per cent, not 70.

The demand curve also tells us that many passengers who paid $50 would have been willing to pay more. They are getting a good deal. The utility or benefit they get from using the service is greater than the price paid. The difference between the $50 fare and the utility they enjoy is called the 'consumer surplus' and is measured by the shaded area in Figure 11.2(a). One aim of revenue management is to maximise revenue by transferring some of the 'consumer surplus' to producers, that is, the airlines. The demand curve also shows us one more important fact – that half the seats are empty if the fare is $50 but that there are people who would be keen to fly at fares below $50.

The airline, aware both of the 'consumer surplus' issue and the need to fill up empty seats, now decides to introduce a three-part tariff: a Flexi Economy fare of $70, a Standard Economy fare of $50 and an Economy Lite fare of $20 (Fares Y, E and A in Figure 11.2). There are various conditions attached. For example, the Economy Lite fare is non-changeable and non-refundable. In practice, because is it so cheap, many passengers opt for the Lite fare (A) and sales boom. But in the end too many seats (40) are sold at this cheap fare, leaving insufficient seats, only 60, for those passengers prepared to pay more but who generally book later. The outcome is shown in part (b) of Figure 11.2 – 40 seats sold at the Lite (A) fare; 20 at the Standard (E) fare and 20 at the Flexi (Y) fare. The seat factor has shot up to 80 per cent, but though revenue has also increased to $3,200 it is still inadequate to cover costs. Moreover, since many passengers are still paying less than what they would be prepared to pay, the airline is still failing to capture for itself an adequate share of the 'consumer surplus'.

In theory, to maximise revenues and capture the consumer surplus the airline should sell each seat at the maximum that each passenger is prepared to pay from $100 down to $1 for the hundredth passenger. This is clearly impractical, but to try to maximise revenue more realistically it might introduce four separate fares: a full Economy Flexi (Y) fare of $80, a Standard (E) fare of $60, a Lite (A) $40 fare and a Super Saver (S) fare of $20. Given the demand curve it could sell 20 seats at each of these fares and its total revenue would be $4,000 per flight, producing a profit of $500 with a seat factor of 80 per cent (Figure 11.2, part c).

The fundamental problem is how to ensure that 20 seats are sold at each fare and more especially how to avoid the situation where too many seats were being sold at the lowest $20 fare. This is the function of revenue management. It is the day-to-day monitoring and control of seat availability in each fare group on each flight to ensure that revenue is maximised. This is done by highly trained staff using the constantly updated information on sales and other key data in the reservations computer.

Traditionally, when fare structures were more rigid, booking conditions attached to different fares and seat availability were the tools used to channel seats to the passengers paying the higher fares. The tariff conditions or 'fences' (Section 11.7) separated the demand for particular fare types into discrete segments, which had different booking characteristics. By controlling the seats available for sale one could then direct that segment of demand on to flights where it was needed to maximise revenues. The need for revenue management arises because passengers who tend to book nearer the departure date are often willing to pay higher fares while many low-fare passengers don't mind booking early, especially if travelling for leisure. The aim is to prevent passengers prepared to pay only low fares from buying seats that could be sold later at a higher price. Today this is done by yield managers.

11.11 Revenue management in practice

Revenue managers have two levers they can use to achieve their primary aim, which is to maximise the revenue per flight. First, they can move the fares for a flight upwards, as departure day approaches, to capitalise on demand becoming less price elastic, or even downwards if demand is weak. Second, if different fares are available on a particular flight they can switch capacity, that is seats, between fare products. The low-cost airlines, because of their simpler fare structures, focus on using the price lever to maximise revenues while network carriers have the complex task of using both the price and capacity levers.

Legacy network carriers face complications in managing their revenues. First, as shown earlier, they offer several fare products on each of their routes and in each cabin. Second, because they operate hubbing networks, seats available in a particular fare category may also be sold as part of a multi-sector flight. For example, a British Airways Economy cabin seat on a London–Frankfurt flight can be sold either as a BA Economy Basic seat or as BA Economy Plus, but may also be sold as part of a New York–Heathrow–Frankfurt ticket or to a Singapore–London–Frankfurt passenger. Each of these will generate different revenues for the London–Frankfurt sector. Similar complications arise with Business class seats on this sector, which may be sold as part of the multiple sector tickets sold by BA or its alliance partners anywhere in the world. Moreover, many such sales will be in different currencies.

International network airlines, such as British Airways or Lufthansa, must control both the fares at which different fare products are sold and the number of seats available for sale at the different fares. This is a dynamic process. It is achieved by putting each of the various fare products into different booking classes or 'buckets'. A flexible economy fare will be in a higher booking class than an Economy fare with numerous restrictions. Seats available for sale as part of multiple sector tickets may be in their own booking class or subsumed in one of the other classes. A year or so in advance, an opening or starting price for each booking class on each flight is fixed as well as the number of seats allocated to that booking class. The opening prices and the rate at which prices change in the future take account of past experience and booking trends but also known holiday periods, sports events, major industrial fairs or other special events likely to generate demand. As a result, the opening fares on such dates may be set high even 12 months in advance.

As, over time, seats from different booking classes on a particular flight are progressively sold, two things may happen. First, if a booking class is selling well and earlier than expected, the fare for that class will increase. This will happen either automatically as a result of an algorithm built into the revenue management system or because of direct intervention by the yield managers for that particular market. Second, in response to actual sales in each booking class the yield managers may move seats from one booking class to another that is selling well especially if it is selling at a higher fare. They may even close down a booking class altogether, forcing potential passengers to look at other booking classes. If later on sales in other classes fail to meet forecasts, then the previously closed booking class may be re-opened for sale.

Most airlines will work with 10 to 12 booking classes, and can go up to 20–25. British Airways in 2017 used up to 40 booking classes on some sectors. Each booking class may contain several fare types. Thus, for the London–Frankfurt sector a BA through ticket sold in New York or Montreal would be put into a low booking class. The lowest booking class is normally for tickets issued in exchange for air miles. Through fares create a major complexity for network airlines, especially those with long-haul routes. While a London–Frankfurt sector on a BA ticket sold in New York may be in a low booking class, the New York–London sector may be in a higher booking class. The airline does not want to lose the revenue from this ticket because its revenue management system will not release a seat for the London–Frankfurt sector, so sophisticated models have been developed to assess through fares on the basis of their total contribution to an airline's revenues as well as their contribution to individual sectors. This then affects the booking class they are put into. The aim of these newer models is to focus revenue maximisation on the end-to-end fare for multi-sector routes rather than optimising the revenue for individual sectors.

The forecasts of sales by class are reviewed periodically in the period starting 12 months before departure and booking classes may be closed or opened accordingly. But it is during the last month that most of the critical decisions and changes are made by the yield managers or controllers. A large airline may employ up to 100 of these working in groups controlling particular parts of its network. Using data from the reservations computer on sales by booking class to date and on past booking trends they must make rapid and critical decisions closing, opening or wait-listing particular booking classes on each individual flight scheduled during the coming month for which they are responsible. The aim is always to maximise revenue per flight. If sales are going badly as the departure date approaches it may mean allocating more seats to lower fare types. Conversely, if demand is high, low-fare booking classes may be closed very early on and before they are sold out. It is a complex and critical task that could not be done without a sophisticated software programme backing up the reservations system. While some decisions on opening or closing booking classes can be made automatically by the pre-programmed computer system itself, much depends on the revenue manager. In British Airways, the European Revenue Manager and his small team will have around 2,500 European flights at any one time on which decisions are pending on whether to change the number of seats allocated to any particular booking class.

There is also the problem of no-shows of passengers with tickets that can be changed or refunded. They may make up to 10 per cent or more of higher-fare passengers. Over-booking can compensate, but one can still end up with off-loading passengers, to whom compensation may have to be paid, or having empty seats. Getting the over-booking right for each flight means more revenue and more satisfied passengers. To do this one must develop models to predict no-show rates, introduce fares with booking conditions that discourage no-shows or even penalise passengers who fail to turn up by cancelling their onward bookings.

Finally, yield managers must constantly monitor the fares being offered by competitors. While they must maximise revenues they must also have an eye to market share. Losing market share may mean higher unit costs.

Numerous studies have shown that legacy airlines can increase their revenues by 5 to 10 per cent when they introduce effective yield management on competitive routes: '*The revenue gains come from forcing consumers to pay fares closer to their willingness to pay*' (Belobaba and Wilson, 1997). The impact is greatest if the competitors have not implemented revenue management themselves. Thus, revenue management may be crucial in ensuring profitability.

For LCCs the relative simplicity of LCC fare structures makes it easier for them to implement effective revenue management. With only one, two or three fares available at any one time for each flight it is possible to use simpler algorithms to move fares up in stages as a certain number of seats are filled and/or as the departure date draws nearer. Alternatively the fare may be moved down, if demand is below expectations.

easyJet illustrates the low-cost airline approach to revenue management. Working more than 12 months in advance, the airline's tariff managers fix the opening or starting fare for each flight on each route. Different flights on the same day on the same route will often have different starting fares. This is because they reflect passenger preferences, known historical demand levels and past booking patterns. Starting fares for flights near to or during religious holidays, school holiday breaks or known special events, such as music or sports festivals, will be at high levels.

As seats on a particular flight are sold or as the departure date approaches the fares will be adjusted upwards. With only one fare available for each flight it is possible to use simple algorithms to move fares up in stages. The process is computerised and automatic though yield managers, specialising in each market area, also monitor fares, including competitors' fares, and intervene manually. The rate at which fares are increased in response to seat sales will differ for each flight and will be based on past years' sale experience for that flight. Fares, as shown in the earlier case study of London–Athens fares in May 2018, can also be moved down when sales are below expectations or targets. easyJet offers a second very much higher 'Flexi' fare on its services and this is managed in the same way.

For LCCs, transfer passengers travelling on two sectors are less of a problem too, since many such as easyJet or Ryanair do not offer many through fares; passengers buy two separate tickets. LCCs that offer through fares such as Southwest still have an easier problem to deal with compared to network carriers that must optimise revenue from a large number of fare buckets and with fares in many different currencies.

With only one or two fares on each flight, low-cost airlines' revenue management is simpler and more effective than that of legacy network airlines, who may have up to 24 or more separate booking classes to deal with. The LCCs only need to use the fare level as their primary lever whereas network airlines, while manipulating numerous fares, also have to juggle with switching capacity, that is seats, between booking classes on the same flight. They must also deal with the problem created by passengers connecting on two sectors. Revenue management is especially complex and cumbersome for network airlines.

Revenue management is an essential concomitant of market-related pricing. While some consumers end up paying more than would otherwise be the case or travelling in more congested aircraft, consumers as a whole should be better off. By mixing high- and low-fare passengers to generate higher revenues, flights are operated that would otherwise not be viable. A wider range of fare products can be made available while protecting last-minute access to seats for those who must travel at short notice and are prepared to pay more for this.

11.12 The tools of dynamic pricing

Where airlines have decided to adopt 'a la carte' dynamic pricing, their marketing directors and pricing managers have complex and inter-related decisions to make. They must resolve the following issues:

- How many fare products or classes should they offer? Should they go for one or two like easyJet, three like Southwest or up to eight or nine, which Singapore Airlines offers? The number they opt for may differ between different parts of their network.
- How many seats should be allocated to each fare class?
- What product or service features should be included in each fare class to make the latter distinctive? The aim is to ensure that each fare class gives value for money for particular market segments (see Tables 11.4 and 11.5).
- What additional product or service features should be available for purchase, where not included in a fare product or class?
- The nature of penalties for breaking the conditions attached to a particular fare. For example, the cost of changing a ticket if not allowed for free under a certain fare.
- Should the fares on all flights on a particular route or on parallel routes be more or less similar or should they vary by day of the week or time of day? In other words, to what degree should fares be standardised or should each flight have its own fares?
- How often should fares for a particular flight or group of flights be changed upwards or even, occasionally, downwards? What should be the trigger mechanism that drives fare changes? After all, that is what 'dynamic' pricing requires.
- At what rate should fares increase – in small or more substantial increments?
- If offering more than two tariff products or classes, at what point in terms of seats sold or time before departure can capacity, that is seats, be moved from one booking class to another, or sales in one class be stopped altogether? In other words, should capacity or seat availability be used as a revenue management tool?

11.13 Passenger tariffs and costs

The aim of revenue management is to maximise the total revenue per flight and in doing this generate a sufficient profit or, at worst, minimise the loss. For low-cost or network carriers with a single cabin class and similar service standards for all passengers this is a straightforward process. The aim then becomes to maximise the average fare or revenue obtained for each passenger carried on each flight, since the average cost per passenger will be the same irrespective of the fare that each one paid.

Where airlines offer a two-class cabin or, as in many long-haul routes, a three- or four-class cabin, they may wish to assess and monitor the costs and revenues per passenger in each separate cabin. This is valuable for two reasons. First, it may be helpful in deciding the pricing policy for each cabin class and more especially the fare differentials between them. Second, it would enable airline planners to decide whether maintaining each separate cabin class is financially justified or whether eliminating one or more of the existing cabins would be a more financially attractive option. It would, for example, help long-haul airlines to decide on the viability of introducing a Premium Economy cabin.

To understand the process whereby one arrives at a cost per passenger in each cabin and the contribution of each cabin to the business it is easiest to examine an example. To do this one might consider the case of a wide-bodied Boeing 777-300ER on a long-haul flight with four cabins each with a different seating configuration and seat pitch producing four First, 48 Business, 28 Premium Economy and 184 Economy seats. This was Singapore Airlines' configuration for this aircraft in early 2018, some of which were being flown to Europe.

If the aircraft was operated with full Economy seating only, it would be possible to arrive at a cost per seat. If the total allocated route costs per economy seat is then assumed to be 100, it is possible to establish what the cost of providing the First and Business class seats should be after allowing for the extra space they require, both because such seats have a longer seat pitch and because there are fewer seats abreast across the aircraft. Such an analysis (using the actual seat pitches and seating layout in 2018 for and SIA Boeing 777-300ER) is shown in Table 11.6. This indicates that, purely on the basis of their space needs, the ratio of costs and therefore of fares in the four classes with the all-Economy cost indexed at 100 should be 569:387:134:100 (line 5 of Table 11.6).

In our example, an adjustment might also be made for the greater proportion of space allocated to toilets and galleys, though this has not been done here. What if the planned load factors of the three classes were different too? Airlines often plan to achieve average year-round load factors of no more than 60 per cent in First and 75 per cent in Business class so as not to turn away any high-yielding demand. On the other hand, they will use promotional pricing and their revenue management systems to try to ensure year-round load factors are close to 90 per cent in the Premium Economy and Economy cabins. We do not know SIA's planning load factors on its 777-300ER flights to Europe, but assuming 60, 75, 90 and 90 per cent in the four cabins as the planned load factors, one can convert the cost index per seat into an index of cost per passenger (lines 6 and 7 of Table 11.6).

Finally, the passenger-specific costs need to be added in to the costing exercise. These include the cost per passenger of the different in-flight services such as meals, drinks, in-flight entertainment, newspapers or magazines and of any exclusive ground facilities. The higher ratio of cabin staff to passengers in First and Business should also be adjusted for. All this is reflected in the assumed passenger-specific costs (line 8, Table 11.6). These are clearly our estimates.

Adding these passenger-specific costs to the passenger cost indices in Table 11.6 produces a final index of relative costs per passenger between the First, Business,

Table 11.6 Estimates of unit costs of different classes on long-haul Boeing 777-300ER flight, 2018

		First	Business	Premium Economy	Economy
1	Cost per seat if all Economy				100
2	Seat pitch (inches)	81	55	38	32
3	**Seat cost index** allowing for seat pitch	253	172	119	100
4	Number of seats abreast	4	4	8	9
5	**Seat cost index** allowing for pitch plus seats abreast	569	387	134	100
6	Planning load factor	60%	75%	90%	90%
7	**Seat cost index** adjusted for load factor	948	516	149	111
8	Passenger-specific costs	70	35	20	10
9	Cost per passenger including passenger-specific costs	1018	551	169	121
10	**Index of cost per passenger if Economy $121 = 100**	841	455	140	100

N.B.: Seat pitch and seats abreast are actual as indicated by Singapore Airline.
Planning load factor and passenger specific costs are author's estimates

Premium Economy and Economy cabins of 841:455:140:100. These suggest that if primarily cost-based, the Business fare in a long-haul Boeing 777-330ER flight should be about four times as high as the normal Economy fare and the First class fare around eight times as high. In so far as passengers in Premium Economy, in Economy and, for that matter, in Business may be travelling with different fare products, this proposed relationship should apply to the average yield per passenger in each class rather than the fare. To what extent do actual long-haul fares and yields for each cabin class broadly reflect a 841:455:140 and 100 cost relationship between the four cabins?

Early in 2018 Singapore Airlines was operating a daily flight between Singapore and Paris with Boeing 777-300ER aircraft with the cabin and seat configuration and density shown in Table 11.6. The fares for a return Singapore–Paris flight, quoted in February 2018, for a flight in mid-March 2018 were examined. Two different Economy fares were available with an unweighted average of the two being S$1,826. The actual average yield in this cabin would depend on the way SIA used its revenue management system to maximise the total revenue from the Economy cabin.

The two Premium Economy fares averaged S$2,494 while the two Business class fares averaged S$7,137 and the First class price was S$10,437. If one indexes the average Economy fare of S$1,826 at 100 then the other ratio of average fares in the four cabins comes out as 571:390:135:100.

These fare ratios show a reasonable relationship to the cost ratios as shown here and on line 10 of Table 11.6, namely 841:455:140:100 with one very marked exception. The First class fare seems much too low in relation to the costs that this cabin class imposes because of the amount of space it occupies and the generally lower seat factor achieved compared to the other cabin classes. With this exception, the fare levels in the three other cabins seem to bear some relationship to cost. Some key assumptions have gone into the costings on Table 11.6, but airlines can do this analysis with their own real data.

This simple case study indicates that, while airline pricing has become increasingly market-related, costs still play an important part in the formulation of pricing policy, especially in longer-haul markets involving aircraft with multiple cabins.

IATA studies in the early 2000s suggested that in many markets First class load factors for many airlines were not high enough to compensate for the high costs involved. If costed as above, First class for many airlines would seem consistently unprofitable. Conversely, Business class fares and load factors were high enough in many markets to ensure profitability. In fact, on many long-haul routes, the Business class was the most profitable market segment. The profitability of the Economy cabin varied between routes and airlines, but when it was profitable its contribution in absolute terms was generally less than that of Business. It seems as if the Economy and Business passengers were subsidising the fat cats sitting in the front of the aircraft. Such studies explain why during the 1990s and later many international airlines dropped First class altogether or reduced the number of First class seats and increased the seating and the quality of service offered for Business class. KLM, SAS, Delta and Air Canada were such airlines. More recently, to bolster Economy yields, many airlines have introduced a Premium Economy cabin on longer sectors offering slightly more space and better cabin service but at a high Economy fare. American carriers were slow to do this.

11.14 Determinants of airline passenger yields

While pricing is an important element in an airline's marketing strategy, from a revenue point of view the level and structure of passenger fares may be less important than the yield that an airline actually obtains. Yield is the average revenue per passenger, per passenger-km or passenger tonne-km performed. These all measure the average revenue per unit of output sold.

For LCCs offering a single-class cabin, the average yield will be close to the average fare charged. On any route, the latter will depend on the mix of different fares purchased as fares increase over time prior to departure dates. These will have been determined by the airline's revenue management. The average total yield may also be dependent on sales of add-ons, such as priority boarding or checked baggage, the revenues from which might in some airlines be considered part of the ticket revenue rather than ancillary revenue. In Europe comparison of average passenger yield (per passenger or passenger-km) between low-cost airlines, operating in the same geographical region, have some validity because generally they will all be short-haul operators offering a single-class cabin with broadly similar stage lengths and operating within a similar market environment. The average yields per passenger will depend primarily on each airline's pricing strategy. Thus, Ryanair or Wizz yields tend to be lower than those of easyJet, in part, of course, because their fares are lower, reflecting their lower unit costs.

When it comes to comparisons of average yield of different network airlines, especially if they operate long-haul as well as shorter routes, one finds wide variations.

The discussion so far has tacitly assumed that an airline can determine its revenue levels and its yields through the pricing strategies it adopts and in particular by the structure and level of passenger tariffs. In practice this is only partly so since the relationship between fares charged and yields achieved is much more complex and is influenced in varying degrees by a number of factors of which the fare structure itself is only the starting point.

A key factor affecting passenger yields is the geographical area in which an airline is operating. For a number of reasons, such as past government controls on fares or, more recently, the impact of increased competition, fare levels vary significantly between different parts of the world.

A 2017 IATA analysis of average passenger yields in different regional markets highlighted the variation in yield levels even in markets with similar average trip lengths (Pearce, 2017). For example, average yields on routes within Europe were significantly lower than on routes within East Asia or those between the ASEAN countries even though trip lengths were similar (Figure 11.3). The highest short-haul fares were on routes within Africa, but even within Europe, fare levels on routes within Northern Europe have tended to be well above those in Southern Europe, reflecting the higher standard and cost of living in the former.

It is evident from Figure 11.3 that where an airline flies and, in particular, its mix of traffic between different markets will have a significant impact on its average passenger yields.

Even when operating within the same geographical markets airlines often find that their average yields may differ widely. Once again, one factor that helps explain such difference is the variation in average sector distances. Since unit costs decline as sector distances increase (Section 4.7 in Chapter 4) fares per kilometre also taper downward

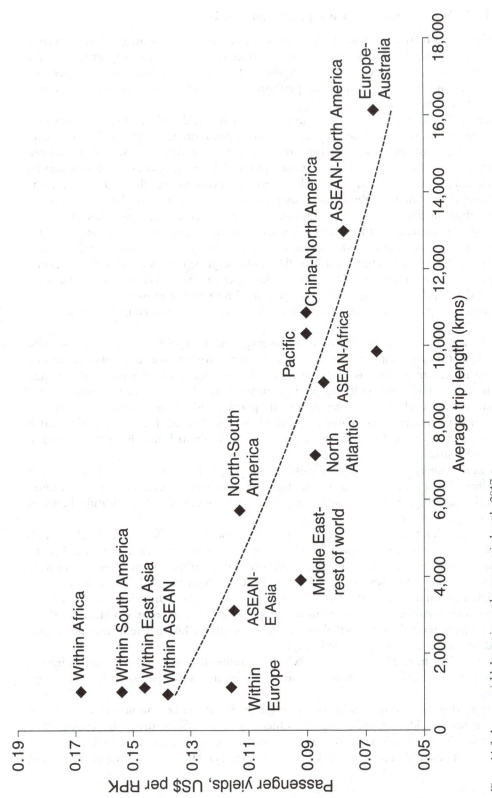

Figure 11.3 Average yields by region and average trip length, 2017

Source: IATA Economics (Pearce, 2017) using data from Paxis+

with distance. As a result, the yields an airline obtains, even compared to others operating in the same region, are very much influenced by the sector lengths it operates. The relationship between average trip length and passenger yields is very evident in Figure 11.3.

But sector length is not the only variable affecting yield. For network carriers, the yield per passenger-km on any route depends not only on the level of individual fares but also on the traffic mix. There are two aspects to this. First is the overall mix between high-yielding First and Business class passengers and the much lower-yielding passengers in the various Economy fare classes or Premium Economy classes if they exist. Some airlines, as part of their marketing strategy, target the business market and plan their products and in-flight services to try to attract high-fare passengers and offer more Business class seats. The improved services may cost more to provide but can be compensated for by the higher fares that passengers may be prepared to pay.

The second aspect of traffic mix relates to the number of seats sold to tour or holiday companies at low promotional fares and used for building up holiday inclusive packages. This will particularly impact on yields within the Economy cabins.

Exchange rates and currency fluctuations also impact on yields. If an airline's home currency is devalued and sales in its home market represent a significant share of its revenues, then its average yield when converted to, say, US dollars will be adversely affected. For large international carriers, exchange rate fluctuations in any one of their major markets can push up or depress their average yields.

Another factor affecting yields is that fares on a route are often not the same from each end. This reflects the different demand elasticities and competitive pressures in each market. Thus, early in 2018 Singapore Airlines was selling Paris–Singapore tickets at lower prices in Paris than when selling the same seats to Singapore-originating passengers. This was because in Paris it had to compete with Air France in the latter's home market where Air France was better known and with a more powerful loyalty programme.

For network airlines another major source of revenue dilution arises from the pro-rating of revenue from passengers on multiple sectors. An interline or online passenger travelling with a single booking on two or more sectors is charged the end-to-end fare, not the sum of the separate fares on each sector. Because of the taper of fares with distance the end-to-end fare to be charged is normally less than the sum of the separate fares. Agreed pro-rating is the method used to share the revenue earned between the different sectors flown, whether they are on the same airline or flown on two separate airlines.

For both network and low-cost airlines, the average yields they achieve will depend both on the prevailing level of fares in the geographical markets they serve but also on the pricing strategies they adopt to generate demand. Fares and therefore yields will also be influenced by the stage lengths being flown. Within that framework of fares it is the traffic mix, that is, the proportion of passengers travelling on each fare or in each fare class, which ultimately determines the total revenue earned and thereby the unit yield. That is why effective yield management is so important. Network carriers face additional problems. Their revenue will be diluted by pro-ration of interline or online tickets. The proportion of connecting multi-sector interline traffic is for them a further important determinant of the yield. For any airline, the final yield in any market or route will bear little relationship to any single published fare. This further complicates the issue of airline pricing. In deciding on its pricing strategy and in working out the tariffs for different market segments, airlines must balance and juggle with all these factors that transform the various fares into an average yield. It is the yield in conjunction with the achieved load factor and the unit costs which will determine whether an airline's revenue and financial targets can be met.

11.15 The power of ancillaries

Air fares are not the only source of passenger revenue. The whole area of pricing for seats has in recent years become distorted by the emergence of so-called 'ancillary' revenues, also paid for by passengers directly and indirectly. For many airlines, ancillary revenues are substantial and clearly reduce the need to ensure that fare revenue on its own is sufficient to fully cover passenger-related costs. This clearly impacts on pricing policies.

The earlier discussions of pricing strategies illustrated the wide range of add-on services or products that passengers could choose to buy as part of their flight package. These are the ancillary sources of revenue. They are not all new. Since the early days, passengers have had to pay for excess baggage, for sports equipment and in some cases for using credit cards. They have long been able to buy duty free and other products on board. But the LCCs, by unbundling their fares and then offering passengers the option of buying a wide range of add-on services and products, introduced several new sources of ancillary revenue. The network carriers adopted some of these add-on charges and also introduced some of their own, such as sale of frequent flyer points to retail companies, banks, etc.

Most LCCs now generate a substantial chunk of their total revenues from ancillaries. In 2016, for Spirit, Frontier and Allegiant in the United States and for Wizz in Europe, ancillaries represented 40 per cent or more of their total revenue (Car Trawler, 2017). At several other LCCs this share was 20 to 40 per cent. For many LCCs revenue from ancillaries makes the difference between profit and loss. For network airlines, ancillaries may be less important in terms of their share of total revenue but they generate very large absolute revenues; additionally, the ancillary revenue per passenger for the best performing network airlines is higher than that of many LCCs. It is clear that ancillaries are playing an increasingly important role in the economics of airline business models. A more detailed assessment of the sources of ancillary revenues and of their relative importance as a revenue source is offered in the next chapter (Chapter 12).

12 The impact of ancillaries

John F. O'Connell

> One day I want to have all the air fares on Ryanair being free. Ancillary revenues already make up 30% of our revenues. We might never get there, but at least it's the objective.
>
> (Michael O'Leary, CEO Ryanair, January 2017)

12.1 A game changer

Ancillary revenue has become a key structural pillar in underpinning the airline industry's financial prosperity over recent years. Airline boardrooms have steered commercial departments to increasingly focus on diversifying revenue streams through ancillary revenue mechanisms. Ancillary revenue is a sizzling new concept that redefines yield management and represents a paradigm leap to produce increasing layers of additional income.

Ancillary revenues are any revenues which are additional to those generated from the sale of the different fare categories or branded fares.

One of the oldest forms of ancillary revenue is in-flight sales of duty free products, and for decades this was the only mechanism by which airlines could capture additional revenues from passengers while on-board. It proved lucrative despite the fact that many passengers had passed through airport duty free shops prior to boarding their flight: globally, $50 billion worth of duty free products are sold annually in airports and on board aircraft each year, indicating the lucrative nature of the business. The indications are clear that passengers are willing to purchase products outside of the air fare. Korean Air, for example, sold $151 million in duty free products in 2017. The Korean incumbent airline has even installed a duty free shop on board its A380s sacrificing 13 seats in the main cabin.

History suggests that airlines may have mismanaged the willingness of passengers to pay as they have previously received a bundled package compartmentalised at an all-inclusive fare that included all aspects of the flight such as baggage, seat assignments, meals, drinks, in-flight entertainment, etc. In comparison, transport substitutes such as ferry boat companies have always charged for meals, drinks, sleeping quarters, access to the cinema, and so forth.

Ancillary revenue grew exponentially from $10.3 billion in 2008 to $82.2 billion by 2017 (Figure 12.1). When this $82.2 billion is compared against the profitability of the world's airlines of $38 billion, its importance becomes indisputably obvious. In comparison, the revenue produced by air cargo (which is not an ancillary item) has been cyclical over the last decade while its revenues in 2017 were close to those produced in 2008 as shown in Figure 12.1. Cargo has been a dominant feature in the

landscape of air transport since the Wright brothers but it remains financially challenged. There is no other business unit (e.g. maintenance, catering, cargo, etc.) within
the airline value chain that is growing its revenues by 26 per cent year-on-year other
than ancillary revenue.

The contribution of ancillary revenues towards the total revenues in percentage
terms for a select number of low-cost and full-service network airlines is shown in
Figure 12.2. It is very noticeable that the low-cost carriers are extremely dependent on
ancillary revenues as Wizz Air, Ryanair and AirAsia Group for example generated 39.4,
26.8 and 18.7 per cent respectively of their total revenues in 2016. Meanwhile the full-
service network airlines have been slower to incorporate ancillaries as part of their core
competency and are distant followers with Air France/KLM, Lufthansa and Emirates
for example earning 7.6, 5.5 and 0.5 per cent respectively.

But in fact, in absolute terms, the US majors generate more ancillary revenue than
other airlines in the world as shown in Table 12.1. Considering the sheer scale of their
operations, United Airlines tops the list with $6.2 billion in ancillary revenue in 2016,
followed by Delta and American Airlines with $5.1 billion and $4.9 billion respectively.
While much of this is generated by various sources, by far the largest single source is
income from the sale of points on their frequent flyer programmes. For other network
or legacy carriers too, such as Qantas or Lufthansa, sales of FFP points/miles is by far
the largest single source of ancillary revenue. In contrast, the low-cost carriers have
never prioritised FFPs as a revenue generator and many do not have such a programme.
But their high ancillary revenue per head emphasises how successful they must be in
generating ancillary revenues from a variety of other sources.

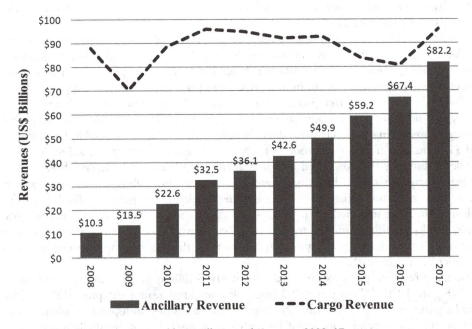

Figure 12.1 Revenues generated by ancillaries and air cargo, 2008–17

Source: Ideaworks, 2018; IATA, 2018

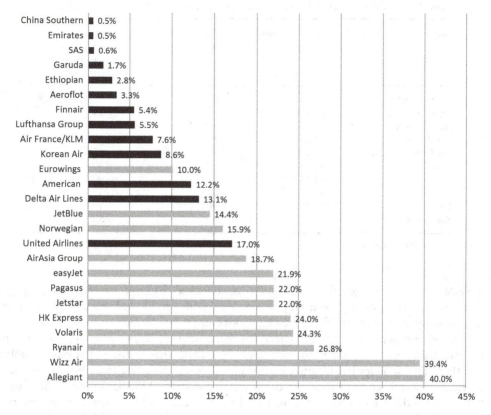

Figure 12.2 Ancillary revenue as a percentage of total revenues, 2016

Note: The LCCs in grey and Full-Service Network Airlines in black.
Source: Ideaworks, 2017

It should also be borne in mind that revenue generated from the sale of FFP points also has a potentially significant cost associated with it. When a proportion of the points are redeemed by those who earned them, airlines will have to offer them seats and bear the costs of carrying such passengers.

Ancillary revenues can be classified into four main groups: a la carte sales, frequent flyer programmes, commission-based products and advertising.

12.2 A la carte sales

A la carte revenue is generated from selling products or services separately, which have been traditionally included in the price of the airline ticket. A la carte can be further divided into two separate entities, (i) unbundled items and (ii) punitive charges.

12.2.1 Unbundled items

The low-cost carriers initiated the a la carte process by deconstructing the fare into its various individual components, becoming known as 'unbundled flight products', which

Table 12.1 Ancillary revenue breakdown for selected airlines, 2016

Airlines	Ancillary revenues (US $billions)	Frequent flyer programme	A la carte (bags, seats, etc.) and commission (hotels, cars, etc.)
United Airlines	$6.2	48%	52%
Delta Air Lines	$5.1	52%	48%
American Airlines	$4.9	43%	57%
Southwest	$2.8	80%	20%
Air France/KLM	$2.1	33%	67%
Ryanair	$1.9	0%	100%
easyJet	$1.4	0%	100%
Lufthansa	$1.3	57%	43%
Qantas	$1.2	90%	10%
Air Canada	$1.1	45%	55%

Source: Ideaworks, 2017

include separate charges for items such as: checked baggage and excess baggage; assigned seating; priority boarding; extra leg room; food and beverages; in-flight entertainment; in-flight wi-fi; fare lock; priority upgrades; lounge access and so forth.

Pricing competition among carriers has become very aggressive and as a result, carriers have detached many of the flight products that were previously bundled together. This strategy has facilitated in stripping down the price to its lowest base fare as internet search engines look for the lowest base fares. This has allowed the legacy full-service airlines to finally compete with low-cost carriers in the distribution systems, which are highly transparent to prospecting travellers across multiple travel search engines and online travel agents. Presenting a seat-only fare and focusing on promoting that price leads customers to think that the fare is the only important consideration. Therefore, unbundling became an essential strategy for the large legacy airlines that had high fares primarily attributable to their high unit costs, which made them uncompetitive against LCCs. The differences in unit costs are very noticeable as Ryanair and easyJet's unit costs (CASK in eurocents) in 2017 were around 3.2 eurocents and 5.5 eurocents respectively, compared to Lufthansa's 8.24 eurocents; Air France/KLM, 7.6; and IAG, 6.6 (author's estimates).

Flybe was the first carrier to introduce *baggage fees* in December 2005 by charging a modest £2 per checked-in bag each way and was followed by Ryanair one month later. Baggage has now become the largest generator of a la carte revenues. US major airlines derive around 20 per cent of their total ancillary revenues from baggage charges while for non-US airlines they generate around 30 per cent of ancillaries. The US DOT (2018a) found that the top US carriers earned around $4.5 billion from baggage fees in 2017 as shown in Table 12.2.

American Airlines alone earned $1.1 billion from checked baggage in 2017, which represented 3.6 per cent of its total operating revenues, while Delta Air Lines made $907 million, equating to 2.3 per cent of its operating revenues. American Airlines was the first major US carrier to introduce charges for checked baggage in May 2008, when oil was reaching almost $150 per barrel. This was an effective mechanism to offset the fuel hike and the impending recession from the global financial crisis. The pace of revenue growth from baggage fees is unprecedented: American Airlines, for example, recorded a rise of 147 per cent in revenue from baggage fees between 2009 and 2017 (Flightglobal, 2018; US DOT, 2018a). Meanwhile, Southwest, which upholds its differentiating characteristic of not charging for bags, clawed in just $46 million in 2017, primarily derived from overweight baggage – the effect on this lost revenue opportunity is highly noticeable as luggage has a negligible impact on its operating revenues. However, it has compensated for this by higher fares.

Baggage charges have now become the norm in the new travelling era and have been largely accepted into people's lifestyles. Across the world's airlines, baggage is also a big ancillary item with AirAsia for example producing 56 per cent of its total ancillaries in Q1, 2018 from baggage fees. AirAsia has applied dynamic pricing to its baggage methodology and now has 60 pricing tiers for checked-in bags; these make the pricing mechanism very sensitive to route demand and the time of booking, with earlier pre-booked baggage allowance commanding a lower price. Because of this new mechanism, the baggage revenue per passenger increased by 9 per cent in 2017 (AirAsia, 2017). Some airlines are now using more sophisticated techniques, including dynamic customer grouping, integer linear programming optimisation and frequent changes based on the observed price elasticity of demand for certain products. British Airways earned around £63 million from baggage fees in 2016, while easyJet made £482.5 million (Ideaworks, 2017).

However, some operational and financial implications still remain as the IT platforms between carriers are not fully standardised to accommodate seamless interline baggage. For example, when passengers and their baggage interline between STAR alliance members such as Egyptair (which does not charge for baggage) and United Airlines (which does charge for baggage), and then onto COPA Airlines (which does not charge for baggage), some IT systems are incompatible and not fully integrated.

Airlines are continuing to push the boundaries of producing revenues from baggage: Spirit Airlines is evolving the concept one step further as it charged $59 in 2018 for carry-on baggage whose dimensions exceed that of a laptop bag. However, if the traveller is a member of Spirit's Fare Club (annual membership fee of $59.95 in 2018) a

Table 12.2 Baggage fees United States airlines, 2017

Rank	Airline	US dollars (000s)
1	American	1,172,728
2	Delta	907,626
3	United	794,489
4	Spirit	492,645
5	Frontier	364,142
6	JetBlue	289,839
7	Allegiant	192,583
8	Alaska	147,243
9	Hawaiian	81,156
10	Virgin America	62,680
11	Southwest	46,111
12	Sun Country	20,056
13	Island Air Hawaii	4,994
	Total	4,576,291

Source: Baggage fees 2007–17. US Bureau of Transportation Statistics, Schedule P-1.2

discount on carry-on and checked baggage is received. Air France and American Airlines have customised the travel experience by offering door-to-door baggage services. Air France can pick up and check in the luggage (up to four pieces) from home/office within the Paris region for flights departing from the Paris airports of Charles de Gaulle and Orly for a fee of €80 in 2018. Meanwhile, American Airlines deliver bags to any location within a 40-mile radius of the arrival airport for $39.95 for two bags in 2018. Meanwhile, AnadoluJet has broken new ground in ground transportation ancillaries by providing passengers with transportation from their homes to the airport at Istanbul and Ankara starting at $6.40 in July 2018.

The revenue-generating success of baggage fees spurred airlines to develop an array of new merchandising offshoots. Air Canada's LCC subsidiary Tango was the first to introduce *seat assignment fees* in 2001. Over the past 10–15 years, leisure passengers have become more knowledgeable about air travel and ask more frequently for window, aisle or emergency exit row seats. Airlines quickly began to capitalise on this opportunity by charging passengers for the privilege of acquiring these unique seats that hold value for them. The onboard real estate in the cabin is finite in capacity and it is essential to maximise its potential; these fees allow the market to determine its real estate value based on demand.

Surveys have shown that passengers were willing to pay for specific ancillary products that were perceived as a 'necessity' such as seat assignment and baggage and together with food and drink, rather than 'nice-to-have' products (Warnock-Smith et al., 2017). A survey on 'willingness-to-pay' in relation to preferred seats on domestic flights within the UK found that over 50 per cent of passengers would advocate paying for certain seats, which is particularly surprising given the short sector lengths. Passengers clearly dislike the middle seat as its visual dimensions give it a reduced stature because it is sandwiched between its neighbouring seats, while its featureless traits of no window, lack of aisle access and accessibility to the overhead-bin space clearly create value for window and aisle seats.

In spring 2018, British Airways offered standard advanced Economy class seating assignment starting at $11 on UK domestic and European flights each way, and more for exit row seats, while on longer international sectors charges of $30+ accrued. British Airways made $66.2 million from seat assignment fees in 2016, while easyJet generated $70 million and the ultra-low-cost carrier Spirit Airlines made $111 million (Ideaworks, 2017).

Exit row seats have a unique selling point due to their increased seat pitch. Qantas has segmented these seats based on distance, with short-haul flights costing between AU$20–60; medium haul: AU$90; while long-haul flights have price points at AU$160. Ryanair has recently created Ryanair Labs, whose aim is to transform the digital experience for its customers. Its creativity is noticeable when compared to other carriers' digital platforms. It has partitioned the aircraft's overall seat configuration into specific colour codes with prices listed under a legend with different price points. Ryanair seats with 'extra legroom' sell at the highest price point, which is followed by a cascading mechanism of pricing zones that stretches from 'front seats' (first off the aircraft), standard seats (window or aisle seat) and 'on sale' seats. Some LCCs offer up to ten different seat zones.

Other airlines also continue to push the ancillary boundaries of seating inventory. Korean JeJu Air offers a 'sleeping seat package' whereby passengers can purchase a configuration of three seats for $100, like Air New Zealand's Sky Couch. Other carriers such as Vueling in Spain allow travellers to block the middle seat for a fee.

Other a la carte products include the *sale of food and beverage*. In 2009, British Airways pared back its onboard catering service by replacing the complimentary sandwich handed out to Economy passengers on short-haul flights with a duration of less than 2.5 hours with a small snack, in a bid to save £22 million a year (Flightglobal, 2018). A fortiori, in 2017, the British airline announced that it would abandon free snacks in Economy cabins but would sell food and beverages on short-haul flights. Meanwhile in the US, United and American Airlines reversed their policy and now offer complimentary drinks and snacks on their domestic networks, while Delta Air Lines commenced serving complimentary economy class meals on several domestic intracontinental routes.

In-flight retail can be a lucrative proposition as Ryanair (2018) made €182 million in 2017 from in-flight sales, equivalent to 10.2 per cent of its total ancillary revenues where a large proportion of this came from the sales of food and beverages. AirAsia's second highest ancillary revenue category in Q1, 2018 came from food and beverages at 8 per cent (AirAsia, 2018).

There are lucrative financial opportunities in selling specific Business class products to Economy class passengers. Austrian, Swiss, British Airways and Air France, for example, sell Business class meals to Leisure class travellers on long-haul flights. In 2018, these meals retailed at around $25, while the option to exchange 8,500 frequent flyer points was also available at Air France.

There is a wide spectrum of other unbundled ancillary products that include priority boarding, upgrades, membership fees (easyJet plus; Wizz Air Discount Club; Volaris VClub), fare lock, lounge access, fast track, wi-fi, IFE, child-free zones, scratch cards and so on.

These a la carte products allow the passenger to personalise their trip. A global study of 1,500 travellers from 20 countries in six regions by travel technology provider Sabre in 2016 revealed that 80 per cent of passengers purchased extras on their latest trip, spending an average of $62. However, the study extrapolated that this would have climbed to $99 if passengers were able to personalise their experience. The survey found that the popularity of each ancillary revenue category varied between travellers from each region, with North Americans and Europeans choosing preferred seating and extra leg room; Latin Americans opting for on-board wi-fi, and Asia Pacific travellers selecting extra checked luggage allowance. For travellers from Africa and the Middle East, on-board food and beverages and fast-track security respectively topped their choice (Sabre, 2016).

To assist its members in encapsulating retail opportunities from ancillary services, IATA launched in 2015 its New Distribution Capability (NDC) programme (IATA, 2015). This is an XML-based transmission standard that improves communication between airlines and travel agents. Airlines can now form transparent, rich-in-content offers of additional products and services to passengers without the intervention of third parties. In this way, airlines can offer a customised service to their passengers accessing at the same time their profiling information. This may prove particularly beneficial in the context of big data analysis and deep personalisation as mentioned later in the chapter.

12.2.2 Punitive charges

Punitive charges are another key revenue driver as consumers may be charged a penalty fee if they choose to alter their travel itineraries or for purchasing tickets with credit (instead of debit) cards. Charges for reservation changes made by passengers travelling on US carriers in 2017 totalled $2.8 billion with American Airlines generating almost $880 million (Table 12.3). The three US major airlines in early 2018 charged $200 (plus any difference in fares) when a passenger changed their itinerary in the domestic market, while international flight changes can cost up to $500. However, due to public outcry, the US Department of Transportation legislated that airlines operating flights within/to the US must refund customers in the original form of payment if the cancellation is made within 24 hours of booking and if the reservation is made more than seven days in advance of departure. Southwest again differentiates as it does not apply any change fees and passengers only pay the difference in fares when changing bookings. It addition the ticket is refundable, except for its lowest fare category called 'Wanna Get Away', but even here, the ticket can be applied toward future travel.

The European or Asian carriers do not aggregate the punitive charges and so must be assessed individually. The UK CAA publishes an Airline Charges Comparison table so that passengers can check the fees associated with different airfares. The following punitive fees were extrapolated and the following data refers to fees set from 25 June 2018 onwards: *easyJet* – cancellation fee, £27; name change, £20–£52; flight change fee, £17–£52 plus fare difference. *Ryanair:* name change, £110–£160; flight change, £30–£90; missed departure fee £100; boarding card reissue, £15 (UK CAA, 2018).

The fastest-growing punitive fee is the credit card burden most carriers pass on to their passengers. In 2018 KLM, for example, charged a 2 per cent fee for bookings paid for through American Express, JCB, Diners Club and UATP/Air Plus.

12.3 Frequent flyer programmes

American Airlines introduced the first airline loyalty programme in 1981 branded as 'AAdvantage'; other competitors quickly imitated the strategy and today such programmes are ingrained as a core competency ethos especially amongst full-service airlines. Frequent flyer programs (FFPs) are primarily regarded as a tool to engage with the passenger and to induce repeat patronage while creating a barrier against leakage when a traveller is prospecting to travel with a competitor. They also act as a powerful data mining tool to create profiles by determining travel patterns and spending capabilities. These profiles provide a platform to engage with the passenger and build loyalty, leading to higher customer lifetime value. FFPs have transformed themselves into an effective revenue-generating mechanism that is producing stellar revenue

Table 12.3 Revenue from cancellation and change fees for US airlines, 2017

Rank	Airline	US dollars (000s)
1	American	878,278
2	Delta	830,644
3	United	709,338
4	JetBlue	135,972
5	Alaska	115,842
6	Spirit	48,934
7	Virgin America	44,352
8	Frontier	36,501
9	Hawaiian	22,826
10	Sun Country	18,616
11	Allegiant	14,533
12	Island Air Hawaii	460
	Total	2,856,296

Source: U.S. Bureau of Transportation Statistics, Schedule P-1.2

performance particularly for full-service network airlines and is becoming an important differentiator when compared to the business model of low-cost carriers (except for Southwest Airlines). This is due to the sheer scale of their member portfolio and because of the length of time that these programmes have been in operation for.

In more recent years, airlines throughout the world have been pivoting their FFPs as profit-centres through two principle drivers. First, carriers are migrating from a distance flown-based methodology of rewarding passengers towards a revenue management-style platform based on the fare paid in conjunction with the tier status of the passenger. The higher the tier status (e.g. Gold, Platinum) the more miles are accrued – for example, a Delta Air Lines passenger with a Platinum status receives nine miles for each dollar spent, while a Silver and General member receives seven and five miles respectively. This increasingly engages loyalty and aspirations to reach higher tiers to gain the induced benefits. The higher the tier level, the more benefits accrue – Tier 1 Gold status at British Airways, for example, yields the following prospects regardless of the class of service flown that day: check-in through First class or Business desks; extra baggage allowance; fast track at security lanes at selected airports; priority boarding; preferred and pre-reserved seating; priority standby and wait-listing; access to first and business class airport lounges (with one guest).

Second, FFPs are fast becoming the 'ancillary engine' as airlines have formulated effective partnerships with banks, which issue airline co-branded credit cards where each dollar spend on the credit card is subsequently rewarded with mileage. Therefore, infrequent travellers but frequent spenders can also benefit from an airline's frequent flyer programme. By using their credit cards to purchase travel or non-travel products or services they accrue points they can redeem for flights.

In the pioneering years when banks were formulating these mutual partnerships with airlines there were limitations on seat availability, which restricted the credit card holders from redeeming accrued miles. This forced airlines to re-engineer the restricted framework by unblocking seat inventory, eliminating or reducing black-out dates (e.g. during Christmas), in order to increase redemption opportunities. Consequently, banks and payment networks, namely Visa, MasterCard and American Express, quickly reacted by pushing the new concept to their customers, which had a catalytic effect in converting an increasing share of bank customers to use co-branded credit cards. United Airlines, for example, committed 7.5 per cent of its total revenue passenger miles in 2017 for mileage redemption and 85 per cent of the total miles redeemed on United were claimed for flights which also included upgrades (United Airlines, 2018).

Banks have a pipeline that reaches deep into communities and subsequently have a lot of market power in society. Co-branded credit cards have become the prominent instrument that is substantially boosting the earning streams of today's full-service network airlines. In addition, there is a wide range of horizontally-related travel products such as hotel accommodation, car rental or travel insurance as well as retail and online providers that also issue airline miles as an incentive. United Airlines and Marriott Hotels, for example, now allow miles and points to be transferred between their loyalty programmes.

Banks or other retailers or service providers pay the airlines for the miles or points they award to their customers. How much they pay will vary. One report has estimated that banks pay between sterling 1.5 to 2.5 pence per mile. Many of the co-branded credit cards have associated annual fees; Citibank Mastercard, which is affiliated to American Airlines, for example, charged US$95 per year in 2018. In addition to the selling price per mile, airlines can negotiate with the card-issuing bank for a share of the annual fees and more critically a share of the transaction-related fee. Bank customers who pay an annual credit card fee typically have higher average earnings and consequently spend more on their cards, generating additional transactional fees for the banks. Such consumers also tend to maintain higher credit scores and are punctual in payment while banks experience fewer defaults. American Airlines (2018) reported that it issued approximately 315 billion AAdvantage miles in 2015, of which approximately 58 per cent were sold to third-party partners such as banks, while the remaining 42 per cent were given to passengers who were being compensated for taking flights.

The financial returns from the sale of FFP points are noteworthy. American Airlines generated $2.4 billion from its loyalty programme in 2017, while United and Delta made $2.3 billion and $1.8 billion respectively. Delta Air Lines stated that its American Express partnership will yield $4 billion per year by 2021, rising by more than $300 million annually until then (American Airlines, 2018; United Airlines, 2018; Delta Air Lines, 2018). Undoubtedly FFPs are expediting the financial transformation of such carriers.

As discussed previously, Table 12.1 shows the contribution of FFPs to the ancillary revenue income for selective carriers. It is evident that a very large proportion of the ancillary income for full-service airlines comes specifically from their frequent flyer programme, particularly for the US majors. Approximately 90 per cent of Qantas' ancillary revenues is also generated in this way.

Some carriers around the world have now separated the FFP from the core business by forming stand-alone enterprises that solely encompass the FFP, which holds the same stature in the annual accounts as the Freight or the Maintenance division. Qantas for example produced over US$1 billion in revenues with EBIT (Earnings Before Interest & Tax) of US$369 million from its loyalty programme in 2017, which was almost eight times more profitable than its freight division. The operating margin of Qantas' loyalty programme significantly outperforms all of its other subsidiaries, returning 24.5 per cent in 2017 – very sizable when compared with the profit margins of the domestic passenger division (11.5 per cent), International (5.4 per cent) and Freight (5 per cent). Qantas' loyalty programme has a very large and deep footprint across the social fabric of Australia's citizens, as 35 per cent of credit card spend in Australia now earns Qantas points on Qantas Frequent Flyer co-branded cards (Qantas, 2017).

The value of these loyalty programmes is equally compelling, as research by Reales and O'Connell (2017) found that the US major FFPs are worth between 25 per cent and 50 per cent of the owner airlines' market capitalisation. As of 10 July 2018, Wall Street valued Delta's loyalty programme at $30.5 billion; United Airlines' programme at $19.6 billion; and that of American Airlines at $17.8 billion.

It is estimated that loyalty programmes presently generate a return on invested capital (ROIC) of 61.1 per cent, compared to 9.2 per cent for US-based airlines, while European and Asian carriers return just 6.2 and 5.7 per cent respectively (de Boer, 2018). Not surprisingly, therefore, and in the context of spin-off corporatisation discussed previously, several airlines in the recent past listed their FFP affiliate companies in the stock market through Initial Public Offerings (IPOs). Thus the 2005 IPO of Aeroplan, Air Canada's FFP, valued the loyalty scheme company at approximately $2 billion; similarly, TAM in Brazil generated about $400 million through the 2010 IPO of Multiplus, its FPP company (Dunn, 2013). In essence, the FFPs have very low capital requirements, high barriers to entry, produce stellar financial results and can be regarded as 'game changing' for the modern airline industry.

12.4 Commission-based ancillaries

Commissions earned from purchases through an airline's website of products or services that are provided by third parties are another important ancillary revenue source. Such purchases may be travel related, such as hotels or car hire, or may be for unrelated goods or services.

Airlines are generating revenues today in the context of dynamic packaging, where pricing, constraints and ultimate choice are determined online based on a real-time inventory. Technology through bolt-on hyperlinks allows a customer to combine multiple travel components such as hotel accommodation, travel insurance and car hire from an airline website, as they are obvious products that naturally complement the sale of an airline seat. The combined travel products are handled as one transaction that requires only one payment. Tourism-related data are integrated onto one transparent platform and, in effect, consumers become travel agents themselves by building a tailor-made package that suits their specific requirements. Commission-based ancillaries are viewed as non-offensive to passengers and considered as value-adding extras.

Airlines are resolutely positioned to offer commission-based ancillaries. Surveys have indicated that purchasing decisions on commission-based products was influenced by the respondents' opinion of the airline offering them (O'Connel and Warnock-Smith, 2013). There was also a general concern that carriers are adding too many ancillary services within the booking pathway, triggering passengers to quickly jump to the final payment thereby bypassing popular key value-adding ancillaries that produce the high margins for carriers. Mobile apps can leapfrog conventional websites when cross-selling these types of ancillaries as connectivity, destination content (car rental, hotels, etc.) and impulse purchasing all converge.

British Airways for example now generates 9 per cent of its ancillaries from its holiday division, which employs dynamic packaging that is personalised. It has diversified its holiday offerings to capture a wider segmentation of customers as it now displays 17 different types of vacations ranging from beach holidays to golfing trips – it offers a combination of hotels that have a wide range of different price points ranging from 'cheap' to 'luxury' on its website, while experiences like theatre tickets, theme parks, etc. can also be added.

Customer centricity and empowerment in an e-commerce environment become the main driving forces of the new tourism market. Airlines now start to move towards an interplay between revenue management, ancillary revenue and customer analytics. Airlines that can integrate these three components together under a unified model will have a clear competitive advantage in the future. Data analytics can weave together services and choices to drive a more customised proposition to each customer. Future profiling of passenger travel purchasing behaviour will be underpinned by mining e-commerce data and by applying algorithms that will tailor the best-fit travel products suitable for the type of trip (leisure or business) being taken based on the client's known data. However, evident weaknesses persist, as Sabre indicated that airlines still use just 12 per cent of their stored passenger data (Flightglobal, 2018).

Airlines have been leaking huge volumes of revenues to third-party suppliers for decades and dynamic packaging aims to significantly curtail this trend. The potential for airlines is enormous as international tourism has exponentially grown from 25 million tourists globally in 1950 to 1.23 billion by 2016, while its international tourist receipts surged from $2 billion in the 1950s to $1.2 trillion by 2016, which has had a multiplier catalytic effect on the global economy. The segmentation of these trips from a global perspective reveals that over half of all international tourist arrivals in 2016 (53 per cent or 657 million visitors) was for holidays, recreation and other forms of leisure, while another 27 per cent travelled for other reasons that include visiting friends and relatives (VFR) – as time moves forward these travellers could increasingly assemble their own personalised travel package through an airline website or app thereby creating enormous volumes of additional revenue layers.

The three biggest commission-based ancillaries are car rental, hotel accommodation and travel insurance. Airlines receive a commission from the supplier each time one of these travel by-products is purchased on an airline website or app. CarTrawler (2014) reported that these three travel-related ancillary products produced 30 per cent of the ancillaries for non-US airlines, while for US airlines it stood at just 5 per cent. Airlines do not report individual commission-based ancillaries in their Profit and Loss statements due their commercial sensitivity.

The global car rental market was valued at approximately $58.26 billion in 2016 and is expected to reach approximately $124.56 billion by 2022, growing at a CAGR of around 13.5 per cent between 2017 and 2022 (Zion Market Research, 2018). Like the airline industry, the car rental market has undergone significant consolidation as Avis-Budget Group, Hertz and Enterprise have now effectively become an oligopoly in the US as they control 90 per cent of the domestic market, while 65 per cent of the European market is controlled by five companies, yielding them enormous market power (Bloomberg, 2016). Around 60 per cent of the car hire occurs at the airport, so there is a huge opportunity for airlines to capitalise by integrating the demand for such services with their partners' inventory within the shopping pathway of the website or app. A round-table discussion at the 2017 Ancillary Revenue World conference indicated that the airline website penetration rate for car hire has risen to around 6 per cent by 2017 and it is fast accelerating due to mobile apps and through personalised profiling. Exclusive car rental deals with a single car hire company usually net the airline a higher commission of between 12 and 18 per cent on the base rental price (Ideaworks, 2011) while commissions of 6 per cent may be more common for carriers with multiple car suppliers.

Hotels are very different, as the penetration rate is around 1 per cent – customers do not have such an affiliation with car rental companies as they do with hotels where they have a significantly higher emotional attachment and because of the fragmented nature of the industry. easyJet's CEO Johann Lundgren reiterated the low penetration rate of hotels by stating that only 500,000 of their customers book through the carriers' website while 20 million book hotels elsewhere (The Guardian, 16 May 2018). However, Ryanair attempted to stop the leakage to third parties by giving passengers a 10 per cent rebate to spend on future flights – for example a customer who books a four-night stay in Dublin for €400 will receive €40 credit to their 'MyRyanair' account. At the 2017 Ancillary Revenue World conference Ryanair declared that it is also seeking to offer hotel distribution through its own website for a 5 per cent commission fee, as opposed to the 12–14 per cent charges levied by other internet booking companies.

In any case, European airlines should now fully comply with Directive (EU) 2015/2302 of the European Parliament and of the Council on package travel and linked travel arrangements. Effective from 1 July 2018, the new Directive offers additional consumer protection compared to the previous framework designed in the 1990s (Directive EU 2015/2302). In particular, airlines offering commission-based travel package services (such as accommodation) on their website at the time of the air ticket booking are now treated as package organisers (similarly to tour operators) and become responsible and legally liable for all the components of the package. Therefore, airlines must now be very selective when choosing travel-related partners as any insolvency of the latter may raise compensation claims from passengers undertaking dynamic packaging over an airline's website (European Commission, 2015).

The travel insurance market is another element of the travel supply chain. With the growing tourist traffic, increased incidences of lost luggage, medical emergencies, lost important documents and natural calamities are being registered. To mitigate the risk associated with such incidences, more travellers opt for travel insurance, while several countries mandate having travel insurance for obtaining an entry visa. Allied Market Research (2016) reported that the global average insurance penetration rate stood at 6.3 per cent in 2015, while the premiums are expected to reach $28.2 billion by 2022. Single-trip travel insurance policies dominated the market in 2015, accounting for around 71 per cent of the overall market revenue owing to increases in popularity and affordability of year-round city breaks, increases in family travellers, shopping trips abroad and winter sun holidays. Travel insurance in the UK is equally a very lucrative enterprise as British consumers took 65.7 million trips abroad in 2015 while spending over £625 million on travel insurance. Meanwhile, the Travel Insurance Market Survey revealed that Americans spent over $2.2 billion in 2014 (US Travel Insurance Association, 2015).

12.5 Advertising

This is the smallest ancillary category and it includes income from advertising across a wide spectrum of related opportunities. It encapsulates the revenue from in-flight magazines, overhead luggage bins, seat backs, air-bridges, exclusive lounges, gate areas and placement of samples and consumer products associated with a commission fee. Such advertising on overhead compartments/bins, tray tables and on boarding cards offers an effective communication platform as the message becomes lodged into the memory of an airline's passengers because these items (i.e. compartments, tables, etc.) are in direct view for the duration of the flight. The inflight magazine is populated with upmarket luxury advertisements together with a wide range of articles from sports to entrepreneurial stories to capture and attract passengers' attention.

Over 150 airlines worldwide now offer in-flight magazines, thus making it a potential revenue generator. In 2009, the Wall Street Journal reported that over 80 per cent of passengers read the magazines that airlines place in front of them and readers spend on average around 30 minutes per flight with the magazines (Michaels, 2009). According to Lufthansa, its magazine reaches the top 20 per cent of households in terms of income in Germany and has more readers than Time Magazine Europe, Newsweek Europe, and The Economist (Huson, 2015). In terms of in-flight magazine advertising costs, a full-colour page in Aeroflot (distributed to all classes) was approximately $16,000 for one month in 2013 (IMM, 2013). Advertising in Cathay Pacific was more expensive, set at $27,120 for a full-colour page for one month; however, this in-flight magazine has a very high circulation and reaches over 1.87 million monthly passengers (IMM, 2013). A 30-second in-flight TV advert on Emirates Airlines started from $114,000 per month upwards whereas a 20- to 45-second on-board TV ad on Air France starts from €64,000.

12.6 The future for ancillaries

Airline marketing departments are beginning to reinvent themselves as their pre-flight, in-flight and post-flight products are changing their integrative shape by pioneering new methods to generate additional income through ancillary revenue streams. These are a sizzling new concept that will represent a paradigm leap to add new layers of revenues, as their profit margins are much higher than the commodity-based pricing of airline seats. Emphasis on ancillary revenue is now a commonplace strategy across the world's airlines and has been gaining much traction in airline boardrooms. Figure 12.3 gives an overview of the four key areas of ancillary revenues today, which include a la carte, frequent flyer programmes, commission-based products and advertising.

Historically, airlines transported a passenger to their final destination for an all-inclusive set fare. Slowly this fare was dismantled, which allowed the carrier to charge separately for each individual flight product as an add-on. This process has now plateaued as there remains very little movement in any further disassembly. On the contrary, as discussed in Chapter 11, airlines have compensated for potential revenue loss through some product re-bundling into different banded fares. These have revolutionised income streams as they were engineered on the principles of passenger segmentation and allowing a specific group of travellers to purchase a specific assembly of flight products at an extra cost. This has been welcomed as airlines have detected that banded fares are up-selling mechanisms that create layers of additional income. However, banded fares have not maximised the potential revenue that airlines can generate from their customers or potential customers; hence, the importance of ancillaries as an additional revenue source, especially as average fares have tended to decline in real terms (Figure 1.1 in Chapter 1).

As shown earlier, earnings from a la carte sales, from commissions earned from other suppliers, from the sale of FFP miles/points and advertising revenues are all significant sources of ancillary revenues. Their relative importance will vary between airlines and in different regions of the world.

Nonetheless, it is the frequent flyer programme and the commission-based ancillaries that have the most potential going forward. The FFPs are 'rich seams' where customers can gain points from a multitude of sources ranging from shoe shopping to purchasing life insurance by using their reward-based, co-branded credit card. Banking customers are increasingly demanding reward cards, thus there exists an insatiable appetite for banks to engage in a bipartisan synergistic relationship with airlines and prosper through deeper integration. The symbiotic relationship being formulated between airlines and banks is unprecedented and the consequential financial endowments are equally unparalleled.

FFPs are becoming an important differentiator for full-service carriers over LCCs due to the sheer scale of their member portfolio and because of the length of time that these loyalty programmes have been in operation.

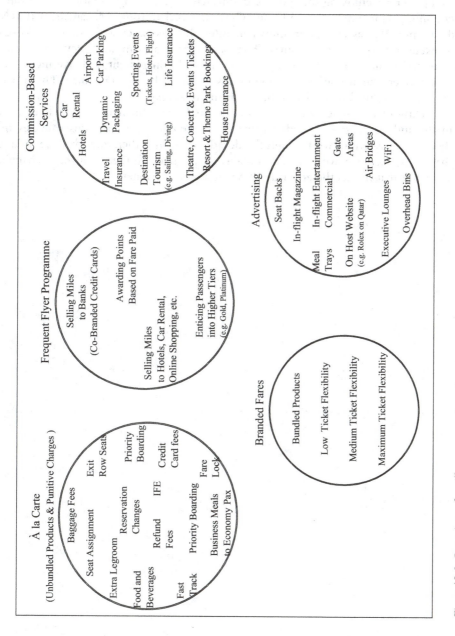

Figure 12.3 Overview of ancillary revenue items by category

The commission-based ancillaries have an equally luminous future as horizontal extensions of air travel such as car rental and hotel accommodation that previously leaked through third parties are being captured by airlines. Big data and customer analytics are the new wave in personalisation whereby predictive algorithms can assess passenger requirements based on previous travel behaviour. Consider for example the case of a passenger enjoying the sport of diving who is travelling to Florida on business – data mining algorithms initiated by the Customer Relationship Management (CRM) could interpret this as an opportunity and offer the passenger a discounted two-day diving excursion to nearby Bahamas. The carrier generates multiple revenue streams from the arrangement as the passenger takes an additional flight and overnights at a hotel; moreover, the airline generates commission from the diving centre. The process in turn builds a value-laden relationship with the passenger.

In conclusion, ancillaries are rich seams packed with financial potential that can sustain the industry's growth and sustainability, even in economic down-cycles that have been so persistent down through the decades. It seems, therefore, that the industry may have engineered a weapon that sustains its financial future in an ever-changing landscape and that merits the accolade of being a game changer.

13 The economics of air freight

Successful companies in our industry will be the ones that re-examine, re-engineer and re-invest to ensure service and profitability going forward.

(Brendan Canavan, President UPS Airlines, August 2015)

13.1 Freight traffic trends

Many of the concepts and principles of airline economics discussed so far apply equally to the cargo side of the industry. At the same time there are particular issues and difficulties that arise in the carriage of air freight and require separate analysis and treatment. The importance of freight is too often under-estimated, yet one-quarter of the output of the airline industry, measured in tonne-kms, is generated by freight rather than passengers and for some airlines it is considerably more than this (Chapter 1, Table 1.2). Though the revenue contribution of freight is much less, generating only around 8 per cent of total revenue, it makes a significant contribution to the profitability of many air services. While there are a number of airlines that only carry freight, air cargo is an integral part of most passenger airlines' operations, though not in the case of low-cost airlines.

The 15 years after 2003 have been much more turbulent for air freight than for the passenger side of the airline industry. Air freight volumes, measured in freight-tonne kilometres performed (FTKs) rose steadily from 2003 until 2007 as did the revenue generated from freight (Figure13.1). Then in reaction to the global economic shock and downturn in 2008–9, freight volumes and revenues collapsed. They shot back up in 2010 but then in the years to 2017, while freight traffic grew spasmodically, revenue generated from the carriage of freight declined.

Air freight faced a major contradiction. Freight volumes were rising but total freight revenues were declining. This could only mean revenue or yield per FTK was also falling. Falling cargo yields during this period were due to more intensive competition between airlines active in international freight markets but were also a response to the fall in aviation fuel prices especially after 2014. The severity of the fall in freight yields is amply illustrated by the example of Singapore Airlines, one of the largest freight carriers. SIA cargo's average yield per revenue tonne-km fell by a third (33 per cent) between 2007/8 and 2016/17. Passenger yields were also declining during the 15 years after 2013 but not to the same extent and the growth in passenger traffic after 2008–9 was sufficiently fast to ensure that global revenues from passenger services continued to rise, as did profits. The years after 2009 were a happy period for the passenger airlines

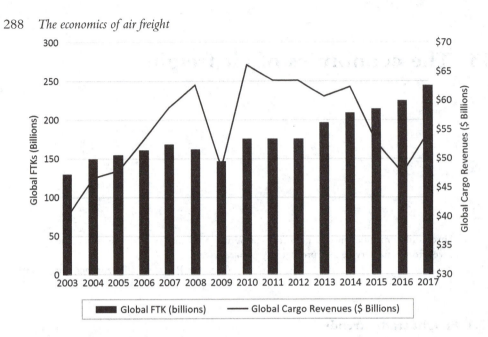

Figure 13.1 Global freight traffic increasing slowly after 2010 but freight revenues fail to grow
Source: Compiled using IATA data

but not for those most heavily involved in air freight. The latter faced greater turbulence. As the world economy accelerated in 2017 so did air freight; but would this upturn last?

Based in export-oriented and rapidly growing economies, the Asian airlines have expanded their international freight traffic particularly rapidly over the last 30 years. Airlines such as Korean Air, Cathay Pacific and Singapore Airlines (SIA) have grown their freight business at annual rates well above the world average and significantly higher than those being achieved by most European or North American airlines. As a result, in 2017 the Asian Pacific airlines dominated the international air freight markets carrying a third (33.1 per cent) of the world's scheduled international freight (Table 13.1). The once-dominant European airlines' share was down to 23.6 per cent and the North American airlines about half of that. In the year 2017 seven of the Asian carriers, Cathay Pacific, Korean Air, SIA, Air China, China Southern, China Airlines and China Eastern, ranked among the world's top ten combination carriers in terms of freight uplifted.

The vast bulk (87 per cent) of the world's air freight is international and about one-eighth domestic. But the largest part of the domestic freight is transported within North America (Table 13.2), mainly by integrators Federal Express and UPS. A significant volume of domestic air freight is also generated in China. When domestic and international freight are combined, the two integrators Fedex and UPS were two of the three largest freight carriers in the world in 2016 in terms of tonnes-km carried (Table 13.2).

Another noticeable characteristic of international air freight is the degree to which it is dominated by two major route groups, namely the Asia to North America routes (22.7 per cent of global freight tonne-kms in 2015) and Asia to Europe (20.3 per cent),

Table 13.1 Distribution of world air freight by region of airline registration, 2017

Region where airline registered	Share of global freight tonne kms
International	%
Asia-Pacific	33.1
Europe	23.6
Middle East	13.7
North America	12.8
Latin America	2.3
Africa	1.9
Total international	87.4
Domestic	
North America	7.7
Asia	3.9
Europe	0.6
Others	0.4
Total domestic	12.6
Total world	100.0

Source: Air Freight Market Analysis, December 2017, Geneva: IATA

and two secondary route groups: intra-Asian routes (14.9 per cent) and transatlantic markets (8.3 per cent). Though the transatlantic market has been declining in importance, these four route groups together generate around two-thirds of the total freight tonne-kms performed on international air services. Interestingly, the very largest international freight carriers, such as Lufthansa, British Airways or Federal Express, as well as the Asian carriers previously mentioned, are all heavily engaged in at least two of these four route groups. This seems to be a prerequisite if an airline aims to be really big in international air freight.

The gradual introduction and spread, during the 1970s and 1980s, of wide-bodied aircraft, such as the Boeing 747, on long-haul routes, and the Airbus A310 and Boeing 767 on medium-haul services, produced a huge jump in belly-hold cargo capacity, compared to that of the narrow-bodied aircraft they were replacing. Moreover, these new aircraft carried large containers and other unit load services (ULD) that facilitated loading and handling of cargo. Airlines discontinued their narrow-bodied and fuel-costly freighters and began switching cargo to the bellies of their new wide-bodied passenger aircraft.

The relative decline of all-cargo scheduled services was reversed in the mid-1990s as a result of the rapid growth in demand for air freight, especially from the export-oriented economies of East Asia. On several trunk routes, belly-hold capacity on passenger aircraft could no longer cope with the demand. In these and other markets airlines began to increase scheduled and charter freighter services. By the mid-2000s the share of international air freight kilometres carried on all-cargo aircraft as opposed to passenger belly-holds had risen to 53 per cent. On domestic services the share was even

Table 13.2 The world's largest global freight carriers in 2017

Rank	Combination carriers		All-cargo airlines		Integrated carriers	
		Total scheduled freight tonne-kms (millions)				
1					Federal Express	16,851
2	Emirates	12,715				
3					UPS	11,940
4	Qatar Airways	10,999				
5	Cathay Pacific	10,772				
6	Korean Air	8,015				
7			Cargolux	7,322		
8	Lufthansa	7,317				
9	Air China	6,701				
10	Singapore Airlines	6,592				
11	China Southern	6,174				
12	China Airlines	5,741				
13			Air Bridge	5,543		
14	All Nippon Air	4,810				
15	Turkish Airlines	4,728				
16			Polar Air	4,378		
17	British Airways	4,364				
18	Etihad	4,303				
19	United Airlines	4,249				
20	Asiana	4,008				

Source: World Air Transport Statistics 2018, Geneva: IATA

higher. This was because of the dominance of the integrators such as Fedex and UPS operating their own freighters in the large US domestic market. In the decade that followed the trend towards greater use of freighters was halted. Systemwide, that is international plus domestic, the freighter's share of global tonne-kms had fallen to 52 per cent in 2017 (IATA, 2018).

Today most intra-regional air freight in Europe is trucked by road. In many cases this is done using scheduled truck services with airline flight numbers. It is cheaper and faster to truck freight in this way, especially as distances are relatively short and most major centres are within an overnight road journey of each other. Even long-haul freight may be trucked by road for the first part of its journey. British Airways, like other major European cargo operators, operates a European freight network. Trucks (generally leased in) collect freight from all over Europe including Scandinavia and Spain and deliver it to BA's cargo centres at Heathrow and Stansted. In this way British Airways can compete with SAS in Scandinavia for freight destined for the United States or Mexico. But SAS also competes for long-haul freight in the UK market by trucking it by road to Copenhagen. Most of Europe's major cargo carriers are heavily involved in trucking. Europe's motorways are criss-crossed nightly by heavy lorries, some with flight numbers, carrying 'air' freight!

International air freight services are regulated by the same bilateral air services agreements as passenger services and broadly speaking in the same way. That is to say that traffic rights and capacity for freight and more especially for freighter services on any international air route could be constrained by the relevant bilateral air services agreement. But in most cases, governments have been willing to liberalise and open up cargo rights and capacity more rapidly than for passenger services. Cargo tariffs were originally regulated and agreed through the IATA machinery, though this is no longer the case (see Section 13.8). Most governments have appreciated the benefits of freeing up air trade and have been loath to interfere in or attempt to control freight tariffs. Tariffs are also difficult to control, but some governments have imposed low tariffs for specific commodities, usually agricultural products such as early vegetables or fruit, in order to stimulate exports from their own countries.

13.2 The key players

Historically, the looser regulation of air freight services compared to that of passenger services has led to the emergence of a fairly heterogeneous industry with several different key players. Clearly a significant group is that made up of the conventional scheduled airlines who transport both passengers and cargo. These are the so-called *combination carriers,* who are of two kinds. Most are airlines who carry cargo but only in the belly-holds of their passenger aircraft. A smaller group of airlines carry freight on their passenger services but also operate or lease in freighter aircraft.

In addition to the combination carriers there are a few *all-cargo carriers,* who tend to operate both scheduled cargo services and ad-hoc charters. The only independent, all-cargo operators of significant size still operating in 2018 were Cargolux, based in Luxembourg, the United States company Polar Air Cargo, where DHL has a 49 per cent shareholding, and the Russian Air Bridge Cargo. These fly primarily scheduled networks, but also offer aircraft for ad hoc charters or for leasing. There are in addition a variety of smaller scheduled and charter all-cargo carriers. These include Nippon Cargo Airlines, Air Hong Kong (now owned by Cathay Pacific), Aerologic in Germany, a joint venture between Lufthansa and DHL, and Kalitta Air and ABX Air in the United States. Some are niche carriers, operating within a particular geographical region as Air Hong Kong does.

The distinction between combination carriers and all-cargo airlines is becoming increasingly blurred as other airlines follow the example of Lufthansa and Singapore Airlines. In the late 1990s, both split off their cargo divisions as separate subsidiary companies with their own accounts, but also with their own staff, pilots and fleets of freighter aircraft. In addition to operating scheduled freighter services, these cargo companies buy and pay for belly-hold capacity on passenger aircraft from the parent airline. They are a different breed of cargo airlines, although in early 2018 Singapore Airlines announced it was re-integrating its cargo subsidiary back into the parent passenger airline.

The third group of key players are the so-called *integrators.* In recent years this has been the fastest-growing and most dynamic sector of the industry. Unlike combination and all-cargo airlines, who traditionally provided an airport-to-airport service with only limited collection and delivery, the integrators provide a door-to-door service. This requires the provision of road trucking for collection and delivery of freight. They were also first in offering guaranteed delivery times and a pricing structure to match. Their success during the last 25 years has been such that integrators are now among the world's largest cargo carriers. Two in particular, Federal Express (Fedex) and United Parcel Service (UPS), are very large. There were, in addition, two medium-sized integrators, DHL Express and TNT, which was bought by Fedex in 2016, and a number of smaller regional companies. These four major integrators together are thought to control over three-quarters of the global air package and express market.

The relevant role in the carriage of air freight of the three key groups discussed so far can be gauged from Table 13.2. This shows the global traffic in 2017 of the world's 20 largest cargo carriers. The industry appears to be dominated by the combination carriers, especially Asian carriers. Eight of the 20 largest cargo carriers are airlines from East Asia. Three all-cargo operators and two integrators appear in the top 20. Within the US domestic market, the large integrators have totally eclipsed the combination carriers. As a result, in terms of total freight, that is scheduled plus domestic, Federal Express is by far the largest cargo carrier in the world and UPS is the third largest. This also explains why there is only one US combination airline among the top 20 cargo carriers. The impact of the integrators needs further examination (see Section 13.6).

A fourth group of players consists of certain *postal authorities*. Traditionally, letters and small packages have been the domain of government postal offices. Domestically and for short international services they have in the past used their own road vehicles, the railways and in some countries their own small aircraft or aircraft chartered in to operate regular overnight services. For longer international distances they handed their mail to scheduled combination carriers, usually their own country's flag carrier. Post offices around the world continue to play a role in air freight, particularly for small parcels. The loosening of international regulations on air freight allowed the integrators to divert a growing share of the documents and small parcels business away from the national post offices.

In the 1990s the post offices began to hit back. In Europe, the German Deutsche Post bought an initial 25 per cent shareholding in DHL and by September 2000 it had acquired a majority stake. In March 2001 it assumed full control of DHL International. Launching a strategy of a 'one-stop shop' for freight, Deutsche Post also began acquiring large freight-forwarding companies. In 1999 it bought Danzas and AEI and in 2005 Exel, a British-based forwarder. It rebranded itself as Deutsche Post World Net (DPWN) and was floated on the stock market. Meanwhile, in 1996 the partially privatised Dutch postal serviced had purchased TNT, the fourth-largest integrator, though two years later TNT was demerged and floated on the stock market. It was eventually purchased by Fedex in May 2016.

Recent years have seen the emergence of a relatively new player in the international air cargo market, the *contract freighter operator,* or *wet-lease provider.* This is the airline that operates all-cargo aircraft but primarily on behalf of other airlines, on a wet-lease contract basis. There are 25–30 such operators. ATSG (Air Transport Services Group) is one of the largest companies, but the best-known and most significant example is Atlas Air in the United States, which started flying in 1993. Early in 2018 Atlas had a fleet of 95 wide-bodied and seven narrow-bodied freighters. These were wet-leased on an ACMI (aircraft, crew, maintenance and insurance) basis to combination carriers, such as Asiana, Cathay Pacific, Emirates and Qantas, to scheduled all-cargo operators, or to integrators such as DHL. In December 2016, 37 of Atlas Air's aircraft were operating for DHL. Normally these are three-to-five-year contracts with a guaranteed minimum number of block-hours per month. A fixed ACMI hourly charge covers the provision by Atlas, or another wet-lease provider, of the aircraft, flight crew, and all maintenance and insurance costs. All other costs, such as fuel, landing fees or crew hotel costs, are met by the lessee. The ACMI charge is in dollars and insulates Atlas from currency fluctuations. Moreover, the ACMI lessor is not exposed to short-term traffic fluctuations or drop in cargo yield since the hourly ACMI charge is totally independent of traffic or revenue levels.

Yet, for passenger or cargo, the airlines' ACMI contracts for leased freighters are attractive. This is because they provide great flexibility in adding or reducing cargo capacity and also because the low-cost structure of a specialist such as Atlas means that this capacity can be provided at rates of 30 per cent or more below the airlines' own costs of providing such capacity. Several all-cargo operators may also lease out their aircraft on an ACMI basis, but often for shorter periods.

For Atlas Air leasing out represents nearly all of their business. In July 2001, Atlas acquired Polar Air, which continues to operate as a more traditional cargo carrier offering its own scheduled all-cargo services. In 2007, the integrator DHL Express acquired a 49 per cent shareholding and 25 per cent voting rights in Polar Air. This deal guaranteed Polar strong freight flows from DHL on many routes. In May 2016 Atlas entered into a long-term relationship with Amazon to provide 20 Boeing 767-300 freighters to support the latter's e-commerce business. An interesting new development!

Atlas Air, in terms of international freight tonne-kms generated, is among the top five or so cargo operators in the world, but none of this traffic is carried in its own name. It is all on behalf of other airlines. More significant is the fact that large ACMI cargo operations are among the most profitable sector of the air freight industry. Atlas Air appears to be relatively free of exposure to risk since the short-term risk of a downturn in traffic is largely borne by the airlines that lease in Atlas' aircraft. As a result, Atlas Air Worldwide Holdings, the parent company of both Atlas Air and Polar Air, has in recent years performed profitably.

The final group of key players in air freight are the *freight forwarders and consolidators*. The largest include DHL Global Forwarding, Kuehne + Nagel, DB Schenker and Panalpina. Their role parallels that of the travel agent and tour operator on the passengers' side. They provide the link between the airline operator and the ultimate customer, the shipper. Some also operate their own freighter services. Their role in this respect is discussed in a later section.

More recently there has been a dramatic new development in the world of air freight. Suddenly in 2016–17 a new player emerged, namely the online retailer flying goods around its warehouses and customer network. As previously mentioned, early in 2016 ATSG agreed to lease 20 Boeing 767 freighters to Amazon to be operated by ATSG airlines but in Amazon colours. ATSG also granted warrants to Amazon to acquire up to 19.9 per cent of ATSG shares. It promptly bought almost 10 per cent. Later, in May 2016, Amazon made a similar arrangement with Atlas Air. The latter was to provide and generate another 20 freighters (Boeing 767-300s) by August 2018 as part of a long-term strategic relationship. Atlas also granted Amazon warrants to purchase up to 20 per cent of Atlas Air Worldwide, the parent company. The retailer branded its operations as 'Prime Air'. Amazon already ships goods by air using a variety of other air freight operators, including the integrators, but 'Prime Air' by 2019 will have a wide-body freighter fleet larger than that of Cargolux. As e-commerce grows rapidly so will 'Prime Air'. It will become a big player and a threat to some of the existing air freight operators.

13.3 The demand for air freight services

Since air freight is much more heterogeneous than passengers there are several ways of categorising it. One may, for instance, consider the commodities being shipped, or one can classify freight by the weight of individual consignments or by the speed of delivery required. As with passenger traffic, it is valuable to try to segment the freight market in terms of the motivation of the shipper rather than in terms of the product, since this has implications for the type of air freight services that need to be provided and for their pricing.

The most obvious role for air transport is the carriage of *emergency freight*. This includes urgently required medicines such as vaccines and spare parts for machinery or for equipment of various kinds, which may be immobilised until the arrival of the replacement parts. Increasingly during the last three decades such emergency freight has also involved documents of various kinds, such as business contracts or other legal papers, medical records, financial papers, articles and reports, as well as films, photographic negatives, artwork and computer tapes or disks. Many such shipments were best handled by the express parcels operators or by the companies providing courier-accompanied services. They provided the basis for the growth of the integrated air carriers discussed later. While the electronic transmission of documents has undermined the traditional courier services, the further globalisation of trade and commerce has ensured the continued rapid growth of express cargo for the carriage of documents and small parcels.

Air is also used in emergencies when surface communications become congested or are disrupted by natural or other causes or when the national postal services are slow or inadequate. In all such circumstances speed is of the essence and cost of shipment is relatively unimportant. Demand to meet emergencies is irregular, intermittent and unpredictable in volume and in the size of individual consignments. It is therefore difficult for airlines to plan for. The need of shippers for high frequencies and good last-minute space availability means that, if adequately catered for, emergency freight demand results in low freight load factors and high unit costs. On the other hand, since the demand is relatively insensitive to price, higher tariffs can be charged.

Goods with an *ultra-high value* in relation to their weight are also normally carried by air primarily because of the much higher security offered. Speed is important not in its own right but because it reduces the time during which the goods are at risk. Gold, jewellery, diamonds, valuable metals and rare furs or works of art fall into this category. Security is of overriding importance, while cost of air freighting, given the value of the goods being shipped, is relatively unimportant.

Both emergency and high-value freight require a high quality of service. Shippers of such consignments normally want to reserve space on specific flights with a guarantee of on-time arrival. They demand preferential handling and clearance through customs and up-to-date information on the progress of their shipments. From this point of view, too, such freight is more costly to handle.

The majority of air freight shipments involve what is called *routine freight*, where the shipper's decision to use air transport is based on an assessment of available transport options and is not a response to a sudden and unexpected problem; nor is it imposed by security considerations. There are many categories of routine air freight. A simple and widely used division is into perishable and non-perishable freight. In the case of *routine perishables*, the market for the commodities being shipped is dependent on air transport. The commercial life of the products – fish, out-of-season vegetables, newspapers, news film, certain pharmaceutical products, high-fashion textiles, to name but a few – is short and the gap between producer and consumer must be bridged before that commercial life expires. Only freighting by air can do that. The freighting costs are quite high in relation to the price of the product, but they can be justified if the final consumers are prepared to pay a premium because no local substitutes are available.

In the case of foodstuffs, the premium consumers are willing to pay for unusual or out-of-season produce is limited. As a result, the demand for air freight is fairly price sensitive. For all foodstuffs being shipped by air there is a tariff level at which the demand virtually dries up because the final market price of the products is no longer attractive to consumers. Since the initial price of many foodstuffs is quite low, that critical tariff level may itself be quite low. Airline pricing strategy then becomes crucial. To develop new flows of perishable freight, airlines may need to offer specific cargo tariffs well below prevailing levels on the routes in question.

The bulk of perishable freight movements are highly seasonable, with very marked and often short-lived demand peaks followed by long periods when demand dries up completely. This happens with the movement of early grapes from Cyprus to the United Kingdom, where the period during which air freighting is viable, despite its high costs, may last only two to four weeks. After that, later grapes transported cheaply by road from Italy or France become available. More expensive air-freighted grapes from Cyprus can no longer compete in the shops. The seasonality of much routine perishable freight means that high year-round load factors are difficult to maintain. On the other hand, the demand patterns are known in advance and airlines can try to stimulate demand from other products during the off-peak periods.

Routine non-perishable freight is shipped by air because the higher transport costs are more than offset by savings in other elements of distribution costs. Any one of a variety of costs may be reduced as a result of shipment by air. Documentation and insurance costs will normally be lower, but the biggest direct cost savings are to be found in packaging, ground collection, delivery and handling. These are all transport-related costs. There may also be savings in other areas from reduced stock-holdings and therefore lower warehousing costs and from the lower capital tied up in goods in transit. When interest rates were high in particular countries shippers and manufacturers became very conscious of the high costs of maintaining large inventories. This pushed them to re-examine their logistics chain with the aim of reducing their stock-holding to a minimum. This is the concept of 'just in time' (JIT). Air freighting is particularly suitable for JIT logistics chains because of its speed and its dependability. These indirect benefits of air freighting tend to be more marked on long-haul routes where a shipment that may take 20–60 days or more by sea and land may reach its destination by air in an elapsed time of two days or less. Taken together, the total distribution costs by air, including the lower costs of holding stock in warehouses or of inventory in transit, should be lower than those or close to those of competing transport modes for air to be competitive.

Routine non-perishable freight consists largely of fragile high-value goods such as delicate optical and electrical goods, clothing and machinery of various kinds, as well as semi-manufactured goods needed in various production processes such as micro-chips. These benefit not only from the higher speed but also from the increased security provided by air transport in terms of reduced damage and loss. This, together with the high value of these commodities, sometimes means air may be preferred even when its total distribution costs are not the lowest. For instance, some shippers or manufacturers may use air freight as a way of breaking into and testing new and distant markets without the need to set up expensive local warehousing and distribution systems. If they are successful, they may then switch to lower-cost surface modes.

Shipments of routine non-perishable freight tend to be regular, known in advance and often of relatively constant size. Although speed is important, small delays of a day or two in collection or delivery can be coped with by the shippers. Non-perishable freight is less price-sensitive than perishable freight because of its high value, but it is nevertheless responsive to the total distribution costs of air transport, especially in relation to the costs of competing surface modes.

Most goods being shipped by air have a high value to weight ratio. Since cargo rates are generally based on weight, the higher the value of an item in relation to its weight, the smaller will be the transport cost as a proportion of its final market price. Therefore, the greater will be the ability of that good to absorb the higher air transport tariffs. This tendency for high-value goods to switch to air transport is reinforced if they are fragile and liable to damage or loss when subject to excessive handling, or if the surface journey times are very long, involving the tying up of considerable capital in transit. Consumer demand in many industrialised countries is switching more and more towards goods with high value to weight ratios such as cameras, laptops and computers, mobile phones, expensive shoes, and so on. It is goods such as these that lend themselves to shipment by air, so the future prospects for air freight must be good. What is more important from the airlines' point of view is that the countries manufacturing such goods will become the largest generators of air freight demand. This is one reason why the growth of freight traffic among East Asian airlines has in recent years far outstripped that of other regions and why Korean Air, Cathay Pacific, Singapore Airlines and Air China are now among the top ten airlines in terms of total freight tonne-kilometres (Table 13.2).

While freight can be categorised and split into market segments in terms of shippers' motivation, it remains very heterogeneous with a wide range of different manufactured and semi-manufactured goods, raw materials and agricultural products that may have little in common. The commodity mix will vary from route to route, but some broad generalisations can be made. Worldwide, about one-third of total international air freight is composed of manufactured goods (Groups 6 and 8 in the Standard International Trade Classification). These include office equipment, computers, electronic goods and components. Another one-third is machinery and transport equipment (SITC Group 7), including motor vehicle parts and equipment, construction machinery, industrial machinery, communications equipment and so on. The remaining third or so is made up of a variety of commodities, among which fresh or refrigerated foodstuffs and other agricultural products, medical and pharmaceutical goods and chemicals and clothing and footwear are all relatively important.

These three product groups are clearly reflected in the composition of goods freighted by air in 2015 from Asia to North America, the densest air cargo market in the world. Telecom equipment made up 32 per cent of the total freight, 16 per cent was electric machinery and appliances and another 13 per cent was apparel. The tonnage going in the opposite direction from North America to Asia had a different mix (Boeing, 2017).

The heterogeneity of goods going by air poses numerous marketing problems for airlines, particularly when trying to identify and develop new markets. This is aggravated by the fact that not only does the commodity mix vary between different routes but also between each direction on the same route. Thus, while in 2015 seafood, flowers and vegetables generated two-thirds (63.7 per cent) of tonnage air freighted from Latin America to North America, such goods were negligible on the return flights (Boeing, 2017).

Another aspect of this heterogeneity is that freight comes in all shapes, sizes, densities and weights. There is no standard unit or size for a freight consignment or any standard unit of space. Freight density is crucial to the economics of air freight. Cargo payload on an aircraft is limited by weight, but also by volumetric capacity. Since generally tariffs are related to weight, an airline can maximise freight revenue on a flight by carrying dense, heavy freight that fully utilises its weight payload. Low-density shipments may fill up the cargo space with a low total weight and a lower total revenue. Surcharges are frequently applied to shipments having a density below a certain level. An airline must try to achieve an average density in its freight carryings that makes maximum use of both the volumetric capacity and the weight payload of its aircraft. Because of the variety of goods being shipped, the risk is that volumetric capacity is used up before the payload weight capacity is fully utilised.

The difficulties of handling large numbers of relatively small individual shipments of different size, shape, weight and density created considerable pressures towards unitisation of air freight, both as a way of speeding up its handling and in order to reduce handling costs. As a result, most air freight now moves in a variety of *unit load devices* (ULDs), which fall into four major groups. There are various built-up or half-pallets, which may be rigid or flexible. Some are no more than a rigid base with netting to cover the goods being shipped. Second, there are IATA-approved lightweight fibreboard or plywood containers or boxes that fit on to full-size or half-pallets. The third group are rigid containers, which come in a number of standard sizes. Most are contoured so as to fit into the holds of wide-bodied aircraft using all the volumetric space. These rigid airline containers now account for the larger proportion of total air freight since much of that freight is being moved on wide-bodied passenger aircraft or freighters. Last, there are ISO inter-modal type containers, which can only be used on wide-bodied freighters such as the Boeing 747F. These various unit load devices may be used and filled by the shippers or the forwarders and presented for carriage to the airline. On many routes the lower costs of handling such ULDs may be passed on to them through low tariffs related to particular ULDs. The fact that much of its freight comes forward in ULDs, each perhaps packed with a variety of different goods, perhaps originating from different shippers, is an added complexity in the marketing of air freight services.

13.4 Freight and passenger services differ

There are a number of significant ways in which the freight and passenger markets differ. While some are self-evident, it is important to emphasise such differences, because they have a major impact on both the economics and the marketing of air freight.

A key characteristic of the demand for air freight is that it is unidirectional. While passengers generally fly round trips or at least return to their origin, freight clearly does not. As a result, considerable imbalances in freight flows can arise. While freight flows on some major international freight routes such as Amsterdam to New York are more evenly balanced in each direction, on most routes there is a marked imbalance. On major freight routes it is common to find that the traffic in the densest direction is twice or more than twice as great as in the reverse direction, as is the case on the Hong Kong to Tokyo or the Bangkok to Hong Kong routes. Between Asia and Europe, a similar pattern has emerged on many major routes, with westbound cargo from Asia being often twice or more than twice as high as eastbound. On secondary but still important freight routes, the imbalances may be even more marked, with the dense flows sometimes as much as three or four times greater than the return flows, as happens on the Hong Kong to New York route. Such imbalances create a major problem, especially for all cargo operators, since very low load factors in the low direction inevitably push down the round-trip load factor.

Wide directional imbalances explain why even major cargo carriers with large freighter fleets appear to achieve relatively poor overall load factors in their freight operations. Certainly, freight load factors tend to be significantly lower than passenger seat factors. For example, in the financial year 2016 Cathay Pacific achieved an overall load factor of 64.4 per cent for the carriage of freight, on its cargo flights and in the belly-hold of passenger aircraft, while its passenger load factor was 84.5 per cent. Even Cargolux, operating only freighters and with no passenger belly-hold space to fill up, only achieved a 67 per cent load factor in 2016.

On many routes the tonnage imbalance is aggravated by cargo pricing policies that try to stimulate demand on the low-density direction by offering lower tariffs in that direction. The result may well be an even more marked revenue imbalance as the low tonnages in one direction end up paying the lower cargo rates. Where freight is being carried largely on passenger aircraft, weight and revenue imbalances are easier to absorb, though sometimes airlines may find themselves with inadequate belly-hold capacity in one direction. Large imbalances are particularly detrimental for the operation of all-cargo services, since they result in low overall load factors with no possibility of compensating revenue from passenger sales on relatively empty return sectors. The absence of assured return loads creates marketing and pricing problems unique to the cargo side of the industry.

A second key differentiator of the air freight market is that whereas the passenger business has tens of millions of individual decision-makers, in freight a few major customers generate the bulk of the traffic. As a result of consolidation among freight forwarders in recent years, the top 20 forwarders control about two-thirds of inter-continental tonnages for heavier air freight, that is, other than the small packages carried by the integrators. This means that in marketing their services, the major cargo airlines must focus on a small number of key customers, the largest freight forwarders in each market. The large volume of business each of these forwarders controls gives them considerable market power. They can play the airlines off against each other to push down cargo rates, especially where there is excess cargo capacity available.

A third difference is that freight decisions are driven by the delivery time at the destination and, unlike passengers, not by the trip duration. The time of a shipment's arrival is the key service requirement of shippers and their forwarders. The total travel time, the routeing taken and whether there is a lengthy intermediate stop and trans-shipment are relatively unimportant. This means that competition for freight on any route is intense as even airlines not operating direct point-to-point services on a route can still offer and sell cargo capacity on that route by carrying cargo via their own hubs. They can do this even if this involves a much longer total flight time and a longer elapsed journey time, provided they can deliver to the ultimate destination within the required target arrival time. Freight will put up with journeys that most passengers would find unacceptable. This means that several airlines can enter the air freight market on any route in addition to the airlines operating direct services. The risk is over-capacity and downward pressure on cargo rates.

The air freight market differs from the passenger market in one further respect. Decisions by shippers or freight forwarders on choice of airline are much more rational.

They are very much based on hard facts – freight rates, collection and delivery times, insurance cost and other service elements. They are not based on taste or a subjective assessment of comfort or convenience or personal likes or dislikes. This again influences the way that airlines market their cargo services.

The importance of objective criteria in decision-making was highlighted in the 2015 IATA Global Shipper survey, which asked 336 shippers to name their three most important criteria for choosing air as opposed to other modes. Close to 90 per cent stated that speed was the number one selling point for air freight. On-time arrival and the reliability of air were also important decision factors (IATA, 2015).

13.5 The challenge of the integrated carriers

The biggest change in the air freight industry in the last 30 years or so has been the growth of the express parcels sectors spearheaded by Federal Express in the United States. Launched in 1971, this company realised that the traditional airlines were ignoring two key needs of a large segment of the potential freight market. This was for high-speed carriage and rapid handling of small parcels, many of an emergency or crucial nature such as legal documents. The second requirement was for door-to-door service with no other intermediary. With these two product features in mind, Federal Express set up a parcels 'hub' in Memphis, Tennessee, and in effect introduced 'hubbing' long before the passenger airlines fully appreciated how to maximise its potential benefits (Section 10.7 in Chapter 10). Complexes of aircraft arriving in Memphis from all over the United States within an hour or so of each other in the middle of the night were able to swap their parcels and leave to return to their origins within a couple of hours. Operating in this way, Federal Express could guarantee overnight delivery anywhere in the United States and could ensure it by providing its own collection and delivery vans in the cities it served.

The freight product was redefined. Instead of weight and price being the key product features, convenience, speed and reliable delivery times became the critical aspects of the product. Today, domestic and international express services are segmented and priced on the basis of speed of delivery as well as weight.

The door-to-door express parcels business in the United States boomed, its growth rate outstripping that of the more traditional air freight sectors. The Fedex model was adopted by others, including United Parcel Services (UPS) in the United States, and DHL International and TNT, which were stronger in Europe. Unlike Federal Express, they did not limit their business to parcels but accepted larger consignments as well. In time, Federal Express began to do so too. Integrators use their own aircraft but also buy space from the scheduled passenger and freight airlines as appropriate. The essence of such integrated carriers is that they provide a total product, including pick-up and delivery, transportation, customs clearance, paperwork processing, computer tracking of individual consignments and invoicing. A single system can handle all kinds of cargo worldwide and guarantee delivery within specified time periods.

Having captured the major part of the US domestic freight market by the late 1980s, the integrated carriers then turned to developing their international operations, focusing first on European and then on Asian markets. This expansion abroad by US companies was accompanied by vertical and horizontal consolidation within the sector. They, together with DHL and TNT, started purchasing courier and road-based freight companies or even airlines in many parts of the world. The integrators also began acquiring freight forwarders in order to attract and handle larger consignments. They too wanted the ability to offer a one-stop shop for shippers, especially for international consignments. Thus in 2001 UPS bought forwarder Fritz and three years later Menlo Worldwide Forwarding. Fedex bought American Freightways, while Deutsche Post, which already owned integrator DHL, bought Exel, one of the largest European forwarders, in December 2005. Consolidation peaked in 2016 when Fedex bought TNT, another large integrator, to further expand its European operations.

By offering speed, on-time delivery, reliability and responsiveness, the integrators have increased their share of the US domestic market to well over 70 per cent. As mentioned earlier, the three major integrators, Fedex (with TNT), UPS and DHL, together control over 75 per cent of the global small packages market, which in most years has been the fastest-growing air freight sector. The size and global impact of the large integrators can be gauged from the fact, pointed out earlier, that in 2017 Fedex was the world's largest cargo operator in terms of freight tonne-kms carried, and this despite the fact that many of its shipments are small in size and over relatively short distances. UPS was third largest (Table 13.2).

A major issue facing the traditional passenger-oriented combination airlines is whether they can successfully meet the challenge of the integrated carriers or whether they are doomed to lose much of their freight traffic as the integrators increase the size of shipments they can accept. To survive that challenge they must capitalise on their major assets, which are high-frequency passenger flights to a wide variety of destinations, and combine these with a high-speed door-to-door integrated service. But this would require large investments in road-based collection and delivery systems. An alternative approach would be to work more closely with the integrators. In fact, all integrators not only use their own aircraft but also send shipments on scheduled passenger flights and may buy space on all-cargo flights, often using block space agreements. Closer co-operation between integrators and combination carriers, especially when the latter are grouped into global alliances, may be a partial answer to the challenge posed by the former.

Lufthansa provides a possible approach. In 2004 Lufthansa started flying five intercontinental routes for DHL using its own freighter. Such co-operation led in early 2009 to the launch by these two partners of a new German joint venture cargo carrier called AeroLogic, with its dedicated fleet of ten Boeing 777 freighters. It operates services to Asia for DHL Express during week days, but also flies some North Atlantic routes for Lufthansa Cargo. In this way Lufthansa is able to participate directly in the high-yielding express parcels business dominated by the integrators.

For freight forwarders, the integrators pose a different challenge. By selling direct to customers and shippers, integrators cut out the middleman or the facilitator, namely the freight forwarders. At first the freight forwarders took the view that the challenge to them from the expansion of the integrators was limited to the small parcels end of the market, which in any case was costly for the forwarders to handle. However, in recent years the integrators have started to go for heavier consignments, a market the forwarders previously thought was their own. They felt, wrongly as it turned out, that the weight and diversity of many such shipments did not lend themselves to the logistics-oriented approach of the integrators. The reaction of the forwarders has been to consolidate and merge into a smaller number of large companies who can offer a global service and economies of scale as a way of attracting and keeping large shippers.

13.6 Role of freight forwarders or 'global logistic suppliers'

The process of moving freight is considerably more complex than that of moving passengers. It involves packaging, more extensive and complex documentation, arranging insurance, collection from the shipper, customs clearance at origin and destination, and final delivery. The complexity involved has encouraged the growth of specialist freight forwarders who carry out some or all of these tasks on behalf of the shipper and provide an interface between shipper and airline. Such firms may be relatively small IATA-approved or non-IATA agents that feed their shipments directly to the airlines or to large freight consolidators. The latter will be handling freight directly for their own customers but may also be collecting and consolidating consignments from smaller agents. There is considerable fragmentation within the industry, with shippers, forwarders, consolidators and airlines all involved to varying degrees with different consignments. Such fragmentation has made the marketing and product planning of freight particularly difficult for the airlines. Any one of the chain of activities necessary to move freight by air may go wrong and undermine the total service being offered. Yet the airline itself may have no control over every activity involved in the transport chain. The airline is also frequently torn between marketing and selling its service direct to the shipper or concentrating its selling efforts on the forwarders.

Larger forwarders or consolidators have expanded vertically to develop and undertake more and more logistic services, in order to provide shippers with a complete end-to-end service. They can offer supply chain design, documentation, customs clearance, warehousing, inventory control, ground collection and delivery and may even publish their own flight or container ship schedules and tariffs. They take the complexity out of planning supply chains for their customers and have become supply chain managers. They can provide the best shipping and routeing option by shopping around between airlines or even chartering their own aircraft, as well as meeting the specialised needs of specific industrial sectors such as the oil or automobile industries. They can be flexible in meeting shippers' specific needs and requirements since, unlike the airlines, they are not tied in to specific flight schedules or the need to push up load factors on individual flights. They can also provide better real-time data on the progress of shipments, their individual cost and other transaction data, since their IT systems are customer-oriented, whereas airline systems tend to be geared to meeting internal operational needs. Finally, the large forwarders can offer their services globally, which few airlines can match. As a result of such advantages, freight forwarders have steadily increased their share of freight shipments. It has been estimated that freight forwarders' share of heavier air freight shipments (excluding the express packages trade) may be around 85 per cent, leaving only 15 per cent of the market to direct sales by the airlines.

Consolidation within the freight forwarding industry has been driven by two requirements: first, by the need to obtain economies of scale and the benefits of vertical integration so as to provide customers with a 'one-stop-shop' service; second, by the need to enter new geographical markets so as to provide global coverage. In short, the twin aims have been to provide total logistic support and worldwide reach. Following numerous mergers and acquisitions some very large forwarders have emerged with a global reach. The largest is DHL Global Forwarding owned by Deutsche Post World Net, which also owns DHL Express. The other big players are DB Schenker and Kuehne + Nagel, both German-based, Panalpina, a Swiss company, and Nippon Express in Japan. Together they have begun to dominate the air freight market, especially for the largest shipment. They have emerged as really *global logistic suppliers*.

In many individual markets, such as UK–North America, a handful of large forwarders and consolidators may come to control over half the freight being shipped. This gives them considerable market power. By consolidating numerous small shipments into large consignments they can obtain substantial bulk discounts. In other words, they buy in bulk from the airlines and sell retail to shippers. On certain routes they can go even further. If the tonnage they ship is high, they can play off the airlines against each other and obtain very low contract rates, particularly on routes where there is over-capacity. In this process airline freight yields are pushed down, but the ultimate shipper may not be given the full benefit of the lower rates the consolidators have squeezed out of the airlines.

On markets where there has been over-capacity, airlines have tried to stimulate total demand or to increase their market share by offering special discounted rates to large forwarders or consolidators. Large numbers of small agents have been unable to generate sufficient freight to take advantage of these special low rates. They have also been wary of shipping via large consolidators for fear of losing their customers to them. Economic pressures from smaller agents eventually led to the establishment of a new specialist, the *freight wholesaler*. They are an important phenomenon. They buy space in bulk at rates comparable to those of the large consolidator and resell to smaller agents. Unlike consolidators, they do not compete directly for the shippers' business and therefore pose no threat to their customers, the smaller forwarders. They are simply brokers of freight capacity.

The growing concentration of freight demand in the hands of small numbers of major global consolidators and wholesalers has created two serious problems for the airlines that supply freight services. First, it has cut airlines off from the ultimate customers, with the result that they become perhaps less aware of and less responsive to customer needs and new opportunities. Some airlines tried to overcome this by acquiring or establishing their own freight-forwarding subsidiaries. These have generally not been successful. Second, and potentially more damaging, was the downward pressure on cargo yields, which, as mentioned earlier, resulted from the activities of large forwarders or wholesalers.

The general impact of consolidators on airline yields can be gauged from the example of a low-density consignment weighing 500kgs (but with a volumetric weight of 700kgs) being shipped regularly from London to Nairobi early in 2018 (Table 13.3). The ready availability of low contract rates on this route, close to the lowest specific commodity rates, encouraged the big consolidators and wholesalers to buy space from the airlines at these very low contract rates.

In the example shown, the consolidator buys space at the lowest contract rate of £0.90 per kilogram. They then sell this space to smaller freight forwarders at a higher rate of £1/kg, who in turn sell it on to the shipper at an even higher rate of £1.60/kg. The shipper pays £1.60/kg for the consignment's volumetric weight of 700kg, a total of £1,120; but the shipper was pleased to be paying much less than the published tariffs.

The smaller forwarder splits the volumetric weight with the consolidator and pays the latter for only 600kgs while the consolidator mixes this bulky low-density shipment with dense cargo so as to lose the volumetric penalty and only pays the airline for 500kgs at £0.90 so £450 in total (see bottom third of Table 13.3).

The result was that the airlines carrying such shipments were often receiving well below half of the money paid by the shippers for the transport of their goods; the balance was going to the middlemen. In the case study shown, the airline carrying this cargo from London to Nairobi would only receive 40 per cent of what the shipper paid for sending their 500kgs to Nairobi. The dilution of freight revenue in this way clearly

Table 13.3 Impact of consolidators and wholesalers on airline revenues: London–Nairobi, 2018

500 kg low-density consignment*	London–Nairobi (£)
Tariff structure	
Normal general cargo rate	6.45
Quantity general cargo rate for 500kg plus	3.27
Lowest specific commodity rate	3.03
Contract rates	0.90–1.60
Selling rates	
Airline's contract rate to consolidator	0.90
Consolidator resale rate to forwarder	1.00
Forwarder's rate to shipper	1.60
Revenues earned	
Shipper pays forwarder for volumetric 700 kg at, say, £1.60/kg	£1,120
Forwarder 'splits' volumetric weight with consolidator. Pays 600 kg at £1/kg	£600
Consolidator mixes with dense cargo to lose volumetric weight penalty. Pays airline 500 kg at £0.90/kg	£450
Airline revenue (£450) as percentage of shipper's payment (£1,120)	40%

* Volumetric weight for charging = 700kg

undermines the profitability of air freight. The growing power of these middlemen, and in particular their ability to force down cargo tariffs when and where there is space capacity, is a continuing problem for international airlines.

For the airlines, the *global logistics suppliers* that have emerged represent really large customers, but also a threat, since they have the market power to squeeze substantial tariff discounts out of the airlines. This will exacerbate the downward pressure on cargo yields.

13.7 The economics of supply

In assessing the economics of carrying air freight and, in particular, the degree to which it is a profitable business, a major dilemma is how combination carriers should allocate costs between passengers and cargo. The problem arises because so many costs are joint costs and are not specific to the carriage of either passengers or freight. For instance, while cabin crew costs are specific to passengers and are only needed if an aircraft is carrying passengers, the costs of the flight crew are joint costs. One needs the pilots to fly the passengers, but, in the process, capacity is also generated for the carriage of freight. Another joint cost is that of the airport landing fees, of which a part is calculated on the basis of an aircraft's maximum take-off weight (MTOW), and are independent of what is actually being transported. The issue of cost allocation arises primarily when freight is carried in passenger aircraft, or in combi aircraft. The latter are aircraft whose main passenger deck is not used only for passengers but part is separated off as a main deck cargo compartment. Once more numerous, very few combi aircraft are still in operation.

13.7.1 Belly-hold capacity

According to IATA, slightly less than half of international air freight and mail (49 per cent in 2016) travels in the belly-holds of the passenger aircraft operated by combination carriers. Traditionally combination carriers have regarded freight as a by-product arising from the supply of passenger services. Provided freight revenues covered those freight specific costs, such as ground-handling, cargo sales and marketing, or extra fuel burn, which could be directly attributed to carriage of freight, any revenue in excess of such costs would make a contribution towards offsetting the costs of passenger services. The significance of this contribution can be gauged from the fact that in the early 2000s British Airways estimated that close to 60 per cent of its freight revenues on passenger flights were sufficient to cover freight-related costs, while the balance of 40 per cent could be used to cover the other costs incurred for passengers carried on the aircraft. The importance of the potential contribution of freight revenues will vary over time as the costs of major inputs such as fuel vary. Nevertheless, belly-hold freight has appeared to British Airways and others to make a valuable contribution to airline profitability. It is for this reason that BA has focused on belly-hold freight and, unlike Lufthansa or SIA or Air France, has not built up its own freighter fleet; however, it has leased in freighters on an ACMI basis for specific high-volume markets.

The by-product approach to costing, however, leaves open the question of whether freight should bear its share of other non-freight-specific costs, such as flight crew costs. Should the major costs of operating a flight be considered to be joint costs that need to be split and allocated in some way to both passengers and freight? This argument is strengthened by the fact that the lower freight decks of wide-bodied aircraft have possible alternative uses as galleys or lounges. Freight must at least cover the opportunity cost of foregoing these alternative uses. One could also argue that the shape, size and capacity of wide-bodied aircraft may have been influenced by the requirement or the possibility of carrying cargo in the belly-hold and that therefore cargo must share all the aircraft-related and direct costs. However, the allocation of joint costs inevitably involves some arbitrariness.

The International Air Transport Association's Cost Committee recommended in 2004 that the profitability of air cargo on passenger and combi aircraft can only be truly assessed after all operating costs have been fully allocated between cargo and passengers. This could be done in three steps as follows:

(1) The direct operating costs of a passenger aircraft carrying belly-hold freight should be apportioned between passengers and freight on the basis of the useable volume of the aircraft allocated to each. These direct costs include the costs of fuel, of flight crews, aircraft maintenance, weight landing fees and aircraft standing charges, that is, depreciation or lease rentals as well as airframe insurance (see Chapter 4, Section 4.3). For example, a wide-body passenger aircraft has total volumetric capacity on its two decks of say 650 cu.m. The main deck's volume as a freighter, that is without overhead bins, galleys, toilets, etc., is 450 cu.m or 69 per cent of total capacity. The lower deck provides for 200 cu.m (31 per cent). On this basis, the main deck, that is the passengers, should bear 69 per cent of the direct operating costs and the belly-hold 31 per cent. However, it is not so straightforward. One should apportion a part of the belly-hold's volume for passengers' bags. Key decisions need to be made on how to calculate the volumetric capacity allocated to freight or passengers. Other

simpler allocative criteria can also be used. For instance, one could allocate direct operating costs in proportion to the revenue generated by the two traffics. In practice, allocation based on volume is more widely used.

(2) All cargo-specific or passenger-specific costs should be separately identified and allocated as appropriate. These include most, but not all, of the indirect operating costs. On the cargo side, specific costs include those associated with cargo sales and marketing, collection and delivery of shipments, ground-handling and warehousing, airport cargo charges and cargo insurance, as well as the administrative costs of the cargo department. On the passenger side one would need to include the costs of ticketing, sales and reservations, of cabin crews, ground-handling and ground staff, passenger-related station expenses, passenger insurance, costs of in-flight catering, airport passenger fees, and so on.

(3) Administration and other indirect overhead costs, which are not passenger- or cargo-specific, should be split between passengers and cargo in proportion to the sum of all the other costs (i.e. (1) + (2) above).

If joint costs are allocated in this way, then the carriage of belly-hold freight becomes marginal or unprofitable. In most markets belly-hold freight fails to cover its fully allocated costs. Nevertheless, the carriage of such freight on some individual routes, such as Europe to/from East Asia, may still be highly profitable. Several airlines, Air France among them, do their cargo costing in this way. Many, however, particularly smaller carriers, still prefer to think of belly-hold cargo as a profitable by-product making a significant contribution to overall revenue, rather than a marginal or loss-making joint product.

The case against allocating 'joint costs' at all, whatever the method used, rests on the view that if no freight is carried none of the joint costs would be reduced. The passenger flight would still go and would have to cover all passenger-specific plus the joint costs; so, it could be agreed that such costs are not truly joint.

From both the suppliers', that is the airlines', and consumers' points of view, belly-hold freight offers numerous advantages. It is certainly low cost if costed on a by-product basis. The higher frequency of passenger services is attractive to shippers, particularly for emergency-type freight, and they are prepared to pay a premium for the better service. This, together with the fact that passenger aircraft tend to carry a higher proportion of small shipments that do not get bulk or quantity discounts, means that average freight yields from belly-hold freight on most routes are generally higher than average yields on freighters flying on the same routes.

A few airlines, Lufthansa, SAS and SIA among them, have separated out their cargo operations as stand-alone businesses. Once this is done the question of joint costs on passenger flights has to be resolved head on. Lufthansa Cargo or SIA Cargo operate their own freighters with their own flight crew and do all the cargo selling and handling within their own facilities and cargo warehouses. Costing all this is not a problem, but they also need to buy space on their parent companies' passenger flights. This now has to be done on a fully-costed basis. In SIA's case, SIA Cargo buys belly-hold space at a price that reflects joint costs allocated on the basis of the volumetric capacity dedicated to cargo. This space has to be paid for by SIA Cargo. In the financial year 2016/17, SIA Cargo paid Singapore Airlines S$903 million (US $625 million) for freight carried on passenger aircraft. This was 46 per cent of SIA Cargo's total costs. Lufthansa Cargo as a company buys belly-hold space from Lufthansa's passenger business, which operates its passenger fleet. With cargo costs made explicit and real, it is easier to assess the true profitability of carrying cargo on passenger flights.

13.7.2 All-cargo aircraft

The major economic advantage of the freighter is that it increases its payload by half or more compared with the same aircraft in a passenger configuration. By stripping out unnecessary and heavy passenger-related facilities such as galleys, toilets, wardrobes or overhead bins, thereby saving weight, a Boeing 747-200 freighter could carry a cargo payload of 100–110 tonnes; the same aircraft with a main passenger deck and belly-hold freight has a typical payload of around 60–67 tonnes. In theory the greater payload should reduce the direct operating costs per available tonne-kilometre (ATK) of freighters by about one-third compared the cost per ATK on passenger aircraft.

The full costs of carrying freight on all-cargo aircraft can readily be identified so that, in theory, tariff strategies could be adopted to ensure that revenues exceeded costs. In practice, over-capacity and competition has meant that tariffs are market-based rather than cost-based. Moreover, yields on all-cargo freight, much of it travelling at bulk discount or contract rates, tend to be lower than those from freight on passenger aircraft. As a general rule, airlines have found that yields on scheduled all-cargo services are around 5–10 per cent or so lower than the yields achieved from the carriage of freight on passenger aircraft, though this varies significantly between different markets. Nevertheless, where airlines have managed to sustain high load factors on scheduled freighter services, such services have proved profitable.

The factors that appear to be necessary to ensure continued viability of long-haul freight services are a high level of demand, preferably from both ends of a route, an insufficient volume of cargo space on passenger aircraft and possibly some constraint on the provision of all-cargo services. In some long-haul markets such capacity control is being achieved by the Third and Fourth Freedom carriers operating freighter services in co-operation rather than in competition. This has been done for many years by SIA and Lufthansa on their Singapore–Germany services. Such co-operative arrangements, especially if they are true joint ventures, avoid over-provision of freighter capacity, which tends to undermine cargo rates.

The danger of over-capacity is present in all markets and as a consequence many airlines are loath to operate freighter aircraft and prefer to concentrate on carrying belly-hold cargo. Yet, there is clearly a role for the freighter. Carriers, who feel that freight is important, will continue to operate freighters as a key part of their overall freight operations. They need them to provide a better overall service for their customers by using them in markets of heavy demand, as from China to Europe or the US, and to transport the 10 per cent or so of freight that is too large or dangerous for belly-holds. All-cargo schedules can also be geared to the delivery time needs of shippers. On some routes, where the demand for passengers is thin, belly-hold capacity may in any case be insufficient to meet cargo needs. This may also be the case on routes where payload or range restrictions reduce the effective cargo capacity on passenger flights.

13.8 The pricing of air freight

13.8.1 Structure of cargo tariffs

The structure of cargo tariffs is very complex. This is because there exists a wide range of publicly available tariffs in parallel with a host of confidential tariffs agreed between airlines and their larger individual customers. In many major markets it is the latter that are more widely used rather than the published tariffs. As with passenger fares, the published international cargo tariffs have traditionally been agreed by the airlines through IATA and subsequently approved by governments, though the latter was a formality. With the spread of liberalisation and with over-capacity in many markets, IATA cargo tariffs have tended to become less significant worldwide. Nevertheless, until 2011 they were negotiated by IATA's Tariff Conferences. These IATA tariffs provided the basis for the interlining of freight between carriers, though this was limited, and also acted as the basic rates the public or an individual shipper saw. However, as a result of pressure from the United States and the European Commission, who considered that fixing cargo tariffs through IATA was anti-competitive, IATA was forced to change.

As a result, since the mid-2000s the process of agreeing freight tariffs has been much looser and airlines are free to use such tariffs or not. IATA publishes 'The Air Cargo Tariffs and Rules' known as TACT. This contains the numerous rules and regulations that apply to air freight such as the type and nature of documents required. TACT also lists five million or so separate cargo rates for 350,000 city pairs, which are circulated electronically worldwide to members and subscribers. Rates shown are of two kinds: first, there are 'industry' rates, which are agreed by e-mail by members of IATA's Cargo Tariff Co-ordination (CTC). These industry rates do not change frequently. In addition to these industry rates, individual airlines are free to file on TACT their own tariffs for particular routes, whether members of CTC or not. Such individual tariffs are frequently for specific commodities. Most airlines use TACT but may not be members of CTC nor are they obliged to use tariffs listed in TACT for specific shipments. TACT tariffs are indicative!

Because of IATA's traditional role in agreeing cargo tariffs, the structure of tariffs today has a certain uniformity whether they are TACT tariffs or those of individual airlines. The basic rate for any city pair will normally be a *general cargo rate*. Like all air freight rates it is expressed as a rate per kilogram and there may be a minimum charge per consignment. An examination of general cargo rates around the world shows that the rate per kilometre tapers with route distance; but the taper that in theory is cost-related is neither regular nor always evident. In addition, there are significant variations in the general cargo rate for opposite directions on the same route. Thus, the general rates from African points south of the Sahara to Europe have traditionally been as low as two-thirds or less of the rates for cargo originating in Europe. Similar north–south imbalances in rate levels have also existed on air routes between North and South America. For instance, the cargo rate from Buenos Aires to Los Angeles has at times been around 40 per cent lower than the return rate from Los Angeles. Such rate variations have clearly been aimed at reducing the imbalances in freight flows and more particularly at generating more northbound traffic. Tariffs are normally expressed in the local currency of the originating point. If this happens to be devalued the rate imbalance in each direction will clearly worsen.

On most routes, tariffs are available that will be lower than the normal general cargo rate. First, there may be *quantity general cargo rates* where the rate per kilogram decreases as the size of the consignment increases beyond certain agreed weight break-points. Most routes may have only one or two quantity rates – 100kgs and 500kgs are common break-points – but routes to and from the United States tend to have many more break-points with successively lower rates as consignment weight increases.

While the quantity general cargo rates encourage consolidation into large consignments they fail to stimulate the air freighting of particular goods or commodities. This is done by *specific commodity rates,* which are individual low rates for specific and clearly-defined commodities. Some routes may have only one or two commodity rates while others may have 40 or more. Such rates will reflect and encourage the types of goods most likely to be shipped by air on each route and in a particular direction. Many commodity rates also include quantity discounts with lower rates as shipment size increases. The level of the commodity rates varies widely but on occasions they may be as low as 40 per cent or less of the general cargo rate. In the London–Nairobi case study used in Table 13.3 the lowest specific commodity rate (£3.03kg) was less than half the normal general cargo rate (£6.45kg).

The third type of discount rate consists of those related to particular unit load devices, known as *ULD rates.* Such rates are not available in all markets. There is a fixed minimum charge per ULD, which declines proportionally as the size of the pallet or container increases. The minimum charge is for a given weight for each type of ULD, known as the pivot weight. If the contents in the ULD weigh more than the pivot weight, then there is a charge per kilogram for each kilogram above that weight. The ULD rates, per kilogram, are normally lower than the quantity general rates or most of the specific commodity rates. Their aim is to encourage shippers and forwarders to use ULDs and to pack as much into the ULDs as possible as ULDs minimise handling costs and handling times. Moreover, by mixing shipments of different weight and density in a container, one can reduce the average cargo rate paid to the airline (see Table 13.3 for an example of such mixing).

A somewhat different category of cargo tariffs were the so-called *class rates,* which involve a reduction (for unaccompanied baggage or newspapers) or a surcharge (for gold or human remains, for example) on the general commodity rate. They have been applied to certain commodities whose carriage calls for special treatment. Only a very small proportion of freight travels at these class rates.

For major cargo carriers such as British Airways as little as 5 per cent or less of their freight is carried at 'IATA' rates posted in TACT. This share will be higher for smaller airlines such as Air India or Philippine Airlines, who traditionally have not attached much importance to air freight. Most freight is carried at tariffs negotiated directly with the larger freight forwarders and are not publicly available. Many airlines will have a special *account holder tariff* or something similar for their regular customers. These are tariffs with a similar structure to the IATA tariffs, that is, with quantity break-points and ULD rates. They are made available to freight forwarders who generate sufficient business to be regular account holders. The latter may also have a Guaranteed Capacity Agreement with the airline. This guarantees space to the forwarder on certain routes or flights for the next six months or for a longer period. Each airline will offer its own rates to regular account holders.

The lowest rates, often reflecting the prevailing market rates on any route, are the *contract rates* negotiated directly between individual airlines and their customers prepared to guarantee a minimum tonnage of shipped freight over a given period. A large cargo airline may find that the 15 to 20 largest global freight forwarders, such as DB Schenker or Nippon Express, with offices around the world, generate two-thirds or more of its business. These, together with very large forwarders in individual countries, can negotiate individual contract rates. The growing market power of freight forwarders and the competitive pressure on airlines to sell excess capacity has created a situation on the North Atlantic, on the North Pacific and some other routes where very low contract rates dominate the market and where freight pricing bears little relevance to published TACT tariffs. Contract rates may fall to 20 per cent or less of the general cargo rate. In addition, to attract and keep business from freight forwarders with offices in many countries, airlines will often offer incentives in the form of rebates payable at the end of each year, if the total business generated exceeds certain agreed levels.

Finally, in order to fill up anticipated spare capacity in certain markets and at particular times, airlines may offer *spot prices*. These are the cheapest rates and are available to all-comers, usually within the last two weeks before the departure dates.

Since the late 1990s, as a response to the challenge posed by the integrators with their door-to-door logistic chains and guaranteed delivery times, several airlines have launched time-definite cargo products and *time-definite rates*. The aim is to increase yields and margins both by offering some collection and delivery and by guaranteeing delivery within specified elapsed times. Whereas traditional cargo products focus on flight schedules and flight departure times, in marketing time-definite (td) services the focus is on minimising the total elapsed journey time, from collection to delivery with a guaranteed delivery time. That is all that concerns the forwarder or the shipper. In Europe time-definite pricing was pioneered by Lufthansa Cargo. In April 1998 it launched three time-definite products: 'td.Flash', which guaranteed delivery within 24 hours, 'td.X' with delivery within 48 hours and 'td.Pro' for delivery within 72–96 hours. The tariffs were obviously higher for the faster services. Within a year of its launch Lufthansa claimed that around 20 per cent of its standard cargo was travelling on time-definite rates and that the average yield from time-definite freight was 30 per cent higher than other cargo (Kraus, 1999). Subsequently, most of the more important air freight carriers, such as Cathay Pacific and Singapore Airlines, also introduced similar time-definite products and tariffs.

In subsequent years, increasing competitive pressure forced the major cargo airlines to develop and further refine their service offering to cater for the specialised requirements of particular product categories. By 2018 Lufthansa Cargo was offering three basic services: 'td.Basic' for shipments where low costs were critical and delivery might take up to three days longer than 'td.Pro', which is for standard cargo. 'td.Flash' is for high-priority shipments. If using td.Flash, shipments can be delivered by the shipper to the airport as late as two hours before departure of the aircraft and can be collected two hours after the scheduled flight arrival time at the destination airport. Additionally, Lufthansa offered specialised services with *specialist product rates*: 'Care/td' for hazardous goods; 'Cool/td' for goods such as pharmaceuticals that need to be transported at constant temperatures; 'Safe/td1' for valuable freight; 'Fresh.td' for perishables; and 'Live/td' for the carriage of live animals. Using different names, Cathay Pacific and other major cargo carriers offer a similar range of specialist products. Inevitably the tariffs for each product tend to reflect both the costs involved for the airline and also the demand elasticity of the shipment involved to the air freight tariff.

13.8.2 Pricing is market- not cost-based

The preceding review of the structure of cargo tariffs suggests that they bear only a tenuous relationship to cargo costs. Different commodities on the same route may be charged at widely different rates with no marked differences apparent in the costs of handling and freighting them. General cargo rates vary markedly between sectors of similar length being operated with similar aircraft. Rates on the same route differ in opposite directions. The taper of rates per kilometre with distance is neither consistent nor closely related to costs. While some airlines have tried to dress up the cargo tariffs as being somehow cost-related, there can be little doubt that the underlying philosophy, especially for commodity rates, is ultimately one of 'charging what the traffic will bear', that is, market-oriented pricing. Such a pricing strategy was encouraged by the by-product view of air cargo. As a by-product of passenger services the carriage of freight appeared to impose low additional costs and any revenue in excess of these low costs made a contribution to the overall profitability of the services.

It could be argued that market pricing is discriminatory since it entails charging some shipments more than the costs they impose and others less. This is undoubtedly the case, but it is difficult to see how market pricing could be avoided given the nature of the air freight market. It has two distinctive characteristics that bedevil any attempt to establish cost-related tariffs. First, the existence of freight consolidators and wholesalers not only cuts off the airlines from their true customers and distorts the pricing mechanism, but also gives such large freight agents considerable market power. Second, the carriage of freight is inherently more competitive even in regulated markets than is the carriage of passengers. This is because most freight, except for emergency freight, is indifferent to the routeing it is offered in order to move from its origin to its destination. A shipper is unconcerned if their shipment goes from New York to Lisbon on a direct flight or via Amsterdam or Frankfurt or Copenhagen, even with a six-hour trans-shipment at one of those airports, provided it gets to Lisbon within the expected time. Few passengers would put up with circuitous and lengthy journeys. Thus, in most cases there are numerous routeings (and airlines) that freight can use to get to its destination. This ensures a degree of inter-airline competition, which may be absent for passengers on the same routes. If one superimposes on these market characteristics the availability on most air services of surplus belly-hold capacity then any attempts to establish cost-related cargo tariffs will inevitably be futile.

Airlines have little choice but to pursue a strategy of setting rates aimed at maximising revenue. In prevailing market conditions on most major routes this means charging what the traffic will bear. Cost-related pricing only becomes possible for products that require specialised handling and storage facilities which are expensive to provide. This is especially so if only a few airlines are able to provide such facilities. Then there is less competitive pressure on tariffs. Pharmaceuticals requiring low temperature transfers and handling are one such commodity, while the transport of live animals may be another.

In an environment of market-oriented pricing, where consolidators and wholesalers have had a major influence on freight tariffs, and where combination carriers are losing market share to the integrators, it seems inevitable that tariffs will increasingly reflect three variables – the speed of delivery required, whether the shipment is loose or in a unit load device, and whether it requires specialised handling. The level of charges within such a structure will of course reflect market conditions in each market or route. They will be highest where the demand for freight capacity exceeds the supply.

13.8.3 Freight yields

As in the passenger market, cargo yields, that is revenue per tonne-km carried, have tended to decline over time. In the 1990s global scheduled freight yields fell each year by about 3 per cent after adjusting for inflation. This decline reflected a downward trend in operating costs of both passenger aircraft and freighters, the increased freight capacity on offer and intensified competition. In the early 2000s freight yields began to rise, especially from 2003 onwards, as fuel and security surcharges were introduced; but then, following the world financial crisis of 2008, cargo yields collapsed by 15 per cent in 2009. They jumped back by 14 per cent the following year before yields entered a period of steady decline. Between 2011 and 2016 they dropped by an average of 8 per cent each year. Not till 2017 was there a slight increase. Collapsing yields were due to a number of factors. Slowing growth in demand for air freight, as key economies slowed down and as sea freight became more competitive, coupled with over-capacity arising from increased competition pushed yields down. Lower fuel prices in 2015 and 2016 depressed yields further. They dropped by over a quarter in those two years. During the 2010s pricing power shifted from the suppliers, the airlines, to the consumers of their services. A bad omen for the future of air freight.

Various factors impact on an airline's cargo yields. The prevailing cargo tariff levels in its major markets and that airline's traffic mix are clearly the major determinants of its freight yields. Other pricing factors also impact on yields. Particularly important is the degree to which the general cargo rates have been eroded by the introduction of low specific commodity rates and ultimately by contract of other deep discount rates. This will be determined by market conditions, notably the availability of spare capacity and the degree of inter-airline competition. Consignment mix in terms of the size of various shipments is important in determining the rates paid to the airline since larger consignments will pay less per kilo. The length of haul of those consignments also impacts on yields since cargo rates per kilometre tend to decline with distance. Similar factors will also affect the freight yields achieved in the various parts of an airline's route network.

For individual airlines, three further factors may impact on the average freight yields they achieve: first, the degree to which they operate all-cargo aircraft, since yields on them tend to be lower than for freight on passenger aircraft. Second, the sector lengths over which they are flying cargo, since shorter sectors tend to produce higher yields because tariffs per kilometre are higher. Finally, the success of the airline in marketing high time-definite rates for rapid delivery or in developing service products requiring specialist handling, such as the transport of pharmaceuticals or very-high-value goods.

13.9 Mixed profitability

Historically, the profitability of air freight in its different formats has been fairly mixed. Freight is no different from passengers in that its profitability depends on the interplay of the same three variables, namely unit costs, unit revenues or yields and the load factors achieved. This varies between different sectors of the air freight industry.

For those airlines who carry the bulk of their air freight on passenger aircraft, and have few or no freighters, cargo profitability depends not only on the freight yields and the freight load factors achieved but also on the method used to allocate costs. In practice, low load factors for freight on passenger aircraft are inevitable. Passenger aircraft generate some cargo capacity on all the routes they operate, irrespective of the level of demand for freight on each route. Most airlines operate many passenger routes where demand for freight is minimal, yet the freight capacity available is substantial either because passenger flight frequencies are high or because wide-bodied aircraft are being used. Put simply, an airline's cargo manager must try to balance unit costs, yield and load factor, yet has no effective control over capacity so as to push up the load factors. An impossible task, since much of their cargo capacity is generated by the demands of the passenger side of the business.

Ultimately, the profitability of freight on passenger aircraft is linked to the costing approach adopted. In the past, IATA recommended the full allocation of joint costs between passengers and freight in proportion to the volumetric capacity used by each (Section 13.7). If fully costed on this basis, freight on passenger/combi aircraft appears in general to be unprofitable for many airlines, though individual routes may be profitable. Many other airlines, including British Airways, consider belly-hold freight as a *by-product* of passenger services, rather than as a *joint product*. They then assess freight in terms of its contribution to the total revenues on their passenger services, after deducting from the freight revenue all costs specific to the cargo operations. On this basis, belly-hold freight appears to make a valuable contribution to the overall profitability of many routes. Cargo managers, especially those in airlines not operating freighters or heavily involved in freight, tend to prefer this approach.

Scheduled freighter services, whether operated by combination carriers, cargo airlines or integrators, are more likely to be profitable in large part because it becomes easier to match the capacity provided with the demand in particular markets. Load factors can be pushed up since they can be influenced directly by an airline's cargo managers and salespeople. But freighter operators face two major challenges in achieving adequate load factors. First, there is a constant risk of over-capacity as other freight operators are attracted to denser markets. Moreover, such competitors may be not only those operating in each specific point-to-point market but also those offering indirect services through their own hubs. Second, they may face major difficulties in achieving adequate load factors because of possible imbalances in freight flows in each direction on the same route. Very high loads in one direction may be offset by negligible flows in the return direction. Where loads are good in both directions and there is no over-supply of freighter capacity it should be possible to achieve good load factors and good yields. Demand and supply conditions in individual markets have a major impact on the profitability of all-cargo services. While such operations in general appear to be marginally profitable results vary considerably both between major markets or routes and between airlines operating freighter services.

A comparative analysis of profit margins, in the ten years 2007 to 2017, of two integrators, UPS and Fedex, of Lufthansa Cargo and of Cargolux, an all-cargo operator, highlights differing financial performances (Table 13.4). Over this period both Fedex and UPS have achieved profit margins of between 5 and 9 per cent every year with only one or two exceptions. These are markedly better and more consistent results then either Lufthansa Cargo or Cargolux. The integrator business, the bulk of it involving the carriage of parcels and smaller air freight, appears to be very profitable. The relatively high tariffs paid by customers to ensure speedy door-to-door trans-shipment more than compensate for the high costs involved, for the integrator, in collecting and delivering shipments.

Some passenger airlines resolved the issue of how to allocate joint costs to the carriage of cargo by setting up cargo subsidiaries, which in addition to operating freighters, bought space on passenger aircraft as needed from the parent passenger airline. Lufthansa Cargo is one such subsidiary. Its financial performance in the ten years after 2007 was reasonable but mixed. There were two years of losses, in 2009 and 2016, but in other years it was profitable though operating margins before interest and tax were generally low, between 2 and 6 per cent (Table 13.4).

Table 13.4 Adjusted profit as a percentage of total revenues – selected cargo operators, 2007–17

	Combination carrier **Lufthansa Cargo %**	All-cargo carrier **Cargolux %**	Integrator **UPS %**	Integrator **Federal Express %**
2017	9.6		8.0	8.4
2016	− 2.4	0.3	8.3	6.1
2015	3.1	2.3	8.4	3.9
2014	4.3	0.1	7.5	8.4
2013	3.6	0.4	7.8	5.8
2012	4.2	− 2.0	8.1	7.5
2011	9.1	− 1.0	9.2	6.1
2010	11.4	3.4	7.0	5.8
2009	− 8.0	− 11.3	6.1	2.1
2008	6.2	− 3.1	5.8	5.5
2007	5.7	− 2.8	8.8	

Source: Company annual reports

However, these results contrast with those of SIA Cargo, another of the major freight operators belonging to a combination carrier. Though not shown in Table 13.4 SIA Cargo made a loss every year between 2007 and 2017 except in 2007/08 and 2010/11. Clearly Lufthansa Cargo has been operating much more successfully than SIA Cargo even though both have similarly large freighter fleets and are in the top ten cargo airlines in terms of freight tonne-kms (Table 13.2). The reason may well be that Germany is one of the world's major exporters and importers of a wide variety of goods that move by air, so Lufthansa is at one end of major air cargo flows. On the other hand, SIA Cargo has to compete by attracting much of its cargo from points outside Singapore to fly to its final destination via its Singapore hub. This means competing in highly competitive markets, which results in strong downward pressure on yields and load factors.

Surprisingly, Cargolux, the largest specialist all-cargo operator, like SIA Cargo, did not perform well financially in the ten years from 2007. In the early period, with one exception in 2010, it made losses every year. After 2012 it recorded only very low marginal profits (Table 13.4).

Clearly, the profit margins of integrated freight carriers such as UPS and Fedex have tended to be much higher than the margins achieved by the traditional combination carriers or the all-cargo airlines such as Cargolux. The integrators' business model gives them a major advantage. By offering a door-to-door service, the integrators provide much more added value and can charge substantially more for their services especially those offering guaranteed and fast delivery. This is why the cargo subsidiaries of airlines such as Lufthansa and Singapore Airlines are focusing increasingly on the provision of door-to-door and time-definite services.

13.10 Future prospects and challenges

In the ten years after 2006, despite one or two good years' growth air freight was sluggish with a compound annual growth rate of close to 2 per cent. Growth in passenger traffic was much faster at around 4.8 per cent per year. In 2017 as the world economy began to accelerate again, the long-term prospects for air freight appeared more optimistic. Airbus and Boeing were forecasting that air freight would grow much faster over the next 20 years to 2036. Boeing's forecast was annual growth at 4.2 per cent while Airbus was predicting annual growth of 3.8 per cent. At the beginning of 2018 that appeared over-optimistic.

The Director General of IATA, Alexandre de Juniac, speaking in December 2017 also sounded optimistic when he stated:

> *We had a very difficult environment (for air cargo) but we have recovered in 2017 with very good figures; capacity increased by less than 4 per cent and demand by 9 per cent. So for once the cargo business will be profitable in many airlines, which has not been the case.*

Whatever the growth rate achieved in coming years, the network airlines will have to adapt and respond to the continued expansion of the integrators and the increased market power of the large forwarders. The traditional view that combination airlines are involved in supplying two joint products, the carriage of passengers and of freight, which are inextricably entwined, will progressively be replaced by the belief that they are two quite distinct products. These two products manifest demand patterns that differ both geographically, in terms of routes, and temporally in terms of seasons and timings. They require airlines to offer different service and product features marketed and sold through separate and different distribution channels. They are two quite separate businesses, and as both are developed further the differences between them will become more pronounced and apparent. Certain sectors of the airline industry have known this for a long time. For the low-cost, no-frills airlines carrying freight is anathema since it would undermine their economics, which are dependent on fast turnarounds and minimal ground-handling. On the other side of the business, the integrated carriers have also seen the advantages of product specialisation – in their case on freight only.

As a result of both economic and operational pressures to separate the two businesses there is likely to be a growing polarisation among combination carriers in their approach to freight. At one end there will be airlines such as Delta, American, Air India or the Polish airline LOT, who will basically see themselves as *primarily passenger carriers*. Such airlines will not view freight as a major part of their business, in which they are prepared to invest substantial financial resources or effort. They will carry some belly-hold freight but will treat it as a by-product, one hopefully making a financial contribution to the passenger side, not as a separate business in its own right. Perhaps up to 20 per cent or less of their revenue tonne-kms will be produced by freight as opposed to passengers but freight will generate less than 10 per cent of total revenues. Moreover, over time both these percentages will be depressed further. Inevitably, these airlines' share of the freight traffic on the routes they operate will also decline.

At the other end of the spectrum will be a few airlines, *true combination carriers*, who see freight as a major and potentially profitable business activity with its own needs and requirements; but an activity sufficiently different from the passenger side of their business to merit separate treatment. These airlines will increasingly follow the example of Lufthansa, Singapore Airlines, Malaysia Airlines and others and operate their cargo operations as separate and independent subsidiary companies or business units. The latter will operate their own freighter aircraft with their own flight crew and will undertake all their own marketing, selling, ground-handling, warehousing, administration and so on. They will buy and pay for belly-hold capacity as required from their parent passenger airline or even from other airlines. Some may in time be floated on the stock exchange, with the parent airline retaining some shares, or they may be sold off entirely. These large, cargo-oriented airlines or airline subsidiaries will be able to concentrate their business exclusively on freight. More importantly, they will refocus their activities away from the traditional view that air freight is about transporting goods from A to B. Success in the future will depend on understanding that is much more than that. Air freight is about providing a delivery service and about supply chain management. This is why the integrators have been so successful and why large freight forwarders and even postal authorities have been making incursions into activities and markets previously the preserve of the airlines.

The *integrators* will continue expanding their business and market, first by going for more non-express traffic and larger shipments; second, by using large forwarders they have purchased to give them greater market spread and facilitate the move into non-core business.

The large air freight airlines, in order to meet the long-term threat of the integrated carriers, will need to face up to several operational challenges. First, they must focus on providing customised services and products to meet the very specific needs of large specialist market segments. As Lufthansa Cargo and SIA Cargo already do, anyone wishing to be a significant player in air freight will need to have customised handling equipment for products such as pharmaceuticals, perishable stuffs, hazardous goods or goods requiring high security and so on. Such services may be costly to provide but should give the providers a marketing advantage and generate higher yields.

Second, freighter fleets will need to be modernised. Older aircraft cannot cope with the needs of tomorrow's air freight market. Yield pressure will require airlines to operate the most fuel-efficient freighters. While fuel prices went down in late 2014, they have moved up gradually since then and are likely in the longer term to stabilise at levels that are still relatively high. For many older-generation freighters, such as Airbus A300F or Boeing 747-400F aircraft, fuel costs may represent 75 per cent of round-trip costs when fuel prices are as high as they were in early 2014. Such aircraft are also too noisy in an increasingly environmentally conscious world. They are old and unreliable and subject to delays, with more and longer maintenance down times. Yet time-definite shipments require punctuality and reliability. In short, freighter fleets need to be modernised. While new-generation freighters will have much higher capital costs, these should be more than offset by lower fuel costs.

Third, airlines with serious commitment to air freight will need to undertake the substantial investments required to improve their IT systems and to re-orient these systems to providing a time-definite integrator type of service. This means high-speed tracing and tracking of shipments, high technology warehousing, automatic and customer-focused reporting systems and the provision, in-house or through ground-handling agents, of time-guaranteed collection and delivery. If the traditional airlines are to succeed in the freight sector, they must appreciate that there has been a logistics revolution. They must invest heavily in distribution networks, in electronic data interchange (EDI) and in other facilities needed to meet shippers' requirements. Their aim should be not just to transport freight by air but to add value to the shipper's products. In doing this they may be able to charge more for their services and thereby counteract any downward pressure on rates.

The final challenge that must be met is how to provide a global delivery service. Big users of air freight such as IBM, Nokia, Ford or General Motors manufacture or source their products in many countries, and sell worldwide. They and most of the other big shippers need global scope and coverage from their providers of air delivery services. For the traditional airlines this means creating cargo alliances, to provide a global network. In theory, this could be done by airlines already within one of the three global alliances, such as STAR or SkyTeam. But differing priorities of the member airlines has meant that cargo alliances have usually been limited to pairs of airlines or a limited number. When they have been launched they have not proved very successful, as was the case with the WOW cargo alliance between Lufthansa, SAS and SIA; launched in 2001, it did not survive for long.

It is not evident that these global cargo alliances have had much success. Establishing genuine co-operation between the partners had proved difficult, as each guarded its own customers too jealously. To be successful in the long run such multi-member alliances have a number of problems to overcome. To be more successful in the longer run, any multi-member cargo alliances must launch a common portfolio of products with common brand names in all markets; they must integrate their IT systems so they can communicate with each other; they must also develop standard handling processes and harmonised service standards and they need to integrate their sales teams and marketing efforts. Such integration will take time.

Perhaps a more realistic next step for airlines heavily involved in air cargo is to create bilateral metal-neutral joint ventures with one or more airlines operating in the same market. Lufthansa's JV with STAR alliance partner ANA, launched in 2015, was ground-breaking because it went further than previous cargo alliances. This JV was approved by the regulatory authorities involved and allowed the two airlines to operate on a metal-neutral basis. They unified their tariffs, aligned their IT systems, warehouses and handling facilities and set up joint cargo sales forces. As the JV is metal-neutral revenues are shared so there is no incentive to sell space on one airline as opposed to the other. Early in 2017 Lufthansa cargo launched another similar cargo JV with Cathay Pacific, member of the Oneworld global alliance. Such JVs generate several benefits for the partner airlines. Capacity offered in key markets is controlled, tariff competition between key players is eliminated and the competitive strengths of the JV partners is reinforced. Some cargo-specific costs can be reduced. Further cargo bilateral JVs as well as cargo JV with three or more partners are inevitable.

It is only through entering more bilateral and widespread JVs, and the more effective integration of marketing and operations that these make possible, that the combination carriers will be able to stand up to the challenge and long-term threat of the integrators and the global logistics suppliers.

14 Strategies for success

The trouble with today is that the future is not what it used to be.

(Paul Valery, French poet, 1871–1945)

In mid-2018 the global airline industry was on a high. It had enjoyed nearly a decade of annual profits, and during the most recent four years its annual returns were, for the first time, higher than the cost of capital (Figure 1.3 in Chapter 1). High profits were also expected for 2018. All this had been achieved despite the slow gradual rise in the price of aviation fuel following its dramatic collapse in mid-2014. There was a prevailing optimism among many airline chief executives who were enjoying unprecedented profits. But this hid a darker reality. In 2017 and 2018 many airlines were operating at a loss, several in Europe and elsewhere collapsed while some were kept afloat only through injections of government capital or aid.

However, this was the longest period ever of sustained profitability for the airline industry. Would it continue? The future is difficult to foresee but historically aviation has been a volatile industry responding to sudden and unexpected external shocks. A global economic slow-down choking off growth in passenger demand, a spike in fuel prices pushing up costs or some other external event, such as a trade war, may push the airlines into a new period of crises. This seems likely to happen sooner rather than later.

How should airlines prepare for such an eventuality? On the basis of the preceding analysis of airline economics it is possible to make some recommendations. First, there are operational and tactical actions that must be considered by all airlines irrespective of their size or business model. Second, there are strategic options that will vary depending on which sector of the industry an airline is operating in.

14.1 Priorities for all airlines

A major priority must be *vigilance on costs*. While at times of crisis airlines take draconian measures not just to contain various categories of costs but to reduce them, in periods of profitability and optimism about the future there is a tendency to be less rigorous in controlling non-fuel costs. Such costs tend to creep up almost unnoticed. As markets become more competitive, cost control must be seen as a long-term necessity not just a short-term response to eroding profits or losses.

Cost control must be exercised in all non-fuel areas but the focus should be on three areas. First, since staff costs are, for all airlines, one of the two largest items of cost, efforts are needed to control or cut labour costs. This can be done by improving labour productivity through changed or re-negotiated work practices or by more efficient management in key areas such as crew rostering. Labour costs can also be cut by reducing staff numbers especially in head office and administration. Computerisation and e-commerce have reduced the need for human hands in many areas. Many airlines have still not taken advantage of the saving in staff numbers that is now possible. Second, airlines must reduce or eliminate commissions paid to third parties such as GDSs, online travel agents or banks. They can also do this by persuading potential customers to avoid using GDSs or OTAs when booking. They can follow the example of Lufthansa or British Airways and penalise passengers who use third parties instead of booking direct with the airlines. Third, airlines can reduce costs by outsourcing various activities to specialist providers who can offer such activities more cheaply. For example, too many mid- or small-sized airlines are undertaking their own maintenance, of various kinds, which could be done more cheaply by specialised maintenance companies because there are significant economies of scale in maintenance provision.

It is not possible for airlines to cut the cost of fuel, except marginally, since the price of aviation fuel is externally determined. But they can reduce the amount of fuel consumed not only by more careful flight planning but by accelerating the introduction of the new generation Airbus NEO, Boeing MAX or Bombardier C-series aircraft that consume 10–15 per cent less fuel than the similar aircraft they are designed to replace. Of course, moving to more fuel-efficient aircraft may not always be possible and, in any case, can only be done gradually as older aircraft are phased out.

For those airlines that have mixed fleets, that is with too many different aircraft types, fleet rationalisations can help reduce costs. By operating with fewer aircraft types, crewing, maintenance and even some ground-handling costs can be cut. If, in the process, the average size of aircraft in the fleet increases, this in itself will result in lower seat-km costs. Fleet rationalisation can also provide an opportunity to replace older aircraft by newer fuel-efficient aircraft.

American Airlines provides a good example of the potential benefits of fleet rationalisation. Following the 2014 merger with US Airways, American by the end of 2017 had inducted 469 newer aircraft into its fleet. The average aircraft age went down from 14 to 10 years. Fleet renewal resulted in a 10 per cent increase in fuel efficiency. This together with a shift from operating 99- to 160-seat aircraft on short-haul sectors to larger aircrafts of 161–200 seats led to a substantial reduction in unit costs. Even for airlines much smaller than American, fleet rationalisation can generate clear cost savings.

At times when fuel prices are tending upwards, fuel hedging can play a significant role both in reducing the cost of fuel in the future but also in providing some certainty about airlines' future cost levels. But hedging is risky, so airlines must implement a well-planned and flexible hedging policy. The key variables in such a policy need to be how far forward they should hedge and what proportion of future fuel needs should be hedged. These variable inputs must be constantly reviewed.

Fuel is paid for in US dollars as are aircraft purchases or leases and some other costs. So many airlines, especially those based in countries with potentially weaker currencies or those earning significant revenues in such markets, need to enter into currency hedges for some or all of their future commitments in hard currencies.

The business world is changing. E-commerce is now at the core of customer-to-business and business-to-business relationships and the internet-based technologies that underpin it are constantly evolving and offering new opportunities. A second key priority for all airlines must be to *maximise the opportunities offered by e-commerce*. They must use it to do much more than traditional online marketing and selling of their services. E-commerce must be at the core of their planning and operations. Each airline's corporate structure must reflect this with responsibility for e-commerce held by executives at very senior level with sufficient human and material resources and with a clear strategy.

An effective e-commerce strategy must be concerned with developing and monitoring e-sales and distribution, with marketing (including effective branding) and with developing a website that provides a good service to customers through a variety of formats including all the different social media. Social media are critical in attracting and maintaining millennials and younger customers. While some airlines, such as Delta, are well advanced in capturing the benefits of e-commerce, others have lagged behind and must prioritise the improvement of their digital involvement.

The final priority for all airlines must be to constantly monitor and *improve revenue generation*. This requires more effective revenue management and inventory control not only to increase the average yield per seat-km, on a route-by-route basis, but also to push up the average seat factor. Many network airlines have much to learn from the LCCs in improving their load factors especially on short- and medium-haul routes. The US major network carriers have done this and operate their domestic services with much higher seat factors than many airlines in Europe or Asia, where especially smaller airlines operate with short-haul seat factors around 75 per cent or less. This is a real challenge for airlines operating a short- to long-haul hub because achieving higher seat factors on short-haul services whose primary purpose is to feed long-haul routes poses particular problems.

Also, as discussed in earlier chapters, all airlines, especially network carriers, must make a greater effort to *maximise ancillary revenues*. They need to learn from the low-cost carriers but also be more innovative in developing new ancillary sources especially on long-haul routes. Effective development of a variety of ancillary revenue sources can be a financial game changer (Chapter 12).

14.2 Large network carriers

In addition to focusing on all these priorities, large traditional network carriers will have to face up to challenges more specific to their sector of the industry. In liberalised long-haul markets they will feel increasingly threatened by the emergence of low-cost competitors as they were previously in short-haul markets. At the same time, they will have to face increased pressure from other network carriers who have entered into new alliances or joint ventures or who have strengthened their existing alliances. What strategies can help them deal with such challenges?

Continued and further consolidation, either through mergers or equity investments, should be a priority. The aim of such consolidation is not so much to reduce costs but to generate additional revenues through both a wider and stronger network spread, that is geographic diversification, but also through creating, in some markets, oligopolistic or monopolistic power. The latter becomes possible when an airline and its partner(s) are so dominant on a particular route that existing competitors are loath to expand capacity while new entrants hesitate. Dominance is reinforced if, as a result of consolidation, the partner airlines effectively control most of the runway slots at key airports at peak times.

Where consolidation of the airline sector within a region or large market area leads to a reduction in the number of major players, then it becomes easier through 'tacit' collusion to rationalise and slow down growth in capacity. In the United States as the large domestic airlines were reduced in number from ten to just four, capacity grew more slowly, load factors increased and profitability improved.

Another effective way of achieving the revenue and market benefits of partial consolidation is through metal-neutral joint ventures that have been fully approved by the regulatory authorities of the states involved (Section 7.5, Chapter 7). They are much more integrative than is the case of membership of a global alliance. Such JVs have the added advantage that they enable partners to more effectively reduce some costs – in marketing, ground-handling and possibly maintenance. They make it easier to rationalise pricing structures so as to compete more effectively. Schedules and seat capacity can be co-ordinated and controlled, making it easier both to achieve higher load factors and to switch to using larger aircraft. If the latter happens then unit costs per seat-km can be reduced. The potential benefits of JVs are such that rapid expansion of JVs must be a key part of any large long-haul airline's commercial and development strategy. Already by mid-2018, both Delta and American were operating more than 55 per cent of their international capacity within existing or pending JVs. This figure was bound to rise.

On dense long-haul routes, such as London–New York, the network carriers can meet the challenge of low-cost competitors by offering very much higher frequencies, which they already do, and by selling just a few seats on each of those frequencies at very low competitive fares. New low-cost entrants may also have difficulty in obtaining sufficient runway slots at major airports to be more than a nuisance to the network carriers. But on thinner long-haul routes and on routes from uncongested airports low-cost long-haul carriers will pose a growing threat, especially if the long-haul LCC operates its own short-haul feeder services.

In the longer term, the legacy network airlines can only meet this threat by setting up their own long-haul LCC subsidiaries to operate in specific leisure markets as SIA has done with Scoot and Air Canada has done with Air Canada Rouge. But for longer-term success, they should not rely on switching older long-haul aircraft and existing flight crew and other staff to their new LCC subsidiary. They should aim to use the newest aircraft with the lowest fuel costs such as the Boeing 787 or Airbus A350, and with staff employed with more favourable terms and conditions. This is, after all, what new entrant true long-haul LCCs, such as Norwegian or Scoot, will be doing.

The biggest challenge for network airlines will be how to compete effectively with LCCs in short-haul markets where the latter are becoming more and more powerful and even dominant. In some markets two approaches have been tried. Some network airlines have tried to replicate the LCC model by slashing costs, putting high-density seating into their aircraft, unbundling the fare and replicating the LCC pricing strategy of offering a low initial fare with a variety of add-on or ancillary charges for different on-board services or products. This has been the Aer Lingus approach in Ireland, and it proved successful. But such a strategy is difficult to implement without the full support of the labour force since, to match or even approach LCC unit costs, existing work practices and even salaries need to be renegotiated.

The alternative approach has been to try to keep or increase the network airlines' market share by differentiating their service so as to justify the higher fares they offer. Some network airlines have tried to differentiate their product by continuing to offer in-flight catering in all classes, free hold baggage and so on or by operating to/from airports that are particularly attractive but where LCCs would have difficulty obtaining sufficient numbers of slots at peak times. But product differentiation means higher costs and there is only limited evidence that such a strategy has proved successful in short-haul markets.

Neither of these responses to the LCC challenge are likely to be successful in the longer term. Replicating the low-cost product model can only succeed if the network carrier can get its unit costs low enough to off-set the low fares it must charge to compete effectively. But, as shown in an earlier chapter, a hubbing network with short-haul flights feeding long-haul suffers some inherent and unavoidable cost penalties (Section 5.7, Chapter 5). Moreover, most large airlines operating such networks have low labour productivity and high legacy labour costs because of out-dated work practices.

The approach of trying to differentiate the network airline product so as to justify higher fares can succeed in maintaining or even increasing traffic levels but market share will be lost to LCCs. This is both because of the lower fares offered by the LCCs and also because the LCCs can, where necessary, upgrade their own product offering, for instance by introducing a Business cabin or offering free hold baggage.

In the long run, to meet the LCC challenge in short-haul markets, network carriers should consider two further alternative strategies. The first would be to set up their own low-cost subsidiary, as many have already done especially in Asia and to a lesser extent in Europe; however, many of those who have done this have made one or both of two mistakes. Some have launched LCC subsidiaries using aircraft and crews from the existing parent airline but hoping to somehow reduce unit costs. The other mistake has been to adopt a half-hearted approach and to keep the LCC subsidiary small with relatively few aircraft so as not to compete too much and too directly with the parent company. This is what Air France has done with Transavia.

Earlier analysis of the LCC model (Chapter 5) showed that there are some limited cost economies of larger size and more substantial marketing and revenue benefits. Lufthansa adopted the correct approach in 2017 in a plan to develop its subsidiary Eurowings into a major LCC with a fleet of 200-plus aircraft operating both short- and long-haul routes. But Lufthansa's error may prove to have been to try to grow Eurowings out of an existing more traditional airline that did not have the very low-cost base that start-up LCCs enjoy. British Airways/IAG adopted an economically sounder approach, which was to buy an existing successful LCC, Vueling, and to allow it to operate at arm's length.

It seems inevitable that all the larger network carriers will end up adopting a multi-brand strategy of some kind. But success of a multi-brand strategy is not necessarily ensured since it can create operational, marketing and management complexities. Qantas, in setting up Jetstar in 2003 as a low-cost airline to fend off competition in the Australian market from LCC Virgin Blue, has shown that a multibrand strategy can succeed. In 2017 Jetstar and Jetstar Asia's total passenger miles were almost half of those generated by Qantas. Both Jetstar and Qantas were highly profitable, with EBIT of $240 million and $546 million respectively in 2017. But several other efforts at setting up joint brands during the early 2000s and later failed. Failures included SAS's LCC airline 'Snowflake', launched in 2003 but collapsing within a year, and United Airlines' launch in 2004 of a lower-cost airline called 'Ted', which only lasted until 2009.

The second strategy might be for the major network carriers to enter into a code-sharing alliance or even joint venture with one of the larger successful LCCs. They can then use their LCC partner in one or both of two ways. The LCC could operate most or all of the feeder services into the network airline's hub, on routes where the latter's own services are no longer viable, while also operating on other short-haul routes. Alternatively, the LCC could operate all non-hub flights, that is flights not serving the main hub, leaving the hub feeder routes to be operated by the parent network airline. This is the way Lufthansa uses its own LCC subsidiary Eurowings. It is inevitable, however, that services operated by Lufthansa itself to feed its hubs at Frankfurt and Munich will be attacked by LCCs such as Ryanair or easyJet.

14.3 Mid- and smaller-sized network airlines

Numerous mid- and smaller-sized traditional hub-based network airlines around the world, many of them fully or partially government owned, must focus on the same priorities and will face many of the same challenges as their larger counterparts. But they also have to deal with a more fundamental structural problem. Most are not big enough to compete effectively in long-haul markets with the large global network carriers while their unit costs are not low enough to compete successfully with LCCs in short-haul markets. Some operate both short- and long-haul services through their major hubs while most operate only medium-haul and shorter international and domestic services from their main hub. They have relatively small total fleets, generally with less than 150 aircraft and in many cases with a lot fewer.

If operating in long-haul markets they are at a disadvantage for several reasons. Their own home market is often a relatively small generator of outgoing long-haul traffic and may not be a major destination for incoming traffic. As a result, their networks are smaller and they serve fewer long-haul destinations. Because their traffic flows are likely to be thinner they may be operating to some long-haul destinations with low frequencies, some less than daily. All this makes them less attractive to potential travellers. As a result they lose passengers, both outgoing and incoming, who flow through the neighbouring hubs of larger network carriers who offer more destinations, higher frequencies, good feed connections and often lower fares too.

In short-haul markets, mid-sized and smaller network carriers often suffer from operating smaller aircraft and more mixed fleets than the LCCs they are competing with. This immediately creates a cost disadvantage. They face further diseconomies from being small or relatively small companies. Being old established airlines, they are frequently over-staffed with out-dated work practices. They may also be highly union-ised and, if government owned, may suffer from too much government interference in labour and operational issues. Management structures may be too hierarchical and bureaucratic. All this creates difficulties in competing effectively with LCCs in short-haul markets.

In addition, where operating in both long- and short-haul markets mid-sized and smaller airlines tend to suffer from diseconomies of small scale particularly in terms of marketing and revenue generation and, to a limited extent, in terms of costs.

Such airlines are not strong enough in long-haul markets and not low cost enough in short-haul markets. If trying to operate a mid-sized hub they are an endangered species. Experience in the United States, where markets were the first to be liberalised, supports this conclusion. Most US mid-sized and smaller network airlines have collapsed, over the years, or have merged with or been taken over by one of the three network majors. In Europe several airlines that were on the endangered list such as Air Berlin, a hybrid carrier, Malev, the Hungarian airline, or Transaero in Russia have collapsed since 2012. Alitalia is in a coma and kept alive by the Italian government. Several other European airlines, especially in Eastern Europe, and Asian airlines, such Air India, as well as several airlines in South America could be categorised as being on the endangered list. What survival strategies should they and other mid- or small-sized network airlines pursue, in addition to the tactical priorities discussed earlier at the start of this chapter?

If operating long-haul services, they may be better off financially by pulling out of long-haul markets altogether or cutting back substantially as some have done in recent years. Instead, they should enter an alliance or code-share agreement with a larger neighbouring airline operating an extensive long-haul network. Or they could enter into several code-share alliances with any long-haul airlines flying into their home hub.

As an alternative they should only maintain or develop their own long-haul network if they can find a specific and sustainable market niche where they have some competitive advantage. Air Portugal has found such a niche by focusing on the Europe to Brazil market and serving more points in Brazil than any other European carrier. In fact, in 2017 it offered 25 per cent of all seats between Europe and Brazil and flew to six points in Brazil not served by any other carrier. However, TAP remained financially weak. Using the geographical location of Helsinki on the shortest Great Circle distance between Europe and East Asia, Finnair has developed a niche market offering very low fares and low elapsed travel times to places like Beijing or Tokyo via their Helsinki hub.

In short-haul markets strategic options for airlines of this size are limited. They could try to reduce their costs, change their product features and operate effectively as a low-cost airline as the Irish airline Aer Lingus has done on its short-haul network. This is difficult to do because they suffer from legacy costs and labour practices that are difficult to change. Even if they manage to do this, in many of their markets they will be competing against much larger LCCs that will enjoy marketing and cost benefits of scale. They could succeed if they have some competitive advantage such as numerous slots at a slot-constrained airport or a particular geographical niche. As an alternative, smaller network carriers may try to position themselves as offering a 'superior' product and service to justify their higher fares; easier to do, but success may be uncertain and in the past up-market positioning has in general not saved airlines when competing with LCCs.

Aegean, the relatively small Greek regional airline, has adopted these strategies. It has managed to achieve low unit costs, in part because as a relatively new airline it had no old-established labour practices to deal with nor was it over staffed. It has also maintained a high level of on-board services, including meals, on its short-haul international services. It has been able to brand itself as an attractive full-service airline. While its predecessor in Greece, Olympic Airways, had originally operated long-haul services to North America and elsewhere, Aegean has steadfastly refused to do so. As a result of the strategies adopted, Aegean has been successful in meeting the challenge posed by several LCCs, which have entered all of its European routes as well as its domestic markets, and has continued to operate profitably.

Another option for such airlines may be to align themselves with one of the global alliances and become a feeder airline serving the alliance's various hubs. This may be attractive to all parties, since the smaller network carrier may have lower short-haul unit costs than its larger alliance partners, though these costs will still be higher than LCC unit costs. Through this link up, the smaller carrier benefits from being able to generate denser feeder traffic to support its short-haul operations. It may also gain marketing support from its alliance partners, but past evidence suggests that this in itself may not be enough. An alternative might be to avoid entering exclusively a single global alliance that may impose restrictions, but to make code-share agreements with airlines from any of the global alliances. This has been the strategy adopted by Air Baltic.

A more serious step might be to sell a minority share to a large network carrier who can provide marketing, managerial and financial support in return for gaining access to and control of the feeder traffic the smaller airline can provide. This was the thinking behind Etihad's acquisition of minority shareholdings in India's Jet Airways (24 per cent) in 2013 and Alitalia (49 per cent) in 2014. These investments helped Jet through a difficult period, though its future in 2018 was still shaky, but have not been able to save Alitalia.

The ultimate defensive strategy for mid- and smaller-sized airlines is to sell out to one of the major global players. Austrian Airlines, SWISS and Brussels Airlines were all sold to Lufthansa when going through a crisis. In this way, these airlines obtained financial support but also marketing support and some limited cost synergies. They have survived but not as independent companies. However, their structural problems remain. In many of their markets, they will continue to face growing and stiff competition from large LCCs with much lower unit costs. Their future profitability may not be assured even if they are units of a larger network carrier.

Collapse and closure or being taken over by larger and more powerful network carriers seems to be the future for mid-sized and smaller network carriers. This, after all, is what happened in the United States. Some of those not bought out may only survive if supported financially by their governments. Others may only survive if they can find a defensible niche market.

14.4 Regional airlines

In order to succeed, smaller regional airlines operating aircraft of around 100 seats or less must focus on the tactics and priorities outlined earlier for all airlines (Section 14.1). In addition, they face a major fundamental problem inherent in the nature of their business model. As was discussed earlier (Chapter 4, Section 4.6), small aircraft, while having lower trip costs, have higher, in some cases significantly higher, unit costs per seat-km than the larger aircraft used by LCCs or most network carriers. The regionals may have lower overhead and other non-aircraft-related costs but these are unlikely to be sufficient to off-set the cost disadvantages of operating their smaller aircraft.

This means that to succeed, regionals must avoid routes where traffic is currently dense enough to attract low-cost operators or routes where low LCC fares can potentially stimulate significant volumes of demand. But operating on thinner routes, many of which are likely to be between secondary or small cities, may not in itself be enough to safeguard the regionals. They need to operate on thin routes on which they can charge high enough fares to cover their higher unit costs. They should therefore focus on thin routes where there is some time-sensitive business traffic prepared to pay such fares or on routes where the surface links by road or rail are slow or inexistent, giving air services a distinct advantage. These will include many thin cross-water routes. Regionals that do not ensure that they primarily operate routes where they can charge high unit fares, at least to some passengers, will be in difficulties.

Another strategy is to link up and code-share with a major network airline feeding thinner flows to its hub(s) on routes the network airline could not operate economically with its larger aircraft with their much higher trip costs. Such feeder traffic can ensure both higher loads and higher average yields. This is the strategy that has kept many US regionals afloat.

14.5 Low-cost carriers

The launch of many new low-cost airlines during the last two decades especially in Asia and Europe has created a multi-tiered structure in this sector of the airline industry. In 2018 there were a few very large LCCs, such as Southwest in North America, and Ryanair and easyJet in Europe, that operated well over 300 aircraft from multiple bases. Then there was a second tier of mid-sized LCCs with around 100 to 150 or so aircraft. These included Eurowings, Norwegian and Wizz in Europe, Westjet in Canada, Gol in Brazil and Air Asia, Indigo and Lion Air in Asia. Some of these had large aircraft orders in hand. Then there was a large number of LCCs with much smaller fleets, many subsidiaries of network airlines.

The LCC majors have been consistently profitable over many years. This was due in large part to their focus on the cost reduction and revenue enhancing strategies outlined earlier (Section 14.1). The mid-sized and smaller ones have enjoyed more mixed fortunes with some, like Indigo, doing well financially while others have not. Large size combined with an extensive widespread network appears to be a key success factor for LCCs. Large fleet size helps reduce some costs, especially aircraft ownership costs when ordering aircraft in large numbers. Additionally, maintenance costs may be lowered. Having a widespread network undoubtedly helps in marketing and branding. The large and well-established also benefit from widespread brand recognition. With very large fleets, these LCCs can dominate markets through offering high frequencies. Thus, a clear survival strategy for mid-sized and smaller low-cost airlines must be to go for size.

In markets that have been liberalised and are open to entry by new, even foreign carriers, smaller LCCs will find it difficult to survive profitably in the longer term. Survival will depend on getting the marketing benefits of large scale and the cost advantages of large fleet size. This means merging with other small LCCs or being taken over by one of the larger LCCs.

The alternative strategy might be to launch a period of very rapid growth involving large aircraft orders, which is what Lion Air, in Indonesia, and Air Asia did in 2017, each placing orders for 250-plus aircraft. This is a high-risk strategy involving very substantial capital investment both in acquiring new aircraft and in developing new markets. Because of this it is not a strategy likely to be undertaken by LCCs that are subsidiaries of network airlines. The parent companies are generally risk averse. As real liberalisation is implemented more effectively in new regions, such as South-east Asia, the smaller LCCs will become endangered.

The larger and mid-sized LCCs will come to dominate most short-haul markets in Europe, large parts of Asia and Latin America. As they capture market share from the legacy network airlines and open new routes they will find themselves increasingly competing, on more and more of their routes, with other LCCs. This will be a crunch time. Success will hinge on a number of factors: large size will be an advantage because of the marketing benefits it creates; low fares will be important, but it is the combination of fare levels and brand that will be key. That is how each airline positions and brands itself in terms of product and service quality. Lower service levels may be acceptable to passengers if combined with very low fares. LCCs must provide value for money.

Competition between LCCs will inevitably lead to attempts by some to differentiate their services and the products they offer. This may be the right strategy for them, but they must ensure that costs, and therefore fares, do not escalate to uneconomic levels.

To be successful, LCCs must also be quick, flexible and decisive in closing routes or bases when they are under-performing in terms of return on the assets employed. Certainly, they must be faster in doing this than network airlines have been in the past.

To achieve the benefits of fleet size and network spread, smaller LCCs must abandon any home country mentality and set about creating a wide matrix of bases (with their own based aircraft and crews) across a whole region spanning several countries or states. This has been done by the largest LCCs in North America, Europe and India. Elsewhere international regulations may prevent this strategy unless an LCC finds ways of bypassing the nationality regulations as Air Asia and Jetstar have done by setting up subsidiary companies in other countries. In South-east Asia already and elsewhere progressively the rules are being relaxed. LCCs must take advantage.

Finally, the largest LCCs need to make a strategic decision on whether they should launch long-haul low-cost services. Outside Europe a few have done this but on a limited scale. These include Air Asia, through Air Asia X, Cebu Pacific and Westjet. In Europe, only Norwegian is making a big effort to develop long-haul routes. Other large European LCCs have talked about doing so but have hesitated.

There are at least two compelling reasons why they should seriously evaluate such a strategy. First, several LCCs while having a main base usually in a capital city also have other large bases in large cities from which they operate many radial short-haul services. Because the network carriers focus their long-haul services on their main hubs they do not offer any such services from secondary airports. An example is Berlin. Lufthansa offers no long-haul services from this large city and tourist destination, but easyJet has several aircraft based there and a radial network of short-haul services that could feed a long-haul route to New York or Bangkok. easyJet could do the same out of Milan–Malpensa. Wizz Air could launch long-haul from its base in Budapest. The economics of such operators should be assessed. The second reason for LCCs launching long-haul low-cost is that the larger network carriers are setting up their own low-cost subsidiaries to do exactly that. Unlike the short-haul LCC airlines, however, the network airlines can only get effective feed at their one or two major hubs. Nevertheless, they should be pre-empted. Those early into long-haul low-cost operations will enjoy first-mover advantage if they succeed.

In Europe, and to a much lesser extent elsewhere, LCCs have launched a multitude of routes from large cities to minor destinations, many of which had few or no air services before but also routes between relatively small cities. The very low fares stimulated a dormant demand and generated enough traffic to support profitable operations. But traffic flows are thin, and many such markets have reached maturity and are unlikely to grow very fast, if at all. To ensure high growth in the future the LCCs need to attack the dense traffic flows to and from the major hubs, flows largely dominated by the large network carriers. easyJet has long followed such a strategy but other European LCCs have mostly not done so. There are problems. The major hubs are generally close to full capacity and a sufficient number of runway slots at suitable times may be hard to access. They also tend to be congested and suffer delays in the air and on the ground, so fast aircraft turn-rounds, which are key to LCC economics, may not always be feasible. Despite all that, European LCCs must target the dense flows to the large hubs of the network airlines.

14.6 Conclusion

The airline industry is very dynamic and fast changing. It is buffeted both by sudden and unexpected external shocks and internal disruptions arising from technological changes or management decisions. A decade of global annual profits from 2010 onwards is likely to be disrupted in the not too distant future. To survive and prosper during a new period of crises and beyond, airline executives must re-examine their current strategies, and assess what new strategies they should be implementing. The present chapter suggests some ideas worth considering, but there will undoubtedly be others.

Appendix A

Freedoms of the air

Negotiated in bilateral air services agreements

First Freedom The right to fly over another country without landing.

Second Freedom The right to make a landing for technical reasons (e.g. refuelling) in another country without picking up/setting down revenue traffic.

Third Freedom The right to carry revenue traffic from your own country (A) to the country (B) of your treaty partner.

Fourth Freedom The right to carry traffic from country B back to your own country A.

Fifth Freedom The right of an airline from country A to carry revenue traffic between country B and other countries such as C or D on services starting or ending in its home country A. (This freedom cannot be used unless countries C or D also agree.)

Supplementary rights

Sixth Freedom The use by an airline of country A of two sets of Third and Fourth Freedom rights to carry traffic between two other countries but using its base at A as a transit point.

Seventh Freedom The right of an airline to carry revenue traffic between points in two countries on services which lie entirely outside its own home country.

Eighth Freedom (or cabotage rights) The right for an airline to pick up and set down passengers or freight between two domestic points in another country on a service originating in its own home country.

Ninth Freedom The right of an airline to pick up and set down passengers or freight between two domestic points in another country on a service entirely outside its own country.

Sixth Freedom rights are rarely dealt with explicitly in air services agreements but may be referred to implicitly in memoranda of understanding attached to the agreement. In practice today most countries have accepted de facto the use of such rights.

Seventh, Eighth or Ninth Freedom rights are only granted in very rare cases, but airlines of member states of the European Union have such rights for services within or between other member states.

Appendix B

Non-economic technical and safety regulation

The large number of such regulations cover every aspect of airline activity and, broadly speaking, they fall into one of the following categories:

i   Regulations that deal with the airworthiness of the aircraft not only in terms of its design and production standards but also in terms of its performance under different operating conditions such as when there is an engine failure during take-off.
ii Regulations covering the timing, nature and supervision of maintenance and overhaul work and the training and qualifications of the engineers who carry out such work.
iii Regulations governing the numbers of flight and cabin crew, their training and licensing, their duties and functions on board and their workloads and schedules.
iv Detailed regulations covering both the way in which aircraft are operated, that is aspects such as flight preparation and in-flight procedures, and also the operation of the airlines themselves. In all countries, air transport operators must be licensed by the relevant civil aviation authority and must satisfy certain criteria and operating standards.
v   Finally, there is a complex profusion of regulations and recommended standards dealing with aviation infrastructure, such as airports, meteorological services, en-route navigational facilities, and so on.

Many of the technical and safety requirements are general, that is not specific to a particular aircraft type, and are promulgated as regulations of the civil aviation directorates or the relevant transport ministries of each country. In the United States they are known as Federal Aviation Regulations. In Europe safety regulations are promulgated by the European Aviation Safety Agency (EASA), which has mandatory powers.

While technical and airworthiness regulations may vary in particular detail from one country to another they are generally based on a whole series of 'International Standards and Recommended Practices' promulgated by the International Civil Aviation Organization (ICAO) as 16 annexes to the 'Convention on International Civil Aviation'. This is the so-called Chicago Convention signed in 1944. For instance, Annex 8 deals with the 'Airworthiness of Aircraft' and Annex 1 with 'Personnel Licensing'. These are constantly revised and updated. As a result, there tends to be considerable uniformity in the technical regulations for air transport in most member states of ICAO.

Operational and safety requirements specific to an aircraft type are contained in its flight manual, but the operational constraints and practices recommended in the flight manuals conform to the more general regulations mentioned above and are approved by the relevant national airworthiness authorities. Among other requirements, the flight manual will impose payload limitations on an aircraft at airports with high temperatures or inadequate runway length. In this and numerous other ways airworthiness and other technical regulations have direct economic repercussions on airlines.

While international technical and safety regulations have been adopted by virtually all countries they are not always fully and adequately implemented. During the 1990s there was growing concern about the airworthiness and safety standards of aircraft registered in certain countries. As a reaction, since 1996 ICAO has operated mandatory audits of individual states' capabilities to oversee the effective application of safety requirements. Additionally, the US Federal Aviation Administration (FAA) has launched its own 'safety oversight' procedures whereby the FAA itself inspects and monitors the degree to which airworthiness and other safety-related regulations are adequately implemented in certain countries where concerns have been raised. The FAA has carried out inspections in well over 120 countries. If the airworthiness standards of a particular country are found to be inadequate, aircraft from such countries may be banned from flying into the United States. Alternatively, their airlines may be prevented from increasing existing frequencies to the US and may be required to abandon code-sharing agreements with US carriers.

Europe through EASA has its own programme of safety assessment of non-European airline aircraft flying into Europe. This differs from the FAA approach in that it is based on ramp inspections of aircraft landing at European airports, but the ultimate sanction is the same: to ban an airline's aircraft from flying to Europe. Each year several airlines are black-listed and not allowed to enter European markets. The threat of such sanctions imposed by major destination countries is a strong incentive on civil aviation authorities of countries with aspiring international airlines to ensure that airworthiness regulations and standards are met. In parallel, IATA airlines have to submit to IATA's Operational Safety Audit (IOSA), which assesses an airline's operational management and control systems. Only airlines that have met the IOSA requirements can now join IATA.

These various technical standards and safety procedures undoubtedly constrain airline managers and, at the same time, impose cost penalties on airline operations. But such external controls are inevitable if high safety standards are to be maintained, and significantly all airlines are equally affected by them. No major international airline can enjoy a competitive advantage by operating to airworthiness standards below the generally acceptable level. The implementation of ICAO standards and the safety oversight procedures together ensure that, unlike the shipping sector, there are very few 'flags of convenience' in air transport, that is, states that allow airlines to circumvent national or international safety or manning regulations as a way of reducing costs. Those few airlines that do bend the rules tend sooner or later to find themselves banned from flying to the major markets.

Glossary of common air transport terms

Aircraft kilometres are the distances flown by aircraft. An aircraft's total flying is obtained by multiplying the number of flights performed on each flight stage by the stage distance.

Aircraft productivity is calculated by multiplying an aircraft's average block speed by its maximum payload in tonnes to arrive at the tonne-kms per hour. Or, one multiplies block speed by seat capacity to produce seat-kms per hour.

Aircraft utilisation is the average number of block hours that each aircraft is in use. This is generally measured on a daily or annual basis.

Available seat kilometres (ASKs) are obtained by multiplying the number of seats available for sale on each flight by the stage distance flown.

Available tonne kilometres (ATKs) are obtained by multiplying the number of tonnes of capacity available for carriage of passengers and cargo on each sector of a flight by the stage distance.

Average aircraft capacity is obtained by dividing an airline's total available tonne kilometres (ATKs) by aircraft kilometres flown. It is a measure of average aircraft size being flown.

Average stage or sector length is obtained by dividing an airline's total aircraft kilometres flown in a year by number of aircraft departures; it is the weighted average of stage/sector lengths flown by an airline.

Block time (hours) is the time for each flight stage or sector, measured from when the aircraft leaves the airport gate or stand (chocks off) to when it arrives on the gate or stand at the destination airport (chocks on). It can also be calculated from the moment an aircraft moves under its own power until it comes to rest at its destination.

Break-even load factor (per cent) is the load factor required at a given average fare or yield to generate total revenue which equals operating costs. Can be calculated for a flight or a series of flights.

Break of gauge is used in air services agreements to allow an airline that has traffic rights from its own country (A) to country (B) and then Fifth Freedom rights onto country C, to operate one type of aircraft from A to B and then a different type (usually smaller) from B to C and beyond. This normally involves basing aircraft and crews in country B. United Airlines and American operated such break of gauge flights from London to European points until the mid-1990s.

Cabin crew refers to stewards and stewardesses.

Code-sharing is when two or more airlines each use their own flight codes or share a common code on flights operated by one of them.

Combination carrier is an airline that transports both passengers and cargo, usually on the same aircraft.

Cost per available seat-km (CASK)   is the total operating cost for a flight, route or network divided by the corresponding seat-kms produced by that flight, route or network. If in miles measure is CASM.

Flight or cockpit crew   refers to the Captain and First Officer (pilot and co-pilot).

Franchising   involves an agreement between a large airline (the franchisor) and a smaller airline (franchisee) under which the latter operates a number of or all its services on behalf of the franchisor, usually with the latter's aircraft colour scheme, uniforms and product features.

Freight tonne kilometres (FTKs)   are obtained by multiplying the tonnes of freight uplifted by the sector distances over which they have been flown. They are a measure of an airline's cargo traffic.

Freight yields   are obtained by dividing total revenue from scheduled freight by the freight tonne kilometres (FTKs) produced (often expressed in US cents per FTK).

Grandfather rights   is the convention by which airlines retain the right to use particular take-off and landing slot times at an airport because they have done so previously, and continuously.

Integrators   are air freight companies offering door-to-door express and small shipment services including surface collection and delivery. Fedex, DHL and UPS are the largest.

Interlining   is the acceptance by one airline of travel documents issued by another airline for carriage on the services of the first airline. An interline passenger is one using a through fare for a journey involving two or more separate airlines.

Legacy airlines   are those old established traditional airlines usually operating a hub-and-spoke network. In this book they are also referred to as 'network' airlines.

Network airlines   refers to airlines operating hub-based networks as opposed to low-cost airlines that operate a matrix network. Most network airlines are also legacy airlines.

Online passenger   is one who transfers from one flight to another but on the same airline.

Operating costs per ATK   is a measure obtained by dividing total operating costs by total ATKs. Operating costs exclude interest payments, taxes and extraordinary items. They can also be measured per RTK.

Operating ratio (per cent)   is the operating revenue expressed as a percentage of operating costs. Sometimes referred to as the Revex Ratio or the operating margin.

Passenger load factor (per cent)   is passenger-kilometres (RPKs) expressed as a percentage of available seat kilometres (ASKs) (on a single sector, this is simplified to the number of passengers carried as a percentage of seats available for sale).

Passenger kilometres or Revenue passenger kilometres (RPKs)   are obtained by multiplying the number of fare-paying passengers on each flight stage by flight stage distance. They are a measure of an airline's passenger traffic.

Revenue per available seat-km (RASK)   is the total revenue for a flight, route or network divided by the available seats offered. Can be compared directly with the unit cost, i.e. CASK. If measuring in miles, it is RASM.

Revenue tonne kilometres (RTKs)   measure the output actually sold. They are obtained by multiplying the total number of tonnes of passengers and cargo carried on each flight stage by flight stage distance. (Revenue passenger kms are normally converted to revenue tonne-kms on a standard basis of 90 kg average weight, including free and excess baggage, although this has been increased by some airlines, e.g. British Airways have increased the average weight from 90kg to 95kg, as a result of a CAA directive.)

Seat factor or passenger load factor   on a single sector is obtained by expressing the passengers carried as a percentage of the seats available for sale; on a network of routes it is obtained by expressing the total passenger kms (RPKs) as a percentage of the total seat-kms available (ASKs).

Seat pitch   is the standard way of measuring seat density on an aircraft. It is the distance between the back of one seat and the same point on the back of the seat in front.

Passenger yield   is the average revenue per passenger kilometre and is obtained by dividing the total passenger revenue by the total passenger kilometres. This can be done for an individual flight or route or for the network.

Slot   at an airport is the right to operate one take-off or landing at that airport within a fixed time period.

Stage or sector distance   should be the air route or flying distance between two airports. In practice many airlines use the great circle distance, which is shorter.

Transfer   passenger is one who changes planes en-route at an intermediate airport.

Transit   passenger is one who continues on the same aircraft after an intermediate stop on a multi-sector flight.

Overall or Weight load factor   measures the proportion of available capacity actually sold. It is the revenue tonne kilometres (RTK) performed expressed as percentage of available tonne kilometres (ATK). The measures might also be in miles.

Wet lease   usually involves the leasing of aircraft with flight crews, and possibly cabin crews and maintenance support as well. A dry lease involves just the aircraft without any additional support.

Wide-bodied aircraft   are civil aircraft which have two passenger aisles (Boeing 767); narrow-bodied aircraft, such as the Airbus A320, have only one aisle.

Yield   is the average revenue collected per passenger-kilometre or tonne-km of freight carried. Passenger yield is calculated by dividing the total passenger revenue on a flight by the passenger kilometres generated by that flight. It is a measure of the weighted average fare paid.

Bibliography

Ainley, J. (2018) *European Airlines – Head to Head*, March 2018, London: Citi Research.

AirAsia (2017) *AirAsia Group Berhad Annual Report 2017*, Kuala Lumpur, Malaysia.

AirAsia (2018) *1Q2018 Results Briefing*, May, Kuala Lumpur, Malaysia.

Airbus (2008) *Global Market Forecast 2007–2026*, July, Blagnac, France: Airbus Industrie.

Airbus (2017) *Global Market Forecast 2017–2036*, Blagnac, France: Airbus Industrie.

Airline Monitor (2017a) *Airline Monitor*, August 2017, Ponte Vedra Beach, FL: ESG Aviation Services.

Airline Monitor (2017b) *Airline Monitor*, October 2017, Ponte Vedra Beach, FL: ESG Aviation Services.

Airline Monitor (2018) *Airline Monitor*, August 2018, Ponte Vedra Beach, FL: ESG Aviation Services.

Allied Market Research (2016) *Travel Insurance Market to Reach $28,264 Million, Globally, by 2022*, London: Hanover Square.

American Airlines (2018) *Annual Report*, Fort Worth, Texas.

Anker (2018) *The Anker Report*, January 2018.

Anna Aero (2017) *The Best and Worst of Ryanair Bases*, 1 February 2017, UK: PPS Publications Ltd.

Belobaba, P. and Wilson, J. (1997) Impact of yield management in competitive airline markets, *Journal of Air Transport Management*, 3(1).

Bloomberg (2016) *Car Rental Companies Discover Mergers, and You're Going to Pay for It*, May 25.

Bloomberg (2017) *Airlines Make More Money Selling Miles than Seats*, 31 March.

Boeing (2017) *World Air Cargo Forecast 2016–2037*, October 2017, Seattle: Boeing Commercial Aircraft.

CAA (2006) *No-Frills Carriers: Revolution or Evolution*, CAP 770. Annex, November, London: Civil Aviation Authority.

CAA (2008) *Recent Trends in Growth of UK Air Passenger Demand*, January, London: Civil Aviation Authority.

CAA (2015) *UK Airline Statistics 2014–15*, London: Civil Aviation Authority.

CAA (2016) *UK Airline Statistics – 2015*, London: Civil Aviation Authority.

CAA (2017) *CAA Passenger Survey Report 2016*, London: Civil Aviation Authority.

Carey (1858) *Principles of Social Science*, (1): 41–43, Philadelphia.

CarTrawler (2014) *Annual CarTrawler Survey of Airline Ancillary Revenue*, July, Shorewood: IdeaWorks Company.

CarTrawler (2017) *Annual CarTrawler Survey of Airline Ancillary Revenue*, July, Shorewood: IdeaWorks Company.

CEC (1983) *Council Directive Concerning the Authorisation of Scheduled Inter-Regional Air Services between Member States*, Brussels: Commission of the European Communities.

CEC (1984) *Civil Aviation Memorandum No. 2 Progress Towards the Development of a Community Air Transport Policy*, COM (84) 72 Final, Brussels: Commission of the European Communities.

CEC (1987a) *Council Directive of 14 December 1987 on Fares for Scheduled Air Services between Member States*, 87/601/EEC, Council Decision of 14 December 1987 on the sharing of passenger capacity on scheduled air services between Member States, 87/602/EEC, Brussels: Commission of the European Communities.

CEC (1987b) *Council Regulations (EEC) No. 3975/87 and No. 3976/87 of 14 December 1987* on the application of rules of competition in the air transport sector, Brussels: Commission of the European Communities.

CEC (1988) *Commission Regulation (EEC) No. 2671/88* of July 1988, *Official Journal*, 24 August, Brussels: Commission of the European Communities.

CEC (1992a) *Commission Regulation (EEC) No. 2407/92*, on licensing of air carriers, *Official Journal*, 24 August, Brussels: Commission of the European Communities.

CEC (1992b) *Commission Regulation (EEC) No. 2408/92*, on access for community air carriers to intra community air routes, *Official Journal*, 24 August, Brussels: Commission of the European Communities.

CEC (1992c) *Commission Regulation (EEC) No. 2409/92*, on fares and rates for air services, *Official Journal*, 24 August, Brussels: Commission of the European Communities.

Clark, P. (2017) *Buying the Big Jets. Fleet Planning for Airlines*, third edition, London: Routledge.

D'Arcy Harvey (1951) Airline passenger traffic pattern within the United States, *Journal of Air Law and Commerce*.

De Boer, E.R. (2018) *The FFP Trinity: Data, Loot and Loyalty*, Airline Leader Summit, Dublin, 17–18 May, Centre for Asia Pacific Aviation.

Delta Air Lines (2018) *Annual Report*, Atlanta, Georgia.

DfT (2014) *Public Experiences of and Attitudes Towards Air Travel*, London: Department of Transport.

DfT (2017) *Air Traffic Forecasts*, October, London: Department of Transport.

Directive (EU) 2015/2302 of the European Parliament and of the Council of 25 November 2015 on package travel and linked travel arrangements, amending Regulation (EC) No 2006/2004 and Directive 2011/83/EU of the European Parliament and of the Council and repealing Council Directive 90/314/EEC.

Doganis, R. (1966) Traffic forecasting and the gravity model, *Flight International*, 29 September.

Doganis, R. (1992) *Flying Off Course*, second edition, London: Routledge.

Doganis, R. (2006) *The Airline Business*, London: Routledge.

Doganis, R. (2017) UK departure opens Pandora's box, *Flight Airline Business*, June, London.

DOT (1990) *Secretary's Task Force on Competition in the US Domestic Airline Industry*, Washington, DC: Department of Transportation.

DOT (2007) *Final Order: International Air Transport Association Tariff Conference Proceeding*, Washington, DC: Department of Transportation, Order 2007.3.23.

Dunn, G. (2013) In a spin over loyalty, *Airline Business* (March): 28–31.

European Commission (2015) *Strong EU Protection for Package Holidays: How Will it Work in Practice?* Brussels: European Commission.

Federal Reserve Bank of Boston (2017) *The 2015 Survey of Consumer Payment Choice*.

Flightglobal (2018) *Analysis: Ancillary Revenue Gains Hinge on Ending Siloed Approach*, 16 February.

Gillen et al. (2003) *Air Travel Demand Elasticities: Concepts, Issues and Measurement*, Ottawa Department of Finance, Government of Canada.

Graham, A. (2000) Demand for leisure air travel and limits to growth, *Journal of Air Transport Management*, 6(2), April.

Graham, A. (2008) *Managing Airports; An International Perspective*, third edition, London: Butterworth-Heinemann.

Grosche, T., Rothlauf, F. and Heinzel, A. (2007) Gravity models for airline passenger volume estimation, *Journal of Air Transport Management*, 13(4), July.

Hanke, M. (2016) *Airline E-Commerce. Log On. Take Off*, London: Routledge.

HSBC (2017) *Airline Analysts Report*, 26 September 2017, London: HSBC.

Huson, S. (2015) *Lufthansa Magazine*.

IATA (2006a) *Profitability: Does Size Matter?* Economics Briefing, June, Geneva: International Air Transport Association.

IATA (2006b) *Airline Cost Performance*, Economics Briefing No. 5, July, Geneva: International Air Transport Association.

IATA (2008) *Corporate Air Travel Survey (CATS)*, Geneva: International Air Transport Association.

IATA (2015) *New Distribution Capability (NDC) Strategy Paper*, Geneva: International Air Transport Association.

IATA (2017) *Global Passenger Survey 2017*, March, Geneva: International Air Transport Association.

IATA (2018) *World Air Transport Statistics*, June, Geneva: International Air Transport Association.

IATA/Tourism Economics (2017) *Overview of Forecasting Framework*, April, Geneva: International Air Transport Association.

ICAO (1980) *Convention on International Civil Aviation*, sixth edition, Doc. 7300/6, Montreal: International Civil Aviation Organization.

ICAO (1997) *Outlook for Air Transport to the Year 2005*, Circular 270, Montreal: International Civil Aviation Organization.

ICAO (1999) *Safety Oversight Manual*. Doc. 9734-AN/959, Montreal: International Civil Aviation Organization.

Ideaworks (2011) *Planes, Cars and Ancillary Revenues*, 31 January, Shorewood: IdeaWorks Company.

Ideaworks (2017) *The 2017 CarTrawler Yearbook of Ancillary Revenues*, Shorewood: IdeaWorks Company.

Ideaworks (2018) *Ancillary* Revenue Defined, Shorewood: Idea Works Company.

IMM (2013) *Inflight Media News*, 24 January.

Kraus, M. (1999) *Time Definitive Services. The Shift of Paradigm for Cargo Airlines*, The 10th world express and mail conference, Brussels: May.

Lill (1889) 'Die Grundgesetze des Personenwerkehrs', *Zeitschrift fur Eisenbahnen und Dampfschiffsfahrt der Osterreichischungarischen Monarchie*, Vienna, No. 35–36.

Lobbenberg, A. (2001) Strategic Alliances, *Air Transport Executive Seminar*, Cranfield College of Aeronautics (unpublished).

Lufthansa (2016) *Annual Report 2016*, May, Germany: Lufthansa Group.

Michaels, D. (2009) *Magazine Publisher Finds Profit in Airlines*, Wall Street Journal, 27 November.

Morrell, P. (2011) *Moving Boxes by Air. The Economics of International Air Cargo*. London: Routledge.

Morrell, P. (2013) *Airline Finance*, 4th edition, London: Routledge.

Nguyen Dai Hai (1982) The Box Jenkins Approach, *ITA Bulletin*, September Paris: Institut du Transport Aérien.

O'Connell, J.F. and Warnock-Smith, D.W. (2013) An investigation into traveller preferences and acceptance of airline ancillary revenues, *Journal of Air Transport Management*, 33, 12–21.

ONS (2016) *Travel Trends 2016*, Office of National Statistics, London: HMSO.

Pearce, B. (2017) *Top of the Cycle or Further Gains for Airline Markets and Profits*, October 2017, Geneva: IATA.org/economics.

Qantas (2017) *Annual Report and Accounts*, Sydney, Australia

Reales, C. and O'Connell, J.F. (2017) An examination of the revenue generating capability of co-branded cards associated with frequent flyer programs, *Journal of Air Transport Management*, 65, 63–75.

Sabre (2016) *Global Study Reveals Travelers Would Spend $100 on Airline Ancillaries to Personalize Travel Experience*.

SIA (2017) *Annual Report 2016–17*, May 2017, Singapore: Singapore Airlines.

Solomko, S. (2009) Forecasting demand in underserved markets, *Marketing and Market Research in Air Transport*, February, London: University of Westminster.

Tae Hoon Oum and Chunyan Yu (1995) A productivity comparison of the world's major airlines, *Journal of Air Transport Management*, 2(3–4): 181–195.

The Guardian (2018) *EasyJet to Expand Holiday Business as It Reduces Losses*, 16 May, London.

UK CAA (2018) *Check the Current Airline Fees and Charges*, June, London: Civil Aviation Authority.

United Airlines (2017) *Annual Report Form 10-K*, February.

United Airlines (2018) *Annual Report Form 10-K*, February.

US DOT (2018a) *Baggage Fees 2007–2017*, Washington: Department of Transportation.

US DOT (2018b) *Reservation Cancellation/Change Fees by Airline 2017*, Washington: Department of Transportation.

US Travel Insurance Association (2015) *More than 152 Million Covered by Travel Protection in 2014*.

Vasigh, B., Fleming, K. and Tacker, T. (2008) *Introduction to Air Transport Economics*, Aldershot: Ashgate.

Warnock-Smith, D., O'Connell, J.F. and Maleki, M. (2017) An analysis of ongoing trends in airline ancillary revenues, *Journal of Air Transport Management*, 64: 42–54.

Westminster (1989) *Air Transport and the Southern Regions of the Community. Vol. IV. Route Forecasts*, London: Transport Studies Group, University of Westminster.

Which? (2018) *Best and Worst Airlines*, January 2018, Hertford: Which?

Zion Market Research (2018) *Global Car Rental Market Share 2016 Will Grow USD 124.56 Billion by 2022*, 30 March.

Index

Note: numbers in **bold** refer to figures and numbers in *italics* refer to tables.